6TH EDITION HAWAII THE BIG ISLAND REVEALED

THE ULTIMATE GUIDEBOOK

ANDREW DOUGHTY

PHOTOGRAPHS BY ANDREW DOUGHTY & LEONA BOYD

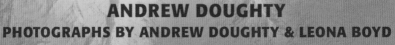

WIZARD
PUBLICATIONS
INC

Hawaii The Big Island Revealed
The Ultimate Guidebook; 6th Edition

Published by Wizard Publications, Inc.
Post Office Box 991
Lihuʻe, Hawaiʻi 96766–0991

ISBN: 978-0-9814610-6-9   2111
Library of Congress Control Number 2010940639
Printed in China

Cataloging-in-Publication Data

Doughty, Andrew
    Hawaii the Big Island revealed : the ultimate guidebook / Andrew Doughty. – 6th ed.
Lihue, HI : Wizard Publications, Inc., 2011
       312 p.: col. illus., col. photos, col. maps; 21 cm.
       Includes index.
       Summary : a complete traveler's reference to the island of Hawaii, with full color
photos, maps, directions, and candid advice by an author who resides in Hawaii.
       ISBN 978-0-9814610-6-9
       LCCN 2010940639

       1. Hawaii Island (Hawaii) – Guidebooks. 2. Hawaii Island (Hawaii) – Description
and travel. I. Title.

DU 622   919.69__dc21

All photographs (except cover & page 16) taken by Andrew Doughty and Leona Boyd.
Cartography by Andrew Doughty.
All artwork and illustrations by Andrew Doughty and Lisa Pollak.

Past and present lava flow information for maps was graciously provided by an over-worked and under-appreciated United States Geological Survey, the silent partner to all mapmakers. Keep up the good work!

Cover space imagery courtesy of Earthstar Geographics (www.earth-imagery.com).

Pages 2–3: Kilauea's Puʻu ʻOʻo vent.

We welcome any comments, questions, criticisms or contributions you may have, and have incorporated some of your suggestions into this edition. Please send to the address above or e-mail us at **aloha@wizardpub.com**.

Check out our website at **www.wizardpub.com** for up-to-the-minute changes.

To Harry and Mary—
Their love of travel lives on…

CONTENTS

ABOUT THIS BOOK
9

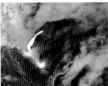

INTRODUCTION
11

11 How it Began
13 The First Settlers
16 Outside World Discovers Hawai'i
18 Kamehameha the Great
19 Modern Hawai'i

THE BASICS
21

21 Getting Here
22 What to Bring
22 Getting Around
25 Getting Married on the Big Island
25 Weather
27 Planning Your Trip
28 Geography
29 So is Hawai'i an Island or a State?
30 Hazards
34 Traveling With Children (Keiki)
34 The People
35 Some Terms
35 Hawaiian Time
36 Shaka
36 The Hawaiian Language
38 Music
39 The Hula
39 A Note About Access
40 A Note on Personal Responsibility
41 Miscellaneous Information
41 A Word About Driving Tours
42 Farmers' Markets
42 Books
42 The Internet

KOHALA SIGHTS
43

43 Up Highway 190 from Kailua-Kona
47 Kohala Mountain Road
47 North Shore of Kohala
49 Pololu Valley
49 Mo'okini Heiau
51 Lapakahi State Historical Park
52 Kawaihae
54 Kohala Resort Area
55 Kohala Lava Desert Area
58 Kohala Shopping
58 Kohala's Best Bets

KAILUA-KONA SIGHTS
59

60 Around Downtown Kailua-Kona
63 Elsewhere Along Alii Drive
67 Up Mauka of Kailua-Kona
67 South of Kailua-Kona
69 Kealakekua Bay & Place of Refuge
74 Kailua-Kona Shopping
75 Kailua-Kona's Best Bets

SOUTH ISLAND SIGHTS
76

79 South Point

VOLCANO SIGHTS

85

86 Will I Get to See Lava Flowing?
87 The Scene
90 A Few Basics
93 Around Kilauea Crater
97 Down Chain of Craters Road
102 Hiking in the Park
102 Outside the Park Entrance
104 The Town of Volcano

HILO & PUNA SIGHTS

106

107 Around Hilo Town
111 Heading South on Highway 11
112 Exploring Puna
121 Hilo Shopping
122 Hilo & Puna's Best Bets

HAMAKUA & WAIMEA SIGHTS

123

123 Leaving Hilo Behind
129 Honoka'a
129 Waipi'o Valley
133 Old Mamalahoa Highway
134 Waimea
134 Parker Ranch
137 Hamakua & Waimea Shopping
137 Hamakua & Waimea's Best Bets

SADDLE ROAD SIGHTS

138

140 Mauna Kea
143 Driving up to Mauna Kea
145 Mauna Loa
146 Approaching Hilo

BEACHES

147

148 Beach Safety
150 Kohala Beaches
159 Near Kona Beaches
170 South Island Beaches
174 East Side Beaches

ACTIVITIES

176

177 ATVs
177 Biking
179 Boogie Boarding
179 Camping
180 Caving
181 Fishing
184 Golfing

("Activities" continued...)

8

CONTENTS

ACTIVITIES
(Continued)
176

ISLAND
DINING
244

190 (Powered) Hang Gliders
191 Helicopters / Airplanes
194 Hiking
207 Horseback Riding
209 Jet Skiing
209 Kayaking
211 Ocean Tours
215 Parasailing
215 SCUBA
220 Snorkeling
223 Snow Skiing
223 SNUBA
224 Spas
224 Stargazing
225 Submarines
225 Surfing
226 Tennis
226 Whale Watching
227 Windsurfing / Kitesurfing
228 Ziplines

244 Island Dining Index
246 Island Fish & Seafood
247 Lu'au Foods
247 Other Island Foods
248 Kailua-Kona Dining
260 Kohala Dining
266 Waimea Dining
268 Hilo Dining
272 Dining Elsewhere
278 Island Nightlife
278 Lu'au
281 Dinner Cruises
281 Island Dining Best Bets

WHERE TO
STAY
282

ADVENTURES
229

229 Manta Ray Night Dive
230 Mauna Ulu Crater
231 Explore a Mile-Long Cave
233 Rain Forest Hike to Pu'u 'O'o Vent
235 Jump Off the End of the World
236 Close Encounter With a Dolphin
237 Boulder-hop to a Waterfall
238 Command Your Own Boat
239 Lose Yourself in Waimanu Valley
240 Hike to Flowing Lava
243 Honokane Nui Hike

282 Where to Stay Index
282 Rental Agents
284 Hotels
284 Condos
285 Bed & Breakfasts
285 Where Should I Stay?
287 Where are the Rest?
287 Kohala
293 Kailua-Kona
300 Hilo Area
301 Volcano Village
303 Waimea
304 Northern Tip of the Island
305 Southeast Part of the Island
305 Honoka'a

INDEX
306

The Big Island has it all. Nowhere else in the world will you find the diversity available here. Pristine rain forests, lava deserts, world-class beaches, snow-covered mountains, an active volcano, dazzling sunsets and just about every activity you can think of. The island is huge—about the size of Connecticut. Navigating your way through this maze of opportunity can be daunting.

Most travel publishers send a writer or writers to a given location for a few weeks to become "experts" and to compile information for guidebooks. To our knowledge, we at Wizard Publications are the only ones who actually *live* our books.

We hike the trails, ride the boats, eat in the restaurants, explore the reefs and do the things we write about. It takes us one to two *years*, full time, to do a first edition book, and we visit places *anonymously*. We marvel at writers who can do it all in a couple weeks staying in a hotel. Wow, they must be *really* fast. Our method, though it takes much longer, gives us the ability to tell it like it is in a way no one else can. We put in many long hours, and doing all these activities is a burdensome grind. But we do it all for you—only for you. (Feel free to gag at this point.)

We have found many special places that people born and raised here didn't even know about because that's *all we do*—explore the island. Visitors will find the book as valuable as having a friend living on the island.

We recognize the effort people go through to visit the Big Island, and our goal is to expose you to as many options as possible so you can decide what you want to see and do. We took great pains to structure this book in such a way that it will be fun, easy reading and loaded with useful information. This book is not a bland regurgitation of the facts arranged in textbook fashion. We feel strongly that guidebooks should present their information so that you don't have to read through every single page every time you want to find something. If you are here on vacation, your time is extremely precious. You don't want to spend all your time flipping through a book looking for what you want. You want to be able to locate *what* you want, *when* you want it. You want to be able to access a comprehensive index, a thorough table of contents, and refer to high-quality maps that were designed with you in mind. You want to know which helicopter, SCUBA, boat tour or lu'au is the best on the island. You want to find special hidden gems most people overlook. You want to be shown those things that will make this vacation the best of your life.

A quick look at this book will reveal features never before used in a guidebook. Let's start with the maps. They are more detailed than any other maps you will find, and yet they omit extraneous information that can sometimes make a chore out of reading a map. We know that people in unfamiliar territory sometimes have a hard time determining where they are on a map, so we include landmarks. Most notable among these are mile markers. At every mile on main roads, the government has erected numbered markers to tell you where you are. We are the first to put these markers on a map so you can use them as reference points. In addition, we repeatedly drove or walked every inch of every road on the maps. This is important because *many* roads represented on existing maps have been shifted, moved or eliminated, making "current" maps obsolete. Where needed, we've drawn legal public beach access in yellow, so you'll *know* when you are legally entitled to cross someone's land. Most guidebooks have the infuriating habit of mentioning a particular place or sight, but *fail to mention how to get there!* You won't find that in our book. We tell you exactly how to find the hidden gems and use our own special maps to guide you.

One of the things unique to this book is the acceptance of change. We produce brand new editions of our books every two years or so, but in the intervening time we constantly incorporate changes into the text nearly every time we do a new printing. We also post these changes on our website. This allows us to make some modifications throughout the life of each edition. We don't have the luxury of making every change that happens on a weekly basis, but it does give us more flexibility than if we only acknowledged changes every two years.

As you read this book, you will also notice that we are very candid in assessing businesses. Unlike some other guidebooks that send out questionnaires asking businesses to *rate themselves* (gee, they *all* say they're good), we've had *personal* contact with the businesses listed in this book. One of the dirty little secrets about guidebook writers is that they often make cozy little deals for good reviews. Well, you won't find that here. We accept no payment for our reviews, we make no deals with businesses for saying nice things, and there are *no advertisements* in our book. What we've seen and experienced is what you get. If we gush over a certain company, it comes from personal experience. If we rail against a business, it is for the same reason. All businesses mentioned in this book are here by *our* choosing. None have had any input into what we say, and we have not received a single cent from any of them for their inclusion. (In fact, there are some that would probably pay to be left out, given our comments.) We always approach businesses as anonymous travelers. This ensures that we are treated the same as you. What you get is our opinion on how they operate. Nothing more, nothing less.

Sometimes our candor gets us into trouble. For instance, this book used to be the only guidebook sold at the Visitor Center in Hawai'i Volcanoes National Park. After undergoing a rigorous multi-month review process by government bureaucrats, this book was deemed "the most accurate book we've ever seen for the Big Island." They even wanted to sell our *Kaua'i* book there, a first at the park, because they liked the way we thoroughly researched things. But thoroughness cuts both ways. When those same bureaucrats later realized that we had revealed a secret but *public* trail (previously unknown to the general public) that led to the erupting Pu'u 'O'o vent through a beautiful forest, they stopped selling this book and fumed over the loss of control to the vent. (The trail is outside the park and therefore outside the control of the bureaucrats.) It's not the first time this book has been pulled from shelves for being too honest, and it won't be the last.

This book is intended to bring you independence in exploring the Big Island. We don't want to waste any of your precious time by giving you bad advice or bad directions. We want you to experience the best that the island has to offer. Our objective in writing this book is to give you the tools and information necessary to have the greatest Hawaiian experience possible.

We hope we succeeded.

Andrew Doughty
Kailua-Kona, Hawai'i

Brand new liquid land flows in a scene as primordial as the island's birth.

As with people, volcanic islands have a life cycle. They emerge from their sea floor womb to be greeted by the warmth of the sun. They grow, mature and eventually die before sinking forever beneath the sea.

HOW IT BEGAN

Sometime around 70 million years ago a cataclysmic rupture occurred in the Earth's mantle, deep below the crust. A hot spot of liquid rock blasted through the Pacific plate like a giant cutting torch, forcing magma to the surface off the coast of Russia, forming the Emperor Seamounts. As the tectonic plate moved slowly over this hot spot, this torch cut a long scar along the plate, piling up mountains of rock, producing island after island. The oldest of these islands to have survived is Kure. Once a massive island with its own unique ecosystem, only its ghost remains in the form of a fringing coral reef, called an atoll.

As soon as the islands were born, a conspiracy of elements proceeded to dismantle them. Ocean waves unmercifully battered the fragile and fractured rock. Abundant rain, especially on the northeastern sides of the mountains, easily carved up the rock surface, seeking faults in the rock and forming rivers and streams. In forming these channels, the water carried away the rock and soil, robbing the islands of their very essence. Additionally, the weight of the islands ensured their doom. Lava flows on top of other lava, and the union of these flows is always weak. This lava also contains countless air pockets and is criss-crossed with hollow lava tubes, making it inherently unstable. As these massive amounts of rock accumulated, their bases were crushed under the weight of subsequent lava flows, causing their summits to sink back into the sea.

What we call the Hawaiian Islands are simply the latest creations from this island-making machine. Someday they will disappear, existing as nothing more than footnotes in the Earth's turbulent geologic history.

Kaua'i and Ni'ihau are the oldest of the eight major islands. Lush and deeply eroded, the last of Kaua'i's fires died with its volcano a million years ago. O'ahu, Moloka'i, Lana'i, Kaho'olawe—their growing days are over, as well. Maui is in its twilight days as a growing island. After growing vigorously, Hawaiian volca-

noes usually go to sleep for a million years or so before sputtering back to life for one last fling. Maui's volcano Haleakala has entered its final stage and last erupted around 1790.

The latest and newest star in this island chain is Hawai'i. Born less than a million years ago, this youngster is still vigorously growing. Though none of its five volcano mountains is considered truly dead, these days Mauna Loa and Kilauea are doing most of the work of making the Big Island bigger. Mauna Loa, the most massive mountain on Earth, consists of 10,000 *cubic miles* of rock. Quieter of the two active volcanoes, it last erupted in 1984. Kilauea is the most boisterous of the volcanoes and is the most active volcano on the planet. Kilauea's most recent eruption began in 1983 and was still going strong as we went to press. Up and coming onto the world stage is Lo'ihi. This new volcano is still 3,200 feet below the ocean's surface, 20 miles off the southeastern

The wonder of creation can still be seen at night at Kilauea Volcano.

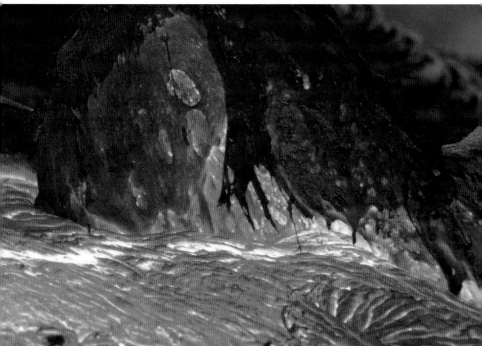

In regions of the island blessed with abundant rains, verdant growth carpets the landscape.

coast of the island. Yet in a geologic heartbeat, the Hawaiian islands will be richer with its ascension, sometime in the next 100,000 years.

These virgin islands were barren at birth. Consisting only of volcanic rock, the first life forms to appreciate these new islands were marine creatures. Fish, mammals and microscopic animals discovered this new underwater haven and made homes for themselves. Coral polyps attached themselves to the lava rock and succeeding generations built upon these, creating what would become a coral reef.

Meanwhile, on land, seeds carried by the winds were struggling to colonize the rocky land, eking out a living and breaking down the lava rock. Storms brought the occasional bird, hopelessly blown off course. The lucky ones found the islands. The even luckier ones arrived with mates or had fertilized eggs when they got here. Other animals, stranded on a piece of floating debris, washed ashore against all odds and went on to colonize the islands. These introductions of new species were rare events. It took an extraordinary set of circumstances for a

new species to actually make it to the islands. Single specimens were destined to live out their lives in lonely solitude. On average, a new species was successfully deposited here only once every 20,000 years.

When a volcanic island is old, it is a sandy sliver, devoid of mountains. When it's middle-aged, it can be a lush wonderland, a haven for anything green, like Kaua'i. And when it is young, it is dynamic and unpredictable, like the Big Island of Hawai'i. Of all the Hawaiian Islands, none offers a larger range of climates and landscapes than the Big Island. The first people to discover Hawai'i's treasures must have been humbled at their good fortune.

THE FIRST SETTLERS

Sometime around the fourth or fifth century AD a large double-hulled voyaging canoe, held together with flexible sennit lashings and propelled by sails made of woven pandanus, slid onto the sand on the Big Island of Hawai'i. These first intrepid adventurers, only a few dozen or so, encountered an island chain of unimaginable beauty.

The ancient Polynesians were exceptional navigators. These stones, at the navigational heiau near Mahukona, were aligned to point the way to other Hawaiian islands, Tahiti and other far away places.

They had left their home in the Marquesas Islands, 2,500 miles away, for reasons we will never know. Some say it was because of war, overpopulation, drought, or just a sense of adventure. Whatever their reasons, these initial settlers took a big chance and surely must have been highly motivated. They left their homes and searched for a new world to colonize. Doubtless, most of the first groups perished at sea. The Hawaiian Islands are the most isolated island chain in the world, and there was no way for them to know that there were islands in these waters. (Though some speculate that they were led here by the golden plover—see box on facing page.)

Those settlers who did arrive brought with them food staples from home: taro, breadfruit, pigs, dogs and several types of fowl. This was a pivotal decision. These first settlers found a land that contained almost no edible plants. With no land mammals other than the Hawaiian bat, the first settlers subsisted on fish until their crops matured. From then on, they lived on fish and taro. Although we asso-

ciate throw-net fishing with Hawai'i, this practice was introduced by Japanese immigrants much later. The ancient Hawaiians used fishhooks and spears, for the most part, or drove fish into a net already placed in the water. They also had domesticated animals, which were used as ritual foods or reserved for chiefs.

Little is known about the initial culture. Archaeologists believe that a second wave of colonists, probably from Tahiti, may have subdued these initial inhabitants around 1000 AD. Some may have resisted and fled into the forest, creating the legend of the Menehune.

Today, Menehune are always referred to as being small in stature. Initially referring to their social stature, the legend evolved to mean that they were physically short and lived in the woods away from the Hawaiians. (The Hawaiians avoided the woods when possible, fearing that they held evil spirits, and instead stayed on the coastal plains.) The Menehune were purported to build fabulous structures, always in one night. Their numbers were said to be vast, as many as

500,000. It is interesting to note that in a census taken of Kaua'i in around 1800, 65 people from a remote valley identified themselves as Menehune.

The second wave probably swept over the island from the south, pushing the first inhabitants ever-north. On a tiny island north of Kaua'i, archeologists have found carvings, clearly not Hawaiian, that closely resemble Marquesan carvings, probably left by the doomed exiles.

This second culture was far more aggressive and developed into a highly class-conscious society. The culture was governed by chiefs, called Ali'i, who established a long list of taboos called kapu. These kapu were designed to keep order, and the penalty for breaking one was usually death by strangulation, club or fire. If the violation was serious enough, the guilty party's entire family might also be killed. It was kapu, for instance, for your shadow to fall across the shadow of the Ali'i. It was kapu to interrupt the chief if he was speaking. It was kapu to prepare men's food in the same container used for women's food. It was kapu for women to eat pork or bananas. It was kapu for men and women to eat together. It was kapu not to observe the days designated to the gods. Certain areas were kapu for fishing if they became depleted, allowing the area to replenish itself.

While harsh by our standards today, this system kept the order. Most Ali'i were sensitive to the disturbance their presence caused and often ventured outside only at night, or a scout was sent ahead to warn people that an Ali'i was on his way. All commoners were required to pay tribute to the Ali'i in the form of food and other items. Human sacrifices were common and war among rival chiefs the norm.

By the 1700s, the Hawaiians had lost all contact with Tahiti, and the Tahitians had lost all memory of Hawai'i. Hawaiian canoes had evolved into fishing, and interisland canoes and were no longer capable of long ocean voyages. The Hawaiians had forgotten how to explore the world.

Hawai'i's First Tour Guide?

Given the remoteness of the Hawaiian Islands relative to the rest of Polynesia (or anywhere else for that matter), you'll be forgiven for wondering how the first settlers found these islands in the first place. Many  *scientists think it might have been this little guy here. Called the kolea, or golden plover, this tiny bird flies over 2,500 miles nonstop to Alaska every year for the summer, returning to Hawai'i after mating. Some of these birds continue past Hawai'i and fly another 2,500 miles to Samoa and other South Pacific islands. The early Polynesians surely must have noticed this commute and concluded that there must be land in the direction that the bird was heading. They never would have dreamed that the birds leaving the South Pacific were heading to a land 5,000 miles away, and that Hawai'i was merely a stop in between, where the lazier birds wintered.*

OUTSIDE WORLD DISCOVERS HAWAI'I

In January 1778 an event occurred that would forever change Hawai'i. Captain James Cook, who usually had a genius for predicting where to find islands, stumbled upon Hawai'i. He had not expected the islands to be here. He was on his way to Alaska on his third great voyage of discovery, this time to search for the Northwest Passage linking the Atlantic and Pacific oceans. Cook approached the shores of Waimea, Kaua'i, at night on January 19, 1778. The next morning Kaua'i's inhabitants awoke to a wondrous sight and thought they were being visited by gods. Rushing out to greet their visitors, the Kauaians were fascinated by what they saw: pointy-headed beings (the British wore tri-cornered hats) breathing fire (smoking pipes) and possessing a death-dealing instrument identified as a water squirter (guns). The amount of iron on the ship was incredible. (They had seen iron before in the form of nails on driftwood but never knew where it originated.)

It's hard to believe that the Big Island will eventually look like this oldest Hawaiian island, Kure Atoll. One day its last ghostly remains will sink forever beneath the sea.

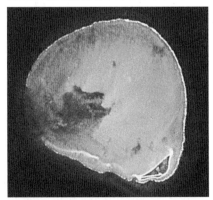

Cook left Kaua'i and briefly explored Ni'ihau before heading north for his mission on February 2, 1778. When Cook returned to the islands in November after failing to find the Northwest Passage, he visited the Big Island of Hawai'i.

The Hawaiians had probably seen white men before. Local legend indicates that strange white people washed ashore at Ke'ei Beach sometime around the 1520s and integrated into society. This coincides with Spanish records of two ships lost in this part of the world in 1528. But a few weird-looking stragglers couldn't compare to the arrival of Cook's great ships and instruments.

Despite some recent rewriting of history, all evidence indicates that Cook, unlike some other exploring sea captains of his era, was a thoroughly decent man. Individuals need to be evaluated in the context of their time. Cook knew that his mere presence would have a profound impact on the cultures he encountered, but he also knew that change for these cultures was inevitable, with or without him. He tried, unsuccessfully, to keep the men known to be infected with venereal diseases from mixing with local women, and he frequently flogged infected men who tried to sneak ashore at night. He was greatly distressed when a party he sent to Ni'ihau was forced to stay overnight due to high surf, knowing that his men might transmit diseases to the women (which they did).

Cook arrived on the Big Island at a time of much upheaval. The mo'i, or king, of the Big Island had been badly spanked during an earlier attempt to invade Maui and was now looting and raising hell throughout the islands as retribution. Cook's arrival and his physical appearance (he was 6 feet, 4 inches) assured that the Hawaiians would assume him to be

The Day the Gods Cried...

At the south end of Alii Drive in Kona, just before it dead ends, there is a lava road leading toward the ocean. This field of lava and an area around the point called Kuamo'o have an extraordinary past. Here occurred an event that forever changed a people. For it was here that the Hawaiians abolished their ancient religion one day in 1820.

The Hawaiian religion was based on the kapu system. A myriad of laws were maintained, with death being the usual punishment for violation. The Hawaiians believed that rigid enforcement for a single violation was necessary, or else the gods would punish the whole community in the form of earthquakes, tsunamis, lava flows and famine. When Captain Cook came, he and his men were unaware of the many laws and inadvertently violated many of them. When natural punishments failed to materialize, many Hawaiians concluded that the gods would not enforce the laws. Since many found the kapu laws burdensome and oppressive, there was pressure to abolish them. While King Kamehameha I was alive, however, none dared challenge the kapu system. Almost as soon as he died, King Kamehameha II, pressured by his stepmother Ka'ahumanu, decided to put an end to the kapu system and destroy the temples around the island. This was before any missionaries ever came to these islands.

It was decided that the action would be consecrated by the simple act of having the king eat with women in public in November 1819. This had heretofore been kapu, and the penalty for breaking this law was death. In breaking this kapu in public, Kamehameha II declared an end to the old ways. One of his cousins, Kekuaokalani, was to be king of the spiritual world and challenged him. The ferocious battle took place near here in early 1820. His cousin was hit by Kamehameha II's forces, and the man's grieving wife ran to his side as he fell. She cried out, begging that her wounded husband's life be spared. Instead she and her husband were summarily executed on the spot, with her body falling on top of his. The Hawaiian religion, as a dominant force, died with them on that bloody day. If you look to the south, you can see what look like terraces cut into the side of the mountain. These are the graves of the many hundreds who died in that very battle.

Today there is a resurgence of the Hawaiian religion. Hawaiians are grappling with their role in the world and are reaching back to their roots. The religion that seemingly died on that raw lava field is being reborn in the hearts of some contemporary Hawaiians.

the god Lono, who was responsible for fertility of the land. Every year the ruling chiefs and their war god Ku went into abeyance, removing their power so that Lono could return to the land and make it fertile again, bringing back the spring rains. During this time all public works stopped and the land was left alone. At the end of this *Makahiki* season, man would again seize the land from Lono so he could grow crops and otherwise make a living upon it. Cook arrived at the beginning of the Makahiki, and the Hawaiians naturally thought *he* was the god Lono, coming to make the land fertile. Cook even sailed into Kealakekua Bay, *exactly* where legend said Lono would arrive.

The Hawaiians went to great lengths to please their "god." All manner of supplies were made available. Eventually, they became suspicious of the visitors. If they were gods, why did they accept Hawaiian women? And if they were gods, why did one of them die?

Cook left at the right time. The British had used up the Hawaiians' hospitality (not to mention their supplies). But shortly after leaving the Big Island, the ship broke a mast, making it necessary to return to Kealakekua Bay for repairs. As they sailed back into the bay, the Hawaiians were nowhere to be seen. A chief had declared the area kapu to help replenish it. When Cook finally found the Hawaiians, they were polite but wary. *Why are you back? Didn't we please you enough already? What do you want now?*

As repair of the mast went along, things began to get tense. Eventually the Hawaiians stole a British rowboat (for the nails), and the normally calm Cook blew his cork. On the morning of February 14, 1779, he went ashore to trick the chief into coming aboard his ship where he would detain him until the rowboat was returned. As Cook and the chief were heading to the water, the chief's wife begged the chief not to go. By now tens of thousands of Hawaiians were crowding around Cook, and he ordered a retreat. A shot was heard from the other side of the bay, and someone shouted that the Englishmen had killed an important chief. A shielded warrior with a dagger came at Cook, who fired his pistol (loaded with non-lethal small shot). The shield stopped the small shot, and the Hawaiians were emboldened. Other shots were fired. Standing in knee-deep water, Cook turned to call for a cease-fire and was struck in the head from behind with a club, then stabbed. Dozens of other Hawaiians pounced on him, stabbing his body repeatedly. The greatest explorer the world had ever known was dead at age 50 in a petty skirmish over a stolen rowboat.

When things calmed down, the Hawaiians were horrified that they had killed a man they had earlier presumed to be a god. See page 71 to see what finally happened to Cook's body.

KAMEHAMEHA THE GREAT

The most powerful and influential king in Hawaiian history lived during the time of Captain Cook and was born on this island sometime around 1758. Until his rule, the Hawaiian chain had never been ruled by a single person. He was the first to "unite" (i.e., conquer) all the islands.

Kamehameha was an extraordinary man by any standard. He possessed herculean strength, a brilliant mind and boundless ambition. He was marked for death before he was even born. When Kamehameha's mother was pregnant with him, she developed a strange and overpowering craving—she wanted to *eat* the eyeball of a chief. The king of the Big Island, mindful of the rumor that the unborn child's real father was his bitter enemy, the king of Maui, asked his advisors to interpret. Their conclusion was unanimous: The child would grow to be a rebel, a killer of chiefs. The king decided that the child must die as soon as he was born, but the baby was instead whisked away to a remote part of Waipi'o Valley to be raised.

The Hawaiians built a highly structured society around the needs, desires and demands of their gods. This place of refuge is called Pu'uhonua o Honaunau.

In ancient Hawaiian society, your role in life was governed by the class you were born into. The Hawaiians believed that breeding among family members produced superior offspring (except for the genetic misfortunates who were killed at birth), and the highest chiefs came from brother/sister combinations. Kamehameha was not of the highest class (his parents were merely cousins), so his future as a chief would not come easily.

As a young man, Kamehameha was impressed by his experience with Captain Cook. He was among the small group that stayed overnight on Cook's ship during Cook's first pass of Maui. (Kamehameha was on Maui valiantly fighting a battle in which his side was getting badly whooped.) Kamehameha recognized that his world had forever changed, and he shrewdly used the knowledge and technology of westerners to his own advantage.

Kamehameha participated in numerous battles. Many of them were lost (by his side), but he learned from his mistakes and developed into a cunning tactician.

When he finally consolidated his rule over the Big Island (by luring his enemy to be the inaugural sacrifice at the Pu'ukohola Heiau near Kawaihae), he fixed his sights on the entire chain. In 1795 his large company of troops, armed with some western armaments and advisors, swept across Maui, Moloka'i, Lana'i and O'ahu. After some delays with the last of the holdouts, Kaua'i, their king finally acquiesced to the inevitable, and Kamehameha became the first ruler of all the islands. He spent his final years governing the islands peacefully from his capital at Kailua Bay and died in 1819.

MODERN HAWAI'I

During the 19th century, Hawai'i's character changed dramatically. Businessmen from all over the world came here to exploit Hawai'i's sandalwood, whales, land and people. Hawai'i's leaders, for their part, actively participated in these ventures and took a piece of much of the action for themselves. Workers were brought in from many parts of the world, changing the racial makeup of the islands. Government corruption became the order of the day, and everyone seemed to be profiting, except the Hawaiian commoner. By the time Queen Lili'uokalani lost her throne to a group of American businessmen in 1893, Hawai'i had become directionless, barely resembling the Hawai'i Captain Cook had encountered the previous century. The kapu system had been abolished by the Hawaiians shortly after the death of Kamehameha the Great. The "Great Mahele," begun in 1848, had changed the relationship Hawaiians had with the land. Large tracts of land were sold by the Hawaiian government to royalty, government officials, commoners and foreigners, effectively stripping many Hawaiians of the land they had lived on for generations.

The United States recognized the Republic of Hawai'i in 1894 with Sanford Dole as its president. It was later annexed and became an official territory in 1900. During the 19th and 20th centuries, sugar established itself as king. Pineapple was also a major crop in the islands, with the island of Lana'i purchased in its entirety for the purpose of growing pineapples. As the 20th century rolled on, Hawaiian sugar and pineapple workers found themselves in a lofty position—they became the highest paid workers for these crops in the world. As land prices rose and competition from other parts of the world increased, sugar and pineapple became less and less profitable. Today, these crops no longer hold the position they once had. The "pineapple island" of Lana'i has shifted away from pineapple growing and focuses on luxury tourism. The sugar industry is now dead on the Big Island, and sugar lands are being converted to other purposes while the workers move into other vocations, often tourist-related.

The story of Hawai'i is not a story of good versus evil. Nearly everyone shares in the blame for what happened to the Hawaiian people and their culture. Westerners certainly saw Hawai'i as a potential bonanza and easily exploitable. They knew what buttons to push and pushed them well. But the Hawaiians, for their part, were in a state of flux. The mere appearance of westerners seemed to reveal a discontent, or at least a weakness, in their system that had been lingering just below the surface. In fact, in 1794, a mere 16 years after first encountering westerners and under no military duress from the West, Kamehameha the Great *volunteered* to cede his island over to Great Britain. He was hungry for western arms so he could defeat his neighbor island opponents. He even declared that, as of that day, they were no longer people of Hawai'i, but rather people of Britain. (Britain declined the offer.) And in 1819, immediately after the death of the strong-willed Kamehameha, the Hawaiians, of their own accord, overthrew their own religion, dumped the kapu system and denied their gods. This was *before* any western missionaries ever came to Hawai'i.

Nonetheless, Hawai'i today is once again seeking guidance from her heritage. The echoes of the past seem to be getting louder with time, rather than diminishing. Interest in the Hawaiian language and culture is at a level not seen in many decades. All who live here are very aware of the issues and the complexities involved, but there is little agreement about where it will lead. As a result, you will be exposed to a more "Hawaiian" Hawai'i than those who might have visited the state a generation ago. This is an interesting time in Hawai'i. Enjoy it as observers, and savor the flavor of Hawai'i.

Going with the flow—Big Island style.

In order to get to the islands, you've got to fly here. While this may sound painfully obvious, many people spend time trying to find an ocean cruise to the Islands. There are no regular cruises between Hawai'i and the mainland.

GETTING HERE

When planning your trip, a travel agent can be helpful. Their commission has been paid directly by the travel industry, though that may change in the future. The Internet has dot.com sites such as Orbitz, Expedia, Cheaptickets, Cheapair, Panda-online, Priceline, Travelocity, etc. If you don't want to or can't go through these sources, there are large wholesalers that can get you airfare, hotel and a rental car, often cheaper than you can get airfare on your own. **Pleasant Holidays** (800) 742–9244 is one of the more well-known providers of complete package tours. They

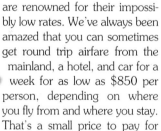

are renowned for their impossibly low rates. We've always been amazed that you can sometimes get round trip airfare from the mainland, a hotel, and car for a week for as low as $850 per person, depending on where you fly from and where you stay. That's a small price to pay for your little piece of paradise.

If you arrange airline tickets and hotel reservations yourself, you can often count on paying top dollar for each facet of your trip. The prices listed in the WHERE TO STAY chapter reflect the RACK rates, meaning the published rates before any discounts. Rates can be significantly lower if you go through a wholesaler.

When you pick your travel source, shop around—the differences can be dramatic. A good source can make the difference between affording a *one-week* vacation and a *two-week* vacation. It's not always a straightforward process; there is an art to it. Look in the Sunday travel section of your local newspaper—the bigger the paper, the better, or check online versions of major papers.

Flight schedules change all the time, but United and others often have *direct* flights to Kona from the mainland. Not having to cool your heels while changing planes on O'ahu is a *big* plus because interisland flights aren't quite as simple and painless as they used to be. Flight attendants zip up and down the aisles hurling juice at you for the short, interisland flight. If you fly to Kona from Honolulu, sit on the left side (seats with an "A") coming in (right side going out) for superb views of several other islands. If you fly into Hilo, sit on the right side coming in. When flying to O'ahu from the mainland, seats on the left side have the best views. Interisland flights are done by **Hawaiian** (800–367–5320), *go!* (888–435–9462) and **Island Air** (800–652–6541), which often has cheap flights between Kona and Hilo.

WHAT TO BRING

This list may assist you in planning what to bring. Obviously you won't bring everything on the list, but it might make you think of a few things you may otherwise overlook:

- Waterproof sunblock (SPF 15 or higher)
- Two bathing suits
- Shoes—flip-flops, trashable sneakers, water shoes, hiking shoes
- Mask, snorkel and fins
- Digital camera
- Extra batteries (which can be hard to find in remote places) for that camera
- Warm clothes (for Mauna Kea or other high-altitude activities) and junk clothes for bikes, etc.
- Fanny pack—also called waist pack, to carry all your various vacation accouterments; waterproof ones are convenient for snorkeling

- Flashlight if you like caves or for the lava field at night if there's a surface flow
- Mosquito repellent for some hikes *(Lotions*—not liquids—with DEET seem to work the longest)
- Light rain jacket
- Shorts and other cool cotton clothing
- Cheap, simple backpack—you don't need to go backpacking to use one; a 10-minute trek to a secluded beach is much easier if you bring a simple pack
- Hat or cap for sun protection

GETTING AROUND
Rental Cars

Rental car prices in Hawai'i *can be* (but aren't always) cheaper than almost anywhere else in the country, and the competition is ferocious. Nearly every visitor to the Big Island gets around in a rental car, and for good reason—it's a *big* island. Fortunately, none have mileage charges.

At Kona Airport, rental cars are a shuttle bus ride away. It's a good idea to reserve your car in advance since companies can run out of cars during peak times.

Many hotels, condos and rental agents offer excellent room/car packages. Find out from your hotel or travel agent if one is available. You can rent a car in Hilo and return it to Kona (or vice versa). There's usually an extra fee of about $50–$100 (depending on the company and car). And prices overall are usually *much* higher in Hilo than in Kona.

Below is a list of rental car companies. The local area code is 808. Some have desks at various hotels.

Alamo	**(877) 222–9075**
	Kona: 329–8896
	Hilo: 961–3343
Avis	**(800) 321–3712**
	Kona: 327–3000
	Hilo: 935–1290

4WDs can unlock some of the Big Island's more secluded beaches, such as this empty black sand beach at Road to the Sea.

Budget	**(800) 527–0700**
	Kona: 329–8511
	Hilo: 935–6878
Dollar	**(800) 800–4000**
	Kona & Hilo:
	(866) 434–2226
Enterprise	**(800) 261–7331**
	Kona: 331–2509
	Hilo: 934–0359
Harper	**(800) 852–9993**
	Kona & Hilo: 969–1478
Hertz	**(800) 654–3131**
	Kona: 329–3566
	Hilo: 935–2896
National	**(877) 222–9058**
	Kona: 329–1674
	Hilo: 935–0891
Thrifty	**(800) 367–5238**
	Kona & Hilo:
	(877) 283–0898

If you're 21–24 years old, most of the companies will rent to you, but you'll pay about $25 extra *per day* for the crime of being young and reckless. If you're under 21—rent a bike or moped or take the bus.

4-Wheel Drive

We *strongly* believe that the best vehicle for the island is a 4-wheel drive vehicle. They come closed (like an Explorer or a Trailblazer) or open (like a Wrangler). They are more expensive, but there are several roads, beaches and sights that you can't visit without 4WD. Even the short paved road into Waipi'o Valley requires the low gear offered in 4WD. Saddle Road (described on page 138) is contractually off limits with half of the rental car companies. That means that if you drive it, the insurance you take out with the rental company is void, so you or your insurance company back home would have to eat it. Different companies have different restrictions, but from a *practical* standpoint, 4WD is the way to go. The drawbacks to *open* JEEPS are more wind and heat and no trunk. Closed 4WDs are best. Expect to pay up to $60–$100 per day for the privilege of cheating the road builders. For some reason, they usually cost much more in Kona than Hilo.

Motorcycles & Scooters

If you really want to ham it up, you can try renting a HOG. *(Disclaimer*—Wizard Publications will not be held liable for bad puns.) **Big Island Harley-Davidson** (329–4464) rents Harleys for $140 per day, $40 extra to keep it overnight. Similar prices at **Big Island Motorcycle** (886–2011) in Waikoloa but insurance is included. Both include helmets, which are *not* required by law in Hawai'i. **Scooter**

Brothers (327–1080) in Kona has scooters for $60 for 24 hours. (These are only useful around Kailua town.)

Motor Homes

The Big Island is the only Hawaiian island where staying in an RV is a viable alternative to hotels. (Ironically, in New Zealand the biggest RV brand is *Maui* brand, but in real life, Maui doesn't *have* any RVs.) With so much territory to cover and good roads leading to so many places, the RV life might be for you, especially if you're traveling with kids.

Some things to consider:

Motor homes are a relatively strange concept here, and you won't find any RV parks or facilities that you might be used to on the mainland.

Beach parks and campgrounds are your best bet for parking. Technically you're supposed to get camping permits to stay at most of them. The best places are Kapaʻa Beach Park in North Kohala (though bees are sometimes a problem there). Spencer Beach Park is also good and Namakani Paio (967–7321) at Volcanoes National Park (it's free), but it was closed for renovations at press time. There are no campgrounds near Kona that we can recommend, but remember, you can park anywhere. See CAMPING on page 179 for more on campsites.

These things don't carry as much waste as you may think, so finding places to empty it will be an ongoing consideration. You can only dump it in Hilo or Kona. Try to use the bathroom facilities at the campgrounds whenever possible.

Harper (800–852–9993) does a pretty good job fixing you up. Their 22-footers are not huge, but they're comfortable. It's not as easy to arrange as a rental car, so do it in advance. You'll need an RV rider from your own insurance. It's $197 per day (plus $220 fee per rental from Kona). 2-day minimum. If you'd like

to pay *way more* than that amount, Island RV (334–0464) will separate you from $320 each day. 5-day minimum.

In Hilo, rent VW camper vans for all you children of the children of the sun. They are like mini RVs with a propane stove, small fridge, drinking water and will sleep four for around $125. **Happy Campers Hawaii** (896–8777). Minimum rental times required.

A Few Driving Tips

Gasoline is *obscenely* expensive here. You may want to have some FedExed to you from home to save money. (OK, maybe not *that* expensive.) Kona is said to have the highest gas prices in the United States (about 15¢ higher than expensive Hilo). Whether that's true or not, prepare to get hammered at the pump. If you're in the Kohala resort area, there's a station off the road to the Waikoloa Resorts at the 76 mile marker. The cheapest gas on the east side of the island is in Hilo or Pahoa, south of Hilo. The cheapest on the *whole island* is in Kona at Costco (but you have to be a Costco member). It's marked on the map on page 164 and not far from the Kona Airport. Many companies charge a top-off fee due to the airport's distance to town, so fill it to the top. And make sure you check your bill. On *many* occasions we've topped off the tank all the way to the brim, only to find a $20 "fuel charge" tacked onto our final tab.

Seat belt and **child restraint** use is required by law, and the police will pull you over for this alone. Wide open roads and frequently changing speed limits make it easy to accidentally speed here. Police usually cruise in their own private, unmarked vehicles, so you won't see them coming. We're not supposed to tell you this, but local protocol dictates that you flash your headlights for a couple of miles when you pass a police car to warn drivers coming the other way. So if you see someone flashing their lights at you, you'd better check your speed.

Cell phone use is illegal for divers unless you have a headset.

It's best not to leave anything valuable in your car. There are teenagers here who pass the time by breaking into cars. Hapuna Beach and several Hilo waterfalls are notorious for car break-ins. When we park at a beach or waterfall, or any other place frequented by visitors, we take all valuables with us, leave the windows up, and leave the doors unlocked. (Just in case someone is curious enough about the inside to smash a window.) There are plenty of stories about someone walking 100 feet to a waterfall in Hilo, coming back to their car, and finding that their brand new video camera has walked away. And don't be gullible enough to think that trunks are safe. Someone who sees you put something in your trunk can probably get at it faster than you can with your key.

Kailua-Kona possesses the dry town syndrome: At the first drop of rain, many Kona drivers become vehicularly uncoordinated, driving like a drunken cat on ice, so beware of this.

Traffic has increased *a lot* in the past few years and you should expect to get stuck in it, especially in Kona. Just remember that it could be worse—you could be in traffic back home *and on your way to work*.

Buses

Our main island bus is called **Hele-On** (961–8744). It was designed for local use, so it doesn't go to all the places that visitors want to go. It's $1 (free if you're over 55, a student or disabled). However, it does go between Hilo and Kona, and they do take luggage (for an extra fee). Call them for a schedule and rates. There are also bus tours from **Roberts Hawai'i** (329–1688) and **Jack's** (969–9507).

GETTING MARRIED ON THE BIG ISLAND

A beautiful beach at sunset—many couples dream of such a background for their special day. 'Anaeho'omalu Beach, pictured on page 43, is one of the more popular spots for sunset weddings. The Big Island offers an almost unlimited selection of wedding, reception and honeymoon possibilities. Although you can set everything up yourself using the Internet and e-mail, it's usually easier and *sometimes* less expensive to use a professional who can assist you.

This one's hard for us. Unlike other activities in this book, we can't exactly get married with all the companies and review them. (The flower bills alone would bankrupt us.) Almost all of the major resorts have wedding coordinators who can offer help. And there are lots of private wedding coordinators. A good resource is **www.bigislandwednet.com**, a wedding network professional exchange.

Expect to pay around $500 for a minimal wedding package (officiant, flower leis and license assistance). Resorts generally charge a hefty fee to use their grounds whether you are a guest or not. All beaches are public, so it won't be a *private* ceremony. Consider renting a private home or an entire B&B in which to hold the ceremony and reception. See our website at **www.wizardpub.com** for links and wedding license requirements.

WEATHER

The weather on the Big Island is more diverse than any island or other comparably sized chunk of land *in the world*. You name it, we got it. According to the Köppen Climate Classification System (which is probably *your* favorite system, too, right?), the Big Island has 10 of the 15 types of climatic zones in the world. (Not *climactic* zones, which we accidentally printed in a previous edition. Boy,

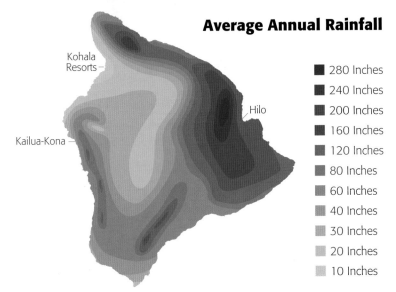

Average Annual Rainfall

Kohala Resorts

Kailua-Kona

Hilo

- 280 Inches
- 240 Inches
- 200 Inches
- 160 Inches
- 120 Inches
- 80 Inches
- 60 Inches
- 40 Inches
- 30 Inches
- 20 Inches
- 10 Inches

people were *really* anxious to find one of *those!*) Only Cold Continental Climate categories are absent. Here we've got tropical, monsoonal, desert and even *periglacial* climates, among others. So no matter what kind of weather you like, we are sure to have it here. As you ascend the slopes of the volcanoes, you lose about 3 degrees for every thousand feet. Call 961-5582 for a recording of today's forecast.

Kailua-Kona has weather that can best be described as eternal springtime. Quite simply, it's almost always warm and wonderful. The average high and low in February (the coldest month) is 80° and 64°, whereas the high and low in August (the warmest month) is 87° and 69°. Humidity is usually between 50% and 80%. The temperature change between night and day is greater than the temperature change between winter and summer, so it could easily be said that nighttime is the winter of the Big Island. Balmy wraparound onshore breezes usually keep it comfortable. The exception is during Kona winds (so named because they come from the Kona direction, rather than out of the northeast as is usually the case). Kona winds occur about 5% of the time and bring stillness or warm air to

Kona, creating uncomfortably humid conditions. Normal conditions in Kona and Kohala mean clear mornings with afternoon clouds created by thermal heating, so morning is usually better for activities such as air tours. During the summer, evening showers often occur as warm moist air is cooled, squeezing rain out of the humidity. Because it is totally protected from the trade winds by Hualalai, Kona is the only place in the state that gets most of its rainfall in the summer afternoons and evenings. The higher up the mountain, the more rain you get.

Hilo's weather is almost always described with one word—*rain*. Hilo is the wettest city in the United States. Annual rainfall is rarely less than 100 inches, usually much more. But rain is not a constant here. Hilo has times of drought like anywhere else. (Like when rainfall was a *mere* 70 inches one year, triggering *rationing*.) Most of the rain falls at night. When daytime showers do occur, they are often intense but short-lived. That said, rain or cloudiness *will* be a factor here. One of the reasons that Kailua-Kona is so much more popular than Hilo is that visitors like sunny weather, and Hilo can't compete in that area. Also, all that rain has to go somewhere, which is why the ocean off Hilo is not nearly as clear as Kona's runoff-free waters.

The Kohala resort area is the driest part of the island, with rainfall usually around 10 inches per year. Sunshine is almost assured (which is why it is so popular). The weather penalty here is the wind. As the lava fields heat up during the day, the air heats and rises. Air from the ocean rushes in to fill the void, creating strong afternoon convective breezes. The hotter, drier and sunnier it is that day, the breezier it may be that afternoon.

The general rule of thumb is that in wet areas like Hilo, most of the rain falls at night and early morning. Dry areas like Kona and Kohala get their rains in the late afternoon and early evenings.

Water temperatures range from 75° at its coldest in February to 82° at its warmest in September/October. It's colder in some areas where freshwater springs percolate from the ocean's floor and float to the top, forming a boundary called a *Ghyben-Herzberg lens*.

PLANNING YOUR TRIP

Visitors are usually unprepared for the sheer size and diversity of the Big Island. The island is over 4,000 square miles, and a circular trip around, on Highways 19 and 11, is a hefty 222 miles. During that drive you pass through dozens of different terrains and climates. (And that doesn't even include Saddle Road, Lower Puna, any of North Kohala or scores of other places.) Put simply, this island is too big and too diverse to try to see in a few days. The graphic on page 29 will put it in perspective.

If you are on the island for three days or less, it's our recommendation that you don't try to see the whole island; you'll only end up touring Hawai'i's exotic blacktop. Pick a side. Since one of your days should be spent at the volcano, that leaves you with a scant two days to experience either Hilo's and Puna's beauty or the Kona side's diversity and activities.

Deciding which side of the island to spend the most time on is a difficult decision, but the numbers are definitely skewed. Most visitors spend most of their time on the western, or Kona, side. There are several reasons for this:

Kona Side

The Kona side has the sunshine. The climate in Kona is as perfect as weather gets, and the Kohala resort area has the highest number of sunny days of anywhere in the state. The Kona side also has *far* more activities available. This leads to another reason—the ocean. Since it's on the leeward side of the island, and because there are no permanent streams on the entire west side of

Only on the Big Island can you experience both conditions on the same day a few dozen miles apart.

the island (except for the one from Kona to Hilo that's filled with tax money), Kona has the calmest, clearest water in the state. Water sports such as swimming, snorkeling, SCUBA, fishing— you name it—are usually unmatched on the Kona side. This side also has the best beaches on the island, with some, such as Hapuna, consistently rated in the top five in the United States. (With a few notable exceptions, the Hilo side has poor beaches.) All this adds up to a traveler's delight, one of the reasons that the Kona side has such a high visitor repeat ratio.

But stand by for a shock when you fly into Kona Airport for the first time. Kona makes a *rotten* first impression on the uninitiated airborne visitor. Part of the airport sits atop a lava flow from 1801, and the first thing you think when you fly in over all that jet black lava is, "I came all this way for *this?*" Don't worry; it gets much better.

Hilo Side

On the other hand, the Kona side is short of what Hilo has in abundance— green. Whereas much of the Kona side is dominated by lava, Hilo is plant heaven. The weather usually comes from the northeast, so Hilo gets around 140 inches of rain per year. This is paradise for anything that grows. Hilo also has breathtaking waterfalls. You won't find *one* on the Kona side unless it's in the lobby of your hotel. Hilo's weather has created beautiful folds and buckles in the terrain. The unweathered Kona side lacks angles—it's mostly gentle slopes. Lastly, Hilo is *much* more convenient for exploring Kilauea volcano.

The Two Sides

The schism between the two sides of the island is wide and deep. Because the two sides are so different and the distances so large (for Hawai'i, that is), most people who live on the west side haven't been to Hilo or Kilauea volcano in years. Most Hilo residents haven't been to Kona in years. Both sides tend to playfully bad-mouth the other. The Kona side creates the tax base, and the Hilo side, the center of county government, spends it (often on Hilo-oriented infrastructure). Hilo has lots of roads that few drive, while Kona drivers curse the traffic on their limited roads.

Suggested Itinerary

If you have a week on the Big Island, you might want to spend four to five days on the Kona side and two to three days in Hilo or Puna. The volcano itself can take one to two days, and you're better off exploring it from Hilo or Puna than from Kona. Hilo all but closes down on Sundays, with most business, even the few tourist-related ones, taking the day off.

GEOGRAPHY

The Big Island is made up of five volcanoes. (See map on the foldout back cover.) Kohala in the north is the oldest. Next came Mauna Kea, Hualalai, Mauna Loa, and finally Kilauea. None of them are truly dead, but only Mauna Loa and Kilauea make regular appearances, with an occasional walk-on by Hualalai. Nearly the size of Connecticut, all the other Hawaiian Islands could easily fit inside the Big Island's 4,000 square miles. And it's the only state in the union that gets bigger every year (thanks to Kilauea's land-making machine).

Gentle slopes are the trademark of this young island. It hasn't had time to develop the dramatic, razor-sharp ridges that older islands, such as Kaua'i, possess. The exception is the windward side of Kohala Mountain where erosion and fault collapses have created a series of dramatic valleys. Two of our mountains rise to over 13,000 feet. Mauna Kea, at 13,796 feet, is the tallest mountain in the world when measured from its base, eclipsing such also-rans as Mount Everest and K-2. Mauna Loa, though slightly shorter, is much broader, earning it the moniker as the *largest* mountain in the world. It contains a mind-numbing 10,000 cubic *miles* of rock.

Another of our mountains is not really a mountain at all. Kilauea, looking more like a gaping wound on Mauna Loa, is the undisputed volcano show-off of the planet. Hundreds of thousands of cubic yards of lava per day issue from its current outlet, Pu'u 'O'o, creating and repaving land on a daily basis.

All this adds up to an exciting and dynamic geographic location. Things change faster here than any place you will ever visit. There have been lots of times that we have gone to a certain beach or area only to find that it has changed beyond recognition. A new black sand beach shifts to another location. Trails become absorbed by a restless and vigorous Mother Nature. Whole roads get covered with lava. Island hopping in this state is like traveling through time. This is an exciting time in the life cycle of this particular island. Enjoy the island in its youth, for like all youths, this, too, shall pass.

SO IS HAWAI'I AN ISLAND OR A STATE?

Both. This island, more than any other in this state, is a bit schizophrenic when it comes to names. This is the biggest island in the state, so it is commonly referred to as (brace yourself) *the Big Island.* Its Hawaiian name is *Hawai'i.* So far, so good. But the whole *state* is called Hawai'i. So you figure the capital must be here, right? Nope, Honolulu is on O'ahu. This must be where most of the people live, right? Uh-uh. O'ahu has 80% of the population. Well, this must be where Pearl Harbor is, correct? Wrong answer—it's on O'ahu, too. So why is the state named after *this* island? Because it's

the *biggest* island, and this is where King Kamehameha the Great was from. It was he who brought all the islands under one rule for the first time. His first capital was here at Kailua (another naming headache—see below). When you do all that, you have some historical influence. In this book we will refer to this island as *the Big Island.* When we say Hawai'i, we mean the whole state. (Even my brother, when he came to visit the Big Island, called from Honolulu to have me pick him up, assuming it must be on the "main" island.) In short, *in Hawai'i* could be anywhere—*on Hawai'i* is on the Big Island.

I won't even get into the name confusion for the town of Waimea. (Or is it Kamuela? See page 134.) Let's tackle a more annoying naming problem. The main town on the west side is called **Kailua-Kona**, **Kona**, **Kailua** or sometimes **Kailua Town**. In the old days it was simply Kailua. Though there are also towns named Kailua on O'ahu and Maui, it didn't present much of a problem to anyone until the Post Office discovered these islands. In order to keep from mess-

How Big is The Big Island of Hawai'i?

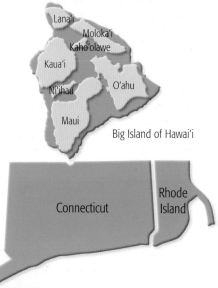

Lana'i
Moloka'i
Kaho'olawe
Kaua'i
Ni'ihau
O'ahu
Maui
Big Island of Hawai'i

Connecticut

Rhode Island

ing up the mail *(don't say it!)*, they decided to rename the town. (Technically, they renamed their post office, but the subtlety is lost on those who have to address mail.) Since this is the *kona* side of the island (*kona* being the name of the less common wind that comes from this direction), they cleverly named the Post Office *Kailua-Kona*. To complicate matters further, the builders of the airport here named it the *Kona Airport*, so people began to refer to a trip here as "going to Kona." All this leaves you with a quandary. What do you call this place? Well, in keeping with our editorial policy of taking gutsy stands, we'll call it Kailua-Kona...except when we call it Kona or Kailua Town. In fairness, that's because most who live here do the same.

HAZARDS
The Sun

The hazard that affects by far the most people (excluding the accommodations tax) is the sun. The Big Island, at $19°-20°$ latitude, receives sunlight more directly than anywhere on the mainland. (The more overhead the sunlight is, the less atmosphere it filters through.) If you want to enjoy your *entire* vacation, make sure that you wear a strong sunblock or cover up, even while snorkeling. We recommend a waterproof sunblock with at least an SPF of 15. Gels work best in the water, lotions on land. Try to avoid the sun between 11 a.m. and 2 p.m. when the sun's rays are particularly strong. If you are fair-skinned or unaccustomed to the sun and want to lay out, 15–20 minutes per side is all you should consider the first day. You can increase it a bit each day. *Beware of the fact that our ever-constant breezes will hide the symptoms of a burn until it's too late.* You might find that trying to get your tan as golden as possible isn't worth it. Tropical suntans are notoriously short lived, whereas you are sure to remember a burned vacation far longer. If, after all of

our warnings, you *still* get burned, aloe vera gel works well to relieve the pain. Some come with lidocaine in them. Ask your hotel front desk if they have any aloe plants on the grounds. Peel the skin off a section and make several crisscross cuts in the meat, then rub the plant on your skin. *Oooo,* it'll feel so good!

Water Hazards

The most serious water hazard is the surf. Though more calm in the summer and on the west side, high surf can be found anywhere on the island at any time of the year. The sad fact is that more people drown in Hawai'i each year than anywhere else in the country. This isn't said to keep you from enjoying the ocean, but rather to instill in you a healthy respect for Hawaiian waters. See BEACHES for more information on this.

Ocean Critters

Hawaiian marine life, for the most part, is quite friendly. There are, however, a few notable exceptions. Below is a list of some critters that you should be aware of. This is not mentioned to frighten you out of the water. The odds are overwhelming that you won't have any trouble with any of the beasties listed below. But should you encounter one, this information should be of some help.

Sharks—Hawai'i does have sharks. They are mostly white-tipped reef sharks and the occasional hammerhead or tiger shark. Contrary to what most people think, sharks live in *every* ocean and don't pose the level of danger people attribute to them. In the past 25 years there have been only a handful of documented shark attacks off the Big Island, mostly tigers attacking surfers. Considering the number of people who swam in our waters during that time, you are more likely to choke to death on a bone at a lu'au than be attacked by a shark. If you do happen to come upon a shark, however, swim away slowly. This kind of movement doesn't interest them. *Don't* splash about rapidly. By doing this you are imitating a fish in distress, and you don't want to do that. The one kind of ocean water you want to avoid is murky water, such as that found near river mouths. These are not interesting to swim in anyway. Most shark attacks occur in murky water at dawn or dusk since sharks are basically cowards that like to sneak up on their prey. In general, don't go around worrying about sharks. *Any* animal can be threatening. (Even Jessica Alba was once rudely accosted by an overly affectionate male dolphin.)

Portuguese Man-of-War—These are related to jellyfish but are unable to swim.

They are instead propelled by a small sail and are at the mercy of the wind. Though small, they are capable of inflicting a painful sting. This occurs when the long, trailing tentacles are touched, triggering hundreds of thousands of spring-loaded stingers, called nematocysts, which inject venom. The resulting burning sensation is usually very unpleasant but not fatal. Fortunately, the Portuguese Man-of-War is very uncommon on the west shore of the island. When they *do* come ashore, they usually do so in great numbers, jostled by a strong storm offshore. If you see them on the beach, don't go in the water. If you do get stung, immediately remove the tentacles with a gloved hand, stick or whatever is handy. Rinse thoroughly with salt or fresh water to remove any adhering nematocysts. Then apply ice for pain control. If the condition worsens,

see a doctor. The old treatments of vinegar or baking soda are no longer recommended. The folk cure is urine, but you might look pretty silly applying it.

Sea Urchins—These are like living pin cushions. If you step on one or accidentally grab one, remove as much of the spine as possible with tweezers. See a physician if necessary.

Coral—Coral skeletons are very sharp and, since the skeleton is overlaid by millions of living coral polyps, a scrape can leave proteinaceous matter in the wound, causing infection. This is why coral cuts are frustratingly slow to heal. Immediate cleaning and disinfecting of coral cuts should speed up healing time. We don't have fire coral around the Big Island.

Sea Anemones—Related to the jellyfish, these also have stingers and are usually found attached to rocks or coral. It's best not to touch them with your bare hands. Treatment for a sting is similar to that for a Portuguese Man-of-War.

Bugs

Though devoid of the myriad of hideous buggies found in other parts of the world, there are a few evil critters brought here from elsewhere that you should know about. The worst are **centipedes**. They can get to be six or more inches long and are aggressive predators. They shouldn't be messed with. If you get stung, even by a baby, the pain can range from a bad bee sting to a bad gunshot wound. Some local doctors say the only cure is to stay drunk for three days. Others say to use meat tenderizer. **Scorpions** are present on the dry, western side of the island. Though not as nasty as the ones you see in the movies, a sting is unpleasant nonetheless. They're usually a couple inches across and mildly aggressive. **Cane spiders** are big, dark, and look horrifying, but they're not poisonous. (Though they seem to *think* they are. I've had *them* chase *me* across the room when *I* had the broom in my hand.) We *don't* have no-see-ums, those irritating sand fleas common in the South Pacific and Caribbean. (A Hawaiian voyaging canoe that traveled to and from Tahiti on a cultural mission several years ago unknowingly brought them back. The crew was forced into quarantine against their will where the tiny biting insects were discovered and exterminated. No-see-ums would have easily spread here and changed Hawai'i forever.)

Mosquitoes were unknown in the islands until the first stowaways arrived on Maui on the *Wellington* in 1826. Since then they have thrived. A good mosquito repellent containing DEET will come in handy, especially if you plan to go hiking. *Lotions* (not thin liquids) with DEET seem to work and stick best. Forget the guidebooks that tell you to take vitamin B12 to keep mosquitoes away; it just gives the lit-tle critters a healthier diet. If you find one dive bombing you at night in your room, turn on your overhead fan to help keep them away. Local residents and resorts often rely on genetically engineered plants such as Citrosa, which irritates mosquitoes as much as they irritate us.

Bees and **yellow jackets** are more common on the drier west side of the island. Usually, the only way you'll get stung is if you run into one. If you rent a scooter, beware; I received my first bee sting while singing *Come Sail Away* on a motorcycle. A bee sting in the mouth can definitely ruin one of your precious vacation days.

Regarding **cockroaches**, there's good news and bad news. The bad news is that here, some are bigger than your thumb and can fly. The good news is that you probably won't see one. One of their predators is the **gecko**. This small, lizard-like creature makes a surprisingly loud chirp at night. They are cute and considered good luck in the Islands (probably because they eat mosquitoes and small roaches).

Leptospirosis is a bacteria that is found in some of Hawai'i's freshwater. It is transmitted from animal urine and can enter the body from open cuts, eyes and by drinking. Around 100 people a year in Hawai'i are diagnosed with the bacteria, which is treated with antibiotics if caught relatively early. You should avoid crossing streams such as Waipi'o with open cuts, and treat all water found in nature with treatment pills before drinking. (Many filters are ineffective for lepto.)

Though not a bug, one animal you are almost sure to see is the **mongoose**. Think of it as a stealth squirrel with mean-looking red eyes. Mongooses (no, not mongeese) are bold enough

With no permanent streams on the west side of the island, fresh water sometimes collects inside lava tubes at the shoreline, such as this one at Kiholo Bay.

to take on cobras in their native India and were brought here to help control rats. Great idea, except mongooses are active during the day and rats work the night shift, so never the twain shall meet. It was a disaster for local birds since mongooses love bird eggs. Kaua'i is the only major island to avoid the mongoose (and vice versa), and the difference between its bird population and the Big Island's is dramatic.

There are no **snakes** in Hawai'i (except for some reporters). There is concern that the brown tree snake *might* have made its way onto the islands from Guam. Although mostly harmless to humans, these snakes can spell extinction to native birds. Government officials aren't allowed to tell you this, but we will: If you ever see one anywhere in Hawai'i, please *kill it* and contact the Pest Hotline at (808) 643–7378. At the very least, call them immediately. The entire bird population of Hawai'i will be grateful.

Frogs

There are some irritating visitors that first arrived on the island a few years back and won't leave. (Well, besides the in-laws.) They're small tree frogs, called Coqui, that emit a whistle all night long. Cute at first, like a bird, but incessant and ultimately irritating. Most of the resorts do their best to deal with them, but there's a chance that some errant froggies may occasionally give you a long night. The Hilo side is froggier (I *swear* that's a real word) than Kona.

Vog

Vog is a mixture of water vapor, carbon dioxide and sulfur dioxide. Each day Kilauea belches 2,500 *tons* of sulphur dioxide. (Since the current eruption began, it has produced enough sulphur dioxide to fill a *half million* Goodyear blimps.) These gases react with sunlight, oxygen, dust particles and water in the air to form a mixture of sulfate aerosols, sulfuric acid and other oxidized sulfur compounds. Why should *you* care? Because our trade winds blow toward the southwest, carrying the vog from its source, down the coast where the winds wrap around Mauna Loa and head up the coast. Then daytime onshore breezes and nighttime offshore breezes rake it back and forth across Kona. If you have a severe lung condition or are very asthmatic, you may experience discomfort. When the volcano is *really* belching, Kona's vog bothers everyone. Those who stay in Kohala and Hilo are usually free from vog. In all, it's probably less than the smog in most mainland cities, but we wanted to alert you to one of the few negatives to living on an active volcano. Call (866) 767–5044 for the vog index.

Dehydration

Bring and drink lots of water when you are out and about, especially when you are hiking. Dehydration sneaks up on people. By the time you are thirsty, you're already dehydrated. It's a good idea to take an insulated water jug with you in the car or one of those 1½ liter bottles of water. Our weather is almost certainly different than what you left behind, and you will probably find yourself thirstier than usual. Just fill it before you leave in the morning and *suck 'em up* (as we say here) all day.

Curses

Legend says that if you remove any lava from the island, bad luck will befall you. *Balderdash!* you say. Hey, we don't know if it's true or not. You don't have to be a believer, but we at Wizard Publications along with resorts and local post offices, get boxes of lava that come in all the time from visitors who brought a souvenir of lava home, only to have their house burn down, have their foot fall off or get audited by the IRS. Coincidence? Maybe. But if you decide to do it anyway, remember... you've been warned.

Also, if the curse isn't enough to dissuade you, the TSA has written us asking us to inform you that they will *confiscate* any large lava rocks, coral or sand found in your luggage.

Grocery Stores

Definitely a hazard. Though restaurants on the Big Island are expensive, don't think you'll get off cheap in grocery stores. You'll certainly save money by cooking your own food, but you'll be amazed, appalled and offended by the prices you see here. If you are staying at a condo, savvy travelers should head over to **Costco** (331–4800) just north of Kona (shown on map on page 164) to stock up. If you're not a member of this national warehouse store, you *might* qualify for membership. (Call 800–774–2678 for info.) If so, the savings on food and everything else are incredible, especially for Hawai'i. Otherwise, ask around to see if any residents you are dealing with will let you go with them.

There are no large grocery stores in the Kohala resort area, just an upscale market in the **Queens' MarketPlace** in Waikoloa. You'll find a larger store 6 miles up Waikoloa Road (which is across from the 75 mile marker) in Waikoloa Village. They're easy to find in Kona and Hilo.

TRAVELING WITH CHILDREN (KEIKI)

Should we have put this section under HAZARDS, too? The Hilton Waikoloa probably has the most extensive children's activity program. Their Camp Menehune (ages 5–12) is a youngster's dream. Several other Kohala resorts also try hard to cater to families. If your keiki (kid) is looking for an adventure, check out page 236 where we have a dandy adventure just for them. **All About Babies** (883–3675) has the usual assortment of keiki paraphernalia for rent, such as car seats, strollers, cribs, bathtubs, etc as does **Baby's Away** (322–5158).

For swimming, the beach in front of the King Kamehameha's Kona Beach Hotel or the tide-pools at the Natural Energy Lab in Kona, and Onekahakaha in Hilo are probably the safest on the island. (Check them out yourself to be sure.) We don't need to tell you that keiki and surf don't mix.

There's a great playground at **Higashihara Park** just south of Kona past the 115 mile marker. Another one is at the corner of Kuakini Hwy and Makala Blvd. at the north end of Kona, and **Waimea Park** in Waimea. See Waimea map. The **Na Kamalei Toddler Playground** in Kailua Park is an entertaining spot for the youngest visitors. And the nearby **Swing Zone** (329–6909) on Kuakini and Makala has batting cages and putt-putt golf for older kids.

'**Imiloa Astronomy Center** (969–9700) in Hilo is a great hands on keiki experience. See page 109 for more.

Kids might enjoy the seahorse tour at **Ocean Rider** (page 57) and if they're old enough, consider SNUBA on page 223.

If you want to eat at a nice restaurant but are afraid the little ones might get restless, we've noticed that many parents often eat at the Kona Inn, where the strip of grass between the restaurant and the shoreline serves as a convenient romping area for kids when they are finished. You can still keep an eye out for them so they don't wander too far.

Lastly, you should know that it's a big fine plus a mandatory safety class if your keiki isn't buckled up.

THE PEOPLE

There's no doubt about it, people really *are* friendlier in Hawai'i. You will notice that people are quick to smile and

A protected tide-pool can be the perfect place to introduce your keiki to the wonders of the sea.

wave at you here. (Those of us who live in Hawai'i have to remember to pack our "mainland face" when we journey there. Otherwise, we get undesired responses when we smile or wave at complete strangers.) It probably comes down to a matter of happiness. People are happy here, and happy people are friendly people. Some people compare a trip to an outer island in Hawai'i to a trip back in time, when smiles weren't rare, and politeness was the order of the day.

Ethnic Breakdown

The Big Island has an ethnic mix that is as diversified as any you will find. Here, *everyone* is a minority; there are no majorities. The last census revealed the ethnic makeup below:

White	68,110
Asian	41,791
Hispanic	21,162
Hawaiian or Other Pacific Islander	20,451
Black	1,778
American Indian or Alaska Native	1,422
Other	23,121
Total	**177,835**

SOME TERMS

A person of Hawaiian blood is Hawaiian. Only people of this race are called by this term. They are also called Kanaka Maoli, but only another Hawaiian can use this term. Anybody who was born here, regardless of race (except whites) is called a local. If you were born elsewhere but have lived here awhile, you are called a kama'aina. If you are white, you are a haole. It doesn't matter if you have been here a day or your family has been here for over a century—you will always be a haole. The term comes from the time when westerners first encountered these islands. Its precise meaning has been lost, but it is thought to refer to people with no background (since westerners could not chant the kanaenae of their ancestors).

The continental United States is called the Mainland. If you are here and are returning, you are not "going back to the states" (we *are* a state). When somebody leaves the island, they are off-island.

HAWAIIAN TIME

One aspect of Hawaiian culture you may have heard of is Hawaiian Time. The stereotype is that everyone in Hawai'i moves just a little bit slower than on the mainland. Supposedly, we are more laid-back and don't let things get to us as easily as people on the mainland. This is the stereotype... OK, it's *not* a stereotype. It's real. Hopefully, during your visit, you will notice that this feeling infects *you* as well. You may find yourself letting another driver cut in front of you in circumstances that would incur your wrath back home. You may find yourself willing to wait for a red light without feeling like you're going to explode. The whole reason for coming to Hawai'i is to experience beauty and a sense of peace, so let it happen. If someone else is moving a bit more slowly than you want, just go with it.

SHAKA

One gesture you will see often and should not be offended by is the *shaka* sign. This is done by extending the pinkie and thumb while curling the three middle fingers. Sometimes visitors think it is some kind of local gesture indicating *up yours* or some similarly unfriendly message. Actually, it is a friendly act used as a sign of greeting or just to say *Hey*. Its origin is thought to date back to the 1930s. A guard at the Kahuku Sugar Plantation on O'ahu used to patrol the plantation railroad to keep local kids from stealing cane from the slow moving trains. This guard had lost his middle fingers in an accident and his manner of waving off the youths became well known. Kids began to warn other kids that he was around by waving their hands in a way that looked like the guard's, and the custom took off.

THE HAWAIIAN LANGUAGE

The Hawaiian language is a beautiful, gentle and melodic language that flows smoothly off the tongue. Just the sounds of the words conjure up trees gently blowing in the breeze and the sound of the surf. Most Polynesian languages share the same roots, and many have common words. Today, Hawaiian is spoken *as an everyday language* only on the privately owned island of Ni'ihau. Visitors are often intimidated by Hawaiian. With a few ground rules you will come to realize that pronunciation is not as hard as you might think.

When missionaries discovered that the Hawaiians had no written language, they sat down and created an alphabet. This Hawaiian alphabet has only twelve letters. Five vowels; A, E, I, O and U, as well as seven consonants; H, K, L, M, N, P and W. The consonants are pronounced just as they are in English with the exception of W. It is often pronounced as a V if it is in the middle of a word and comes after an E or I. Vowels are pronounced as follows:

A—pronounced as in *Ah* if stressed, or *above* if not stressed.
E—pronounced as in *say* if stressed, or *dent* if not stressed.
I—pronounced as in *bee*.
O—pronounced as in *no*.
U—pronounced as in *boo*.

One thing you will notice in this book are glottal stops. These are represented by an upside-down apostrophe ' and are meant to convey a hard stop in the pronunciation. So if we are talking about the type of lava called 'a'a, it is pronounced as two separate As (AH-AH).

Another feature you will encounter are diphthongs, where two letters glide together. They are ae, ai, ao, au, ei, eu, oi, and ou. Unlike many English diphthongs, the second vowel is always pronounced. One word you will read in this book, referring to Hawaiian temples, is *heiau* (HEY-YOW). The e and i flow together as a single sound, then the a and u flow together as a single sound. The Y sound binds the two sounds, making the whole word flow together.

If you examine long Hawaiian words, you will see that most have repeating syllables, making it easier to remember and pronounce.

Let's take a word that might seem impossible to pronounce. When you see how easy this word is, the rest will seem like a snap. The Hawai'i State Fish is the humuhumunukunukuapua'a. At first glance it seems like a nightmare. But if you read the word slowly, it is pro-

nounced just like it looks and isn't nearly as horrifying as it appears. Try
it. Humu (hoo-moo) is pronounced
twice. Nuku (noo-koo) is pronounced
twice. A (ah) is pronounced once. Pu
(poo) is pronounced once. A'a (ah-ah) is
the ah sound pronounced twice, the
glottal stop indicating a hard stop between sounds. Now you can try it again.
Humuhumunukunukuapua'a.
Now, wasn't that easy? OK, so it's not
easy, but it's not impossible either.

Below are some words that you might
hear during your visit.

'Aina (EYE-na)—Land.

Akamai (AH-ka-MY)—Wise or shrewd.

Ali'i (ah-LEE-ee)—A Hawaiian chief; a
member of the chiefly class.

Aloha (ah-LO-ha)—Hello, goodbye
or a feeling or the spirit of love,
affection or kindness.

Hala (HA-la)—Pandanus tree.

Hale (HA-leh)—House or building.

Hana (HA-na)—Work.

Hana hou (HA-na-HO)—To do
again.

Haole (HOW-leh)—Originally foreigner,
now means Caucasian.

Heiau (HEY-YOW)—Hawaiian temple.

Hula (HOO-la)—The story-telling dance
of Hawai'i.

Imu (EE-moo)—An underground oven.

'Iniki (ee-NEE-key)—Sharp and piercing
wind (as in Hurricane 'Iniki).

Kahuna (ka-HOO-na)—A priest or
minister; someone who is an expert
in a profession.

Kai (kigh)—The sea.

Kalua (KA-LOO-ah)—Cooking food
underground.

Kama'aina (KA-ma-EYE-na)—Long-time
Hawai'i resident.

Kane (KA-neh)—Boy or man.

Kapu (KA-poo)—Forbidden, taboo;
keep out.

Keiki (KAY-key)—Child or children.

Kokua (KO-KOO-ah)—Help.

Kona (KO-na)—Leeward side of the island; wind blowing from the south,
southwest direction.

Kuleana (KOO-leh-AH-na)—Concern,
responsibility or jurisdiction.

Lanai (LA-NIGH)—Porch, veranda, patio.

Lani (LA-nee)—Sky or heaven.

Lei (lay)—Necklace of flowers, shells or
feathers. The lehua blossom lei is the
lei of the Big Island.

Liliko'i (LEE-lee-KO-ee)—Passion fruit.

Limu (LEE-moo)—Edible seaweed.

Lomi (LOW-me)—To rub or massage;
lomi salmon is raw salmon rubbed
with salt and spices.

Lu'au (LOO-OW)—Hawaiian feast;
literally means taro leaves.

Mahalo (ma-HA-low)—Thank you.

Makai (ma-KIGH)—Toward the sea.

Malihini (MA-lee-HEE-nee)—A new-
comer, visitor or guest.

Mauka (MOW-ka)—Toward the mountain.

Moana (mo-AH-na)—Ocean.

Mo'o (MO-oh)—Lizard.

Nani (NA-nee)—Beautiful, pretty.

Nui (NEW-ee)—Big, important, great.

'Ohana (oh-HA-na)—Family.

'Okole (OH-KO-leh)—Derrière.

'Ono (OH-no)—Delicious, the best.

Pakalolo (pa-ka-LO-LO)—Marijuana.

Pali (PA-lee)—A cliff.

Paniolo (PA-nee-OH-lo)—Hawaiian
cowboy.

Pau (pow)—Finish, end; *pau hana*
means quitting time from work.

Poi (poy)—Pounded kalo (taro) root that
forms a paste.

Pono (PO-no)—Goodness, excellence,
correct, proper.

Pua (POO-ah)—Flower.

Puka (POO-ka)—Hole.

Pupu (POO-POO)—Appetizer, snacks
or finger food.

Wahine (vah-HEE-neh)—Woman.

Wai (why)—Fresh water.

Wikiwiki (WEE-kee-WEE-kee)—To
hurry up, very quick.

Quick Pidgin Lesson

Hawaiian pidgin is fun to listen to. It's like ear candy. It's colorful, rhythmic and sways in the wind. Below is a list of some of the words and phrases you might hear on your visit. It's tempting to read some of these and try to use them. If you do, the odds are you will simply look foolish. These words and phrases are used in certain ways and with certain inflections. People who have spent years living in the islands still feel uncomfortable using them. Thick pidgin can be incomprehensible to the untrained ear (that's the idea). If you are someplace and hear two people engaged in a discussion in pidgin, stop and eavesdrop a bit. You won't forget it.

Pidgin Words & Phrases

An' den—And then? So?
Any kine—Anything; any kind.
Ass right—That's right.
Ass why—That's why.
Beef—Fight.
Brah—Bruddah; friend; brother.
Brok' da mouf—Delicious.
Buggah—That's the one; it is difficult.
Bus laugh—To laugh out loud.
Bus nose—How one reacts to a
   bad smell.
Chicken skin kine—Something that
   gives you goosebumps.
Choke—Plenty; a lot.
Cockaroach—Steal; rip off.
Da kine—A noun or verb used in place
   of whatever the speaker wishes.
   Heard constantly.
Fo Days—plenty; "He got hair fo days."
Geevum—Go for it! Give 'em hell!
Grind—To eat.
Grinds—Food.
Hold ass—A close call when driving
   your new car.
How you figga?—How do you figure
   that? It makes no sense.
Howzit?—How is it going? How are
   you? Also, Howzit o wot?

I owe you money or wot?—What to say
   when someone is staring at you.
Mek ass—Make a fool of yourself.
Mek house—Make yourself at home.
Mek plate—Grab some food.
Mo' bettah—This is better.
Moke—A large, tough local male.
   (Don't say it unless you *like beef*.)
No can—Cannot; I cannot do it.
No mek lidat—Stop doing that.
No, yeah?—No, or is "no" correct?
'Okole squeezer—Something that suddenly frightens you ('okole meaning
   derrière).
O wot?—Or what?
Pau hana—Quit work. (A time of daily,
   intense celebration in the islands.)
Poi dog—A mutt.
Shahkbait—Shark bait, meaning pale,
   untanned people.
Shaka—Great! All right!
Shredding—Riding a gnarly wave.
Sleepahs—Flip-flops, thongs, zoris.
Stink eye—Dirty looks; facial expression denoting displeasure.
Suck rocks—Buzz off, or pound sand.
Talk stink—Speak bad about somebody.
Talk story—Shooting the breeze; to rap.
Tanks eh?—Thank you.
Tita—A female moke. Same *beef* results.
Yeah?—Used at the end of sentences.

MUSIC

Hawaiian music is far more diverse than most people think. Many people picture Hawaiian music as someone twanging away on an 'ukulele with his voice slipping and sliding all over the place like he has an ice cube down his back. In reality, the music here can be outstanding. There is the melodic sound of the more traditional music. There are young local bands putting out modern music with a Hawaiian beat. There is even Hawaiian reggae. *Hawaiian Style Band*, the late *Israel Kamakawiwo'ole* (known locally as Bruddah Iz) and *Bruddah Waltah* are excellent examples. Even if you don't always agree with all of the messages in the songs, there's no denying the talent of these groups.

THE HULA

The hula evolved as a means of worship, later becoming a forum for telling a story with chants (called mele), hands and body movement. It can be fascinating to watch. When most people think of the hula, they picture a woman in a grass skirt swinging her hips to the beat of an 'ukulele. But in reality there are two types of hula. The modern hula, or hula 'auana, uses musical instruments and vocals to augment the dancer. It came about after westerners first encountered the islands. Missionaries found the hula distasteful, and the old style was driven underground. The modern type came about as a form of entertainment and was practiced in places where missionaries had no influence. Ancient Hawaiians didn't even use grass skirts. They were later brought by Gilbert Islanders.

The old style of hula is called hula 'olapa or hula kahiko. It consists of chants and is accompanied only by percussion and takes years of training. It can be exciting to watch as performers work together in a synchronous harmony. Both men and women participate, with women's hula being softer (though no less disciplined) and men's hula being more active. This type of hula is physically demanding, requiring strong concentration. Keiki (children's) hula can be charming to watch as well.

The world's best gather each year in Hilo for a week starting the first Thursday after Easter Sunday for the **Merrie Monarch Festival** (named after the 19th-century king credited with reviving the hula). Tickets are often hard to come by if you wait too long. Call (808)

935–9168 *right* after New Year's Day if you want to be assured of getting a seat. Otherwise, check it out on TV. It will utterly dazzle you.

A NOTE ABOUT ACCESS

If a lawful landowner posts a NO TRESPASSING sign on their land, you need to respect their wishes. That seems simple enough. But here's where it gets tricky.

It's common in Hawai'i for someone who doesn't own or control land to erect their own NO TRESPASSING, KEEP OUT and ROAD CLOSED signs. Picture a shoreline fisherman who doesn't want anyone else near his cherished spot, putting up a store-bought sign to protect his solitude. Or a neighbor on a dirt road who hates the dust from cars driving by, so he puts up a sign that he knows locals will ignore, but it might dissuade unwary visitors.

In the past we did our best to try to ferret out when NO TRESPASSING signs were valid, and when they were not and we took *a lot* of heat from residents who thought we were encouraging trespassing when we weren't. But the current environment doesn't permit us to do that anymore. So if you're heading to one of the places we describe and you encounter a NO TRESPASSING sign, even if you think it's not authorized by the landowner (and even if it's on *public* land), we have to advise you to turn around and heed the sign. All descriptions in our book come with the explicit assumption that you have obtained the permission of the legal landowner, and unfortunately it'll usually be up to you to determine who that is and how to get it. But please, under no circumstances are we suggesting that you trespass. Plain and clear. Don't trespass…ever…for any reason…period.

You stay safe by staying smart. You don't need a guidebook to tell you that this is a really bad idea.

A NOTE ON PERSONAL RESPONSIBILITY

In past editions we've had the sad task of removing places that you can no longer visit. The reason, universally cited, is *liability*. Although Hawai'i has a statute indemnifying landowners, the mere threat is often enough to get something closed. Because we, more than any other publication, have exposed heretofore unknown attractions, we feel the need to pass this along.

You need to assess what kind of traveler you are. We've been accused of leaning a bit toward the adventurous side, so you should take that into account when deciding if something's right for you. To paraphrase from the movie *Top Gun*, "Don't let your ego write checks your body can't cash."

Please remember that this isn't Disneyland—it's nature. Mother Nature is hard, slippery, sharp and unpredictable. If you go exploring and get into trouble, whether it's your ego that's bruised or something more tangible, please remember that neither the state, the private land owner nor this publication *told* you to go. You *chose* to explore, which is what life, and this book, are all about. And if you complain to or threaten someone controlling land, they'll rarely fix the problem you identified. They'll simply close it... and it will be gone for good.

Sometimes even good intentions can lead to disaster. At one adventure, a trailhead led hikers to the base of a wonderful waterfall. There was only *one* trail, to the left at the parking lot, that a person could take. Neither we, other guides nor websites ever said, "stay on the trail to the left" because at the time there was only one trail to take. The state (in their zeal to protect themselves from liability at an unmaintained trail) came along and put up a DANGER KEEP OUT sign at the trailhead. Travelers encountering the sign assumed they were on the wrong trail and started to beat a path to the right instead. But that direction started sloping downward and ended abruptly at a 150-foot-high cliff. Hikers retreated and in a short time a previously non-existent trail to the right became as prominent as the correct (and heretofore *only*) path to the left. Not long after the state's well-intentioned sign went up, an unwitting pair of hikers took the new, incorrect trail to the right and fell to their deaths. They probably died because they had been dissuaded from taking the correct trail by a state sign theoretically erected to keep people safe.

Our point is that nothing is static and nothing can take the place of your own observations and good judgment. If you're doing one of the activities you read about in our book or someplace else and your instinct tells you something is wrong, *trust your judgment* and go do another activity. There are lots of wonderful things to do on the island, and we want to keep you safe and happy.

And also remember to always leave the island the same way you found it.

MISCELLANEOUS INFORMATION

It is customary here for *everyone* to remove their shoes upon entering someone's house (sometimes their office).

If you are going to spend any time at the beach, woven bamboo beach mats can be found all over the island for about $3. Some roll up, some can be folded. The sand comes off these easier than it comes off towels.

Around the island you'll see signs saying VISITOR INFORMATION, VOLCANO UPDATE or something similar. Allow me to translate. That's usually code for WE WANT TO SELL YOU SOMETHING.

The **area code** for the state is 808. **Daylight Saving** isn't observed here.

If you wear **sunglasses**, *polarized* lenses are highly recommended. Not only are our colors more vivid here, but the lower latitudes of Hawai'i make polarized lenses particularly effective.

If you want to arrange a lei greeting for you or your honey when you disembark the airplane, **Greeters of Hawai'i** (800) 366–8559 can make the arrangements for around $25. Nice way to kick off a romantic trip, huh?

A WORD ABOUT DRIVING TOURS

The Big Island is, to use the scientific term, *one big bugga*. With this in mind,

we have decided to describe the various parts of the island in a series of tours. You're not being pigeonholed into seeing the island in this order, but we had to organize the regions in some fashion, and this seemed the logical way to do it rather than a scattershot description. You can take these tours from any place you are staying, but we have described most of them (except the Hilo tour and the Hamakua/Waimea tour) on the assumption that you are starting from the west (Kona) side because the majority of Big Island visitors do just that. The Hamakua/Waimea section is described from the Hilo side first because it's convenient to see it that way after traveling via Saddle Road.

Nearly every guidebook divides the Big Island and its sights by districts. (See graphic on fold-out back map.) While this land division made perfect sense to the ancients who divvied up the island among themselves, it is not real helpful to the modern traveler who cruises the island by car. So we have divided the island up in a way that makes more sense to today's visitor. It takes into account where most people stay and how they drive. Look at the inside *front* cover to see how we have divided the island and on what pages we describe the sights.

Most main roads have mile markers erected every mile. Since Hawai'i is mostly void of other identification signs, these little green signs can be a big help in knowing where you are at a given time. Therefore, we have placed them on the maps represented as a number inside a small box ⬛. We will often describe a certain feature or unmarked road as being, "⁴/₁₀ miles past the 22 mile mark." We hope this helps.

For directions, locals usually describe things as being on the **mauka** (MOW-ka) side of the highway—toward the mountains or **makai** (ma-KIGH)—toward the ocean.

Beaches, activities and adventures are mentioned briefly, but described in detail in their own separate sections.

FARMERS' MARKETS

Kailua-Kona—The **Kailua Village Farmers' Market** (Wed.–Sun.) at the corner of Hualalai and Alii Drive is the biggest in town. There are tons of cheap, foreign-made crafts. Open 7 a.m. to 4 p.m. The **Alii Gardens Marketplace** near the 2½ mile marker on Alii Drive focuses more on crafts and local hand-made items with a few decent food vendors. Open 9 a.m. to 5 p.m. daily. The **Keauhou Farmers' Market** (Sat.) at the Keauhou Shopping Center claims to sell only locally grown products such as coffee and mac nuts. Open 8 a.m. to noon.

Hilo—The **Hilo Farmers' Market** on the corner of Mamo Street and Kamehameha Avenue has mostly produce and flowers with a few booths of crafts and gift items. Open every day 7 a.m. *till it's gone*. Wednesdays and Saturdays have the most vendors and open at 6 a.m.

Waimea—The **Waimea Homestead Farmers' Market** is small but has a lot to offer. Among the food, flower and plant vendors, you'll find some great locally made items like goat cheese, chocolate and vanilla beans. Saturdays only, on Hwy 19 near the 55 mile marker. Open Saturdays from 7 a.m. to noon.

Pahoa—The **Maku'u Farmers' Market**, on Sundays, just south of the 7 mile marker on Hwy 130 has reached flea market (or possibly bazaar) status. Open Sundays from 8 a.m. to 2 p.m.

BOOKS

There is an astonishing variety of books available about Hawai'i and the Big Island. Everything from history, legends, geology, children's stories and just plain ol' novels. **Kona Stories** (324–0350) in the Keauhou Shopping Center on Ali'i Drive has a large selection of Hawaiiana titles. Walk in and lose yourself in Hawai'i's richness. **Kona Bay Books** (326–7790) on Kaiwi Street is one of the largest *used* bookstores in the state. **Basically Books** on Kamehameha in Hilo (961–0144) also has a superb collection of Hawai'i titles. They also have the best selection of topographic maps on the island.

THE INTERNET

Our website, **www.wizardpub.com** has recent changes, links to cool sites and the latest satellite weather shots and more. We also show our own aerial photos of nearly every place to stay, so you'll know if oceanfront *really* means oceanfront. It also has links to every company listed in the book that has a site—both those we like and those we recommend against. For the record, we don't charge a cent for links (it would be a conflict of interest), and there are no advertisements on the site. (Well…except for our own books, of course.) We could have listed all of the Web addresses in the book, but it seemed pretty mean to make you type in all of those URL addresses. We also have a calendar of upcoming events.

If you're on-island and need Web access (to check your mail, etc.), most of the big resorts have business services available for around $20 an hour. **Kona Business Center** (329–0006) in Kona has Internet access for $8 per hour. **Island Lava Java** in Kona (see ISLAND DINING) has Web access and good cinnamon rolls—what a combo!

If you brought your computer… shame on you, you're on vacation. Anyway, **Wavecom Solutions** (331–0897) can set you up with a temporary local dial up account for $10 set-up fee plus a $20 per month. If you have Wi-Fi, **Kona Brewing Co.** and a gathering area at the Kona Coast Shopping Center have free Wi-Fi.

'Anaeho'omalu Beach is a sunset photographer's dream come true.

Kohala is the oldest volcano on the island, having last sputtered 60,000 years ago. It contains lush forest, dry lava desert, windswept grassy plains and outrageous beaches. Some of the most expensive resorts on the island are along the Kohala Coast.

This is a large, diverse area to cover in one section, but because of the way the island's resorts are distributed and the roads are laid out, most will see this area in a circular driving tour, so that's how we'll describe it. We're going to start as you leave Kona (see map) heading up Hwy 190. If you're staying in Kohala, you can come up Waikoloa Village Road and pick up the description on Hwy 190 heading north. If staying in Hilo, pick it up from Waimea.

UP HIGHWAY 190 FROM KAILUA-KONA

As you leave Kona, you'll take Palani Road, which becomes Mamalahoa Highway (190) heading north. (See map on page 45 or 61.) From near sea level, you will be heading up to 3,564 feet then down again into Hawi, so gas up on that cheap *(ha!)* Kona gasoline.

Leaving Kailua-Kona, it's hard to believe that just above the town is a beautiful fern and 'ohi'a **cloud forest** steeped in fog and moss. Weather here is determined by altitude because the mountain literally creates its own rain through convection. You can see it by taking **Kaloko Drive** just south of the 34 mile marker. Follow it for 7 miles as it winds upward into another world. Just before the end of the road, turn left and it will

DIVERSION ALERT!

dead end at 5,000 feet with expansive views (clouds permitting) of Kona below. Morning is best for this drive; don't ride your brakes on the way down.

As you leave Kona, you'll get some good views down the coast. Keep an eye out for renegade peacocks (which sound like cats being tortured) from the Makalei Golf Course around the 32 mile marker.

The highway bisects several channels and tubes in the lava between the 28 and 26 mile markers. Rivers of molten stone coursed down the mountain here during the 1800 Hualalai lava flow. If you look down the coast, you'll get an idea of the scale of a "typical" lava flow. On your right before the 21 mile marker is road to the Puʻu Waʻawaʻa trailhead described on page 203.

By the 19 mile marker you have passed from Hualalai Mountain to the slopes of Mauna Loa. Proof is in the form of a lava flow here that ran for 30 miles in 1859 all the way to Kiholo Bay, destroying Kamehameha's fishpond (see BEACHES). If

clouds are absent, you may see the top of Mauna Kea and its many dome-enclosed telescopes ahead and on your right.

As you continue, you'll notice cactus scattered about, and trees appear again. **Parker Ranch** starts at the 14 mile marker, part of a colossal 130,000-acre cattle ranch.

At the 11 mile marker is the road through **Waikoloa Village**, which leads down to the Kohala mega-resorts. It's marked by a giant obelisk erected by Waikoloa Land Co. in a fit of psychedelic creativity. Waikoloa Village is a relatively stark community. Due to its location, on the leeward side of the saddle between Mauna Loa and Mauna Kea, it's usually pretty windy. *(How consistently windy? When the wind stops, the cows fall down.)* If you are staying at a mega-resort in Kohala, you'll want to know that there is a fairly large grocery store here.

Still on Hwy 190 between the 5 and 2 mile markers off to your right (up mauka), there's a large hill called **Holoholoku**. Everyone has seen the famous WWII photo and statue of the scene where Marines on Iwo Jima raised the American flag over Mt. Suribachi. Possibly the most dramatic WWII photo ever taken, it puts a lump in your throat every time you see it. What you don't know is that those very guys practiced storming the hill right there on Holoholoku because it was thought to be similar to Suribachi in size and shape.

As you approach the town of **Waimea** (Kamuela), you may decide to check it out now. Since this is the crossroads between the east and west sides of the island, we could have included it here or in the section on Hamakua. After careful analysis of driving patterns, accommodation indexes and topography…we flipped a coin and put it in the HAMAKUA chapter. Waimea has an incredibly colorful history

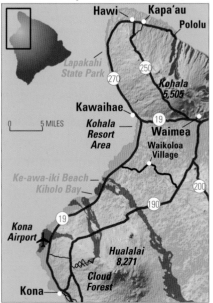

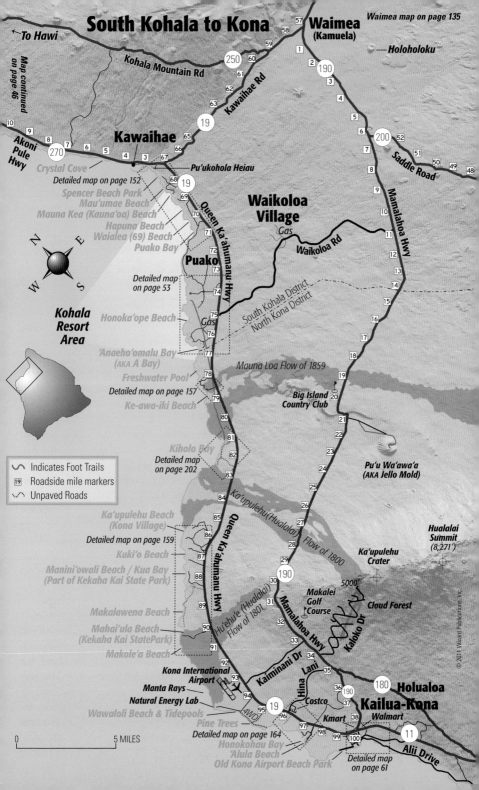

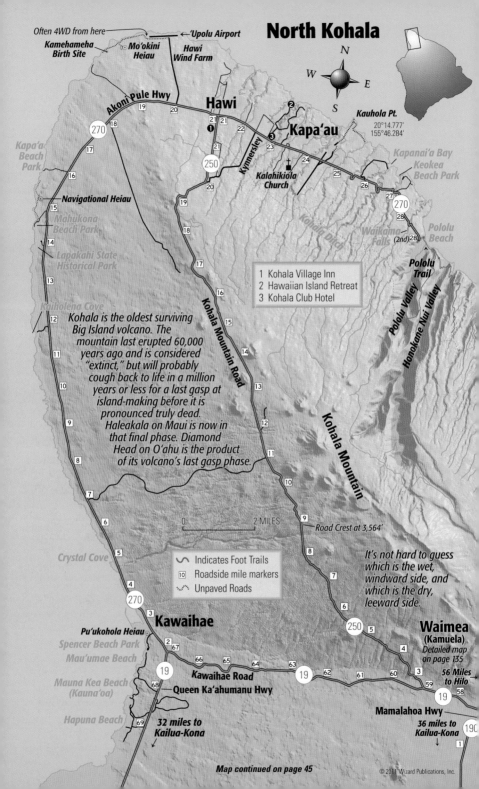

North Kohala

Often 4WD from here

Kamehameha Birth Site

Mo'okini Heiau

'Upolu Airport

Hawi Wind Farm

Akoni Pule Hwy

Hawi

270

18

17

16

250

20

21 21

22

1

21

20

19

18

17

16

15

14

13

12

Kymersley

23

3

Kapa'au

2

24

25

26

27

Kalahikiola Church

Kauhola Pt.
20°14.777'
155°46.284'

Kapani'a Bay
Keokea Beach Park

270

28

(2nd) 28

Waikama Falls

Pololu Beach

Pololu Trail

Pololu Valley

Honokane Nui Valley

Kohala Ditch

Kohala Mountain Road

Kohala Mountain

Kapa'a Beach Park

Navigational Heiau

Mahukona Beach Park

Lapakahi State Historical Park

Kaiholena Cove

15

14

13

12

11

16

15

14

13

12

11

10

Kohala is the oldest surviving Big Island volcano. The mountain last erupted 60,000 years ago and is considered "extinct," but will probably cough back to life in a million years or less for a last gasp at island-making before it is pronounced truly dead. Haleakala on Maui is now in that final phase. Diamond Head on O'ahu is the product of its volcano's last gasp phase.

1	Kohala Village Inn
2	Hawaiian Island Retreat
3	Kohala Club Hotel

10

9

8

7

6

5

4

270

3

Kawaihae

Pu'ukohola Heiau

Spencer Beach Park

Mau'umae Beach

Mauna Kea Beach (Kauna'oa)

Hapuna Beach

2

67

66

65

64

63

62

61

60

19

59

58

Road Crest at 3,564'

It's not hard to guess which is the wet, windward side, and which is the dry, leeward side.

250

5

4

3

Waimea
(Kamuela)
Detailed map on page 135

56 Miles to Hilo

0   2 MILES

~⌢~ Indicates Foot Trails
⑩ Roadside mile markers
⋰⋱ Unpaved Roads

Kawaihae Road
Queen Ka'ahumanu Hwy

19

68

69

32 miles to Kailua-Kona

Mamalahoa Hwy

36 miles to Kailua-Kona

190

1

Map continued on page 45

and is worth exploring. If you do it now, turn to page 134 before continuing on.

KOHALA MOUNTAIN ROAD

See map on facing page or on page 135 to get to Highway 250 (left at the Chevron station). You are traveling up the spine of the sleeping Kohala Volcano. (They say you shouldn't honk your horn, or you may wake it up.) You're still on the dry, leeward side and will crest at 3,564 feet before descending to the sea.

Around the 14 mile marker you'll start to see a huge mountain looming in front of you. That's not on this island; it's **Maui**, 30 miles across the sea. On clear days, the island of Maui seems to tower over the little town of Hawi even more than the Big Island's own volcanoes. Sometimes it looks gigantic, and sometimes it's less impressive. It's the same reason the moon always looks enormous when it's near a mountain horizon or through trees—it gives your brain some scale to compute its size. Maui looks biggest when you see it *with or through* something other than on the ocean's horizon.

NORTH SHORE OF KOHALA

Be sure to take the road to Hawi, not Kapa'au, near the 20 mile marker. As you pull into Hawi, you're greeted by a couple of old banyan trees on your right. You'll want to head right (east), but if you're hungry for a treat, across the street from **Bamboo Restaurant** on your left is **Kohala Coffee Mill**, which has **Tropical Dreams**, an *outstanding* ice cream made here on the island. We unselfishly review it *every* time we are on the north shore, just to be thorough.

The sleepy little towns of **Hawi** and **Kapa'au** lie at this northernmost point of the island. Until the '70s, this was sugar country. When Kohala Sugar pulled out,

this area was left high and dry. Rather than let their towns die, residents stuck it out, opening shops and other small businesses. Today, this area is enjoying a comeback of sorts. There are lots of artists who call this area home. A Japanese investment company bought most of Kohala Sugar's land assets (19,000 acres) in 1988 when land here was cheap and has *plans* for a resort at Mahukona, a restaurant at the end of the road overlooking Pololu Valley and more. But they've been *planning* for a long time. In the meantime, this is a quiet, peaceful community. It's said that the investor bought all this land after simply flying over it in a helicopter—without ever touching it!

Heading east, you come to the town of **Kapa'au**. On the mauka side of the highway in Kapa'au is a statue of **King Kamehameha the Great**. If it looks just like the famous one standing in front of the Judiciary building in Honolulu, that's because it's the same…sort of. When the Hawaiian Legislature commissioned the statue in 1878, it was cast in Paris and put on a ship. Unfortunately, the ship and its cargo were lost at sea near the Falkland Islands in the South Atlantic. Since they had shipping insurance, they used the money to order a new one. Meanwhile, the captain of the wrecked ship later spotted the "lost" statue standing in Port Stanley (somebody had salvaged it). He bought it for $500 and shipped it (this time successfully—must have FedExed it) to Hawai'i where its broken arm was repaired, and it was erected where you see it now. On King Kamehameha Day (June 11) the statue is piled high with leis and other decorations and is quite a sight to see. There are public restrooms here behind the building.

Continuing east, just before the 24 mile marker, is the road to **Kalahikiola**

Church, originally built in 1855. It was ravaged by a strong earthquake in 2006. The current building is new, but the stones from the original building, hand-carried from the ocean and rivers of the area in 1850, were used to build the wall around the new church.

If you want to see some raw coastline and have a 4WD vehicle, take a left ½ mile past the 24 mile marker onto Maulili (which is just after Old Halaula Mill Road). After ⅓ mile it becomes dirt. Turn right when it ends and the short paved section leads to an unpaved road that goes to Kauhola Point. In 1933, they built a lighthouse at this point that was 85 feet away from the edge of the cliff. In 2009, they had to destroy the lighthouse because it was only *20* feet from the shoreline and ready to topple into the sea. If you look at the sides of the cliffs, you can *see* how they're getting munched away by the waves. This area is wild and undeveloped and sports nice views of the sea cliffs that wrap around the north shore. The area a few hundred yards to the right (east) is full of abandoned sugar equipment and cars. Many are actually embedded in the *side* of the cliff, evidence of the rapid pace of cliff erosion. Just a few decades ago the

Though the Pololu Lookout is nice, you'll get a much better vantage point if you go part of the way down the trail.

cars were buried in "stable" ground and the cliffs were farther out.

Back on the highway, look to your left just before the 25 mile marker. There is a large banyan tree with an old **tree house**. Wouldn't you have *loved* a tree house like that when you were a kid?

There are ATV **Tours** of the coastal cliffs along here as well as other **Land Tours**, all described in ACTIVITIES.

POLOLU VALLEY

The end of the highway (which lacks a turnaround for some reason) is the **Pololu Valley Lookout**. This outstanding vista displays the raw, untamed side of the Big Island. (Unfortunately, the state some- **A REAL GEM** times lets the vegetation block out some of the view. The view's *much* nicer halfway down the trail mentioned below.) Nearly vertical cliffs are battered unmercifully by the winter north shore surf. Four hundred feet below is **Pololu Beach**, accessed via a 15–20 minute trail down through lush vegetation. (If you make it back *up* in 15 minutes, we're proud of you. It means you didn't stop once.) If it's been raining much, the trail may be slippery. At the bottom, in several spots, you'll find black sand dunes over 100 feet high, now mostly covered with vegetation. This type of black sand beach is formed as water constantly chips away at the lava river bed. Though the beach is not very swimmable (the surf and current are usually too violent), it's very picturesque and a nice place to observe Mother Nature's force. During the week you may have it nearly to yourself down there. Halfway down the trail is a small natural platform that looks out over the beach—a good photo op.

The beach is prettier from below than above. On the opposite side of the valley, a trail leads up the wall over to the next valley, called **Honokane Nui**. These seven valleys, from Pololu to Waipi'o, are the only part of this new island that show much sign of erosion.

In ancient times Pololu Valley was a bountiful source for waterworn stones. Thousands of tons of stones have been hauled from here to build temples, houses and other structures. The massive Pu'ukohola Heiau, 25 miles away at Kawaihae, was built from stones from this valley. A gigantic chain of people passed stones hand to hand all the way. If one was dropped, it was left where it lay (unless it was on his foot) to prevent the cadence from being interrupted. When you're ready, head back west past Hawi.

MO'OKINI HEIAU

Near the 20 mile marker is a sign saying simply "Upolu Airport." This road (unpaved *past* the airport) leads to the northernmost tip of the island and past two important sites. The impressive 10½ megawatt **Hawi Wind Farm** is just before the airport. Though it looks peaceful, to any pilot who has ever landed at 'Upolu, the location is horrifying. That's because during normal winds, your approach to the airport places you in the gut-wrenching, scream-for-Mama prop wash from the turbines, turning a previously turbulent runway (before they built the turbines in 2006) into a delightfully terrifying experience.

You head left when you reach the quiet 'Upolu Airport. The county does a *terrible* job maintaining the unpaved portion. If it's dry and they've scraped it lately, you *may* make it in a regular car the 1½ miles to the heiau described below. Otherwise, it's 4WD on at least *part* of the unpaved section, and the last part might even scare 4-wheelers. Puddles last a *long time* here, and some of them are large enough

to have nearly spawned their own unique ecosystem. Even during bad weather we've seen rental cars back here, giving legitimacy to the question: *What's the difference between a rental car and a 4WD? A rental car can go* **anywhere**...

This area is dominated by the legacy of two influential men—an ancient priest named **Pa'ao** and **Kamehameha the Great**. Pa'ao is said to have arrived in the 11th or 12th century and changed the islands. He was born in Tahiti or on one of its neighbor islands. It is said that the islands were in a state of anarchy when Pa'ao arrived. He restructured society, introduced the concept of human sacrifice and brought other similar traditions. Here he built the Mo'okini Heiau, where countless people were put to death to please Pa'ao's hungry gods. You'll have to park at the gate and walk five minutes to the heiau.

Even before we knew the gory details about Mo'okini Heiau's history, the place gave us the heebie-jeebies. We aren't the only ones who have noticed that the area around the temple is filled with an eerie, ghostly lifelessness, and it's the only place on the island that we like to avoid (not counting the Department of Motor Vehi-

cles). Used for human sacrifices, the area feels devoid of a soul. The quiet is not comforting, but rather an empty void. The walls of Mo'okini are extremely tall and thick—oral tradition says that some of the rocks were passed by hand from Pololu Valley, 9 miles away. Just in front of the heiau is a large lava slab with a slight dip in it. In front of it is a raised stone. It takes little imagination to see that this slab was the *holehole* stone, where unfortunate victims were laid while the flesh was stripped from their bones. These bones were then used to make fish-hooks and other objects. The number of Hawaiians sacrificed here ran into the tens of thousands.

There were no signs at this heiau at press time to orient you to the timeline here. Although people from the Marquesas Islands settled on the Big Island around 300 AD, they were eventually overwhelmed by the Tahitians who came with Pa'ao around 1000 AD. It was the Tahitians who built this heiau and became the Hawaiians we know today.

Farther down the road is the **Kamehameha Akahi Aina Hanau Heiau**. This is where Kamehameha the Great, who conquered all the islands, was said to have been born. (Actually, many think he was born nearby, but not right here.) Kamehameha means "the lonely one," which seems ironically fitting given the almost palpable loneliness this area of the island exudes.

After Kamehameha's birthplace, you will come to an old Coast Guard LORAN station where you'll probably encounter boulders blocking the road. If so, retrace your route to the highway.

As you pass the tip of Kohala on 270, take note of how quickly you go from green to lots of dry scrub and an arid feel. That's the rain shadow effect, when the mountain causes it to rain more on one side than on the other.

There are a couple of places along this stretch to swim or snorkel—**Kapa'a Beach Park** and **Mahukona**, both described in BEACHES.

Near the 15 mile marker, look toward the ocean in the distance, and you can see stones sticking up in the air from a fascinating *navigational* heiau where the stones are aligned to point to other Hawaiian islands, Tahiti and more. You can walk to it from Mahukona. We took a GPS here and were able to verify that the stones *really do* align with Polynesian destinations. Pretty impressive.

By the way, Mahukona is also the name given to the Big Island's first and now-forgotten volcano, located offshore. This volcano started it all but sank beneath the water less than half a million years ago.

On a clear day, you can't miss seeing Maui from here. But on *very* clear late afternoons, in addition to Maui's two mountains, you may see the islands of Lana'i, Kaho'olawe (in front of Lana'i from this angle) and Moloka'i between Lana'i and Maui. Look at the island chain map on the front inside cover to orient yourself. Sunsets from this area can be superb.

LAPAKAHI STATE HISTORICAL PARK

At the 14 mile marker is **Lapakahi State Historical Park**, which consists of the remains of an old Hawaiian village. There is a trail running through the village, complete with markers noting interesting spots. Open 8 a.m. to 4 p.m., admission is free. This self-guided tour takes around 45 minutes, and the brochure does a reasonable job of explaining what you are seeing. Lapakahi is interesting at times and worthwhile for anyone interested in a taste of how the ancient Hawaiians may have lived in such an inhospitable place. The park rangers here can be inhospitable as well. Sometimes surly to the point of being comical, they occasionally convey some of the worst and most inaccurate information we've run across in any park in the state. An example: "This area was once lush rain forest until western man came along and cut it down, causing the rainfall to go from 100 inches to 10 inches annually." (In reality, this was originally a thin, rocky and scrubby *dryland* forest until *the Hawaiians* burned it down to plant crops after they discovered Hawai'i. This area is dry because it is, and always has been, in the rain shadow of Kohala Mountain.)

One often overlooked aspect to Lapakahi is the fabulous water in **Koai'e Cove** (described in BEACHES). But don't expect to get the warmies from the staff, who seem to resent snorkelers here.

The highway between the 14 mile marker and Kawaihae (4 mile marker) is replete with dirt roads leading toward the ocean. You may be tempted to explore them, especially if you have 4WD. With that in mind, using a variety of vehicles and on foot, we traversed nearly every inch of all of them, including their branches (and we can cough up the dust-balls to prove it). The result? We can say with complete confidence that most of these roads are utterly wretched and lead to absolute squat. The entire coastline in this area is rocky and mostly unprotected. There are *no* beaches. It's pretty but not beautiful, and the land is harsh and unforgiving. (The real beauty of this area is underwater, with lots of extensive coral formations and ultra-clean water.) The only people who bother to make their way to the coast along this stretch are shoreline fishermen or hopeful whale watchers. So don't bother unless you have *way* too much time on your hands. The only exception is **Kaiholena Cove** between the 11 and 12 mile markers. The snorkeling is outstanding and fairly easy to access. (See BEACHES for more.)

Look to the shoreline from this area. Somewhere around here you'll usually find a place where to the left, the ocean looks calm and inviting, whereas to the right it looks choppy and frothing, and the line of demarcation is pretty defined. This is a terrifying place (if you're a pilot). It's the transition zone from waters that are wind-protected to waters that are whipped up from nukin' gales that slither around the tip of North Kohala. The turbulence in this area would make the toughest ULTIMATE FIGHTER scream like a little girl if he were flying here. (I've tried taking aerial photos of Kaiholena Cove, but that pesky emotion called *fear of death* keeps turning me away.) So if you see any low flying aircraft around here—salute 'em.

Like an old commercial says, sometimes you feel like a nut. If so, just over ½ mile past the 5 mile marker is a road that leads to the **Hamakua Macadamia Nut Co.** (882–1690). They have all things mac nut. Super friendly folks, they'll give you a quickie tour of the processing facilities behind the glass.

KAWAIHAE

The tiny port town of Kawaihae has a few places to eat and shop and is the launching area for some fishing and SCUBA operations. Otherwise, there's not much to see. There's an ice cream place on the back side of Kawaihae Center that

Kamehameha was instructed to build Pu'ukohola Heiau in order to conquer all the islands.

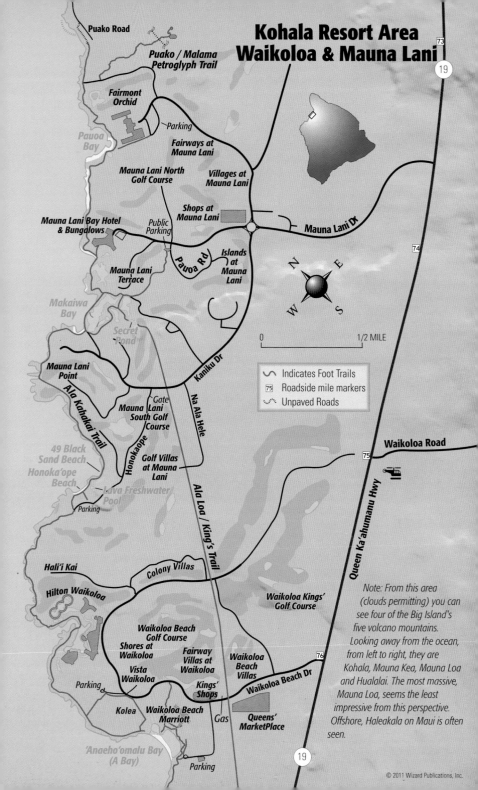

has fairly good ice cream. Café Pesto is your best bet for food.

This is the driest part of the state, with annual rainfall averaging less than 10 inches. (Contrast that with 240 inches on the slopes northwest of Hilo.)

At the junction of Highways 19 and 270 is the impressive **Pu'ukohola Heiau.** (Entry is free and a very impressive visitor center is open 7:30 a.m. to 4 p.m.) Check out their incredible weapons display. This massive structure was built by King Kamehameha in 1790–91. He had sent his wife's grandmother to visit a kahuna on Kaua'i to ask how he could conquer Hawai'i. The kahuna said that if he built a fabulous heiau (temple) at Kawaihae and dedicated it to his war god, he would prevail. Thousands of "volunteers" worked on the project, carrying boulders from miles away. Workers were routinely sacrificed at different portions of the structure during construction to ensure that the gods would be pleased. When the temple was completed, Kamehameha dedicated it by inviting and then sacrificing his enemy Keoua (see page 91). During construction Kamehameha himself participated to inspire his workers. When his brother picked up a boulder to help, Kamehameha slapped the rock out of his hand saying, "No, brother, one of us should keep the kapu" (meaning staying pure). Kamehameha then instructed that the rock his brother had touched be taken far out to sea and dumped into deep water. Pu'ukohola Heiau is best viewed from Kawaihae Harbor Road (the one that leads out to the breakwater) in the late afternoon with Mauna Kea in the background. Just offshore are said to be the remains of a shark heiau, called **Hale-o-Kapuni,** where human remains were offered to sharks. Its precise location is unknown, and it has been buried for decades.

KOHALA RESORT AREA

Continuing *south* onto Highway 19 (called *Queen K* by most locals, short for Ka'ahumanu) toward Kailua-Kona, you will pass the **Kohala mega-resort area.** Ensconced in this desolate sea of lava and scrub, multi-zillion dollar resorts dot the coastline offering the luxury and amenities that have made this region famous. Golfing is top notch (and *expensive*) here; see ACTIVITIES. Ocean activities, such as snorkeling and SCUBA, are very good. Though you wouldn't suspect it from the road, some of the best beaches in the state lie between here and Kailua-Kona. Some, such as Hapuna and Mauna Kea, are well known. Others, such as Manini'owali and Makalawena, are less known or deliciously secluded. The chapter on BEACHES describes them all in detail and tells you *exactly* how to get to each one of them.

See that barren lava field on the mauka (mountain) side of the highway? A Japanese company purchased the 3,000 acres in 1990 for a *mere* $45 million. They had big plans for it, including six golf courses and 2,600 homes. After paying taxes on it for nine years, the shrewd investors unloaded it in 1998 for $5 million.

Most of the lava you see here flowed thousands of years ago. In other parts of the island it'd be covered with forest. But the very thing that brings visitors here— the utter lack of rain—keeps the lava looking so uninviting.

Hold on to your hat along this stretch. The wind can be fierce in the afternoon. As the lava fields heat up during the day, it causes the air to heat and rise. Air from the ocean rushes in to fill the void, creating strong afternoon breezes.

Hapuna Beach is off the road near the 69 mile marker. This beach is often featured in travel shows and is a *superb* place to frolic. We like to snorkel from

Even the harsh lava deserts hide jewels, such as the golden pools of Ke-awa-iki.

there to Beach 69 on calm days, or boogie board till we're raw. Otherwise, just gallivant on the fine sand.

The road to the Mauna Lani between the 73 and 74 mile markers is worth consideration. See map on page 53. To the north is the **Puako/Malama Petroglyph Trail.** This simple 25-minute walk through kiawe forest leads to a very large field of petroglyphs—or carvings—in the lava. Though not as extensive as the Pu'u Loa field at Kilauea Volcano, it's one of the largest in the state and worth a stroll if you want to see how ancient Hawaiians expressed themselves through their tenacious carvings.

The **Mauna Lani Bay Hotel** sits adjacent to some of the most fascinating grounds of any Big Island resort. Huge fishponds surrounded by palm trees to the south make for wonder-filled strolling. We like to wander back to Secret Pond (see map) for a cool, refreshing dip in the crystal clear water. (I know: The other ponds aren't clear—*this* one is.) Park at the public parking area (6:30 a.m. to 6:30 p.m.) and wander along the trail toward the fishponds. Allow an hour for this pleasant diversion.

Continuing south, the road at the 76 mile marker leads to **'Anaeho'omalu Beach.** If you're low on gasoline, there is relief on this road. 'Anaeho'omalu has a gorgeous palm-fronted fishpond behind the beach. If you're looking for the perfect location to take a **sunset photo,** the backside of the fishpond is as good as it gets. When clouds cooperate, even the most photographically challenged (present reader excluded) can take postcard-quality shots.

KOHALA LAVA DESERT AREA

Back on Highway 19 heading south, the large cluster of palms toward the ocean at the 79 mile marker surround a large freshwater pond and a pretty but secluded beach called **Ke-awa-iki.** The pond itself is not available to visitors (the barbed wire, half-starved Dobermans, and snipers with night vision glasses see to that), but the beach is accessible via a 15-minute walk, and there is a special freshwater golden pool available to hikers. (See Ke-awa-iki hike in ACTIVITIES.)

Take a look at the "graffiti" strewn about the lava field. It's sort of an island tradition to compose messages from pieces of coral on the black lava canvas, and families often come out here to do it together. They're almost always friendly messages, like *Al* ♥ *Sandy, I Love You Mom,* or *In Memory of Dan,* and rarely contain the nasties often seen in real mainland graffiti.

The scenic turnout at the 82 mile marker overlooks **Kiholo Bay**. Down there you will find a saltwater bay with freshwater calmly floating on top, lots of turtles and a lava tube with fresh spring water just 80 feet from the ocean. Intrigued? I hope so. You can drive part of the way during daylight hours and hike around. (See HIKING on page 200.)

Throughout this part of the island you'll occasionally see palm trees along the barren coastline. These are almost always an indication of freshwater spring-fed pools. Since there's no permanent stream on the entire west side of the island, water percolates into the lava and often bubbles to the surface near the shore, forming pools. We look for them when we're hiking along the coast. When you're hot and tired, you can't beat splashing like a fool in a cold, clean freshwater or brackish pool.

If you're looking for a stunning, secluded beach, and don't mind walking for 15–20 minutes, **Makalawena Beach** (described in BEACHES) is west of the 89 mile marker.

You may still see some DONKEY CROSSING signs along here. Until the turn of the century there was a small herd of wild donkeys that crossed the highway at night and early mornings on the older lava north of the 85 mile marker. They came down out of the mountains to lick the salt off rocks by the shore, drink from springs and occasionally putt on the Hualalai Golf Course. (Now *there's* a hazard.) Known locally as **Kona Nightingales**, (because they would call, or "sing" to each other at night), they were the descendants of coffee-hauling pack animals that escaped a century ago. Every so often one got whacked by a passing car, leaving both pretty bent out of shape. They were finally rounded up and hauled away to a corral near Waikoloa Village, but many have escaped and now similarly terrorize the golf course off Waikoloa Road. Wild goats still work this area and are fairly easy to spot.

Just north of the 91 mile marker is a **large lava tube** from the Hualalai lava flow of 1801 that bisects the highway. On the ocean side of the road it has collapsed, leaving a large chasm in the lava. On the mauka side it forms a cave, which is collapsing in several spots. This cave looks rickety and unstable.

Located just south of the Kona airport is the **Natural Energy Laboratory**. This is a classic example of unintended consequences. Started by the government in the 1970s, they monkeyed with making electricity using temperature differences between 80° surface water and 37° deep sea water. Yeah, it worked. But the technology wasn't particularly scalable and has since been abandoned at this location. But their giant 55-inch pipe sucking water from 3,000 feet down has become a magnet for dozens of private companies taking advantage of easy access to cold seawater and year-round sunshine. Industries, such as those raising clams, coral, sea horses, blue green algae, oysters and mushrooms, are thriving out here.

An example is **Kona Cold Lobster**. When the lobsters arrive from the mainland, they have a nasty case of jet lag. (If you flew here from the East coast, you can probably relate.) The beasties are put in the cold water to rejuvenate so that they are bright and alert when you boil them for dinner.

A nice tour here is at **Ocean Rider** (329–6840). They have 1-hour tours of their seahorse farm *(Hey, shouldn't this be called a ranch?)* for $35. The price is pretty steep, but there's something undeniably endearing about these critters that have been nearly wiped out in the wild. At the end of the tour you'll get to have one of them wrapped around your finger. (More likely it'll be the other way around.) Good for kids and adults.

Surprisingly, once you pump seawater out of the ocean, federal environmental laws make it *illegal* to return it, even if it's perfectly clean. So they're forced to pump it into a deep hole (more like a *loop*hole) where it naturally seeps back into the ocean. The energy lab gives about a 90-minute lecture/presentations Monday through Thursday at 10 a.m. for $8. Reserve at 329–8073. A mile offshore here is **Kona Blue**. It's an open-sea fish farm that raises a delicious fish called *Blue Kampachi,* which is available at Roy's and Merriman's restaurants. Normally tasty but inedibly wormy in the wild, these farm-raised kahala fish are worm-free.

An excellent tide-pool is nearby at **Wawaloli Beach**. (See page 163.)

Near the 97 mile marker is the parking lot for **Kaloko-Honokohau National Historical Park**. Despite its appearance, this area was once a thriving community, and Hawaiian artifacts are still scattered

The Green Flash

Ever heard of the green flash? No, it's not a super hero. We'd heard of the Green Flash for years and assumed that it was an urban myth, or perhaps something seen through the bottom of a beer bottle. But now we know it to be a real phenomenon, complete with a scientific explanation. You may hear other ways to experience the Green Flash—but this is the only true *way.*

On days when the horizon is crisp and clear with no clouds in the way of the sun as it sets, you stand a reasonable chance of seeing it. Avoid looking directly at the sun until the very last part of the disk is about to slip below the horizon. Looking at it beforehand will burn a greenish image into your retina, creating a "fool's flash" (and possibly wrecking your eyes). The instant *before the last part of the sun's disk disappears, a vivid flash of chartreuse is often seen. This is because the sun's rays are passing through the thickest part of the atmosphere, and the light is bent and split into its different components the way it is in a rainbow. The light that is bent the most is the green and blue light, but the blue is less vivid and is overwhelmed by the flash of green, which lingers for the briefest of moments as the very last of the sun sets.*

For a variety of reasons, including our latitude, Hawai'i is one of the best places in the world to observe the Green Flash. North Kohala is usually better than Kona due to the clarity of the horizon, but we've seen excellent Green Flash from all along the West coast.

If you aren't successful in seeing the real Green Flash, try the beer bottle method—at least it's better than nothing.

about the lava field. There's even a holua (stone slide) that was used by chiefs. (See page 67 for more on holua.)

If you are into deep sea fishing, you'll want to check out **Honokohau Harbor** listed in the BEACHES chapter. Fishing boats leave from here, and weigh-ins take place daily at 10 a.m. and 6 p.m. (You can tell what they caught by the fish flags they hoist.)

KOHALA SHOPPING

While in Hawi, pick up some **Tropical Dreams** ice cream at **Kohala Coffee Mill. L. Zeidman** has wood bowls and vases. **Mother's Antiques & Fine Cigars** is a good place to stop if you appreciate a smoke. Their Hawaiian brand cigars ironically are rolled in Nicaragua. We really love the jewelry designs at **Olivia Clare.** See **Elements Jewelry & Fine Crafts** for exciting artwork, jewelry and items made from recycled materials. **Lighthouse Liquors** has unique beers, wines and other spirits. On the other end of town, don't miss the excellent contemporary gallery called **Kohala Artworks.**

Heading north in Kapa'au, grab a coffee drink or sandwich at the **Nanbu Courtyard.** Across from the Kamehameha Statue the **Ackerman Galleries** has a great assortment of original artwork, glass and woodwork, though their hours *may* be a bit odd, so call ahead at 889–5971.

All of the mega-resorts have shopping areas, but especially noteworthy are the shops at the **Hilton Waikoloa** and the **Mauna Lani.** An additional shopping area at the Mauna Lani Resort called the **Shops at Mauna Lani** has a few places worth a stop, such as **Tommy Bahama** for clothes and **Lahaina Galleries** for art.

The main shopping area in South Kohala is the **Kings' Shops** located at the Waikoloa Beach Resort. Just about any-thing can be found here from **Tiffany & Co.** to **Sunglass Hut.** Don't miss **Noa Noa** for Polynesian print clothes for both men and women. **Kilauea Clothing Co. Vintage Aloha Wear** has great retro-style Hawaiian shirts—*mostly* made in Hawaii, but not all. **Making Waves** is a good place to get a new swim suit, while **Waking in Paradise** is a sandal collector's dream. A few art galleries here are worth a stop, such as **Genesis Gallery. Under the Koa Tree** has artwork, home decor, and where else can you buy a koa skateboard for $450? Directly across the street is **Queens' MarketPlace.** You'll find some similar stores here as in the Kings' Shops. We love **Giggles!** for anything kid-related. If you've been wanting a T-shirt with a gecko playing cards on it, you'll find it at **Local Lizard and Friends. Hawaiian Quilt Collection** has some outstanding examples of quilts and home decor. There's also a food court if you're hungry. Expect higher prices here.

KOHALA'S BEST BETS

Best Sunsets—Behind the fishponds at 'Anaeho'omalu Beach

Best Place to Get the Willies—Mo'okini Heiau, Hawi

Best Treat—Tropical Dreams, Hawi

Best Pizza—Café Pesto, Kawaihae

Best Koa Carvings—Gallery at Bamboo

Best Secluded Beach—Makalawena

Best Resort Grounds to Stroll Around— Mauna Lani Bay Hotel & Bungalows

Best Lu'au—Kona Village

Best Golf—Mauna Kea Golf Course

Best View of Maui—Coming down Highway 250 into Hawi

Best Overlook—Pololu Valley

Best Boogie-Boarding—Hapuna or Mauna Kea Beach

Best Remnant of Ancient Hawaiian Art—Puako Petroglyph Field

Kamehameha the Great, the first king to rule all the islands, could live anywhere he wanted. He chose Kailua-Kona. This is his 'Ahu'ena Heiau.

Kailua was a tiny fishing village in days gone by. Fishermen would haul in giants from the deep, bountiful waters, while farmers tended their fields up the slopes of Hualalai. Many of the great chiefs of old chose this part of the island as their home. Kona weather and Kona waters were known throughout the islands as the very best, and that hasn't changed. Though no longer the sleepy little village of yesteryear, this is a charming seaside town where the strolling is pleasant, the sunsets are mesmerizing, the food is diverse, and the activities are plentiful. Some people bad-mouth Kona because it's not the same as it was 20 years ago—what is? Kona is still great; there are simply more people who know it.

The town is alternately referred to as Kailua-Kona, Kona, Kailua, or some-times Kailua Town. See page 29 for an explanation of this confusing situation.

Kailua-Kona is nestled in the lee of Hualalai Volcano, meaning that it is sheltered from the trade winds coming from the other side of the island. The winds we do get are usually from wraparound sea breezes. The rains from them have already been wrung out.

The heart of Kailua-Kona is the mile-long oceanfront stretch of Alii Drive starting at the Kailua Pier. As with any town, traffic can be heavy. Alii Drive is a particularly good area to take a walk after a meal. There have been times that unsavory-looking characters made night walks intimidating, but shop owners have banded together to hire private patrollers, and it has helped tremendously. Public parking is pretty limited and is shown on the Kailua-Kona Map.

This part of town has lots of shops and restaurants overlooking the water. If you start strolling from the Kailua Pier, keep an eye out for some of these sights.

AROUND DOWNTOWN KAILUA-KONA

To the right (north) of the pier is the ʻAhuʻena Heiau. Now wonderfully maintained and very picturesque, this was King Kamehameha the Great's personal heiau (temple) that he had restored in 1812, and it was here that he spent his later years until his death in 1819. Note the bird on top of the tallest kiʻi akua (statue of a god). It is a golden plover, the bird that may have guided the first Polynesians here. (See page 15.) Kamehameha dedicated this heiau to the god Lono and filled it with European and Chinese furniture. Nearby is Nane Mahina ʻAi, where the king went to get away from it all. There was a famous portrait painted here of Kamehameha wearing a red vest, white shirt and a yellow silk necktie. The artist pleaded with him not to wear the fancy sailor's outfit, but Kamehameha insisted.

The tiny beach in front of the heiau is Kamakahonu Beach, one of the calmest beaches on the island. There you can rent kayaks, paddle boats, stand-up paddle boards, snorkel gear, etc. (though at confiscatory prices).

To the left of the pier is the starting gate to end all starting gates. Every year in October an athletic event occurs on the Big Island that draws national attention. The Ironman Triathlon is a profound testimony to the power to challenge, to the ability to reach down to the very core of our spirit and summon the impossible. Three events, any one of which would seem *insurmountable* to most of us mere mortals, are stitched together in a triathlon that seems almost ludicrous. Swim 2.4 miles in the open ocean, then get out and ride a bike 112 miles on a hot road cut through a lava field. Finally, dismount and run a 26.2 mile marathon. All this is done consecutively under the tropical sun. This is the best opportunity you'll ever have to look into the faces of mass excellence, and not just the young. We had a friend who, even in his mid-60s, would blow by most of the 25-year-olds and complete the race in under 12 hours.

The seawall near the pier is usually a great place to fish. During abnormally high seas, water crashes over the wall and is quite a sight to see. Even better fishing is at the wall in front of the Huliheʻe Palace (329–1877) farther down. This palace, **A REAL GEM** built in 1838 by Governor Kuakini, quickly became the house of choice for vacationing Hawaiian royalty until 1914. Now a museum lovingly run by the Daughters of Hawaiʻi, inside you'll find a nice collection of koa furniture, including some stunning armoires, and a 6-foot diameter table cut from a single piece of koa. Most of the furniture was auctioned off in the 1920s but fortunately was cataloged. Later, the buyers were

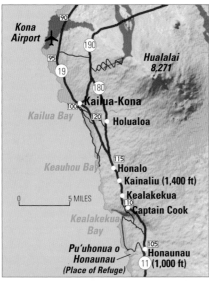

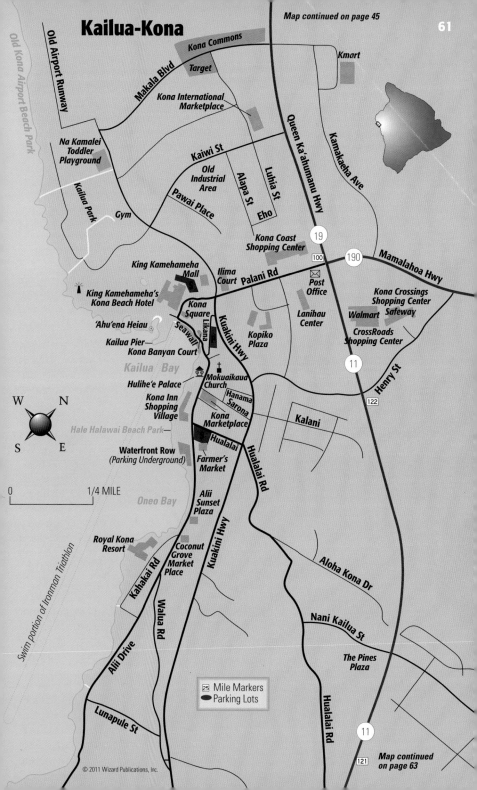

Kailua-Kona

Old Airport Runway

Old Kona Airport Beach Park

Makala Blvd

Kona Commons

Target

Kmart

Kona International Marketplace

Queen Ka'ahumanu Hwy

Kamakaeha Ave

Na Kamalei Toddler Playground

Kaiwi St

Kailua Park

Old Industrial Area

Alapa St

Luhia St

Gym

Pawai Place

Eho

19

100

190

Mamalahoa Hwy

Kona Coast Shopping Center

King Kamehameha Mall

Ilima Court

Palani Rd

Post Office

Kona Crossings Shopping Center

King Kamehameha's Kona Beach Hotel

Kona Square

Lanihau Center

Walmart

Safeway

'Ahu'ena Heiau

Likana

Kuakini Hwy

Kopiko Plaza

CrossRoads Shopping Center

11

Kailua Pier — Kona Banyan Court

Seawall

Henry St

Kailua Bay

Hulihe'e Palace

Mokuaikaua Church

122

Hale Halawai Beach Park

Kona Inn Shopping Village

Hanama Sarona

Kalani

Kona Marketplace

Waterfront Row (Parking Underground)

Hualalai

Farmer's Market

Hualalai Rd

Oneo Bay

Alii Sunset Plaza

0   1/4 MILE

Royal Kona Resort

Coconut Grove Market Place

Kuakini Hwy

Kahakai Rd

Aloha Kona Dr

Swim portion of Ironman Triathlon

Walua Rd

Nani Kailua St

Alii Drive

The Pines Plaza

25 Mile Markers
● Parking Lots

Lunapule St

Hualalai Rd

11

121

Map continued on page 63

© 2011 Wizard Publications, Inc.

contacted, and many have graciously lent the items to the museum for display. There are many photos of Hawaiian royalty, including Princess Ruth. (History books *never* mention her without mentioning her size, but we're above that... no, we're not. Estimates range from 6-foot-2 to 6-foot-10, 400–450 lbs. She slept in a hut outside.) Spears, fishhooks and other artifacts make this museum a worthwhile stop. Most who give the tours (under an hour) are very knowledgeable and friendly, but occasionally you'll get some bad historical information. Admission is $6. Open Wednesday through Saturday. The Palace Gift Shop next door has interesting items and hard-to-find books and is worth a peek.

Outside, on the south side of the Palace *was* a rock with a hole in it. It was the top of a Pohaku Likanaka. This was used for executions out at Kahalu'u Beach Park. People would be forced to stand in front of it while a rope was passed through the hole, around the neck, and back out. The executioner would then pull back for a few minutes...and that was that. Some palace personnel used to grumble that the darkly historic stone shouldn't be there. In 2006 an earthquake damaged the palace, forcing its closure and refurbishment. When they reopened, *wadayano*? The stone had simply vanished. They don't know where it went, and they don't seem too unhappy about it.

Across the street from Hulihe'e Palace is the Mokuaikaua Church. This was the first Christian church built in the islands, in 1820. The initial building was a thatched hut, with the current structure erected in 1837. You're welcome inside; admission is free. Built of lava rock and crushed coral with koa hardwood gracing the tall interior, this is a magnificent remnant of the era. Look at the joints inside the building, which were painstakingly attached with pins made from gnarly 'ohi'a trees. There are exhibits relating to early Hawai'i and the work of the missionaries, along with a model of the *Thaddeus*, which brought the first missionaries here.

With moonlight on one side and sunlight on the other, altars (called lele ho'okau), such as this one at the Ku'emanu Heiau, are still used by some for a morning prayer.

Sometimes referred to as the Mayflower of Hawai'i, the *Thaddeus* left Boston in October 1819 for a five-month trip to the islands. These men and women left comfortable lives in the United States to come to an alien and mysterious land. Unbeknownst to them, their chances for success were greatly enhanced en route when Kamehameha II and his step-mother Ka'ahumanu orchestrated the overthrow of the Hawaiian religion less than a month into their journey to the islands.

There's a large shopping area at Kona Inn. If you're looking for a place to watch the sunset or have a picnic, the grass on the ocean side of this center is ideal.

If you want to watch the sunset from a restaurant along here, the best views (from south to north) are: Don the Beachcomber, Lulu's (powerlines take away from their view), Huggo's, Bubba Gump, Kona Inn and Kona Canoe Club. See individual reviews in ISLAND DINING. During months around the summer solstice (June 21), the sun may set behind the point from the northernmost restaurants.

ELSEWHERE ALONG ALII DRIVE

As you drive farther south along Alii Drive, keep an eye out for joggers. They trot up and down Alii Drive in large enough numbers to constitute a flock. (Or is it a gaggle?) There are mile markers every half mile here, which we put on the Alii Drive map. Between Kona By The Sea and Kona Isle is a 100-yard access trail that leads to something that even most longtime Alii Drive residents don't know about. It's a public saltwater swimming pool fed by the splashing of waves. It was privately built decades ago and reverted to the state when the owner died without heirs. The pool directly abuts the ocean and even has some fish in it most of the time. There's

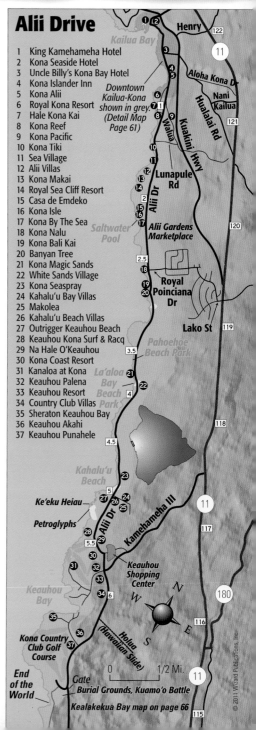

Alii Drive

1 King Kamehameha Hotel
2 Kona Seaside Hotel
3 Uncle Billy's Kona Bay Hotel
4 Kona Islander Inn
5 Kona Alii
6 Royal Kona Resort
7 Hale Kona Kai
8 Kona Reef
9 Kona Pacific
10 Kona Tiki
11 Sea Village
12 Alii Villas
13 Kona Makai
14 Royal Sea Cliff Resort
15 Casa de Emdeko
16 Kona Isle
17 Kona By The Sea
18 Kona Nalu
19 Kona Bali Kai
20 Banyan Tree
21 Kona Magic Sands
22 White Sands Village
23 Kona Seaspray
24 Kahalu'u Bay Villas
25 Makolea
26 Kahalu'u Beach Villas
27 Outrigger Keauhou Beach
28 Keauhou Kona Surf & Racq
29 Na Hale O'Keauhou
30 Kona Coast Resort
31 Kanaloa at Kona
32 Keauhou Palena
33 Keauhou Resort
34 Country Club Villas
35 Sheraton Keauhou Bay
36 Keauhou Akahi
37 Keauhou Punahele

Downtown Kailua-Kona shown in grey. (Detail Map Page 61)

Henry
Kailua Bay
Aloha Kona Dr
Nani Kailua
Hualalai Rd
Kuakini Hwy
Walua
Lunapule Rd
Alii Dr
Alii Gardens Marketplace
Saltwater Pool
Royal Poinciana Dr
Lako St
Pahoehoe Beach Park
La'aloa Bay
Keauhou Beach Park
Kahalu'u Beach
Ke'eku Heiau
Petroglyphs
Alii Dr
Kamehameha III
Keauhou Shopping Center
Keauhou Bay
Kona Country Club Golf Course
Holua (Hawaiian Slide)
Gate
Burial Grounds, Kuamo'o Battle
Kealakekua Bay map on page 66
End of the World

0   1/2 Mi.

© 2011 Wizard Publications, Inc.

a smaller tide-pool to the left. If you want to swim in seawater but are hesitant to go into the ocean, here's your chance. Unmaintained, the pool occasionally isn't refreshed enough if the surf has been flat for too long, meaning it sometimes gets green and yucky.

Keep an eye out on the mauka side of Alii Drive for a farmers' market called Ali'i Gardens. Near the 3½ mile marker is Pahoehoe Beach Park. No sand here, but it's a nice place to have a picnic, or to just sit on a bench and watch the surf. White Sands Beach (as it's known by locals or La'aloa as the sign says) is a little farther down with good boogie boarding when the sand is in town. (See BEACHES.)

There are scads of oceanfront condos and apartments along this road. Traffic noise is going to be your penalty for staying on Alii Drive, but it's a penalty most are quite willing to endure.

Soon you'll come to the quaintest little church you've ever seen. St. Peter's Catholic Church is known locally as the "Little Blue Church." This tiny building, with its picturesque location and less than a dozen simple *small* pews, is the most photographed in the islands. Weddings of all denominations take place there almost every weekend. If the doors are unlocked, sunsets through the etched glass can offer dramatic photo opportunities.

To the right of the church is the Ku'emanu Heiau. This is the only heiau (temple) in the state known to be associated solely with surfing. This surf spot was available only to chiefs (commoners caught surfing here were put to death), and they came here to pray for gnarly conditions. (They usually got them, too. Even today this is one of the most dependable breaks in Kona.) To this day, Hawaiians still come here to pay homage to the spirits. The small notch in front was a luapa'u, where discarded bones were tossed—perhaps bones of commoners caught surfing. Incidentally, surfing in the old days was usually done naked (giving new meaning to the term *hang loose).

Next to the church is Kahalu'u Beach Park where you'll find some of

In ancient times Kahalu'u Beach was heavily populated. Today, it is heavily snorkeled.

A Fish Story

Keauhou was dominated by the legacy of a king in the 1600s named Lonoikamakahiki (called Lono by his friends). Lono (not to be confused with the Hawaiian god of the same name) got into a series of bets with the king of O'ahu. Each time Lono won. On one occasion, Lono and the O'ahu king were out fishing. Lono's advisor told Lono not to go because he (Lono) didn't know how to fish. They went anyway, and while fishing, Lono got all worked up while the O'ahu king was hauling in a beauty and asked to borrow fishing gear. As Lono's advisor feared, the O'ahu king mocked Lono for not bringing his own gear. Lono's advisor, in order to save his master's honor, volunteered the solution to Lono. He whispered it into his ear and Lono agreed. Lono then shouted, "Hey, I don't need your gear. I'll bet you I can catch a fish on my own." The O'ahu king accepted, knowing that Lono had not brought any fishing gear with him. Then Lono, at his advisor's suggestion, clubbed his advisor to death, ripped open his belly and used his intestines for fishing line. Lono splintered the man's thigh bone for a fishhook. His flesh was used for bait and his head for a sinker. He lowered the gear into the water and immediately caught an ahi. Lono won the bet (a large piece of O'ahu) and later went on to win all of O'ahu in another bet.

The moral: If you think you sacrifice a lot for your boss, try working for Lono.

(Incidentally, Lono's bones were in the Bishop Museum in Honolulu until 1994 when they were stolen by Hawaiian activists and buried in Waipi'o Valley.)

the easiest access to good snorkeling on the island. It gets crowded on weekends. See BEACHES for more on this gem. Kahalu'u had a large population in the old days, and there are very extensive lava tube caves tucked away in the jungle up mauka (toward the mountain).

After you pass the Outrigger Keauhou Beach Resort, you'll see a parcel of land to its left. Fronting this parcel on some of the lava at low tide, you can see petroglyphs carved in the rock. They are at the northern end of the salt-and-pepper sand and gravel beach kitty-corner to the heiau described below. In the 16th century, Kamalalawalu, the King of Maui, was impaled alive by Lonoikamakahiki at Ke'eku Heiau for 10 or 11 days. Kamalalawalu was then taken to a flat rock nearby and slain. His body was towed out to sea and fed to the sharks. The petroglyphs on the

rock date back to that incident and detail the event. (Lonoikamakahiki had a good reason to be miffed at Kamalalawalu. His general had been captured by invading Maui forces, had his eyes gouged out and his eye sockets pierced with darts *before* being killed. That was considered uncool even by the standards of the time.)

The land contains several heiau, including one where thousands of Hawaiians were sacrificed to their gods. Local lore says that any business that operates there is cursed. If you don't believe it, ask the Japanese company that paid millions for the lease to a 454-room hotel here in 1988. They closed the hotel, called the Kona Lagoons, planning extensive renovations. Then they ran out of money. It sat vacant and dilapidated, until they finally gave it up in 1994 to the landowner, Bishop Estate, which bulldozed it a

Greenwell Coffee
Farm 1 mile north
on Hwy 11.

Alii Drive map on page 63

Kealakekua Bay to
Honaunau

1300'

11

110

This 4WD road is very nasty &
should only be used as a hiking trail.

11

Mamalahoa Hwy

109

**Captain Cook
Monument**

Napoopoo Rd

*Exceptional
snorkeling here*

10

108

Kealakekua Bay
(Great place to spot dolphins)

Hikiau Heiau

11

Napo'opo'o Beach Park
(Sand mostly gone now)

Napoopoo Rd

Old Coffee Mill

160

11

Manini Beach

Kahauloa St

Kayakers
usually launch
here

8

10'

Keawiki

Ke'ei Beach

Middle Keei Rd

Moku-a-Kae Bay

Moku'ohai Battlefield

160

Painted Church Rd

19°26.016'
155°55.215'

N

† **Painted
Church**

W   E

Arch City

S

105

0   1/2 MILE

2

Honaunau

1

Honaunau Bay
Keoneele Cove

3

Ke Ala o Keawe Rd

160

104

**Pu'uhonua o Honaunau
National Historical Park**
(AKA **Place of Refuge**)

**Picnic
Area**

1871 Trail

11

⌇ Indicates Foot Trails

3 Roadside mile markers

⋰ Unpaved Roads

© 2011 Wizard Publications, Inc.

South Island map on page 77

decade later. The re-created heiau you see here are a far cry from the rubble you would have seen at the turn of the century. They are part of a long rebuilding project begun in 2008 by the landowner.

As you ascend Alii Drive toward the Keauhou Shopping Center, keep an eye on your right, in the golf course, for the strangest corkscrew-shaped palm tree we've ever seen. No interesting story here—just weird. There's a flock of imported wild parrots that cruises around these parts. Keep an eye (and ear) out for them.

If you stay on Alii for a moment, pull over at the service entrance for the Kona Country Club golf course and look up mauka. It looks like a wide path that was bulldozed through the lava. That was done *by hand* to create the Keauhou Holua. In ancient times Hawaiians would fill these holua (slides) with dirt and wet grass, then Alii (Hawaiian royalty) would race down these slides at rippin' speeds on wooden sleds while commoners screamed and cheered them on. These holua remains are 2,500 feet long (not 1,200, which is listed in most references) and at one time extended to Keauhou Bay.

Right after this, Alii ends near the shoreline. (The road extending south is a bypass used by folks living up in coffee country.) There is a lava road near the dead end. If you walk on the road for a minute (actually you can see it from your car), you'll be able to see, on your left, terraces in the side of the mountain. You are at an extraordinary place. It might not look like much, but this is where the battle between Hawaiians to kill their religion took place one day in 1820. (See page 17 for the amazing story.) The terraces are the graves from that battle.

With a name befitting the area, a cliff-jumping spot past the battlefield called *End of the World* is listed in ADVENTURES on page 235.

UP MAUKA OF KAILUA-KONA

Hualalai Volcano erupts sporadically every few hundred years. The last time was in 1801 when it covered part of what is now Kona International Airport. The top of Hualalai is mostly covered with 'ohi'a and eucalyptus forest with occasional koa and pine. The clouds usually roll in around mid-morning, blanketing the 8,271-foot summit in a rich fog that can reduce visibility to zero. Wild goats and pigs scramble about the uninhabited top portion of the mountain. The views of Mauna Kea and Mauna Loa, as well as its own caldera, make Hualalai a hiker's haven. Unfortunately, it's all owned by Bishop Estate, which routinely denies access to the public. (Bishop Estate is a trust set up in the 1800s to help Hawai'i's kids. It has grown to where it now owns 11% of the state and has astonishing power. Many of the houses you see on the island are actually on Bishop land leased for several decades by individuals.)

Hovering above the town of Kailua-Kona is the "artist community" of Holualoa on Highway 180. There are several galleries (and one excellent restaurant called Holuakoa) worth stopping for if you are in the neighborhood. Hours can be sporadic. Otherwise, there is not as much to offer the visitor in this quiet, peaceful bedroom community as visitor literature might imply.

Although Kona itself doesn't convey the lushness many associate with Hawai'i, it *does* exist on this side of the island. Kaloko Drive meanders up into a luxuriant cloud forest. See page 43 for more.

SOUTH OF KAILUA-KONA

If you head south out of Kona, you'll come to a series of small towns, all above 1,000 feet. It's usually cool up here, sometimes even foggy. The theme of these towns is often coffee. Free sam-

Kona Coffee

Of all the products produced on the Big Island, none is more well known or has received more accolades than Kona coffee. Though now out-produced in quantity by

Kaua'i, Kona coffee is unmatched in terms of quality. With the possible exception of Jamaican Blue Mountain coffee, Kona coffee is widely considered to be the best in the world. Good Kona coffee lacks the bitterness of coffees from other parts of the world. By the way, contrary to nearly everyone's belief, lighter roasts have more caffeine than darker roasts. (Caffeine cooks away during the roasting process.)

A quality cup of coffee has little resemblance to mass-produced coffee you see on most supermarket shelves. (Of course, you pay more for the good stuff.) Good Kona coffee will set you back $20 or more per pound. Surprisingly little profit is made by the farmer at that price. Most small farmers grow coffee as a labor of love. If you see 100% Kona coffee (not a blend) selling for $12 per pound, it might be poorly chosen, broken or contain poorly roasted beans. You usually get what you pay for. And if you're told in a restaurant that they serve Kona blend because pure Kona is too strong, it's like saying that champagne needs to be blended with gasoline because pure champagne is too strong. Kona blends (which are blended with cheap beans from elsewhere) are less mellow than pure Kona. Blends are usually served because they're cheaper, not better.

Being wretched coffee addicts, we've tried them all. For what it's worth, we like **Pau Hana Estate** (808–328–8099), **Holualoa** (800–334–0348), **Greenwell** (808–323–2275) and **Kona Blue Sky** (877–322–1700). Some aren't available in stores, only by phone or mail order. **Kona Joe** (866–566–2563) grows their trees on a trellis, like grapes, and the Trellis Reserve medium roast is very good. But at $55 per pound you'll be forgiven if you want to pursue less expensive vices, such as caviar or Cristal champagne.

Coffees that we've tried and didn't like are Bad Ass Coffee, Ferrari Mountain Gold, Royal Aloha, and Starbuck's Kona coffee. (The last one is surprising.) We are not saying that these companies are bad, just that we didn't like their coffee and didn't think it was worth the money.

Coffee tours are available from many growers, but coffee farms that claim to offer tours are often poorly marked, and owners and employees sometimes seem shocked when you show up to buy coffee. **Greenwell** and **Hula Daddy** (327–9744) have good tours. Greenwell is on the map on page 66.

ples are offered at many establishments. Some are mediocre. Others, such as Greenwell and Bayview, sell very good quality coffee to take with you. There are places to eat along here, such as Ke'ei Café (for dinner) and The Coffee Shack, (for breakfast). Look for Discovery Antiques—Ice Cream on the ocean side of the highway in Kealakekua. They serve Tropical Dreams ice cream, as sinful here as in Hawi on the north shore. Just after the Aloha Theater in Kainaliu, stop at the Donkey Ball Store for some of their namesake treats. (Wonderful chocolate covered mac nuts with thick chocolate.) Available in any quantity. (Not just pairs.)

In Kealakekua (you'll be forgiven if you don't readily see the transition between towns up here) between the 112 and 111 mile markers on the ocean side of the road is the Kona Historical Society Museum (323–3222). Located in an old general store built during the 1800s, there are lots of old coffee-related photos and other items of historical interest. Worth a stop if you have an interest in the past. Closed Friday–Sunday, $7 admission ($3 for kids).

There are good views down the coast from some spots along here. After you pass the 111 mile marker on Highway 11, you'll see Napoopoo Road on the ocean side of the road—take it. There are lots of coffee farms down here. (See gray box on facing page.) A coffee tour might be worth the effort. You may get to try delicious coffee or meet offbeat characters you'll remember for years to come.

Napoopoo comes to an intersection of itself and Middle Ke'ei Road. Turn right here and head toward the ocean. The old Mauna Loa Coffee Mill near the 8 mile marker is now a tourist shop run by another company and is of marginal interest. Stop only if you need to stretch.

KEALAKEKUA BAY & PLACE OF REFUGE

When you get to the sea, hang a right to Napo'opo'o Beach Park. The stone structure you see in front of you at this southern end of Kealakekua Bay (at the end of the road) is Hiki-au Heiau. This was a luakini (a temple where human sacrifices were made). Here Captain Cook was first worshipped as the returning god Lono. During the ceremony, an elder priest named Koa, in the honored tradition of the Hawaiians, chewed the food first before spitting it out and offering it to Cook. (He politely declined.) It was also here that the first Christian ceremony was held in Hawai'i. Ironically it may have contributed to the death of Captain Cook. When one of his men died, Cook ordered him buried near this heiau and personally read the service. This event was proof to some Hawaiians that the strangers were mere mortals, not the gods others felt them to be.

Napo'opo'o Beach used to be a fabulous beach fronting the heiau. It had been eroding for years, being gradually replaced by boulders. When Hurricane 'Iniki sideswiped the island way back in 1992, its surf removed most of what sand was left. Over the decades very little has returned.

One mile across the bay you can see a white obelisk, the Captain Cook Monument, which was erected in 1874 by British sailors. It was near this spot (a rarely visited plaque to the left of the monument marks the *actual* spot) in 1779 that Cook was killed by the Hawaiians. (See INTRODUCTION for more on this event.) You won't need your passport to go there, even though it is British soil that the monument rests on. The small plot was deeded to the United Kingdom by Princess Likelike.

Kealakekua Bay is also popular with dolphins. A large number of spinners reside in the bay, so keep an eye out for them. We see them almost every time we kayak to the monument. Toward the monument side on the bay, up the steep cliff, there is a grayish impression. Local lore says this was made by a cannonball fired from Cook's ship.

These cliffs hold even more secrets. In the past, important chiefs were buried in small caves in the cliff face. After the bones had been separated, volunteers were lowered down the face of the cliffs by rope to place the bones in crevices. No one had a long résumé in this line of work. That's because the person doing the burying, once finished with his task, would signal to those above that he was done. The officials on top would promptly cut the rope, sending the burial person, and all knowledge of the location of the bones, crashing to the rocks below. (It was actually considered an honor to be the volunteer at the end of the rope.) All this was to prevent the bones from being desecrated. Bones were often turned into fishhooks and other implements. Skulls were turned into refuse pots or toilets. *(Really* good joke edited out here upon further reflection.)

Today, if you hear something fall from the cliff, it won't be a person. Brainless cows from above occasionally wander off the ledge, pleasing the fish below with a refreshing change from their seafood diet.

The waters near the monument are crystal clear and teeming with coral and fish. This is some of the best snorkeling in the state. The local community wants to keep it somewhat difficult to access to prevent it from being overrun with "casual" visitors. If you are wondering how to get there, you have several choices:

You can swim it. This takes us about an hour each way with fins and is guaranteed to tucker you out.

You can walk along the edge of the bay for about 98% of the distance. You'll have to scramble on boulders the whole way and will have to swim for a couple of short patches. You expose yourself to the ocean's whims and falling rocks with this method. Not a great way to get there.

You can rent a kayak and paddle over. (See KAYAKING on page 209.) This is our favorite method. It's a relatively easy 30-minute paddle across the usually

Is there anything more tranquil than coconut trees, like those here at Honaunau?

peaceful bay, and you stand a good chance of cruising among dolphins along the way. Make sure you bring water, lunch and snorkel gear. This is an excellent way to spend the morning.

Another way to get to the monument is to take the trail near the intersection of Highway 11 and Napoopoo Road. (The trailhead is a little over ¹⁄₁₀ mile from the highway across from 3 large palm trees. See map. You may have to park a short distance up the road.) It used to be a road but is now suitable only for hiking. It's 2 miles each way with a 1,300-foot constant descent to the water. It's a pretty good puffer coming back up with little shade and some obnoxious footing. It takes most people more than an hour each way. Drink *plenty* of water before and during the ascent, and be careful not to pull your calves during the steady, grueling climb. Along the way you'll pass (but won't see due to brush) the Puhina o Lono Heiau. It was here that Cook's bones were…well, cooked. (See below.)

Lastly, you can take one of the boat trips on page 211. They stop for snorkeling near the monument. They also offer SCUBA, SNUBA, and all-around fun.

What Finally Happened to Cook?

The Hawaiians traditionally scraped the flesh off the bones of great men. The bones were then bundled together and burned or buried in secret so they wouldn't be desecrated. If the dead person was really loved, the bones were kept in a private home for a while. Because Cook was so respected by the Hawaiians, his body parts were distributed among the chiefs. His head went to the king, his scalp went to a high-ranking chief, his hair went to Kamehameha, etc. Some of his organs, including his heart and liver, were stolen and eaten by some local children who mistook them for dog innards. *(Yuck!)* Eventually, when two Hawaiians brought

a bundle to the ship, the British solemnly unwrapped the bundle and discovered a pile of bloody flesh that had been cut from Cook's body. Even though the Hawaiians were bestowing an honor upon Cook, the British sailors didn't see it that way and were naturally shocked and horrified. The anguished sailors begged Captain Clerke to allow them to go into the village and extract revenge, but he refused, fearing a bloodbath. Some went anyway, killing several villagers. Most of the bones were eventually returned to the British, and Cook was buried at sea in Kealakekua Bay. The ship's surgeon wrote, "In every situation he stood un-rivaled and alone. On him all eyes were turned. He was our leading star which, at its setting, left us in darkness and despair."

The steep cliffs around Kealakekua Bay seem strangely out of place on this otherwise gently sloping mountain. There's a good reason, and it happened in one day. See page 77 for the explanation.

As you leave Napo'opo'o Beach, stay on the oceanmost road heading south. There is a side road leading to Ke'ei Beach. Pretty but not real usable, its historical legacy is a Hawaiian legend, bolstered by Spanish records, which states that white men straggled ashore in the 1520s, 250 years before Cook arrived.

Lots of blood has been spilt on this part of the island. One particularly important battle took place just south of Ke'ei Beach at Moku-a-Kae Bay called the Moku-'ohai Battlefield. You only access it via a hike, but it was near here in 1782 that Kamehameha the Great finally became king of this half of the island after defeating Kiwala'o. During a bloody battle, one of Kamehameha's generals, named Ke'eaumoku (call him Ke for short), got tangled in his own spear and tripped, savagely impaling himself. Presuming Ke to be mortally wounded, Kiwala'o ran over to the enemy general to finish him off and

Lawbreakers had one chance to escape the inevitable death penalty: Reach the area's place of refuge before your enemies reached you, and all was forgiven.

seize his prized neck ornament. (Taking it off your enemy's body was symbolic of defeating him.) As he was leaning over Ke's body, Kiwala'o was beaned on the head by a sling stone hurled by one of Kamehameha's warriors, and fell backward. Ke, who wasn't dead from his spear wound, painfully crawled to the unconscious Kiwala'o and slit his throat with a leiomanu (a Hawaiian version of brass knuckles, but with razor-sharp shark's teeth embedded on the outside). Thus Kamehameha was able to defeat his nemesis and rule western Hawai'i.

Battles such as these are a constant throughout Hawaiian history after the 12th century. Rival chiefs or kings were quick to take each other on. Warriors would often congregate on opposite sides of the battlefield and shout insults at each other in an attempt to intimidate. (Insults about lineage were always a real hit.) During battles, spears, sling stones and clubs were used with remarkable efficiency. Shark tooth-studded leiomanus

were often given to old men who would go out onto battlefields after the fighting was over to slit the throats of those still alive. Though it may sound harsh (OK, OK—it *is* harsh), this was their way and not considered abhorrent to them.

Soon you come to Pu'uhonua o Honaunau (pronounced HOE-NOW-NOW). Also called Place of Refuge, this is an *awesome* spot to visit. It is a site of great importance and a fun place to explore. In ancient times, commoners' lives were governed by the kapu system. There was a dizzying number of laws to observe. Those of lower classes weren't allowed to look at or even walk on the same trails as the upper classes. Men and women were forbidden to eat together, citizens were not allowed to get close to a chief or allow their shadows to fall across them, etc. All manner of laws kept the order. The penalty for breaking any of the laws was usually the same—death by club, strangulation, fire

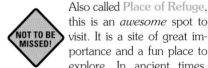

NOT TO BE MISSED!

or spear. (Well, it's nice to have choices, at least.) If the offense was severe enough, the offender's *entire family* might be executed. It was believed that the gods retaliated against lawbreakers by sending tidal waves, lava flows, droughts and earthquakes, so communities had a great incentive to dispatch lawbreakers with haste. If a lawbreaker could elude his club or spear-wielding pursuers, however, he had one way out of his mess—the area's Pu'uhonua (Place of Refuge). This predesignated area offered asylum. If a lawbreaker could make it here, he could perform certain rituals mandated by the kahuna pule (priest). After that, all was forgiven and he could return home as if nothing had happened, regardless of the violation. Defeated warriors could also come here to await the victor of a battle. They could then pledge their allegiance to whoever won and live out their lives in peace.

Pu'uhonua o Honaunau is such a place. Designated as a national park by Congress in 1961, it is the finest example of a Place of Refuge in all the islands. Here you will find neatly kept grounds featuring a remarkable stone wall, called the Great Wall. Built in the 1500s, this massive wall is 1,000 feet long, 10 feet high and 17 feet thick in most places. It separated the Pu'uhonua from the Ali'i's palace grounds. Though the wall has a chiseled appearance, it was made without dressed (cut) stones and without mortar. Also on the grounds you will find reconstructed Hawaiian houses, temples, and a few petroglyphs (rock drawings). There are wood carvings of gods (including one that is anatomically correct, assuming that's how the gods were endowed). The reconstructed thatched structure called Hale-o-Keawe was originally a mausoleum, containing the bones of 23 chiefs. Bones were thought to contain supernatural power, or *mana*, and there-fore ensured that the Place of Refuge would remain sacred.

There are many other sights here, as well. Overall, this place is easy to recommend. The walk around the grounds is gentle, and there are facilities such as drinking water and restrooms. Coconut trees (which have an almost magical, calming effect) are scattered all over. There is a $5 per car entrance fee, but sometimes no one is there to collect it because they "can't afford the manpower to collect the money." (Only the government could come up with that kind of logic.)

Honaunau is particularly enchanting an hour before sunset, the best time to visit. Swaying coconut trees have a golden glow as large turtles munch limu in the water near the canoe landing. You won't find a more relaxing or soothing place to finish off the day. Then head over to the middle/southern end of the park where picnic tables and BBQS await. Local families often bring their keiki (kids) to play in the nearby tide-pools. Drive to that area using the dirt road to the left of the visitor center after you enter the park.

For the less cerebral, you'll find unbeatable snorkeling and SCUBA diving in Honaunau Bay to the right of the boat launch. There are also hiking trails, including the 1871 Trail, so named because area residents paid their taxes in 1871 by fixing up this formerly dilapidated trail. (We have a call in to the IRS to see if the offer's still good.) The trail goes all the way to Ho'okena Beach, but the portion outside of the park is pretty bleak.

Leaving Honaunau, you'll continue up Ke Ala o Keawe Road to Painted Church Road. Hang a left onto it to get to St. Benedict's Catholic Church, known simply as the Painted Church. It's a charming little **A REAL GEM** building dating back to the 1800s. Between 1899 and 1904, Father

Wake me when the mai tais are ready.

John Velge dedicated himself to creating frescos on the inside walls and ceiling. Everything from hell to the Temptation of Christ is represented in loving detail. There is a sign on the door explaining in detail Father Velge's efforts. Termites and age are starting to take their toll, but this is always worth a stop.

Either continue on Painted Church Road to Middle Keei Road, or backtrack to get back up to the highway. (See map.)

When deciding where to eat in Kailua-Kona, see ISLAND DINING on page 248.

KAILUA-KONA SHOPPING

There are many small shopping areas in, around and south of Kona to keep your stomach filled and wallet emptied. Kona Commons is a big box shopping center north of Kona on Makala Blvd. off Hwy 19. The main store here is Target, but you'll want to check out Kona Wine Market for their extensive selection of wines.

The Kona International Marketplace in the old Industrial Area north of Kona on Kaiwi and Luhia Streets is a great one-stop shopping spree. Though some stalls are so-so, others are pretty nice. There's also a Farmers' Market there.

Continuing south on Kuakini is the King Kamehameha Mall where you will find Quilt Passions for original quilts and quilting supplies. Across the street from the King Kamehameha Kona Beach Hotel is the Cindy Coats Gallery, whose artwork reflects the colors of the island in a whimsical way.

Along Alii Drive there are many shops. A few of our favorites are: By the Sea at the Kona Seaside Shopping Mall, a good place to pick up sandals and clothing—especially Hawaiian shirts for men. At the Kona Square is Country Samurai Coffee Company where you can get the shakes off their Buzz Beans, a coffee and chocolate jolt that will wake the dead.

In Kona Banyan Court, next to the free parking lot, don't miss Elementz Designs whose unique jewelry is made from burning patterns in leather and ox horns (from Waimea) and then hand painted.

Other shops to visit along the north end of Alii Drive are Crazy Shirts for T-shirts and Na Hoku for pearl jewelry. Check out The Eclectic Craftsman for wood carvings and bowls, and Lava Light Galleries for photos of the island that you can't capture with your pocket camera. Across the street at the Kona Inn Shopping Village you'll find Honolua Surf Co., and for casual island-style clothing. Try Kona Inn Children's Wear for kids' clothes and books, Tropical Heat Wave for island-style housewares and Mermaids Swimwear, which is great for women's swimsuits and accessories.

Other stops in Kona are Hilo Hattie across from Kopiko Plaza for reasonable prices and a great selection of aloha wear and souvenirs. Walmart in the Crossroads Shopping Center offers good prices on souvenirs. Don't forget about Costco (near the airport) for the best gasoline prices in Kona.

South along Alii Drive, on the mauka side of the road, is Ali'i Gardens Marketplace, a place to pick up some last-minute souvenirs with smaller crowds than downtown Kona. In Keauhou Shopping Center, visit Kona Stories, a well-stocked bookstore and place to connect your laptop to the Internet for free.

Above Kona in Holualoa you will want to stop at some of the most original galleries on the island. Don't miss Ipu Hale Gallery, on the north end of town, for bowls and vases made from gourds dyed in a traditional Hawaiian way. Some of our other favorites are: Dovetail for contemporary art, Cliff Johns Gallery for woodworking, Holualoa Gallery and Pacific Island Gallery. At Holualoa 'Ukulele Gallery you can make your own 'uke, if you have a spare 8 to 10 days in your schedule, or just buy one created by their many artists. Hawaii Treasure Mill has some affordable smaller pieces to pack in your suitcase.

In Kainaliu, there's Showcase Gallery for paintings and sculptures by artists from all over Hawai'i. Lavender Moon has works by Big Island artists. To pick up an uke ('ukulele, that is) try Just Ukes or Kiernan Music. At Paradise Found, Sweet Surrender and Yoganics Hawaii

you'll find island-style clothing for women—sorry, guys. Kimura's Fabrics has an outstanding selection of Hawaiian print fabrics and quilting supplies.

In Mango Court, visit Divine Goods Hawai'i for an eclectic assortment of gifts, jewelry and clothing.

Past the 111 mile marker on your left is a beautiful antique shop called Antiques & Orchids. Before the 109 mile marker on the makai side of the road is Sacred Grounds Coffee Farm & Paradise Pottery Studio. They grow mac nuts here, too. Their reasonably priced ceramics are covered with ginko leaf patterns.

Coffees N' Epicurea across from the 106 mile marker in Honaunau is a nice stop to grab a fresh pastry (but it's hard to choose just one) and fresh coffee. Just south of here is Bong Brothers & Sistahs, a good stop for a smoothie, fresh fruit, coffee or some Bong Brothers logo items. Gotta love the name.

KAILUA-KONA'S BEST BETS

Best Place to Meet Fish for the First Time—Kahalu'u Beach Park
Best Pizza—Kona Brewing Company
Best Fish Sandwich—Quinn's
Best Treat (Despite the Name)— Donkey Balls
Best Sunset Cocktail Location— Verandah at Keauhou Beach Resort
Best Place for a Coffee and Cinnamon Roll in the Morning—Island Lava Java
Best Snorkeling—Captain Cook Monument or Honaunau
Best Place to Spot Dolphins— Kealakekua Bay
Best Sunset Picnic—The BBQS at Honaunau or the tide-pools of Wawaloli Beach, if the surf's crashing
Best SCUBA Adventure—Manta Ray Night Dive
Best Way to make your Lips Numb— Kanaka Kava

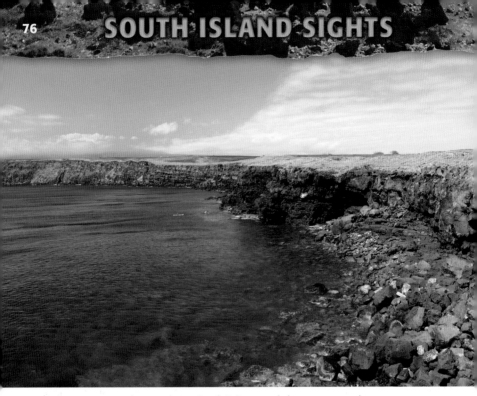

At Broken Road near South Point, crystal clear waters are the norm.

The southern end of the island from Honaunau (near the 104 mile marker on Highway 11) to Hawai'i Volcanoes National Park is the least developed part of the Big Island. Long stretches of lava fields on the western side of Mauna Loa's flank give way to green as you round the southern part of the island, where rain is allowed to fall with less interference from Mauna Loa volcano. Along the way you'll pass roads leading to, among other things, a (usually) deserted black sand beach, a lightly inhabited 11,000+ acre housing subdivision and the southernmost place in the United States. Since most people drive this stretch on their way to the volcano from Kailua-Kona or Kohala, we'll describe it from that direction.

These districts, called **South Kona** and **Ka'u**, are littered with the financial corpses of big businessmen with big plans and big wallets who took a big bath. Most didn't have a clue how business in Hawai'i works and lost their 'okoles as a result. Three examples, all mentioned in detail later, are:

HOVE—*If you build it, they won't come...not for a generation.*

Hawaiian Riviera—*He who underestimates his opponents will ultimately be crushed by them.*

SeaMountain—*How to turn $30 million in cash into $3 million in real estate.*

From Highway 11 heading south from Honaunau, you'll have several opportunities to visit beaches below the road. **Ho'okena** (a decent gray sand beach) and **Pebble Beach** (a violent 'okole kicker) are described in BEACHES. Distances between gas stations are large, so gas up when you can. Just after Honaunau between the 104 and 103 mile marker is the best fruit stand we know of on the west side. **South Kona Fruit Stand** usually has excellent quality fruits all organically grown on the adjacent farm.

While driving along the flanks of Mauna Loa along here, consider this: Mauna Loa was built from countless thin layers of lava flows, usually less than 15 feet thick. (Flows since 1800 are shown on the map.) About 120,000 years ago, there was a plain below you where there are now steep hills. At that time, a humongous piece (that's a technical term) of the island, from roughly around the 109 mile marker to an area north of Miloli'i (20 miles to the south), broke off and slid into the ocean, creating what is now Kealakekua Bay and the steep hills south of Honaunau. The resulting tsunami (tidal

wave) was so huge that it washed completely over the 1,427-foot-high island of Kaho'olawe, continued on and washed almost completely over the 3,370-foot-high island of Lana'i, where it deposited chunks of coral over a thousand feet up the mountain. This area is, geologically speaking, still unstable. Just didn't want you to run out of things to worry about.

Usually referred to as the last remaining fishing village on the island, **Miloli'i** is just past the 89 mile marker. As a beach destination, it won't offer you much (especially on the weekends—see BEACHES for more information). From the highway, 2²/₁₀ miles into the beach access road, look off to your left, and you will see a narrow a'a lava flow. The nearby village of **Ho'opuloa** was wiped out entirely when the lava marched down the slopes of Mauna Loa in 1926. Miloli'i's residents gained notoriety when they and their

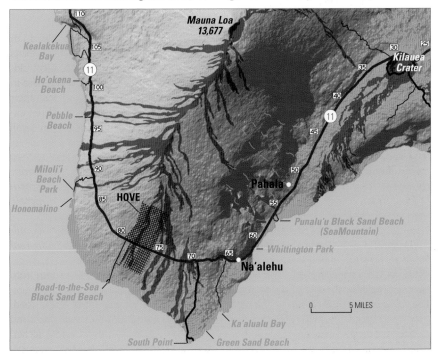

lawyer managed to kill the Hawaiian Riviera Resort, 17 miles to the south. (See below.) A 20-minute walk from Miloli'i leads to an exceptionally picturesque coconut-lined bay called Honomalino. It's usually deserted and worth the walk. See page 170 for more.

The main highway, called the Hawai'i Belt Road, follows an old Hawaiian road called the Mamalahoa Highway. If you want to see what driving this area *used* to be like (and why it took so bloody long to circle the island), take the 2-mile stretch of the old road. The intersections are at the 88 and 86 mile markers on the mauka (mountain) side of the road.

You'll see lots of macadamia nut trees along this stretch of the island. (By the way, keep the mac nuts away from dogs; they cause paralysis in certain breeds.) The Big Island is a major player in the macadamia nut world. The inner shell of the macadamia nut is impossibly hard. We've been told by nearly every macadamia farmer we know that if you roll over them with your car, they won't break. So we did it. The result? They all broke. Another urban legend shot to...

Back on the highway, Manuka State Park is near the 81 mile marker. There's a 2-mile loop trail that wanders through lava flows of several ages, giving you perspective on how things grow over different times. There are restrooms and phones.

The arrow-straight dirt road ⅔ mile past (south of) the 80 mile marker off Highway 11 is a perfect example of why 4WD vehicles are so useful here. It's called Road to the Sea. (Gee, I wonder where it goes...) Two stark, deserted black sand beaches, unknown even to the vast majority of island residents, are at the end. (See BEACHES on page 171 for an explanation.) It's hard to conceive of a lifeless, arid area being inviting, yet these beaches somehow are. We've even seen plankton-eating whale sharks more than once near the beach. The road is a *public access*, misleading sign notwithstanding.

Another beautiful bay south of here is called Pohue, but access to it from the lava road has been scuttled for decades by lawsuits and general bickering. Separately, there was a several *thousand* acre resort called Hawaiian Riviera slated to be built from Road to the Sea to Pohue Bay. Even though the developer had big bucks, he was thwarted by a handful of residents from Miloli'i, 17 miles to the north, who protested that a planned marina here (and the resort in general) would interfere with their rich fishing grounds and their way of life. They got a lawyer to take up their cause, and together they successfully killed the project. The land has changed hands several times since then, the last time for $13 million, and the current owners resurrected giant development ideas (including an airport) for the area in 2009, but so far it's going nowhere.

Continuing along, Hawaiian Ocean View Estate (known locally as HOVE) lies up mauka of the highway along here. They have gas, nice grocery stores and a few restaurants. HOVE is sort of a new community and an old one at the same time. Look at the map on the previous page. Notice all those roads? About 11,000 one-acre parcels on harsh lava are spread among those roads. An oil company built it in the '60s, with the dream of creating a new community. Acre lots originally sold for $995 each, and until the early 2000s you could still pick up lots for $1,500. Prospective buyers were lured by photos of palm tree-backed Pohue Bay (which is distant, private and not reachable) and talk of the HOVE Yacht Club (which never existed). For over 30 years the vast majority of the lots remained unbuilt. They used party line phones until

1998 and around that time they got electricity. Rain catchment has been their lifeline. There's not even a school. Streets have lovely sounding names like *Paradise Parkway* and *Tree Fern Avenue.* But after driving around, you'd expect names like *Lava Lane* and *Rocky Road.* Most of the lots were sold or given away free with a full tank of gas (just teasing). Not to be outdone, another company built a subdivision below the highway (also shown on the map) with 1,200 three-acre lots. It took the short-lived land boom of around 2005 to finally shake up HOVE real estate values and draw residents.

To be fair, everyone we've met who lives in HOVE loves it there. They have formed a tight-knit community and seem happy as can be with their location. Whenever we drive around here, however, we're reminded that the Big Island is often rumored to be one of the largest repositories of people from the FEDERAL WITNESS PROTECTION PROGRAM. What a perfect place to lose one's self.

There's not much to eat down here. Check out ISLAND DINING on page 277.

SOUTH POINT

Between the 69 and 70 mile markers is the road to South Point (called Ka Lae meaning "the point"). This is the southernmost part of the island, making it the southernmost spot in the entire nation. (Not the Florida Keys, as most trivia books claim.) At one time the road was nasty and very hard on rental cars. It has since been repaved and is in fine condition the whole way. The only hazard is that the road is one lane for much of its length. It is mostly straight, and there is space to pull over for oncoming cars. Try to resist the temptation

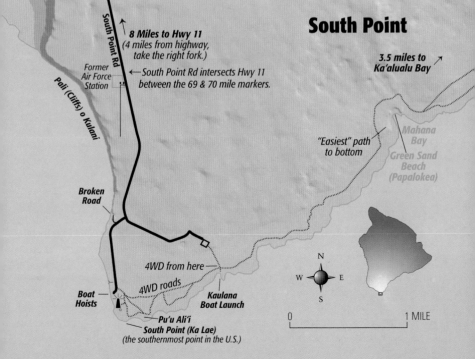

South Point

South Point Rd

↑ **8 Miles to Hwy 11**
(4 miles from highway, take the right fork.)

Former Air Force Station

← *South Point Rd intersects Hwy 11 between the 69 & 70 mile markers.*

Pali (cliffs) o Kulani

3.5 miles to Ka'alualu Bay ↗

"Easiest" path to bottom

Mahana Bay

Green Sand Beach (Papalokea)

Broken Road

Boat Hoists

4WD from here

4WD roads

Kaulana Boat Launch

Pu'u Ali'i

South Point (Ka Lae)
(the southernmost point in the U.S.)

N W E S

0   1 MILE

NOT TO BE MISSED!

Massive turbines are one indication of the ever-present winds in this area.

to speed on the seemingly wide open parts of this road; there are some surprise blind hills and turns.

The wind is always blowing out on this grassy plain, hence this location for the old **Kamoa Wind Farm** you cross on South Point Road. At press time it looked sad and abandoned and was overshadowed by the much larger **Pakini Nui Wind Farm** beyond and behind them. The trees here are all wind-blown in the same direction (west), vividly showing what happens to deflected trade winds coming from the northeast. (The foldout back cover map puts it in perspective.)

As you get near South Point, turn right at the fork after the KALAE entrance sign. (The sign looked rickety at press time—the fork is a mile south of some abandoned buildings on the right.) South Point is the site of some of the oldest artifacts yet discovered in Hawai'i (as early as 300 AD) and was probably the first place the Polynesians came ashore and settled when they discovered these islands. Dry and desolate with no permanent streams, this might seem a surprising place for people to settle. The reason for its settlements, however, lies offshore. The waters off South Point are incredibly rich fishing grounds. Large pelagic game fish, such as tuna, mahimahi and marlin are plentiful. The ancient Hawaiians quickly discovered this but had a problem harvesting the fish. The wind and current together form such a strong offshore force that it would require all their attention just to stay put in a canoe. Those who went out too far were considered lost due to these forces since fishing canoes were not as maneuverable as voyaging canoes, and since the currents are uninterrupted all the way to Antarctica. The bottom drops to great depths quickly, so anchors aren't the answer. Their clever solution was to carve holes into the rock ledge and feed ropes through them so their canoes could be tied to shore while fishing. Some of those holes are still visible near the boat hoists at the cliffs.

Freshwater is very scarce here, even from wells, and what is available is barely potable. In the 1700s a chief named Kalani'opu'u, tired of having to bathe several miles away, asked his kahunas if there was water under the ground. One know-it-all assured him there was water at a certain spot if he dug *really* deep. After much digging, they found nothing. The big-mouth kahuna was promptly executed for his bad advice.

Today, you're likely to see long lines strung from the sea cliffs just to the northwest of the actual South Point. These lines are usually held afloat by empty bleach bottles and are sometimes pulled so taut by the wind and current that you'd swear you could walk on them. Fishermen use toy sailboats to drag the rope out to sea and dangle 10 foot leaders from the main line at every bleach bottle. When they get a strike, they haul the whole line in.

At the cliffs near South Point are old hoists, used to lower small boats from the low cliffs. Metal cliffside ladders are present, as well. Larger boats use the Kaulana boat launch less than a mile to the east. People lived at Kaulana until the beginning of the 20th century. Most visitors make the mistake of assuming that the cliffs with the boat hoists *are* South Point. The real South Point is past the light beacon to the left of a place where a rock wall trails down into the sea. There is no cliff there. The beacon will be behind you. Next to the beacon is the small Kalaea Heiau.

Since ancient times this entire area has had a reputation for having exceptionally strong currents, and during all but calm seas this is no doubt true. Even so, we know people who love nothing better than to leap into the water from the boat hoist area and come back up via the metal ladder adjacent to a boat hoist. There are also a few spots along the cliffs where you can scramble down to the water. Some people even like to snorkel here at night when fish and clouds of small, beautiful shrimp greet the eye. The water is unbelievably clear and seems quite inviting when calm, especially when you can see lots of fish swimming below.

With this in mind, I've repeatedly snorkeled here below the boat hoists to assess the currents. I was so wary the first time out that I tied myself to the cliff ladder with a long rope—just to be safe. It turned out to be unnecessary. *When calm, I have yet to detect much current below the boat hoist area,* probably because it's protected by the point. The water is teeming with life and visibility is usually over 100 feet. But (and I can't stress this enough) I've *never* gone into the water when it's not calm, I don't swim too far, and I don't endorse swimming there. The surge there demonstrates the extreme power of the ocean, and I'm excited and nervous every time I swim at that spot. South of the cliffs at the actual South Point, the water is always violent and unswimmable. I mention all this so you will

Here's another. Bring your extra-strength hairspray when you visit South Point.

know what I've experienced here in case you are crazy enough to do it on your own. Check to see that your life insurance policy is in order before you go, and buy a good guidebook to Antarctica—just in case.

South Point was used during WWII for army barracks. Later, the Navy installed a missile tracking station on 33 acres. Not to be left out, the Air Force later took over the facilities and renamed it South Point Air Force Station. The station was closed in 1979, and little remains except the shabby buildings on your right as you are approaching South Point. Look for horses in the buildings' remains.

Just north of the boat hoists (see map) is a road that leads off a cliff. The road was built in 1955 along with a concrete landing below to service fishing boats. Representing the finest county quality, it lasted less than a year. The surf erased the landing and part of the road. What remains is called (you see this one coming, don't you?) **Broken Road**. The view from the end of Broken Road is spectacular, but the snorkeling isn't as good here as it is below the boat hoists. Off in the distance you see Pali o Kulani, which rises 350 feet from the ocean. At the place where the cliff appears to end, it actually turns inland and runs north to an area just south of Highway 11. The inland cliff was caused by another catastrophic landslide, similar to (but pre-dating) the one described earlier. It slid to the west and caused a similar splash.

If you had gone left at the aforementioned fork, you'd come to all that remains of former military housing. We were thrilled when state authorities leveled them a while back. Until then, militant squatters had occupied the crumbling buildings for many years, extracting "Green Sand Parking Fees" from visitors and often threatening car break-ins if they didn't comply. It was a well-known problem and generated over 150 police reports in one year

alone. Authorities seemed paralyzed until finally, in 2007, 21 officers converged here, brought a BBQ, grilled up burgers for themselves and the squatters, then proceeded to bulldoze all the structures.

When the pavement ends, a dirt road leads to a boat launch ¼-mile away.

Off to the east of South Point is a strange phenomenon called **Green Sand** **Beach**. (See BEACHES.) It features a beautiful mixture of green and black sand and is a fascinating place to visit. If you have 4WD you *might* be able to drive it. It's 2¼ miles each way on the flat but sometimes *deeply* rutted, grassy plain. Sometimes even timid 4WDers can make it. Other times, you'll want to bring along four sumo wrestlers to help you carry your car out of the ruts. Many readers have written us to say we're *way* off on that distance, by the way. We promise, we're not. We've checked it by car odometer and on foot with GPS. It just *seems* longer since the wind is in your face going out.

A REAL GEM

Back on Highway 11, as you continue, you'll wrap around the island and enter the wetter, windward side. Almost instantly, our old friend green has returned to the scene. This was the edge of sugar country. Big Island sugar died here in 1996 (as a business—some of the cane still lives on), and many of the fields here have been replaced with the more profitable macadamia nut trees. Coffee has also been planted upslope of the highway. It's not in the same league as Kona coffee. We've had some good Ka'u coffee, but a lot of bad cups. (Ka'u growers write to us telling us we're dead wrong and have no taste. *Sorry*, it's just our opinion.) Both coffee and mac nuts can be found at roadside stands and local markets.

Waiohinu and **Na'alehu** are the first towns you come to. Waiohinu's claim to

Don't adjust your book. The sand really is green here.

fame was the **Mark Twain Monkeypod Tree**, planted by the author himself. It blew down in the '50s, but its shoots have grown into a respectable new tree. You'll find restrooms down the road at Waiohinu Park.

While in Na'alehu, stop by the best restaurant along this part of the island, **Hana Hou Restaurant and Bakery**.

As you come down the hill near the 62 mile marker, you'll see **Whittington Park** and the remains of its wharf in the distance. From the vantage point up the hill you truly appreciate the vastness of this Big Island. Whittington is picturesque from a distance and makes a decent rest room pit stop if you're in need.

Just after the 56 mile marker is the road to **Punalu'u Black Sand Beach**. This is the easiest volcanic black sand beach to access on the island now that the more famous one in Puna is gone. (That one was buried by lava in 1990—see page 119.) The water here is cold due to the large amounts of freshwater percolating from the floor just off-

NOT TO BE MISSED!

shore. At one time the ancient Hawaiians at Punalu'u (which means *spring dived for*) obtained their freshwater here by diving down with an upside-down, dried, hollow gourd to where the freshwater was streaming out. There they would flip the gourd, fill it with fresh water, put their thumbs over it, and come to the surface.

There are scads of turtles in the bay, and it's one of the few areas where we've seen them beach themselves. There is also a picturesque fishpond backed by lots of coconut trees. (Incidentally, there were no coconuts in Hawai'i before the Polynesians came. Though ubiquitous in the South Pacific, Hawai'i is fed by the North Pacific Current, precluding the possibility that a live coconut could have floated here from any place warm. Just thought you needed to know that for your next appearance on *Jeopardy.*) The only eyesore at this exotic black sand beach is the closed and ramshackle restaurant behind the fishpond. Fortunately, it's mostly covered over from the beach side, which tells you how long it's been closed—long enough to choke off their lovely view with vegetation. It's been condemned and might be bulldozed by the time you arrive.

When the Japanese attacked Pearl Harbor in 1941, Army troops dynamited the concrete wall over near the boat launch to keep it from being used by the enemy in case of an invasion.

Tour buses sometimes bring groups to Punalu'u, but it *usually* isn't crowded since it is 60 miles from both Hilo and Kona. Forgive us for nagging, but please resist the temptation to take black sand home as a souvenir. Since it is finite, it would eventually deplete the beach for everyone. (Or you can see CURSES in BASICS.) The sharp edges of the sand grains ensure that swimmers will inadvertently take some home anyway. You will find plenty of stowaways in the lining of your bathing suit, which will stay there for years. The concessionaire at Punalu'u sells black sand and, though they *claim* it's from another beach consumed by the volcano, that certainly can't be said of their green sand, so we hope you won't buy any. OK, end of nag.

This area is sometimes called Sea-Mountain, named by a developer for the Lo'ihi Seamount. That undersea volcano, 20 miles offshore from here, will be the Big Island's next volcano attraction. It's still 3,200 feet underwater and won't surface for another 100,000 years, but be sure to look for it when we release our 99,000th edition of this book. (Call now to reserve your copy early.) The whole property was purchased by a Japanese investment company for more than $30 million at the height of a real estate boom in 1989. After five years and countless challenges to their plans by local residents, they sold it for less than $3 million, not even a *tenth* of what they paid for it. *(Ouch!)* There are older condos here and a golf course. See BEACHES for more on Punalu'u.

From Punalu'u you'll start your gradual 4,000-foot ascent to Kilauea Volcano. Along the way you pass Pahala, a former sugar town. (This is also a speed trap, so watch it. Another bad speed trap is when the limit changes after the 38 mile marker.) Though friendly, the town is quiet and a little depressing, and the economic harm is, to a certain degree, self-inflicted. Pahala residents were crucial in killing the expansion plan at Punalu'u in the mid '90s, confident that their sugar plantation jobs were sufficient and fearful of altering their way of life. After that, the coastal land below Pahala was slated to be a spaceport where private satellites would be launched. Again Pahala residents were able to successfully fight the plan, even though it was backed by the state, the governor and the mayor.

Then in the late '90s the last Big Island sugar plantation opened the books and told the workers they either needed to accept a 15% pay cut or the company would have to close down due to ongoing losses. (Every other sugar plantation on the island had failed in the previous years due to a changing marketplace.) The sugar workers voted to reject the pay cut, and the sugar company promptly shut down, putting nearly every resident of this one-industry town out of work. Their way of life changed anyway, but they had nothing to fall back on. For a decade they paid the price in the form of a downward economic spiral. Only after the short-lived 2005 land boom did some prosperity finally start to trickle down to this part of the island.

A couple miles past the edge of Hawai'i Volcanoes National Park, take note of the rugged looking a'a lava. It's hard to believe that barefoot armies marched through this stuff, but they did—sometimes under extraordinary circumstances like those described on page 91.

Lava sometimes forms surreal images as it's flowing.

If you had to name the one thing the Big Island is most famous for, it would undoubtedly be **Kilauea Volcano**. In all the world there isn't a more active volcano, and none is as user-friendly as Kilauea. People often refer to it as the drive-in volcano.

Kilauea is an enigma—you can't really see the mountain from anywhere on the island, or even recognize it when you are standing on it. It seems more like a wound on Mauna Loa, whose flanks it resides upon. In the past, everyone thought that it was *part* of Mauna Loa, but today we know that it is separate and distinct, with its own separate (though possibly interrelated) magma chamber. One part of Kilauea, the actual Pu'u 'O'o vent itself, is teasingly inaccessible. You can't get very close to it without a long hike.

The "quickest" way is described in ADVENTURES on page 233.

We feel strongly that most people allow far too little time for visiting **Hawai'i Volcanoes National Park**. Many simply blow through on an around-the-island driving frenzy, stopping long enough to snap a shot of Kilauea Caldera. There is much more here than meets the eye, and this might be the highlight of your Hawaiian trip. Whether Kilauea is erupting or not, this park is the most fascinating place you may ever visit, and you *surely* don't have anything like this back home. The finest hiking on the island is here. The lushest rain forest you've ever seen is here to stroll through. Vents spewing steam, brand new land, birds-a-plenty, giant chasms, ancient Hawaiian petroglyphs, lava craters, walk-through lava tubes, unrivaled vistas—it's all here. Once you know what to look for, you will want to spend *at least* a whole day, preferably two. Since driving to the volcano can take four hours round trip from Kona and five hours from Kohala, consider reserving a place to stay in the town of Volcano (see WHERE TO STAY). This allows you to experience it at a more leisurely pace and is a nice way to go, if you can swing it. You'll probably want to stay until after dark if there are accessible surface lava flows, and the drive back to Kona or Kohala is a drag. If you are staying in Hilo, it's an easy drive back.

WILL I GET TO SEE LAVA FLOWING?

Historically (meaning since 1778), most eruptions have lasted days or weeks, rarely months. Until this eruption, only once, from 1969–1974 at Mauna Ulu, has an eruption outside the crater lasted more than a year. The current eruption, originating from a newly created vent called Pu'u 'O'o, is redefining our understanding of an eruption. It started on January 3, 1983, shifted to a vent called Kupaianaha from 1986 to 1992, then shifted back toward Pu'u 'O'o and was still going strong as we went to press with an occasional hiccup in its flowing activity.

When you visit Kilauea, you either *will* or *won't* get to see a surface lava flow. (Now *there's* a gutsy prediction!) Hawai'i Volcanoes National Park has a recording at 985–6000. They also have weather info. You can also get updates from the USGS at 967–8862. As we went to press, there were no signs of an impending work stoppage by Madame Pele, the fire goddess of Hawai'i, but that doesn't mean you can come here and be assured of being able to stick your toe into liquid lava. Madame Pele can be kind of a tease. The lava has stopped and started many times, shifted from vent to vent, gone straight into the ocean from underground lava tubes, and flowed in inaccessible places. It has also flowed just feet from the end of Chain of Craters Road, in Kilauea Caldera and other very accessible places. It's a gamble as to whether you will get to see it. Kilauea might go months without *accessible* lava flows, then put on a flawless show for months after that. If you have Internet access, we have an eruption update on our website at www.wizardpub.com. We also have links to other eruption websites.

When you hear that the volcano is erupting, you might think of a cone-shaped mountain, of going up to the top and peering into a boiling lake of molten

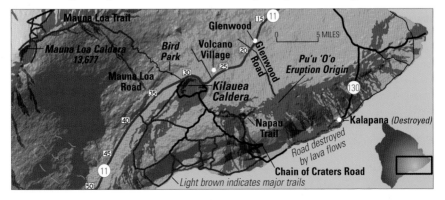

Light brown indicates major trails

rock. Maybe some will be pouring rapidly down the mountain, consuming everything in its path as people flee in panic. In Hawai'i, things are *far* different. Here, even the volcano is laid-back. Though it has erupted from the main crater in the past, most of the time (including the current eruption) the lava breaks out from a vent along what's called the rift zone, a linear belt of fractured rock on the flank of the volcano. From this vent the lava travels downhill, usually to the sea. After it starts flowing, pahoehoe lava rivers crust over, forming tubes. These tubes act as excellent insulators (the lava usually loses a mere 20°F over miles of travel in these tubes) and carry the lava to the ocean. Sometimes these tubes break the surface downhill of the source, forming surface flows. When this happens, you can often walk right up to it. Otherwise, there might be an enormous steam plume at the sea (which glows at night).

Many activity companies and nearly every guidebook shows photos of a helicopter or viewer directly in front of gigantic fountains of lava. You won't see any pictures like that in our book for two reasons. One, you're more likely to see a *balanced federal budget* than to see

that. It might happen a few times each decade for a few hours. What are *your* chances? The other reason is that a few of those photos are fake. (A stock government photo of a Kilauea lava fountain taken by scientists, a shot of a helicopter or person, a computer, and *voilà*—the unreal looks real.) The close-up photographs of surface lava flows you see in this book were all taken by us at accessible sites. We didn't get special permission to go to special spots or go through any unusual procedures. We didn't use a camera lens longer than a rental car to make it *seem* like it was close (and I've had the singed leg hairs to prove it). We also didn't charter helicopters and use zillion dollar cameras on loan from NASA. Granted, we didn't get to see this kind of lava our first time out there, but these are the kinds of things that mere mortals like us might get to see *if* Madame Pele is cooperating.

THE SCENE

We've been to the volcano countless times, with and without surface lava. It's always a fantastic experience, though not what people expect.

During a relatively calm flow, pahoehoe lava is silvery coated, red or yellow as it oozes its way toward the sea. It is a humbling experience to stand there and observe Earthly creation, like seeing the planet during its fiery adolescence. In most parts of the world, people dread active volcanoes, fearing death and destruction. A huge explosion will send clouds of ash and pumice into air, killing everything in its path. (Or screwing up travel to Europe.) In Hawai'i, people drop whatever they are doing and drive out to see it. Rather than apocalyptic explosions, Kilauea mostly drools and dribbles. (In historic times, it has exploded only a few times, and one had astonishing consequences—see page 91.) Though the total volume of lava erupting ranges from 300,000 to more than a million cubic yards *per day,* it is so spread out that it rarely rushes down the mountain in a hellish river of liquid stone. Usually, it's small rivulets of molten lava separated by large distances from other rivulets. When it hardens (which occurs very quickly), it crunches beneath your feet like shards of glass.

There are not many places on this planet where you can walk on ground younger than you are, where you can be assured that there is absolutely nothing alive beneath your feet except for the earth itself. We've been there when people from all over the world stand in awe, tears streaming down their cheeks as they tell their children, "You may never see anything like this again in your lifetime."

As freshly hardened pahoehoe lava cools, it stresses the silica coating on the outside. This natural glass then crackles and pops off the rock, creating subtle sounds that bewitch viewers. Heat from the flows can be intense. Many times we've been less than a yard from the molten lava and felt like we would suddenly burst into flames. Other times, the wind has blown from the other direction so we could enjoy the liquid earth in comfort. Sometimes there is unpleasant black smoke and fumes (especially when the volcano is gobbling up more road or forest). Other times it seems to have ab-

A father and daughter standing around watching the world get made. Not a bad way to spend the afternoon.

Lava comes in many flavors and textures.

solutely no fumes or smoke and no offensive smell. (What smell it does have is hard to describe but never forgotten.)

At night, the lava may glow in numerous spots like a prehistoric scene from yesteryear. Sometimes, as the lava flows into the ocean, brilliant red and orange steam clouds light up the immediate area, creating dazzling light shows as the flow drips or gushes into the ocean. Sometimes, when it burns scrub vegetation at night, the methane emits a blue flame. A scene at night might go like this: A crowd of about 50 people on a bluff overlooking a field of fresh pahoehoe. It pops, crackles and glows as the night consumes all. What amazes us is how reverent everybody is. Couples hold each other tight. People speak in soft whispers. They try not to move much for fear of disturbing others as they watch Earth's most primordial show. Nobody wants to leave. Watching the lava enter the sea at night never fails to impress, and we've been told more times than we can count by visitors that it is an unsurpassed highlight.

A FEW BASICS

Despite the fact that it is operated by the federal government, the park seems very well run. Much of the staff are friendly and professional. (We've seen other parks where the staff can be real curmudgeons.) The rangers are pretty good at letting you see the action close up. We've been there when they lead people across smoldering lava, the heat coming up through their shoes. They will only keep you away if they *truly* perceive danger, unlike some other parks where they sometimes keep you away from imaginary dangers on orders from the lawyers. Because of this, you should heed their cautions seriously. If they say you can't go to a certain area because they expect a lava bench might collapse, don't go there. At least one person has died because he didn't heed this warning. (The ocean drops quickly off the coast of the park, and new lava land is usually destined to break off when it reaches a critical mass.) If rangers say an area is off limits because of the dangers of methane explosions, believe it. Methane from plant matter in older flows can heat up when a new flow covers it. This usually escapes by hissing or by small pops, but sometimes it can be more dramatic. We were there once with many other visitors when a large methane explosion occurred 25 feet from us. It was powerful enough to rip through 12-inch thick lava, pieces of which jumped into the air. Under certain circumstances, these explosions occur 100 yards in advance of a lava flow.

In the park we like to arrive at surface flows about an hour or two

A river of stone plunges into the sea.

before sunset. That way we get to see it during the day and at night. As the sun sets, the light-emitting lava doesn't have to compete with the sun, resulting in brighter and seemingly more abundant lava. Bring a polarizing filter if you have a camera that will accept it. (Wipe your camera off when you are finished; the air can be acidic and is hard on electronics.)

The best shots will be late in the afternoon. If you get close to the lava, the heat might consume your camera battery faster than you think. (Trust me on that one.) Bring water—you'll get hot and thirsty. If it rains, you'll be grateful for something waterproof, and so will your camera. Depending on the flow, a flashlight might be invaluable. At times,

The Explosion That Changed History

Mild-mannered Kilauea has exploded on a large scale only twice in recorded history, once in 1790 and once in 1924. (There is evidence that it may have exploded more often in the distant past.) These eruptions are phreatomagmatic, meaning steam-induced (but you knew that).

In 1790, Kamehameha ruled much of the island. While he was distracted with plans to invade Maui, a rival chief named Keoua seized control of this part of the island. Kamehameha sent troops to do battle. Eventually both armies pulled back to their strongholds. As Keoua's troops and their families camped at Kilauea that night, fire and rock spewed from Kilauea Caldera. Keoua thought he had offended Pele, the volcano goddess, by rolling stones into the crater the day before and spent two days trying to appease her. It didn't work. On the third day they tried to leave, organized in three divisions. Right after the first division left, the mountain exploded. Darkness enveloped the area, punctured by volcano-induced thunder and lightning, and streams of red and blue light from the crater. Huge amounts of hot ash rained down, then a suffocating gas belched up from the volcano.

The first division to depart escaped mostly intact. The second division disappeared. When the third division came to the scene, they found their comrades of the second division huddled in circles, some hugging each other with their noses pressed together. Relieved, the third division rushed forward to greet them, only to discover that every last member of the second division—around 400 men and their wives and children—were dead. (Not 85 as the park sign says.) Most had been asphyxiated by the noxious gas. The only survivor was a solitary hog. If you take the Ka'u Desert Trail (page 102), you can see the faint outline of steps preserved in the ash—steps created by other soldiers at the time of the disaster.

As for Keoua, everyone now knew that Pele was against him and his army. He kept fighting more battles but never turned the tide. Not yet defeated, he was invited by Kamehameha to peacefully dedicate the new Pu'ukohola Heiau in Kawaihae. When Keoua's boat approached the shore of Kawaihae, he was immediately murdered by one of Kamehameha's officers and had the dubious honor of being the temple's first official human sacrifice. Thus was Kamehameha's rule over the island forever solidified.

Kilauea Crater

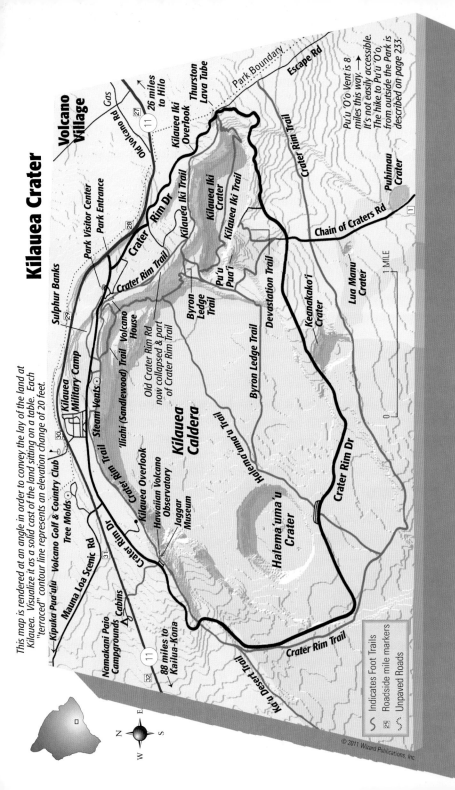

This map is rendered at an angle in order to convey the lay of the land at Kilauea. Visualize it as a solid cast of the land sitting on a table. Each "terraced" contour line represents an elevation change of 20 feet.

Pu'u 'O'o Vent is 8 miles this way. → It's not easily accessible. The hike to Pu'u 'O'o, from outside the Park is described on page 233.

Volcano Village

Gas

26 miles to Hilo

11 27

Park Boundary

Escape Rd

Thurston Lava Tube

Kilauea Iki Overlook

Old Volcano Rd

Rim Dr

Crater

Park Visitor Center
Park Entrance

28

Kilauea Iki Trail

Kilauea Iki Crater

Kilauea Iki Trail

Crater Rim Trail

Crater Rim Trail

Puhimau Crater

1

Chain of Craters Rd

Sulphur Banks

29

Byron Ledge Trail

Pu'u Pua'i

Devastation Trail

Keanakako'i Crater

Lua Manu Crater

1 MILE

0

Military Camp

Volcano House

Kilauea Military Camp

Steam Vents

'Iliahi (Sandlewood) Trail

Old Crater Rim Rd now collapsed & part of Crater Rim Trail

Byron Ledge Trail

30

Crater Rim Trail

Kilauea Overlook

Hawaiian Volcano Observatory

Jaggar Museum

Kilauea Caldera

Halema'uma'u Trail

Crater Rim Dr

Kipuka Pua'ulu Volcano Golf & Country Club

Tree Molds

Mauna Loa Scenic Rd

31

Crater Rim Dr

Halema'uma'u Crater

Namakani Paio Campgrounds Cabins

11

88 miles to Kailua-Kona

32

Ka'u Desert Trail

Crater Rim Trail

Indicates Foot Trails
25 Roadside mile markers
Unpaved Roads

N E S W

© 2011 Wizard Publications, Inc.

they let you walk to places at night that can be spectacular. Contact lens wearers will want to bring drops—maybe even your glasses if it gets uncomfortable. Bring sunscreen if you are there for the day. Add more water. What you don't want to bring are your preconceptions. No matter what you expect, the flow will be different. Come with a blank slate, and you will leave full of wonder.

And remember, if there are no accessible surface flows (which is quite possible), don't despair. The volcano area is eminently fascinating and exciting, with or without surface flows, and is always worth at least a day of exploration. Below are some of the other delights waiting for you at Hawai'i Volcanoes National Park.

AROUND KILAUEA CRATER

A quick note: We decided not to use our **Real Gem** and **Not To Be Missed** icons in this section because they would fill the pages. The entire park is *a real gem* and is *not to be missed*.

A REAL GEM

As you arrive at the park, which is open 24 hours a day, there is a recording playing on 530 AM radio. It has information that is promptly updated every leap year or so, so don't expect up-to-the-minute reports.

Remember that Kilauea Caldera is located at an altitude of 4,000 feet, so make sure you bring your warmies for those days when it's misty and chilly at the summit.

After paying your $10 car entrance fee (what a deal!) at the gate, stop by the Visitor Center on your right. They have up-to-date information, a nice display of books, videos, artifacts, a movie showing and—most important if you've driven a long way—restrooms. Check out the 3-D miniature of the island near the restrooms to get a perspective of the island. Some

guided hike notices are sometimes posted at the Visitor Center if you're interested. From the Center, you might want to walk across the street to **Volcano House** for your first peek of Kilauea Caldera from their enviable view, though at press time it was closed for renovations.

We should probably take the opportunity to confess here that the park used to sell this book at the Visitor Center. After undergoing a lengthy reviewing process, they called it the most accurate book they'd ever seen on the Big Island, and it became the only guidebook sold there. Quite a coup. The book's not there anymore. Why? Because some park bureaucrats became upset when they realized that we revealed things, such as a trail to Pu'u 'O'o that doesn't go through their park, the hike to Mauna Ulu, and several other things. Well, we're not going to stop telling you about these attractions even if it means they won't carry our book at the Visitor Center. The trail to Pu'u 'O'o is described in ADVENTURES on page 233; Mauna Ulu is on page 230. (A few other things we revealed also got under their skin.)

You'll want to do a counter-clockwise tour of the caldera to start. The first thing you come to are the **Steam Vents** on your left. Here, rain that has seeped into the ground is heated by Kilauea and issues forth as steam. The amount varies daily depending on the level of rain in the past few days, and it is rarely smelly like Sulphur Banks listed below. In fact, there is usually no smell at all. Make sure you take the trail for 2–3 minutes toward the crater rim for a smashing view of the crater, and where additional, more powerful and unobstructed steam vents are present.

From the steam vent parking lot, back up the road on the opposite side (toward the visitor center), is the Sulphur Banks Trail. It leads 5 to 10 minutes through a

'A'a lava on the left (named by the first Hawaiian to walk on it bare-footed?) is rough and clinkery. Pahoehoe on the right is smooth and ropy, like thick cake batter.

pretty forest to a boardwalk at the **Sulphur Banks**. This colorful but stinky phenomenon is where hydrogen sulphide gas and steam form deposits of sulphur, gypsum and hematite on the ground. This should be avoided by those with a heart condition, respiratory problems, children or anyone eating lunch.

Rounding the crater, you come to **Kilauea Overlook**. This is a different perspective on Kilauea Crater and its progeny, **Halema'uma'u Crater**, and is definitely worth a stop. Look for white-tailed tropic birds soaring on the thermals down in the crater.

Just past the overlook is **Jagger Museum** and the **Hawaiian Volcano Observatory**. The museum has some very interesting exhibits and is worth a stop. (The view is *da kine,* as well.)

Continuing on, you start to round the bottom of the crater. Note that there are no walls here. The crater summit is tilted, and lava has spilled over the sides at the southern end many times in the past. At times when Halema'uma'u is venting, they close the road past here.

Soon you come to **Halema'uma'u Crater**. This crater-within-a-crater is said to be the home to Madame Pele, the Hawaiian volcano goddess. Though crusted over now, for most of the 19th century this was a boiling lava lake. Mark Twain and other celebrities of his time visited here, and described it as viewing the fiery pits of hell. When Isabella Bird saw it in 1873, she wrote:

Suddenly, just above, and in front of us, gory drops were tossed in air, and springing forwards we stood on the brink of Hale-mau-mau, which was about 35 feet below us. I think we all screamed, I know we all wept, but we were speechless, for a new glory and terror had been added to the Earth. It is the most unutterable of wonderful things. The words of common speech are quite useless. It is unimaginable, indescribable, a sight to remember forever, a sight which at once took possession of every faculty of sense and soul, removing one altogether out of the range of ordinary life. Here was the real "bottomless pit"—the "fire which is not quenched"—"the place of hell"—"the lake which burneth with fire and brimstone"—the "everlasting burnings"—the fiery sea whose waves are never weary. There were groanings, rumblings, and detonations, rushings, hissings, and splashings, and the crashing sound of breakers on the coast, but it was the surging of fiery waves upon a fiery shore.

Halema'uma'u is quieter now with the lava action occurring elsewhere. It takes a few minutes to walk to the crater overlook and is well worth the walk. Though usually not as strong, fumes *can* call for similar warnings as at Sulphur Banks. And when it's venting, as it did starting in 2008, the fumes can be deadly. The crater has risen and fallen over time—going from 1,335 feet deep to overflowing its top. Right now, it's less than 300 feet deep and 3,000 feet across.

Some Hawaiians today still make offerings to Pele. You might see these gifts near the edge of the crater, though most of the time these come from visitors and are considered an irritant by park personnel. It is said that Pele will appear as a beautiful young woman in the mountains and as a very old and very ugly woman at the shoreline. (Hence the Hawaiian saying, "Always be nice to an old woman; it might be Pele.") Though Halema'uma'u is said to be her home, she seems to be spending more time these days at her summer house at Pu'u 'O'o.

Continuing, you come to another crater called **Keanakako'i**. The Hawaiians used to fetch abnormally hard rock from here until it was covered by subsequent lava flows. Across the road from Keanakako'i is a lava fissure. These fissures are usually long cracks where lava erupts in a curtain of fire, as this one did in 1974.

Past Keanakako'i you will notice a gravel-like substance on the ground. That's **tephra**, airborne gas-frothed lava from fountains, which cools as pumice cinders.

Soon you pass **Chain of Craters Road**, which leads 19 miles down to the shore and ends abruptly where the current lava flow has cut it off. Just pass it by *for now.*

The road will pass through an incredibly lush area. Ferns and 'ohi'a trees rule this forest—it's hard to believe that a few minutes ago you were in a lava desert.

On your left will be a road to the **Pu'u Pua'i Overlook**. The overlook just past the parking lot is great. It overlooks **Kilauea Iki Crater** and **Pu'u Pua'i**. This crater (meaning little Kilauea) had been asleep for almost a century when it became active in 1959. Then it erupted into gargantuan fountains of lava, some reaching a staggering 1,900 feet—that's more than four times the height of the crater walls and is the highest on record. Scientists had warnings that an eruption was going to occur. Earthquake swarms and a swelling of Kilauea told them it was coming. So they set up their instruments and waited for the inevitable—*at Halema'uma'u.* They were stunned when the lava instead shot from the southwest wall of Kilauea Iki (right below you) 2 miles away. Ground zero was near the Pu'u Pua'i (meaning gushing hill) cinder cone. It was created as fountains of lava, blown southwest by the trade winds piled high into a cone. The vent spewed enough lava at one point to bury a football field 15 feet deep in lava—*every minute!* Each time the showers ended, the lava would drain back into the vent opening, only to be shot out again. When it ended, 36 days after it began, the crater floor was a dead zone with a lava bathtub ring above the floor to tell how high the lava lake had reached.

The lava lake cooled and cracked as sheets of lava buckled and warped, giving the crater the look of dried, crusted-over gravy. Today, steam usually issues from cracks in the crater floor, and the rock is still molten a couple of hundred feet down. There are still vents on the crater, though the main vent was covered by falling cinders. Kilauea Iki offers one of the best hikes on the island. See HIKING on page 194.

From here you can stroll for 10–15 minutes along the **Devastation Trail**. This is where the fallout from the 1959 Kilauea Iki eruption killed the fern and ʻohiʻa forest. The line of demarcation is abrupt, going from healthy forest to a field of tephra littered with bleached tree trunks. The forest is working to come back, and you will see the results along the way. You can either walk back the way you came, loop around on Crater Rim Road, or have someone pick you up at the other end.

Back on Crater Rim Road, you come to a parking lot (probably full of buses). This is **Thurston Lava Tube**. If you are looking for an easy way to see what the inside of natural lava plumbing looks like, Thurston Lava Tube is worth a stop. It is considered one of the "must sees" at the volcano. If you get there between tour buses, it can be an interesting experience. The entrance is a few minutes walk from Crater Rim Drive (see map). You exit about halfway through the tube. This part of the tube is lighted and is the most widely visited. Most of the lava stalactites have been removed over the decades, but you can still see enough tube detail to get the idea of how the lava travels. Undisturbed tubes often have floors littered with rocks that fall from the ceiling (either from when the tube cooled or from rainwater seeping through the cracks over the years). Thurston has been cleaned up and lighted to make it easy to visit. The more adventurous might want to see Thurston's *darker* half. At the stairs at the end of the tube tour and past the gate, Thurston continues for another 1,000 feet (it seems like more) before it ends abruptly. You are welcome to go. (The rangers used to keep a book for visitors to sign at the end of the tube, protected by a pvc pipe, but say they had to pull it out because visitors kept mistaking the pvc for a pipe bomb.) Make sure you bring a good flashlight (or two) for the journey, as you will be in total darkness most of the way. At the end, turn off the light. You've never seen *real* blackness until you've seen *this* blackness.

If you want to get a feel for what Thurston Lava Tube looked like before it was tamed, see ACTIVITIES.

That dirt road that leads south of Thurston Lava Tube is an **escape road**. It is well maintained in case Chain of Craters Road is ever obliterated by a lava flow (again). That dirt road is the only place in the park where **mountain bikes** are allowed. It goes through very lush forest and is a delight. Just make sure you close all gates behind you. Some areas are fenced off to prevent pig damage. Wild pigs are amazingly destructive, and rangers fight an unending war to minimize their impact.

Just past Thurston Lava Tube is the **Kilauea Iki Overlook**. This, too, is worth stopping for. You look at Kilauea Iki from the other side. The Kilauea Iki hike mentioned a moment ago starts from here. Kilauea Iki is separated from Kilauea by a narrow shelf of land called **Byron Ledge**. It was on this ledge in 1824 that Princess Kapiolani publicly stood and, to the horror and fear of many, denied the volcano goddess Pele

The 1959 eruption of Kilauea Iki punished this part of the forest when it showered the land with falling bits of gas-frothed lava from the 1,900-foot-high fountains. But it's the forest that will prevail. Take the short Devastation Trail and see for yourself.

and embraced Christianity. She initiated this by eating 'ohelo berries without offering any to Pele first. (It was thought that Pele would strike you dead if you didn't offer her some first by tossing a fruiting branch into the crater.) When the Princess didn't die after snubbing and denying Pele, Christianity was more widely embraced by her people.

If you continue on Crater Rim Drive, you will end up back at the Visitor Center. If you need a break, walk over to the building on your left, the **Volcano Art Center Gallery**. Built in 1877, this was the original Volcano House before it was moved here to make way for another building. Now an art gallery, they have an exquisite selection from some of the island's top artists, including higher-end wood carvings, glassworks, paintings, and the like. This is also a good place to check out what's going on in the area in terms of events and demonstrations. Open 9–5.

There is another nice hike called the Earthquake Trail that starts near Volcano House. (See HIKING on page 197.) Part of it is on the *old* Crater Rim Drive—before it fell into the crater in 1983—and the results are dramatic.

DOWN CHAIN OF CRATERS ROAD

From the Visitor Center, you could head back the way you came on Crater Rim Drive, past Kilauea Iki and onto **Chain of Craters Road**. This is a 19-mile descent to the sea. (At least it was 19 miles when we went to press, and getting shorter from time to time.) The road was so named because it passed numerous craters along the rift zone before veering off to the shore. It was rerouted after Madame Pele repaved 12 miles of the road with lava during the 1969–74 Mauna Ulu flow and now visits fewer craters than it used to. Mile markers are on alternating sides of the road, and we will refer to some of them. There are still some craters along the way you might want to check out (but don't bother with Ko'oko'olau). Remember to check your gas gauge; we've seen people run out of gas coming back up.

A little more than 2 miles into Chain of Craters Road is **Hilina Pali Road**, 8³⁄₁₀ miles long. It may be closed during nene nesting or if there is a perceived fire danger. The drive isn't impressive, but at the end is **Hilina Pali Lookout**. Walk down the path for 100 feet or so, and you are treated to an amazingly expansive view. You're perched above the vast shoreline below, and on a clear day you can see the entire shoreline for over 30 miles south. It's very quiet, desolate and peaceful, with the sound of the distant ocean sometimes present. If you take it, please drive very slowly as the endangered nene are usually in the road and aren't very impressed by cars. The Kulanaokuaiki campgrounds are also on Hilina Pali Road.

Lava sometimes bursts from fissures such as this one from the 1970s Mauna Ulu eruption. But life always reclaims the land.

Less than ¹/₁₀ mile past Hilina Pali Road, on the left (east) side is a 60-second walk to **Devil's Throat**. (It's unmarked.) This small collapsed crater is impressively sheer and a genuine heart-stopper. It's *straight* down. Be careful at the edge; it looks pretty fragile.

Along this stretch of Chain of Craters Road, keep an eye to your left. You *might* see steam coming from a hill. This is **Mauna Ulu**, the source of the second longest flank eruption of Kilauea. From 1969–1974 it poured lava and harassed park road builders, forcing Chain of Craters Road to be rerouted. There is a trail off the spur road past Pauahi Crater that goes near Mauna Ulu. (See ADVENTURES on page 230.) In 1997 a couple camping way out at Napau Crater (3½ miles east of Mauna Ulu) were awakened when lava suddenly began gushing from the ground half a mile away.

Just east (to the left) of the 4 mile marker is a field of gravel-like tephra. We've walked along here (staying mostly to the left side of the flow) and discovered incredible lava fissures and colorful blobs from four decades ago (such as the one shown in the photo), with ferns and trees already growing in them. But there is no trail, so you are on virgin, and untested, ground. This is an area where lava fountains shot into the air, and the violence from the event is evident.

Proceeding down the road, you will get an appreciation in several spots of how lava actually flowed down the mountain during the 1969–74 Mauna Ulu eruption. At the **Alanui Kahakai turn-out** (near the 14 mile marker) you will see a segment of the old, partially covered Chain of Craters Road. At the **Holei Pali Lookout**, just before the 15 mile marker, there is a great view of the mountain lava flows, where you get a feel for the volume of 'a'a and pahoehoe that drooled down the mountain. The newer highway cutting through the lava flow is dramatic.

About ⅓ mile past the 15 mile marker, you will pass by a lava tube on your left. Road crews bisect them every time they cut a new road in this area.

Past the 16 mile marker you will see the **Pu'u Loa Petroglyph Trail**. This 15–20 minute walk is over an old pahoehoe lava flow with cairns (mounds of rock) marking the way. (The undulating lava is a bit more tiring than flat ground.) It leads to an area studded with thousands of petroglyphs (rock carvings) representing everything from birth to death. This is the largest petroglyph field in the state. A circular boardwalk has been built near some of them to allow you to view them without walking on them. If you circle the boardwalk from both directions you notice some you didn't see on the first pass. *Many* more carvings are located past the boardwalk, but they request that you avoid walking around to protect the perishable petroglyphs from wear. The small holes bored in the rock were usually cut by parents who placed the umbilical cords from their newborns there for good luck. The area is very peaceful and worth your time if you wish to see a direct expression of ancient Hawaiian life. It's 1½ miles round trip.

The Hawaiians, like people since the dawn of time, were compelled to leave a lasting legacy of themselves to the ages. These ancient petroglyphs are on the short Pu'u Loa trail.

After the 18 mile marker is where you'll probably have to park and walk the last ½ mile or so to the **Holei Sea Arch**, where the ocean has undercut the rock, leaving an arch.

Past here should be the **end of Chain of Craters Road** (unless the lava advances to the sea arch). This is where the lava usually flows, sometimes on the surface, sometimes into the sea, sometimes too far inland to walk to, sometimes outside the park boundary. Old maps showing Kamoamoa Campgrounds, a visitor center, Waha'ula Heiau, Lae 'Apuki, Waiaka Pond, Queen's Bath, Royal Gardens, Kalapana Gardens and more are all tragically out of date. These were victims of the current eruption. Before you is a newly paved lava wasteland, where liquid rock has poured above and below ground, reaching the ocean and building more land. The park "Visitor Center" at the bottom is now a motor home, which has had to be moved many times to avoid the fate of the last visitor center down

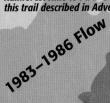

← **Rainforest Hike to Pu'u 'O'o on this trail described in Adventures.**

1983–1986 Flow

← **10 miles to Kilauea Caldera**

Pu'u 'O'o Crater
(Heart of current eruption)

Kupaianaha

2500'

2000'

N
W · E
S

Park Boundary

2002–2004 Flow

2004–2007 Flow

1992–2002 Flow

2000'

1500'

1000'

500'

Royal Garde Subdivision

Visitor Center
(Closest Parking)

End of Chain of Craters Road

19

Former Campground

Kohola

Wilipe'e

W. Highcastle

Laeapuki

Kamoamoa
Pre-eruption coastline

Brand new land

Kamokuna

Wahaʻula H
(now destro

0   1 MILE

© 2011 Wizard Publications, Inc.

The Current Eruption

Since the eruption began at Pu'u 'O'o (which conveniently materialized just within the park boundary) on January 3, 1983 the lava flows have been quite prolific. Each day 300,000 to 1,000,000 cubic yards of lava erupts, which has dramatically changed the landscape. Note how the lava concentrates in one area until another area opens up. The town of Kalapana was erased from the map in 1990. The famous Black Sand Beach at Kaimu is gone, now under 50–75 feet of lava. But a new, unnamed black sand beach now exists a third of a mile in front of where the old one was.

One of the most important heiau on the island was Waha'ula Heiau. Oral tradition states that it was constructed by Pa'ao, a priest from Tahiti who arrived during the second wave of colonization in the 12th century. It was he who was said to have introduced the concept of human sacrifice. Mu, whose role was to gather people to be sacrificed, would go out at night in parties of three and eavesdrop on houses, listening for any breach of kapu (rules of conduct). When one occurred, they would rush in and seize the victims and lead them off to this heiau. Sacrifices here were deemed so important that priests were sometimes sacrificed if others could not be found by the required time. Even smoke from its altars was sacred, and it was death to anyone who passed under the shadow of the smoke. Abraham Fornander states in his epic work of the late 19th century that this was the last heiau to be destroyed after the kapu system was abolished by King Kamehameha II in 1819. The heiau's foundations were finally buried by lava in 1997.

The doomed village of Kalapana is said to be named after an old man from Kaua'i trying to make a pilgrimage to Pele. He landed at what was Kaimu Beach and tried to make it to Kilauea but was unsuccessful due to severe storms. That night Pele came to his hut and appeared to him. The next morning nearly all of the old man's long hair was burned off. When he died some time later, the people named their village after him. It is said that because Kalapana could not make it to Pele's house, she sometimes visits his.

Interesting facts at a glance...

Total lava erupted since 1983–4,600,000,000 cubic yards
Number of dump trucks that would fill–Over 300 million
Temperature lost while traveling in lava tubes–20 °
Average temperature of flowing lava–2,000 °
Length of public highway covered–8.5 miles
Amount of new land created–475 acres
Owner of all new land–State of Hawai'i
Total area covered–47 square miles
Number of structures destroyed–213

1500'

1986–1992 Flow

2007–Current Flow

1000'

500'

Kalapana Gardens and most of Royal Gardens were destroyed by lava flows in 1990.

18

130

19

20

21

21

22

137

**Former Kaimu
Black Sand Beach**

Kalapana

**Kalapana Gardens
Subdivision**

End of lava road
(at press time)

2WD Lava Road

Pre-eruption coastline

New Kaimu Black Sand Beach

Brand new land

Brand new land

Punahaha

Cave of Refuge

Kupapau Point

here. Check with the rangers to see what's shakin'. Ask if nighttime offers good viewing conditions. Often at night the skylights, holes in the ceiling of a lava tube, are visible in the distance. Usually the only way to see a skylight during the day is on a helicopter flight. When the lava is flowing inland, you are usually allowed to hike to it. (They may *imply* that you can't but will usually admit that it is permitted if pressed.) See ADVENTURES on page 240.

HIKING IN THE PARK

Much of the best hiking on the island is in Hawai'i Volcanoes National Park. The ACTIVITIES chapter has a HIKING section on page 194, which lists scads of great hikes in the park. There's also a couple of spookier park hikes listed in ADVENTURES. Note that strolls of less than 30 minutes were described above in the tour of the volcano.

OUTSIDE THE PARK ENTRANCE

Just outside the park entrance there are a few sights that are worth checking out, either before or after your park visit.

Mauna Loa Scenic Road leads past the **Tree Molds**. These holes are created when a lava flow encounters a sopping wet tree trunk, which resists bursting into flames just long enough to harden the lava around it. They look a little like water wells with the texture of the tree bark and some of the trees must have been pretty large. No walking required, the tree molds are right at the parking area. Farther up the road is **Kipuka Pua'ulu (Bird Park)**. A trail goes through a kipuka, an old growth of forest surrounded by newer lava flows. This kipuka features many native trees and plants, but is less visually dazzling than other hikes nearer the crater.

Birds abound in this park—hence its nickname, Bird Park. The entire 1-mile stroll takes only 30 minutes plus stopping time. There are several benches scattered along the trail, which ascends gently for the first half.

Mauna Loa Scenic Road becomes very winding past here and switches to one lane (with several blind turns), as it passes through a pretty forest that is different from other forests in the area. No big payoff here, just a lonely road that often ascends into the clouds, usually with lots of pheasants around. At the end of the 13-mile road (at 6,650 feet) is the trailhead to **Mauna Loa Trail**. This is where you start your multi-day trek through the cold and altitude to ascend the summit of Mauna Loa. (Maybe another day.) There are picnic tables and a nice view of the park at the road's end. Though pleasant, this road is dispensable if you are budgeting your time.

Off the main highway south of the park entrance near the 38 mile marker is the **Ka'u Desert Trail**, which leads less than a mile to **Footprints**. Most of these were created during the explosion of 1790 (plus a few from an earlier explosion in the 1500s). You may read or be told that the footprints are worn away because they were vandalized. The truth is apparently a little more embarrassing. Park sources have told us that park personnel tried to protect the footprints many years ago by placing a glass case over them. Their intentions were pure, but when it rained, water condensed on the underside of the cracked glass and dripped onto the prints, wearing them away. That's why the display case is gone, but the vandalism rumor persists. Most personnel believe the vandalism explanation to be true to this day. Regardless, if you look around, you can still

Creation meets destruction. The ocean begins dismantling the land even before it cools.

Why you Shouldn't Pick a Lehua Blossom off an 'Ohi'a Tree

According to legend, 'Ohi'a was a young, handsome Big Island chief. The volcano goddess Pele knew that 'Ohi'a was courting a beautiful young girl named

Lehua. Pele became enamored with 'Ohi'a and desired him for a husband. One day as 'Ohi'a went up into the mountains to cut kukui bark to stain his surfboard, Pele appeared to him. She was dressed in her finest clothes and was quite striking. After a time, she announced to 'Ohi'a who she was and asked him to be her husband. Nervously but very diplomatically, he turned her down, professing his eternal love for Lehua. In her anger, Pele told him he was as gutless as a piece of wood, and changed him into a gnarled tree with grey-green leaves. When the other gods saw what Pele had done, they felt bad and tried to reverse it, but failed. The best they could do to reunite the broken-hearted Lehua with her beloved 'Ohi'a was to turn Lehua into a beautiful blossom on the same tree. To this day, it is said that picking a lehua blossom off an 'ohi'a tree will produce rain. These are the tears from heaven for separated lovers everywhere.

find better footprints elsewhere when shifting ash dunes permit.

Just outside the park is **Volcano Golf and Country Club** (see GOLFING in ACTIVITIES). Their restaurant (see IS-LAND DINING) has pretty good food. A mile down Piimauna Road, you'll find **Volcano Winery** (967-7479). This is a good place to stop for a sip of some lo-cally made wines. They have several un-usual wines, including a local favorite, Mac Nut Honey Wine. They also have wines made from fruits—*even grapes.*

Hard-core oenophiles might turn up their noses, but less finicky palates might enjoy a snort or two of the exotic. A sign there says NO LARGE TOUR BUSES. Wow, *that's* a switch.

THE TOWN OF VOLCANO

When you first see the town of **Vol-cano** on a map, you figure they must spend all their time biting their nails over the active volcano crater less than 2 miles away. In fact, since they're upslope of the crater, they're safer from lava flows than Hilo or even the Kohala Resort area 50 miles away, as far as the geologists are concerned. Though extensive lava flows did cover this area about 500 years ago, the summit has since been reshaped so that today nearly all the lava flows happen on Kilauea's southern flank (away from the village). Their main threat is from falling tephra or ash from the occasional crater explosion like the one in 1790—annoying, but not as bad as a lava flow. And as for volcano smoke, normal trade winds send the smoke around the bottom of the island and up the coast where it harasses Kailua-Kona. It's ironic that this dreamy little community, set in a misty, lush fern-filled forest, can be so snug living on an active volcano.

Volcano is also a convenient place to pick up some supplies and gas (which is *breathtakingly* expensive here). If you enter the loop road from near the 27 mile marker, you pass by the **Volcano Store** and **Kilauea General Store and Gas Station** farther down. If you're driving back to the west side of the island, you can grab some gas or a snack before the long drive back. We often pick up some tasty pumpkin bread, mac nut bars, ginger cookies, or sandwiches on Hawaiian sweetbread at Kilauea General before heading back. Baked Mon., Wed. and Fri.

In addition to the hotels and inns, there are cabins and free tent camping at **Namakani Paio Campgrounds** (967–7321) and **Kulanaokuaiki**, both in CAMPING on page 179. Current and retired military can rent clean cabins at **Kilauea Military Camp** (967–8333) right in the park. Higher rank, higher rent.

Looking more like the gates of hell, a rare vertical skylight allowed us to peek into a lava falls. You never know what you'll discover on an ever-changing lava field.

If you like waterfalls, Rainbow Falls is a perfect example of why you'll want to drive to the Hilo side.

Hilo is a charming mix of old and new Hawai'i. Once a thriving town bolstered by limitless sugar revenues, the demise of the sugar industry has kept Hilo in a time warp. And that's the charm. Though a full-fledged city, things move slower here, and the community is tight. They've been through a lot. Lashed by tsunamis, threatened by lava flows, racked by a changing economy, Hilo has withstood it all. Hilo is also a strikingly beautiful town. Abundant rains give the flora a healthy sheen that soothes the soul. Though the exodus of business has left many of its buildings looking worn and neglected, Hilo's charms lie deeper.

Hilo's Achilles' heel is weather. Only in Hilo would water officials quake in fear and declare a drought, even encouraging water conservation, when they receive *only* 70 inches of rain in a year. (All you Arizona residents can stop laughing now!) This rain translates to an unacceptable gamble to many visitors. People are hesitant to spend precious Big Island days in a place that might get rained out. But they forget that even if it's rain-city here, elsewhere along the eastern side things might be sunnier. Hilo is the logical gateway for exploring Puna, the easternmost part of the island, where you'll find lush rain forests, a black sand beach, thermally heated pools and volcano-ravaged towns.

Puna is also famous for its outlaws from the 20th century, guerrilla gardeners and bizarre characters.

Hilo has a reputation for being less friendly to visitors than other parts of the island. Sort of a *let da buggahs go to Kona* mentality. Though this reputation is not entirely unearned, it is also not entirely accurate. Some of the friendliest, nicest and most helpful people we've run into have been in Hilo. But we've also gotten more blank expressions and outright nastiness here.

Hilo is a ghost town on Sundays. Don't expect much of anything to be open. We'll describe sights around Hilo in a scattershot manner before heading toward Puna.

AROUND HILO TOWN

Starting at the corner of Kamehameha (which fronts the bay) and Waianuenue (in northern Hilo), head southwest on Waianuenue. (See map on next page.) When you pass the Hilo Public Library on your right, take a look at that oblong stone out front, six full strides long. Think you can move it? At age 14, Kamehameha risked death (if he failed) and agreed to try to move that Naha Stone (estimated at 7,000 pounds). He did it because legend said that whoever could overturn the stone would be the first king of all the islands. At that time the stone was slightly imbedded in the ground. The ox-like youth, whose strength was unprecedented, squatted and gave a huge push— nothing. He tried and tried but could barely nudge it. As people gathered round and the priest started to come over (to condemn him to death), he summoned a final burst of strength and overturned the boulder, shocking everyone and beginning the fulfillment of his destiny.

Just off Waianuenue Street, on the corner of Haili and Kapiolani, the Lyman Museum (935–5021) is worth a stop. The Earth Heritage exhibit alone justifies the $10 admission. It has incredible dis-

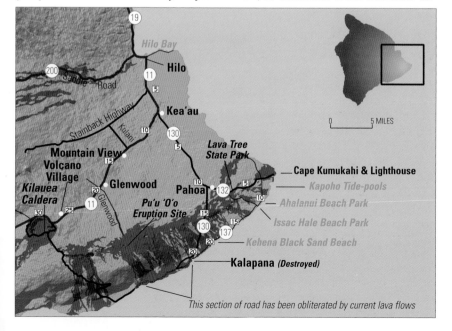

This section of road has been obliterated by current lava flows

Hilo

Hamakua Coast map on page 125

Lower Puna & Kilauea Volcano map on page 113

To Puna & Kilauea Volcano

Kaumana Coast map on page 125

Kalanianaole Ave

Hilo International Airport (General Lyman Field)

Kanoelehua

Kalanikoa

Ho'olulu Park

Hinano

Kekuanaoa St

Kawili

Maka'ala

Waiakea Center Walmart

Maka'ala

Puainako Town Center

Kanoelehua

Prince Kuhio Plaza

Manono St

Kamehameha

Wailoa River State Park

Hilo Shopping Center

Kilauea Ave

Kinoole

Puainako St

Kawailani

Hilo Bay

Reeds Bay

Ice Pond

Banyan Dr

Naniloa Golf Course

Clock Tower

Lihiwai

Coconut Is.

Lili'uokalani Gardens

Hilo Bayfront Beach Park

Bayfront Hwy

Kilauea

Pauahi

Kupunu

Hualalai

Kinoole

Mohouli

University of Hawai'i at Hilo

Lanikaula

Kawili

Kumukoa

Nowelo

'Imiloa Astronomy Center

Komohana

Naha Stone

Wainaku

Ualili

Keawe

Kaiulani Av

Lyman Museum

Haili

Ponahawai

Kapiolani

Punahele

Waianuenue Ave

Kaumana Dr

Lava Flow of 1881

Waianuenue AV

Moo'oilo River

Rainbow Falls

Boiling Pots

Pe'epe'e Falls

Waiale Falls

Pe'epe'e Falls Street

Akolea Rd

Kaumana Cave

Bypass Starts Here (You'll have to watch for your chance to stay on Kaumana Drive/Hwy 2000.)

1 Inn at Kulanaiapia Falls
2 Shipman House
3 Dolphin Bay Hotel
4 Wild Ginger Inn
5 Hilo Bay Hostel
6 Hilo Hawaiian Hotel
7 Uncle Billy's Hilo Bay Hotel
8 Naniloa Volcanoes Resort
9 Country Club Hawaii Condo Hotel
10 Hilo Seaside Hotel

Bayfront Hwy
Kamehameha
Waianuenue
Keawe
Kinoole
Kalakaua
Mamo
Ponahawai
Haili
Kilauea
Kamehameha
Shipman

1/2 MILE

N W S E

Indicates Foot Trails
Roadside mile markers

© 2011 Wizard Publications, Inc.

plays of Hawaiian geology, plant, animal and fish life (nicely done), plus an exceptionally beautiful rock and mineral collection from around the world. Elsewhere **A REAL GEM** they have Hawaiian history displays and a few other interesting items. Tours of the Lyman missionary house next door are given at various times throughout the day.

Take the right fork after the 1 mile marker and follow the signs to Rainbow Falls. These falls change dramatically depending on water flow. Moderate flow is best. (Too little and the wishbone shape is gone; too much and it's an undefined, roiling mess.) The falls are best seen in the morning when the sun is behind you. (Rainbows can only be seen when the sun is behind you, so if you ever see a photo with the sun and a rainbow in the same frame, it's fake.) The cave below the falls is where Kamehameha is said to have buried the bones of his father. Take the trail to the left for different views and the shady comfort of a large banyan tree. From the left, a trail leads to the top of the falls, but you are on your own in assessing whether to go down there.

A mile farther up the road is Boiling Pots. This series of bowl-shaped depressions roil and boil when the water flow is heavy, creating dramatic photo opportunities. (Although sometimes the county lets the vegetation grow enough to block your views.) To the left is Pe'epe'e Falls. (No, it's *not* pronounced pee-pee, but rather PEH-EH PEH-EH, so wipe that smirk off your face.) One look and it's obvious you can't swim in Boiling Pots when it's boiling. (During calmer times we see daring dudes jumping from pot to pot to pot, but even in calm times Boiling Pots tends to claim the lives of swimmers.) There's a trail to the right of the viewing area that leads down to the rocks below. From there you could scramble over the boulders to the other side (without getting your feet wet if the flow is low enough, as in our photo on the next page) and continue to Pe'epe'e Falls. This waterfall and deep pool are an idyllic place to sit in solitude and ponder. You'll usually have it to yourself. Be careful on the rocks; don't go if the river is raging, and don't fall in. Also, don't go down to the falls without mosquito repellent unless you've checked with your life insurance company to see if excessive bloodletting is considered an accident rather than suicide. While we're nagging, this is probably a good time to tell you that Boiling Pots and Rainbow Falls are common places for car break-ins. We often see thieving scum casing the lots looking for unsuspecting tourist cars to rob while they are away lost in the beauty.

Less than a mile up Waianuenue the road veers right. From a bridge you can see Wai'ale Falls. The amount of water is considerably more than what you saw downstream at Rainbow Falls, an impressive demonstration of how much actually seeps into the porous lava bed along the way. (It's *not* tapped at the nearby dam.) You can hike there and enjoy some wonderful pools. See HIKING on page 205.

Over on Kaumana Drive (see map) is Kaumana Cave. This lava tube can make for fun exploring and is described in detail in SADDLE ROAD SIGHTS on page 146 since it's usually visited by those coming into Hilo from the Saddle.

Off Komohana St. is the 'Imiloa Astronomy Center (969–9700), a good hands-on exhibit for kids and a pretty cool planetarium that will make you dizzy. $17.50 for adults, $9.50 for kids.

Along the bay, the grassy park fronting the town is the Hilo Bayfront. It used to be the main Japanese district, Hilo's

Offerings are common at Pe'epe'e Falls.

road on Kamehameha Street in front of Naniloa Golf Course stands with its hands frozen in time—1:04 a.m.—from the 1960 tsunami. Townsfolk refurbished the clock but refused to rebuild it to working order in honor of those who died.) Tsunamis have unimaginable power. The water first recedes, exposing the ocean's floor, and then bulldozers of water come crashing in. The event can last for hours.

The **Pacific Tsunami Museum** (935-0926) is on Kamehameha and Kalakaua. (Open 9 a.m. to 4 p.m.) It's in the old First Hawaiian Bank Building. (You sit in the old bank vault while they show a movie of the tsunami.) They haven't had docents on recent visits, so you're probably on your own. Lots of photos, and you'll leave with a good understanding of what a tsunami is—and why it's not really a wave. It's $8, closed Sundays.

Banyan Drive, where most of Hilo's hotels are located, is named after the graceful and stately banyan trees that line the road. If a tree can look wise, then banyan trees definitely qualify. Each tree was named after the person who planted

Japantown. On April Fool's Day 1946 a tsunami (tidal wave) of unprecedented size was generated from a horrific earthquake off Alaska. The tsunami lashed the entire state, but punished this part of the Big Island the most. In all, 159 people, including 21 school children in Laupahoehoe, were killed in one of the worst natural disaster in Hawai'i's history. After another tsunami killed another 61 people in 1960, town fathers decided to make this area a park rather than risk more lives during the next tsunami. (The clock on the side of the

A REAL GEM it. Familiar names such as Amelia Earhart, King George V, Babe Ruth, FDR and Richard Nixon. (In one of those ironies of life, the first tree Nixon planted was washed away on election day when he became VP.) Also on Banyan Drive is Lili'uokalani Gardens. This is one of several graceful and serene parks in the area and is our favorite place in Hilo for a great early morning or late afternoon stroll. If you're a bit warm, look for the nearby ice pond. (See map.) Cold water intruding into this part of the bay (you can sometimes see it percolating to the surface) creates water so cold it'll give you *chicken skin kine.*

If you were to continue east along the shoreline on Kalanianaole, you would pass most of Hilo's beach parks. See BEACHES for more on these. On your way out to the parks check out a beach access across from Lokoaka Street. It is very jungly and draped with vines. The beach is worthless, but the short walking road is kind of cool as is the trail on the left, which ends at the more desirable Carlsmith Beach Park. You'll also pass Hilo Homemade Ice Cream (935–3895) on the ocean side. Although owned by our favorite, Tropical Dreams, this ice cream is not as sweet or rich as other gourmet ice creams, has more air and less butter fat. Lots of exotic flavors like ginger and 'ohelo.

HEADING SOUTH ON HIGHWAY 11

As you head out of town, you will pass by Hilo's biggest shopping area. Prince Kuhio Plaza, Waiakea Center, and Puainako Town Center are where you will find Safeway grocery store, Longs Drugs, Walmart, and a zillion fast food restaurants. On Hinano Street off Kekuanaoa is Big Island Candies (935– 8890). Their locally made chocolates and cakes are *excellent*, though their prices are confiscatory. (This is a favorite stopping place for tour buses.) Good place for chocolate if you don't mind paying double-extra-super-retail. You can see their impressive operations behind giant glass windows. On the highway before the 4 mile marker, Makalika Street heading east leads to Nani Mau Gardens (959–3500), 20 acres of flawlessly groomed tropical and sub-tropical plants. Most of their business

comes from Japanese tour groups (who are fussy about their gardens). Whereas the mother of all gardens, Hawai'i Tropical Botanical Garden (on your way out of town heading north, described on page 124), is much more exotic, Nani Mau Gardens will appeal to those who want a more manicured, controlled and artistically arranged setting. Nani Mau is also a popular place to get married. Allow 30–60 minutes, cost is $10 (for the garden, not the wedding). They also have a lunch buffet for $13.

The road past the 4 mile marker heading west leads to Stainback Highway and the Pana'ewa Rain Forest Zoo & Gardens (959–7224). We've never been very impressed with this zoo, but they've really put in the effort at places, and it shows. The grounds are lush and beautiful, to the point that they have added the word "garden" to their name. It's a small zoo with minimal animals (they do birds the best), but kids should enjoy it as a brief diversion and parents will enjoy the price—it's free.

Between the 5 and 6 mile marker is Macadamia Road and the Mauna Loa Visitor Center (966–8618). This is the mac nut giant's main processing plant, popular with tour buses and cruise ships. You can see the process through the glass or pick up some of their products; otherwise, it's expendable.

If you're going to explore Puna, your best route is to take Highway 11 to 130, then take 132 to 137, and 137 to Kalapana where you link back up to 130. See maps on pages 107 or 113 if you aren't too dizzy to flip the page. If you want a meaningless diversion, you could continue along Stainback Highway past the zoo until it ends at the Big Island's least popular visitor attraction—our prison. This one-lane road goes for miles through an otherwise impenetrable forest, ending at over

5,000 feet elevation. There are signs saying that it is illegal to drive the road, but they were put up by the prison to cover their 'okole—they told us that it's perfectly OK to drive it as long as you're not planning to spring anyone. Some 13¾ miles into the one-lane (and dead-on straight) road is the Pu'u Maka'ala Forest Reserve. The roads in there are 4WD only, and the trails (if you can find them) are lush and wet.

EXPLORING PUNA

Head south on Highway 130 and you come to the town of Pahoa. Known as the Big Island's outlaw town, this is where guerrilla gardeners (pakalolo farmers),

Free energy. In Puna they don't drill for oil; they drill for steam.

dreadlock enthusiasts, FBI fugitives and the never-bathe crowd coexist without stepping on each other's toes—usually. You'd be surprised to learn how many homes you see are built on vacant land—at least according to the County Tax Assessor's Office. Permit? What's that? To be honest, Pahoa's reputation is a little exaggerated—probably. People-watching here can be a hoot sometimes. There are a couple places to eat here that you may like, reviewed in ISLAND DINING. By the way, Pahoa usually has *comparatively cheap gas*.

After Pahoa, turn onto Hwy 132 and you'll soon come to Lava Tree State Park. Lava trees form when fast flowing pahoehoe encounters wet 'ohi'a trees. As the flow drains away, it leaves a thick coating around the dying tree. Most of these free-standing tubes are moss-covered. You can saunter around the park in 30–60 minutes. Look for the huge chasms created during the explosive eruption of 1790. Even if you don't want to hike (there are better lava trees on the Napau Crater Trail), take a minute to drive into the park and gawk at the regal trees that dominate the area.

Past Lava Trees, the canopy of trees is absolutely lovely. If you have a convertible, look up; it's kind of hypnotizing. If it's after sunset, pull over and listen. Millions of tiny coqui frogs fill the air with their whistle. Islanders consider these new arrivals a pest and are trying to eradicate them by spraying various chemicals, including caffeine.

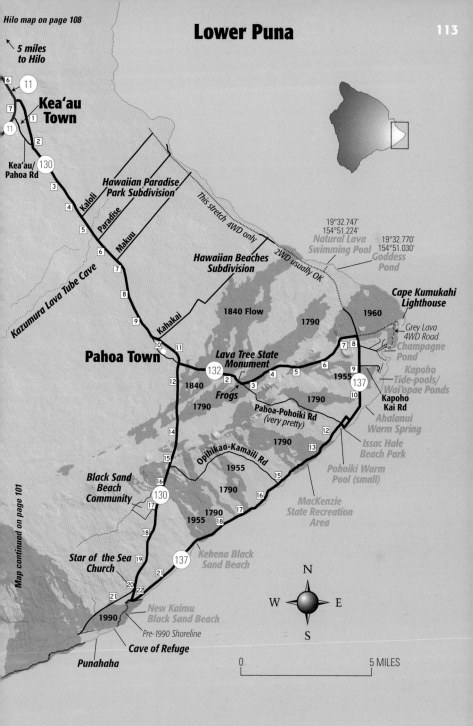

Lower Puna

5 miles
to Hilo

6
11

7

**Kea'au
Town**

1

11

2

Kea'au/
Pahoa Rd

130

3

Kaloli

4

Paradise

5

**Hawaiian Paradise
Park Subdivision**

Makuu

6

7

Kazumura Lava Tube Cave

8

9

Kahakai

This stretch 4WD only

2WD usually OK

**Hawaiian Beaches
Subdivision**

19°32.747'
154°51.224'
*Natural Lava
Swimming Pool*

19°32.770'
154°51.030'
*Goddess
Pond*

**Cape Kumukahi
Lighthouse**

*Grey Lava
4WD Road*

1840 Flow

1790

1960

10

11

Pahoa Town

*Champagne
Pond*

**Lava Tree State
Monument**

132

7   8

6

9

1955

137

*Kapoho
Tide-pools/
Wai'opae Ponds*

1840

2

Frogs

3

4

5

10

**Kapoho
Kai Rd**

1790

1790

Pahoa-Pohoiki Rd
(very pretty)

*Ahalanui
Warm Spring*

*Issac Hale
Beach Park*

12

13

14

Opihikao-Kamaili Rd

1790

15

*Pohoiki Warm
Pool (small)*

15

16

**Black Sand
Beach
Community**

1955

1790

16

17

130

1790

17

*MacKenzie
State Recreation
Area*

17

18

1955

1790

18

N

18

19

**Star of the Sea
Church**

137

*Kehena Black
Sand Beach*

W   E

20

21

21

22

S

21

1990

*New Kaimu
Black Sand Beach*

Pre-1990 Shoreline

Cave of Refuge

Punahaha

0   5 MILES

Map continued on page 101

Though it gives you and me a morning lift, it'll make these little guys...croak. (Sorry, I just *had* to get that one in.)

Shortly after Lava Trees take the left fork (near a papaya grove) where Hwy 132 continues toward Kapoho. Ever wonder where people on an island get their electricity? Well, here on the Big Island, 20% of our juice is volcano-powered. They drilled a basketball-sized hole a *mile* deep and when they did, steam shot up at pressures similar to what you'd find inside a SCUBA tank. They use the steam to turn turbines. The underground water source is naturally replaced by the ocean's pressure, so it'll last indefinitely—at least until the surrounding rock cools. Interestingly, though the land is private, *all* mineral rights in Hawai'i belong to the state government (as all first-time landowners here discover to their shock). This includes "any steam over 150°." So, even though the private company returns the water vapor back to the ground, they have to pay the state almost $2 million a year for the steam they temporarily borrow because it's considered *state steam*. (Just thought we'd pass that along, in case you were thinking of opening a gold mine here.) By the way, the cost of steam has risen proportionally with the price of oil.

Across from the 5 mile marker on the left (north) side is the lava vent from the 1955 eruption. The vent is interesting to walk on. It's made up of loose and cemented blobs of airborne lava (called tephra) that fountained out of the vent. It's worth a few minutes if you want to poke around. There are opportunities for a good fall, so be careful.

The end of Hwy 132 is on lava flows from 1960. A dirt road leads out to the point. Fountains of lava ³/₁₀ mile high produced enormous amounts of lava that wiped out the town of Kapoho, leaving only two subdivisions. Having hiked through countless lava fields on the island, this wins the prize as the harshest and most difficult to walk through we've ever encountered. (You'd have an easier time walking through the minefields of the demilitarized zone between North and South Korea than hiking through this stuff.) At the end of the unpaved road leading to the sea is a light tower.

Take a deep breath. This is the easternmost part of the island, and since our winds come from that direction, scientists use it to test "virgin air" that has drifted over the landless Pacific for many weeks. Air from here is considered as pristine as any in the world, and it is analyzed by governments around the globe and used as a benchmark to compare to their air.

While you're out on this point, you'll see a 4WD gray lava road on the right. If you take it and a right, then left onto the lightest gray road at the first confusing intersection, it heads for 1²/₁₀ miles to Kapoho Bay. Why would you want to do that? Simple. A truly awesome experience called Champagne Pond awaits.

Imagine a calm, protected ocean inlet filled with *crystal* clear water. A scattering

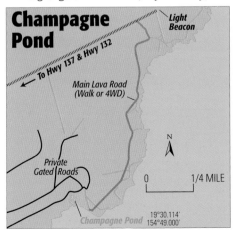

Champagne Pond

Light Beacon

To Hwy 137 & Hwy 132

Main Lava Road (Walk or 4WD)

N

Private Gated Roads

0   1/4 MILE

19°30.114'
154°49.000'
Champagne Pond

An oceanside natural lava swimming pool—the original black bottom pool.

of fish and sometimes a turtle or two (or *nine,* our personal record here) await. Fine, you say. There are lots of places with that. Maybe. But how many of them are *heated*? Sparkling clean fresh- **A REAL GEM** water heated by the volcano percolates from the ground. It's not Jacuzzi-hot, but rather relaxing-warm (around 90° on top) and changes with the tide. The more it's been raining lately, the deeper the floating warm water goes. Bring a mask and you can *see* the layers of temperature differences (warm is on top). This isn't Ahalanui Park (listed later). This is in a gated residential community, and the cove is next to an A-frame house. But from the 4WD public *lava* road, *anyone* can access it. Weekends and holidays are crowded with locals, and it's best to leave it to them during those days. But during the week it's *usually* lightly used. Make sure you take out anything you brought in, and wear water shoes in the water or you are *guaranteed* to stub your toes. Don't worry if the water's cool when you first get in, just head to the back of the cove where it's warmer. And remember: The best way to avoid scaring a turtle away is to act disinterested and keep your distance.

Back at the corner of Hwys 132 and 137, you'll want to head south on 137. But if you feel like a different kind of forest drive, head north first for 5 miles or so. It goes from stark lava to a luxuriant jungle filled with birds almost instantly. Along the way there's a delightful natural lava swimming pool if you don't mind walking ³⁄₁₀ mile (each way.)

The enormous pool (250 feet long) is naturally ensconced in a rugged lava shoreline. It's 5 feet deep in spots and backed by a thick grove of lovely hala trees. (Sometimes unusually ultra-low tides virtually erase it.) Meandering around the pool is fun while you scramble over the occasional lava obstacle. (If you don't have some cheap water shoes, navigating the rounded-boulder floor will be unpleasant.) There is shade near the pool until noon. Water splashes into the pool from the ocean. Only during big surf or very high tide is it anything but gentle in the pool. Bring a mask (though the water is so incredibly clear, you almost won't need one). Fishermen sometimes use it on weekends, but it's usually vacant during the week.

To get there, drive about 1½ miles from the end of the pavement (or 2⁷⁄₁₀ miles from the corner of Hwys 132 and 137—see map on page 113). The beautiful jungle-side road (which looks more like a tunnel drilled through hau bush) is easy to find: It's the first road on the right at the bottom of a short paved segment on the otherwise unpaved main road. It's 1,500 feet to the shoreline, and the pool is another 100 yards to the left.

Return to Hwys 132 and 137 when you're done.

Heading south on Hwy 137 leads past Kapoho-Kai Road. This road goes to one of the more unusual locations on the Big Island. Dozens and dozens of spring-fed, brackish pools and tide-pools, some volcanically heated, are strewn throughout the area known as the Kapoho Tide-pools. Many of the land-locked pools have been incorporated into people's front and back yards as swimming pools. The large pools adjacent to the ocean (called Wai'opae Ponds) are on public property and contain some of the most fascinating snorkeling around. If you wish to snorkel here, take Kapoho–Kai Road (just before the 9 mile marker). When it seems to dead end (on Waiopae), turn left to the parking lot. (If it's full, there's an access at the end of Kapoho-Kai Road.) Snorkel exploration is possible even for novice snorkelers. The largest pool snakes its way to the ocean and rises and falls each day with the tide. This creates slight currents that are fun to ride if the surf's not high. These pools are usually (but not always) very calm and protected. Closer to the reef edge brings more fish, but sometimes there's a current. We've spent many hours here and counted eight kinds of coral. Toward the back (west) a couple of pools are slightly heated by the volcano. The weather is sometimes snot-

A vast area of interconnected tide-pools await at Kapoho, providing endless snorkeling possibilities.

Though it looks like an ordinary swimming pool, Ahalanui boasts a natural heating system powered by Kilauea Volcano.

ty in the morning but usually clears up in the afternoon.

Note that the tide-pools are best visited during the week. Weekends are crowded since Puna residents have comparatively few beaches to choose from. A couple hours _before high tide_ is our favorite time. The water is deeper and usually very clear. It also coincides with local residents' belief that at _low_ tide, septic systems from nearby houses could leach into the tide-pools, causing higher bacterial counts at _low_ tide.

There are lots of vacation rentals available here (called Vacationland) and next door in the gated community of Kapoho Beach Community. Make _sure_ you see what you're getting beforehand because there are a number of charming-sounding dumps there alongside wonderful vacation rentals.

Farther down Hwy 137 past the 10 mile marker is Ahalanui. (Formerly called Pu'ala'a, the state discovered that they had accidentally misnamed it for decades—_oops_.) This delightful gem is **A REAL GEM** definitely worth stopping for. It's a spring- and ocean-fed pool with a man-made wall and an inlet separating it from

the ocean. Although the original builders created this spot when the water was _ice cold_, the Kapoho eruptions of 1955 and 1960 reworked the lava plumbing here so that now, instead of coming out cold, this pool is _volcanically heated_ to a toasty 91–95 degrees. The temperature is influenced by several factors, including tide. At high tide the ocean floods the pond with cooler seawater, making the pond more brisk. At these times, if you were to grope your way through the jungle to the left for 50 yards, you'd find the heater for Ahalanui in the form of a small, shallow warm pond in the lava where freshwater heated by underground rocks seeps to the surface.

With palm trees all around and the sound of the surf over the seawall, you may have trouble hauling yourself out once you've experienced this genuine Pele bath, and it's easier to access than Champagne Pond, though it's more crowded, as well. _On occasion_ we've noticed a slight sulphur smell on the skin when we've gotten out, but even then it's worth it. Plus there's a shower there. Closed Wednesdays.

As mapmakers we couldn't help but notice that this area called Puna, which

A lonely Puna road.

receives *lots* of rain and is the size of Moloka'i, doesn't have a *single* river or stream—not even an intermittent one. The reason? The land's too new. Rain that falls simply seeps into the porous lava. If you get a chance to hike in a lava tube, you'll see it dripping from the ceiling on its way to recharging the vast water table below.

Isaac Hale Beach Park farther down the road is where local fishermen launch their boats, and they are not known for extending gobs of aloha to visitors. (There's often a lunch wagon here that serves the worst shave ice we've had on the island.) The swimming is poor and the surfing is for experts. So why bother? Because if you take the shoreline trail to the right of the boat launch for two minutes, where it veers inland, you'll come to a surprise. There, set in the vine-covered jungle but only 40–50 feet from the shore, is a small (8-feet by 14-feet) warm water pool (called Pohoiki) similar to Ahalanui but completely natural. The setting is heaven sent. The only caveat is that some residents don't always appreciate the par-

adise that they live in and occasionally spoil the area with litter. But if you come during the week, there's a chance you may have it all to yourself. It's cut off from the ocean, but the level follows the tide, so it's deeper and more desirable (unlike Ahalanui) at high tide.

As you drive along this stretch, realize that this is one of the least known parts of the Big Island. The vast majority of island residents and visitors never see this area, and that's a shame. It is mostly untouched and exceptionally beautiful. Take your time here.

Less than 2/10 mile past the 13 mile marker is a turnoff to the ocean. Check out the massive squared-off rock at the lava bluff's edge. Then try to imagine the kind of wave it takes to *toss* it up from the ocean, because that's how it (and others you see around you) got here. This area is a nice place to watch the humbling power of the ocean when the surf's up. Just be careful not to let a monster wave surprise you. Another good wave-watching place is 2/10 mile past the 14 mile marker. It's a 700-foot walk if you don't have 4WD and leads to a series of tide-pools that are created on this short bluff when waves explode against the lava, showering the pools.

If you look at the map, you'll see that this part of the shoreline was covered by a lava flow in 1790. The flow killed everything in its path, leaving nothing but barren, unforgiving rock for new life to work with. Yet look at what life has managed to accomplish in these two centuries. Remember this natural rejuvenating power when you come to the modern devastation that lies ahead on this road.

Near where the 19 mile marker *should* be (but was missing on our last visit) is Kehena Beach. This is a powerful testament to the changing nature of the Big Island. This beach wasn't even here until it was created by the 1955 lava flow you just drove through. Officials created stone steps leading down to the western part of the beach. Then an earthquake in 1975 sank the beach 3 feet all at once. The lower portion of the stone steps collapsed. The steps are still there (now blocked by vegetation), ending abruptly 10 feet above the shoreline. The trailhead to the beach itself is to the left of the parking area. Swimming is dangerous during high surf, and the beach is often used by nudists (who don't take kindly to cameras on the beach). Be careful not to leave anything in your car here, as we've noticed lots of thieving scum casing cars.

Shortly after the 22 mile marker, you're confronted with the consequences of the current Kilauea eruption. A rolling sea of hardened lava stretches in front of you. This particular flow occurred in 1990, annihilating the towns of Kalapana, Kaimu and the Royal Gardens subdivision beyond. (See map on page 100 to get an idea of the scale of the devastation.) Kalapana was a treasured Hawaiian fishing village, richly steeped in the traditions of the past. Its loss was a stunning blow to those wishing to keep the old ways alive.

Until the 1990 lava flow, this was also the site of the most famous black sand beach in the world. A long curving bay of jet black sand with numerous stately palm trees sprinkled about, the black sand beach at Kaimu was universally regarded as the finest. Today, it is gone, forever entombed under 50–75 feet of lava.

When the road stops, get out and walk to the top of the lava and look toward the shore. You'll notice young, sprouting coconut trees in the distance. The campaign to bring the plantings was begun by a local resident. She encouraged others in the community to take trees out to the new black sand beach ⅓ mile in front of you to begin the process of rebuilding their precious beach. Even as she was dying of cancer, residents and school children continued the tradition in her honor. Today, there are vast numbers of sprouting coconuts along the new black sand beach, a testament to the vision of one resident who refused to let her community die, even in the face of her own death.

Like people, black sand beaches have limited life spans. Once the lava flow stops, the source of the sand disappears as well, and the ocean begins robbing the sand. The new Kaimu Beach was born in 1990, but after two decades, it was mostly gone. There still some black sand that was tossed up beyond the low sea cliffs and a thin padding of sand that's best appreciated at low tide. But the new Kaimu Beach is now mostly a memory. A hundred years from now, when every grain of black sand is gone, visitors may wonder why there are

The Star of the Sea Church had to be pulled from its foundations and moved to avoid being destroyed by an advancing lava flow.

so many coconut trees along a sandless lava shoreline.

Imagine what it must be like to have grown up in Kalapana. Sights that seemed so permanent to you like the freshwater queen's bath you played in as a child, the fishing shrine that your grandfather used every day before he went fishing, that beautiful coconut grove where you had your first kiss. All these things that seemed so timeless, that came before you, and you *knew* would always be there, are now gone, erased without a trace, as if your whole world had been nuked. Kalapana residents didn't just lose their home; they lost all traces to their past and share the unique experience of having outlived their world.

A 5–10 minute walk straight out across the lava field on crushed red rocks leads to what's left of the new black sand beach. Don't even consider swimming there for the surf is treacherous. To the right of the trailhead are some perfect impressions of palm trees. Their dying act was to cool and harden the lava around their trunks, forever capturing the bark texture of a vanished Kalapana coconut tree. There are even some hala tree fruit moldings in the lava.

If you look at the map on page 100 you'll see another road, Hwy 130, leading toward a demolished neighborhood. Most of the subdivision is now buried under lava. There's not much to see in the area itself: A handful of hardy souls still live, on and off, in the ravaged subdivision without power or water. Birds have rediscovered this island of green in a sea of lava (called a kipuka). During the devastating lava flows, the media and the public focused their sympathy on the people who lost their homes. The *real* people to feel sorry for are the people who *didn't* lose their homes. You see, insurance covers loss of property, not loss of *access* to property. Imagine an insurance adjuster walking up to your now worthless house, surrounded but untouched by a sea of hardened lava and saying, "Nothing wrong with this house; claim denied."

The narrow paved access road at the end of 130 is a *public* road and you *are* allowed to drive on it, despite any misleading NO TRESSPASSING or RESTRICTED AREA signs you may see. (The land on *either side* is private, but not the road.) Depending on *where* the ever-changing lava is flowing during your stay, you might have to drive on it to see lava flows. When lava viewing requires this road, the county *sometimes* charges $5 per car, which is very reasonable when you consider how much work it is to keep the road open. Less than two weeks after the state's grand opening of this road, lava crossed it again, requiring yet another trip for the bulldozers. See page 240 for more on lava viewing.

You may be wondering what happens if you own oceanfront property, and the volcano creates new land in front of you (called *accreted land* for the trivia deprived). Do you now own a larger parcel? No. You don't even own oceanfront anymore! Apparently Madame Pele signed a quitclaim deed over to the state, because all newly created land goes to our hungry state government.

As you head north on Hwy 130 on your way back toward Hwy 11, look for the church on the right (east) side of the road near the 20 mile marker. Called the Star of the Sea Church, it was built in 1928 by the same priest who did the Painted Church near Honaunau. The building was in the path of an advancing lava flow in 1990. Community members had to wrench it from its foundations to save it just in the nick of time. After sitting on the side of the road for

years without a home, it was finally placed on a foundation and can now be visited. Watch for aggressive wasps flying around inside.

Subdivisions in East Hawai'i often have names at odds with reality. Places like HAWAIIAN BEACHES SUBDIVISION (there are *no* beaches there), PARADISE PARK (it's not a park and it sure ain't paradise) and our personal favorite that you pass, up the mountain of the 17 mile marker on Hwy 130. It's surrounded by jungle, miles from the ocean, and is called BLACK SAND BEACH COMMUNITY. (The lots were probably easier to sell than if they had named it SURROUNDED BY JUNGLE COMMUNITY.)

When you take Hwy 130 back to Hwy 11, you can either head to Hilo or toward the volcano. If you head to the volcano, look for the Hirano Store before the 20 mile marker. You used to be able to see Pu'u 'O'o belching 7½ miles away from their parking lot, and tour buses still stop here, but someone let vegetation block it across the street. Drive past the store to Glenwood Road on your left. About 100 feet down this road you should be able to see it, clouds permitting. This is the headline-grabbing vent that has been the lava source for most of the current eruption. Unless you hike to it or fly over it, this is as close as you'll come. If you *are* up to a long hike, the trek through the virgin rain forest to Pu'u 'O'o is the trek of a lifetime. See ADVENTURES on page 233 for more on this beautiful hike.

Kilauea Volcano is just ahead.

HILO SHOPPING

Hilo has lots of shopping opportunities. Bear in mind that some chain stores aren't as responsive to local conditions. For instance, we went in to Ross in May looking for a raincoat. They didn't have any because their mainland buyers said it's "not the season." *Really*. It's *Hilo!* It's *always* the season.

Farmers' Markets are big here. See BASICS on page 42. Start at the Farmers' Market at the corner of Kamehameha and Mamo and head north. There are many shops worth a stop, but here are some of our favorites. In the Hata Building, Burgado's Fine Woods for everything made of wood from doorstops to rocking chairs. Dreams of Paradise is an excellent gallery featuring local artists and has a very knowledgeable and helpful staff. Also look for High Fire Hawaii Gallery & Studio near the Tsunami Museum. The Grove Gallery has silkscreened towels, sheets and clothing with island plant motifs, quilts and other smaller art pieces. Fabric Impressions has an extensive selection of quilting fabrics. Hawaiian Arts makes unique T-shirt designs. Hana Hou has boutique Hawaiiana clothing women, men and accessories, and Sig Zane, next to the Tsunami Museum, offers truly original clothing in native Hawaiian plant prints for men and women. Basically Books is a great bookshop for anything Hawai'i-related. Feel free to explore the streets just off Kamehameha for some great shops, such as Kathmandu Trading Co. for antiques from Tibet and Arthur Johnsen Gallery for local artists and reasonable prices both on Waianuenue Street.

Try some saltwater taffy from Sugar Coast Candy—only the Kona coffee and coconut flavors are made locally. (Whatever you do, don't leave it in your hot car!) Also on Kamehameha is Abundant Life Natural Foods if you are craving a healthy snack. And a couple of doors north of the Farmers' Market is Nutty Guys Hawaii, which has

some really unique flavors of nuts, like Cajun (super hot), sweet varieties and candies, too.

On Hwy 11 heading south you'll see Waiakea Center, which has a Walmart Superstore and a Down to Earth natural food store. Across Maka'ala Street is Prince Kuhio Plaza, which has Sears, Macy's, Longs Drugs and other popular mainland chain stores. Hilo Hattie on the corner is the popular stopping place for visitors, and for good reason—their aloha wear is good quality and priced right.

If you're interested in the beautiful bonsai plants you've seen on many countertops around the island, Fuku-Bonsai (982–9880) is 10 miles south of Hilo in Kurtistown. Call first to be sure they'll be open.

HILO & PUNA'S BEST BETS

Best Cerebral Stimulation—Lyman Museum

Best Snorkeling—Tide-pools at Kapoho

Best Place to Soak Your Bones—Champagne Pond or Ahalanui Park

Best Way to Pull Your Back—Duplicating Kamehameha's Feat of Lifting the Naha Stone

Best Waterfall—Rainbow Falls

Best *Secluded* Waterfall—Pe'epe'e Falls

Best Shakedown—State Charging for Use of Steam at Puna Geothermal

Best Healthy Food—Island Naturals Deli in the Hilo Shopping Center

Best Margarita—Luquin's in Pahoa

Best Chance of Finding Turtles—Champagne Pond

Best Place to Nuke Your Cholesterol Count—Café 100

Best Burger—Hilo Burger Joint

Best Place to Catch an Easy Glimpse of Erupting Pu'u 'O'o—Glenwood Road near the Hirano Store

The lush waterfalls of the Hamakua Coast contrast with this rolling countryside of Waimea, creating one of the best drives on the Big Island.

When local residents speak of driving between Hilo and Kona, they either "drive the saddle" or they "take the upper road." The upper road is the stretch of Highway 19 between Hilo and Waimea. It passes through magnificent country reminiscent of old Hawai'i. Along the way you can check out numerous waterfalls, drive along stunning gorges, gaze over (or go into) an Eden-like valley, or check out Hawai'i's premiere ranch town, home of the country's largest private ranch, Parker Ranch. Part of this drive is actually in the districts of North and South Hilo, but that distinction is lost on the driver.

We'll start our description from the Hilo side. (If you're coming the other way, just turn the book upside down.) It's best to start this drive in the morning since the waterfalls and much of the best scenery face east.

Highway 19 was constructed to make it easier and faster to travel this part of the island. Consequently, most people are totally unaware of the almost forgotten stretches of road that make up the old highway. We have a particular fondness for these diversions off the highway and point them out as DIVERSION ALERTS.

LEAVING HILO BEHIND

Heading north (see map on page 125) you will see a sign on the ocean side past the 4 mile marker that says ALAE. Take Nahala Road, then turn left at the T. You pass by **Honoli'i Beach Park**. This is the primo surfing and boogie

DIVERSION ALERT!

boarding spot on this side of the island. There are stairs leading down to the black sand beach. The road continues around the back of the stream. When it ends, hang a right to go back to the highway, then left. This is probably a good time to mention that, while stopping at scenic spots along here, during certain times of the year, it's a good idea to have mosquito repellent. Sometimes they are absent; other times they are ferocious. Feeling lucky?

Past the 7 mile marker is the only part of the old highway that is marked. This 4-mile **scenic route** is breathtaking—do *not* miss it—and leads past the **Hawai'i Tropical Botanical Garden** (964–5233). (Consider the 4-mile drive a NOT TO BE MISSED.) You don't have to be a "garden person" to appreciate this *stunningly* **A REAL GEM** beautiful area that fronts Onomea Bay. For $15 ($5 for kids 6–16 years old), you wander on a self-guided tour for about an hour through over 2,500 exotic types of marked flora. (Umbrellas are thoughtfully

provided, but mosquito repellent is extra.) Birds abound in this Eden-like setting. The smell of flowers and fruit (especially mangos) fills the air. Onomea Falls is located on the grounds, which makes a nice place to stop and take in the surroundings. Views of the bay are unbeatable. $15 is pretty steep for a garden, but this is the Big Island's best. A mile past the garden is a food stand called **What's Shakin'** (964–3080) that serves exceptionally good smoothies. (They make 'em the way you're *supposed* to make 'em—starting with frozen bananas, not ice—*oh, yeah...*) They also have a small lunch menu with dependably great food.

Back on the highway between the 13 and 14 mile markers is a 3¾-mile road through former sugar land to **'Akaka Falls.** This free-fall plunge of 420 feet is best seen in the late morning. (It's $5 per car to park or $1 per person to walk in.) If you're in a hurry, walk left 3–5 *beautiful* minutes through lush vegetation and over streams to the falls. There

NOT TO BE MISSED!

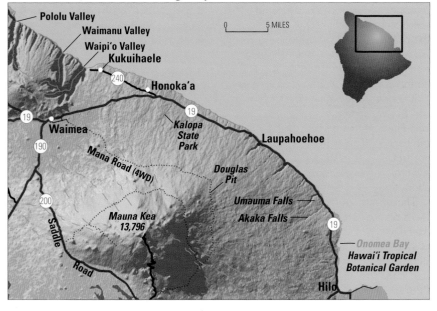

Pololu Valley
Waimanu Valley
Waipi'o Valley
Kukuihaele
240
Honoka'a
19
19
Waimea
Kalopa State Park
Laupahoehoe
190
Mana Road (4WD)
Douglas Pit
200
Umauma Falls
Akaka Falls
Mauna Kea 13,796
19
Saddle Road
Onomea Bay
Hawai'i Tropical Botanical Garden
Hilo

0   5 MILES

you'll find silver/white strands forming as the water hits the rocks on the way down. Otherwise, there is a ½-mile, 15-20-minute amble (with *lots* of steps) through the lush bamboo-filled woods along with another waterfall. (Though the latter, Kahuna Falls, is largely blocked by vegetation.) The full loop is recommended if you have the time. Everything's paved. After visiting 'Akaka Falls, you'll want to stop at the Woodshop Gallery and Cafe for some homemade ice cream and the best collection of Hawaiian wood products we've seen on the island. Woodworkers can even purchase a plank of Hawaiian hardwood to take home. For food here, see ISLAND DINING.

As you continue on Hwy 19, there is another piece of old road to take. It's shortly after the 14 mile marker on the mauka (mountain) side. It leads past Kolekole Park. The massive highway bridge in front of you was part of an old railway. The great tsunami of 1946 carried away many of the girders, rendering the bridge useless. This was the deathblow for the railway, sparking the construction for the entire highway. During the week this is a great place to bring your briquettes and cookables to make good use of the stone BBQs, full facilities and tranquil setting. (Though quiet during the week, it gets too rowdy on weekends to recommend.) The small waterfall and swimming hole is where most swim when the river isn't raging, since the black sand beach itself is too hazardous to swim. This is where the water from 'Akaka Falls ends up, so if you lost something up there, maybe you'll see it again here.

If you stay on this road, it crosses the highway, curves left and empties into Hakalau Bay. A rich, vine-filled forest dripping with life ushers you into the bay. The ruins at the mouth on the east bank are from a mill destroyed during the tsunami. The swimming here is poor, but you can't say that about the view. Backtrack to the highway.

The bridge past the 16 mile marker boasts nice views of two waterfalls. As impressive as they are, they don't even come close to the multi-tiered beauty of Umauma Falls upstream. This may be the most stunning waterfall setting in the state. You can only see it by visiting the Umauma Experience (page 228) and paying $6 or going on one of their zipline

DIVERSION ALERT!

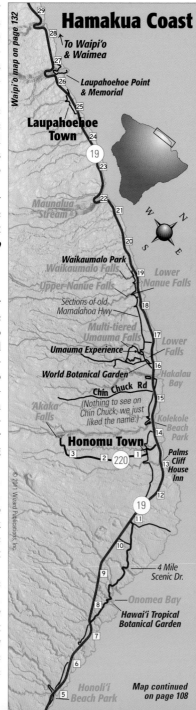

Waipi'o map on page 132

Hamakua Coast

To Waipi'o & Waimea

Laupahoehoe Point & Memorial

Laupahoehoe Town

19

Maunalua Stream

Waikaumalo Park
Waikaumalo Falls   Lower Nanue Falls
Upper Nanue Falls

Sections of old Mamalahoa Hwy

Multi-tiered Umauma Falls   Lower Falls
Umauma Experience

World Botanical Garden   Hakalau Bay

Chin Chuck Rd
(Nothing to see on Chin Chuck; we just liked the name.)

'Akaka Falls   Kolekole Beach Park

Honomu Town   Palms Cliff House Inn

220

19

4 Mile Scenic Dr.

Onomea Bay
Hawai'i Tropical Botanical Garden

Honoli'i Beach Park

Map continued on page 108

tours. (See the photo on page 128 to see if it's worth it to you.)

Whether you want to pay for the falls or not, while you're on the highway, *be sure* to backtrack ²⁄₁₀ mile from the highway bridge turnout, then take the road on the mauka side across from the 16 mile marker and turn right at the T. This 4-mile-long, one-lane country road passes through sugar land before it takes you to a small tree tunnel and several striking gulches. This is the Hawai'i of yesteryear, when life moved a bit slower. You might want to do the same. Stop at one of the old bridges and enjoy the peace. Vine-covered trees and ever-

chirping birds give this area an unforgettable feel.

Early into this road is the **World Botanical Gardens** (963–5427). Started in 1995, it's still a bit stark for a garden, though it's starting to fill out. They used to control access to the Umauma Falls lookout, which was their most compelling asset. Now that they don't have the waterfall, it's hard to get excited about this garden.

Just past the botanical gardens, across from a sign that says THE UMAUMA EXPERIENCE, is a bridge. If you park across from that sign there is a super-short, steep, treacherous (especially when muddy) trail that leads down to a pretty waterfall and perch from with to observe it. From looking at county TMK maps it *appears* that the land here is part of a roadway easement, meaning you're allowed to be there, but it's hard to say for certain.

Still on this 4-mile back road, one of the small Depression-era bridges crosses **Nanue Stream** (it's stamped into the bridge). The nearside of the bridge has a crude and *steep* trail that leads down to the stream. From there a person could walk over to the top of the falls (don't fall off), or go upstream where another waterfall awaits. (The upstream falls, though only 900 feet away, require *very* awkward stream hiking. See ADVENTURES on page 237.) If you don't have mosquito repellent, be prepared for the bloodletting of a lifetime.

DIVERSION ALERT!

Bypass any opportunities

What a drop! 'Akaka Falls tumbles 420 feet.

From a picnic table at Kolekole Beach Park you can either watch the ocean or watch kids swinging off a rope swing next to a waterfall. Talk about an embarrassment of riches!

to reconnect with the highway until you pass rarely used **Waikaumalo Park** near a pretty stream.

When you reacquire the highway just north of the 19 mile marker, you may want to backtrack less than a mile to see the densely jungled gulch and waterfall visible from the highway that you missed before continuing north.

As you effortlessly cruise these gulches on our modern bridges of today, try to visualize what a nightmare it must have been to cross them in days gone by. It took many days to get from Hilo to Waipi'o Valley. When author Isabella Bird toured this area by horse in 1873, she wrote of the utter dread she felt as she plunged down and then trudged up gulch after harrowing gulch on her way to Waipi'o, fording raging streams on a snorting, terrified horse. Today, the hardest thing about traversing these gulches is resetting the cruise control after a sharp bend.

Just past the 25 mile marker is the road leading mauka to the town of **Laupahoehoe**. (The short road on the ocean side sports a nice view of the point mentioned below.) The town itself doesn't offer much other than a '50s-style restaurant (see ISLAND DINING), plus a store down a road on the *ocean* side of the Hwy $^{3}/_{10}$ past the 24 mile marker. It's just a store, and they usually only have one hot meal to eat, so just ask what's for lunch today. (Their curry stew's not bad.)

Also on the highway is the **Laupahoehoe Train Museum** (962–6300). This assortment of artifacts and photos of Hamakua's history with trains is somewhat interesting. They have over a dozen volunteers. Some are extremely knowledgeable...and some aren't. It's $4.

Just past the 27 mile marker is a road on the ocean side that leads 1 mile down the cliffs to **Laupahoehoe Point**. To

many on the Big Island, Laupahoehoe is associated with tragedy. During the April Fool's Day tsunami of 1946, twenty-one schoolchildren and three adults were swept to their deaths. Following this, the village was moved topside. The views from the road down to the rugged point sport dramatic views of the sea cliffs beyond and is well worth the

Umauma Falls is the only waterfall on the island you have to pay to see. Is it worth it? You decide...

stop. There is a memorial at the bottom to those who lost their lives. From out on the jetty, the ocean's energy feels raw and menacing. Waves come in with powerful anger. You feel (and are) exposed to the ocean's fury on the jetty. Here it's not the calm, soothing ocean of Kona, but rather the unpredictable, hot-tempered ocean of Laupahoehoe. Away from the jetty the surf pounds against the twisted and jagged lava and is spectacular to watch, especially when surf's up, but don't even *think* of swimming here at any time. In 1985 a barge full of brand new Toyotas broke loose from its tug and washed ashore near here, spilling the entire cargo. When an insurance adjuster from Lloyd's of London came to check it out, he insisted on landing on the deck of the wrecked ship in a helicopter. Then a wave knocked the chopper over, drowning the adjuster. Surf is almost always violent here.

This whole area was once dominated by sugar. Over 70,000 acres of the Big Island were under cultivation. Even with generous government subsidies, the last mill shut down in 1996, ending 150 years of sugar production. Today this area has a different look and a different crop. More than 24,000 acres of fast-growing eucalyptus trees were planted with the idea of turning them into paper pulp. But the pulpers got their plans shot down *after* the trees were planted and no one has figured out a way to harvest them here and turn a profit. So although they're more than mature enough to cut, they're still standing.

Between the 39 and 40 mile markers is the road to **Kalopa Native Forest State Park**, which offers nice hiking and camping.

HONOKA'A

Near the 42 mile marker is a road through the town of **Honoka'a**. Most merely use it to get to **Waipi'o Valley**, described below. There are a few places to eat available that are mentioned in Is-LAND DINING.

WAIPI'O VALLEY

Waipi'o Valley is as beautiful a place as you will ever visit. With unimaginably steep walls on all sides, waterfalls etching the perimeter, fields of taro and a luscious **A REAL GEM** mile-long black sand beach, Waipi'o never fails to impress. The instant you arrive at the lookout above this awesome spectacle, you realize why this place was so special to the ancient Hawaiians. Because of its inspiring and tranquilizing effects, Waipi'o was often chosen as the meeting place for chiefs when important decisions, such as the succession of the king, were made. Even the kings who resided in sunny Kona had residences in Waipi'o Valley. According to Hawaiian legend, Waipi'o Valley was gouged out by a powerful warrior with his club to demonstrate his power. (Unfortunately, the warrior was himself clubbed to death by the one he was trying to impress.)

At one time thousands of people lived here, meticulously cultivating the lush valley floor with everything from bananas to taro to coconuts. Even Waipi'o pigs were considered tastier here in the Big Island's breadbasket. During times of famine, you could always count on Waipi'o Valley for much-needed sustenance. Fifty generations of Hawaiians have lived and died here, and they believe that the spiritual *mana*, or supernatural power left by those departed, is preserved and felt to this day.

As an infant, Kamehameha was hidden away here soon after he was born to avoid a death sentence by the king of the Big Island, who feared the prophecy that the child would one day rule the island. (And he was right to fear it.)

The peace of Waipiʻo Valley was shattered by the great tsunami of 1946 that washed away nearly everything. Most people moved away and the valley was left mostly wild for two decades. Then in the '60s and early '70s people started trickling back in. Most were hippies and recently discharged veterans who wanted to "get away from it all." Others soon joined. These days Waipiʻo is populated by a colorful assortment of 50 or so characters (including an inordinate number of guys named Dave). Many have turned their backs on traditional society; others simply live there to experience the grace of nature at its grandest. Lots of feuds take place down here, and it's not uncommon for one to result in a building getting torched. Police hesitate to get involved in Waipiʻo disputes, so residents usually settle things on their own.

Those who live in the valley have no power, water, sewage, phones, cell or TV coverage. Solar power and generators provide the electricity they need. (A few nearside residents have phones and power courtesy of small lines stretching down into the valley.) They share their valley with two herds of wild horses (the swamp horses and the bush horses) that were left by the departing residents after the tsunami of '46. The horses can get pesky if they want something (such as apples, which they *love*) so don't turn your back on 'em. There are people who live "topside" and come down daily or on weekends to tend their taro patches.

Land ownership is a big issue. Even the biggest, most powerful landowner in Hawaiʻi, Bishop Estate, has trouble proving how much of the valley they own. Dueling surveyors keep boundaries in flux. When Bishop tried to block access to a beach parcel in 1997, all of their signs were torn down and Bishop gave up.

Today the allure of Waipiʻo Valley is beckoning outsiders. Visitors and residents alike enjoy the splendor of Waipiʻo. Experienced surfers and boogie boarders ride the waves off the black sand beach. Horseback rides are popular. And Waipiʻo Valley Shuttle takes groups down the steep road. Does all this mean that Waipiʻo is ablaze with activity? Not really. To you and me, Waipiʻo is a quiet, peaceful place. But if you've had the place all to yourself for years, even a few people a week would seem like a crowd. The residents here range from the friendly to the grouchy to the *very* weird. We've found that we are less likely to get a smile or a wave in this valley than anywhere else on the island, in sharp contrast to the friendly folks in Kukuihaele and Honokaʻa above. Stink eye (dirty looks) and overall unfriendliness from some residents is common. Perhaps it's because they see visitors as antithetical to the reason they chose to live in Waipiʻo in the first place.

Getting Into the Valley

Don't even *think* about driving a regular car down Waipiʻo Valley Road. The paved one-lane road down into the valley has a ridiculously steep *25%* grade. Vehicles with 4WD and low gears (so you don't burn up your brakes) can make it down the 900-foot descent (in less than a mile). Regular cars simply can't. (There is a wad of metal that was once a two-wheel drive truck below one of the turns left by someone who thought otherwise. He miraculously survived by jumping from the vehicle just as it started tumbling down the almost vertical plunge.) You would probably be violating your rental car agreement if you brought your SUV down here, meaning that they won't come save your bacon if it breaks down. Downhill traffic yields to uphill traffic, so use the turnouts. While driving back up the road, the extreme angle makes it feel like the vehicle is about to flip over backward. (Lance Armstrong once biked up the road on a bet in just over 9 minutes.)

While the overlook sports an unforgettable view of the valley and along the coast, it gives you only a taste of what the valley has to offer. The view from the valley floor with its numerous waterfalls is even better. If you don't have an SUV (or nerve), you can take **Waipi'o Valley Shuttle** (775–7121). For $55 they'll take you into the valley on a 1½-hour *limited* tour. You can get off and arrange for a pick up for $60. They are nearby in the town of Kukuihaele (shown on map on next page). A better way is **Waipi'o Valley Wagon Tours** (775–9518). For $55 they take you on the same 1½-hour tour in a mule-driven wagon. (A half hour of it gets you into and out of the valley by 4WD.) Wagons hold 8 passengers and the driver narrates the sights in a similar way, but with the added charm of being in an open-air wagon. Neither operate on Sunday.

If you want a better tour, **Na'alapa Stables–Waipi'o** (775–0419) has outstanding horseback rides in the valley. They'll shuttle you down into the valley and take you back a ways. See HORSEBACK RIDING.

If you want to hike down into Waipi'o Valley, just walk the road to the bottom. (Oh, is *that* all?) Though less than a mile going down, you'd swear it was 5 miles coming up. Just take your time. Waipi'o is a great place to spend the afternoon. At the bottom, the beach is to your right. **Waipi'o Beach** is often treacherous to swim unless the surf is real calm. Rip currents are

a problem, and the power of the waves is impressive. Legend states that the door to the underworld is near Waipi'o Beach, so Hawaiians were always careful where they camped, lest they should take the one-way trip there themselves.

The back part of Waipi'o Valley is awesome. In the first nook you'll see twin falls of staggering heights. One of the falls are periodically shut off by Bishop Estate. *(Grumble, grumble.)* The falls on the right, **Hi'ilawe Falls**, is 1,450 feet high with a free fall of 1,200 feet, the highest on the island. You'll see it when you head inland after you've reach the bottom of the road.

Mosquito repellent should be required by law for visitors here. The bugs are not always around, but when they are in a foul mood—watch out!

Waipi'o Valley is a lush wonderland where taro farming is still the main occupation.

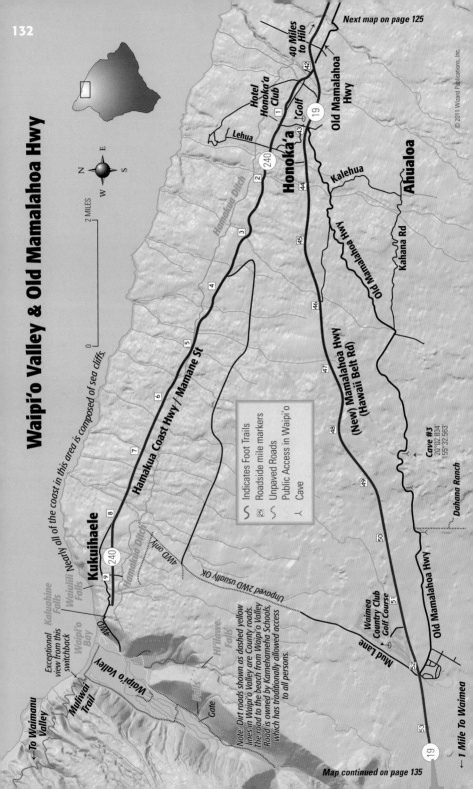

Waipi'o Valley & Old Mamalahoa Hwy

Next map on page 125

40 Miles to Hilo

Hotel Honoka'a Club

Golf

Old Mamalahoa Hwy

Lehua

Honoka'a

Kalehua

Ahualoa

Kahana Rd

Hamakua Ditch

Hamakua Coast Hwy / Mamane St

Old Mamalahoa Hwy

(New) Mamalahoa Hwy (Hawaii Belt Rd)

Cave #3
20°02.834
155°32.563

Dahana Ranch

Nearly all of the coast in this area is composed of sea cliffs.

2 MILES

N
W · E
S

Legend

- Indicates Foot Trails
- 25 Roadside mile markers
- Unpaved Roads
- Public Access in Waipi'o
- Cave

Kukuihaele

Hamakua Ditch

4WD Only

Unpaved 2WD usually OK

Waimea Country Club Golf Course

Mud Lane

Kaluahine Falls
Wailulli Falls

Waipi'o Bay

Exceptional view from this switchback

Hi'ilawe Falls

Waipi'o Valley

Mullwai Trail

To Waimanu Valley

Gate

Note: Dirt roads shown as dashed yellow lines in Waipi'o Valley are County roads. The road to the beach from Waipi'o Valley Road is owned by Kamehameha Schools, which has traditionally allowed access to all persons.

Old Mamalahoa Hwy

1 Mile To Waimea

Map continued on page 135

© 2011 Wizard Publications, Inc.

Getting Around the Valley

Waipi'o seems so idyllic and peacefull you'll be forgiven if you feel compelled to dig in and explore. But the fact is that, other than the roads we show in yellow on the map, the rest of the valley is privately owned and jealously guarded. Many Waipi'o residents get downright grumpy toward visitors wandering around. This has always been the case with Waipi'o, but we feel some responsibility for steering visitors into the back of the valley.

When we did our very first edition, we went down to the county building to diligently research road access in the valley. County personnel took out great big TMK maps and showed us that the roads leading to the back of the valley were "government roads," and we eagerly labeled them as such on our maps. For this edition, we went back to the county and were shown the same TMK maps. But this time we dug deeper. We looked up ownership of every single parcel that *make up* the road. Lo and behold, most of the "government road" is actually private. So feel free to go to the bottom of Waipio Valley Road. Go as far back as the second stream crossing where you'll see an END OF COUNTY ROAD sign. If you want to head to the beach, visitors are traditionally allowed to go to and use the beach, despite a variety of odd signs over the years. (We like the far side of the beach best, if the stream is low enough to cross.) And if you're hiking to Waimanu Valley (see below), go right ahead. But that's it, unless you have the blessing of one of the residents or if you're on a commercial tour.

The trail you see zig-zagging up the wall on the far side of Waipi'o Valley goes up, then down into the next valley, Waimanu. The third switchback (400 feet up the trail cut pretty deeply into the mountain) offers a far grander view of the valley than from the automobile lookout. You can see the back of the valley, the twin falls and lots more. Waimanu is much farther along the trail. It is utterly gorgeous, devoid of residents, and camping is allowed for those who are willing to make the trek. See ADVENTURES for more on accessing Waimanu Valley. Don't try to go and come back as a day hike. It's too long, and you can't see Waimanu Valley from the trail until you have mostly descended.

OLD MAMALAHOA HIGHWAY

Leaving Waipi'o and Honoka'a behind, get back on Hwy 19. Along this stretch of the highway, between the 43 and 52 mile markers, there is another forgotten piece of the Old Mamalahoa Highway. Again the scenery on Old Mamalahoa is much nicer than Hwy 19 and worth the diversion. Lush, green hillsides bracket this old country road. Mist and rain mean that lovers of green will be very happy. If you like caves, there are several along Old Mamalahoa Highway. The best, by far, is labeled on the map as cave #3. You should bring two flashlights. (There are lots of long chambers snaking pitch black into the mountain and, though tall enough to walk upright in, you'd be groping till the cows come home if you lost your only flashlight toward the back of some of these chambers.) The entrances are often dripping with ferns. Cave #3 has lots of structures inside (such as walls and platforms), presumably built by early Hawaiians, and a few empty drinking bottles, presumably left a bit later. It's 1½ miles from Dahana Ranch Road or 2¼ miles from where Kahana meets Old Mamalahoa Highway. The other caves labeled are much less impressive. These caves are in old Mauna Kea flows, and it's unusual for lava tube caves to last so long.

DIVERSION ALERT!

WAIMEA

This town is often labeled Kamuela on maps. That's because there are two other Waimeas in the state, so the Post Office named the local branch Kamuela—Hawaiian for Samuel (as in Samuel Parker; see below). Many locals object to the use of Kamuela, so we will use the original name in deference.

On the surface, Waimea seems like the least Hawaiian town in Hawai'i. In fact, if Scotty had beamed you here and asked you where you were, Hawai'i would probably be the last state you'd guess. At 2,600 feet, the air has a cool crispness to it. Clouds slither over the saddle between Kohala and Mauna Loa volcanoes, often bathing Waimea in a cool fog. Evergreen trees and cactus sit side by side, and the trees all seem blown in one direction. (Kind of like your hair if you've rented a convertible.) Rather than seeing surfers in shorts and aloha shirts, you're more apt to see Hawaiian cowboys (called paniolo) wearing blue jeans and driving pick-up trucks. (A brief visit to a magazine rack, and you'll think, "Wow, I never knew there were so many *truck* magazines.")

Life runs a little slower here, and families are a bit closer knit. Many people compare its appearance to a Northern California rural town, but prettier. As you drive through town from the east side of the island, note how quickly the terrain changes from lush upland forests and green pastures to dry lava scrubland. If it's raining in Waimea (a common occurrence) and you're heading to Kohala via Hwy 19, it'll stop raining less than 5 minutes after you leave Waimea—*guaranz, brah.*

Don't be lulled into thinking that Waimea is a hick town. It is remarkably over-represented when it comes to fine shopping and has several restaurants that are utterly superb. Some of the homes up in the Waimea Homesteads where the descendants of cattle magnates live are absolutely beautiful.

PARKER RANCH

The town is dominated by the legacy of John Palmer Parker. When Captain George Vancouver brought long-horned cattle to Kamehameha as a gift in 1793, the king made them kapu (off limits) for 10 years to build up the numbers. By 1815 the wild herds that roamed Kohala were so ferocious that locals steered clear of them. Marauding cattle were known to drive Hawaiians from their homes by munching and goring everything in sight—even the homes themselves. Kamehameha the Great hired Massachusetts-born John Palmer Parker to shoot them, salt the meat and bring it to the harbor to sell to passing ships. This was no easy task. Long-horned cattle of that time were not like the tame, mindless morons we know today. They were wily, lean and stealthy. They would charge men on horseback, goring them. They lived in the valleys and canyons as well, making them very difficult to detect. Good horses became the equivalent of hunting dogs—they would smell the wild cattle before they saw them, and their ears would perk up, warning their rider to the danger. Because Parker possessed a musket and good shooting skills, Kamehameha made him the first person ever allowed to kill the cattle. Parker took great pains to select cattle with favorable traits and kept them for himself as payment. These he domesticated, starting the Parker herd.

As a totally irrelevant aside, one of the casualties of these cattle was the Scottish botanist David Douglas. He's the guy for whom Douglas fir trees were named. He was walking near Mana Road on the slopes of Mauna Kea one day when he fell into one of the covered pits used as a cattle trap. (Some said he was thrown

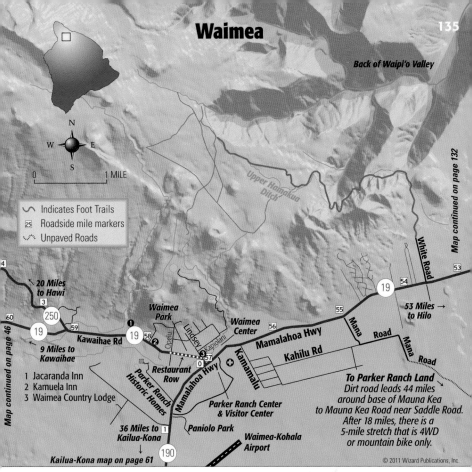

Back of Waipi'o Valley

Map continued on page 132

Map continued on page 46

Upper Hamakua Ditch

Indicates Foot Trails
25 Roadside mile markers
Unpaved Roads

20 Miles to Hawi

9 Miles to Kawaihae

Kawaihae Rd

Waimea Park

Waimea Center

Waimea Hwy

Mamalahoa Hwy

Kahilu Rd

Mana Road

Mana Road

53 Miles → to Hilo

1 Jacaranda Inn
2 Kamuela Inn
3 Waimea Country Lodge

Restaurant Row

Parker Ranch Historic Homes

Parker Ranch Center & Visitor Center

Paniolo Park

Waimea-Kohala Airport

36 Miles to Kailua-Kona

To Parker Ranch Land
Dirt road leads 44 miles around base of Mauna Kea to Mauna Kea Road near Saddle Road. After 18 miles, there is a 5-mile stretch that is 4WD or mountain bike only.

Kailua-Kona map on page 61

in.) Although he was lucky enough to survive the fall, so was the bull already occupying the pit. The unhappy bovine made his displeasure known by goring Douglas to death. Douglas Pit is 28 miles into Mana Road from Waimea.

John Parker himself was a colorful character. A lover of adventure, he was a natural born risk-taker who, though a long-range planner, felt strongly that part of wisdom is to know the value of today. He was well loved and respected by his contemporaries. (But he sure wasn't very photogenic—in his sour photo he makes Ebenezer Scrooge look like Barney the dinosaur.)

In 1816 John Parker married Kamehameha the Great's granddaughter, forever cementing the bond between him and the royal family. He was eventually allowed to purchase two acres of land. His wife, because of her royal blood, was later granted 640 acres, and he bought another 1,000 acres. Thus was born what would become the largest privately owned cattle ranch in the entire United States, peaking at over 225,000 acres, 9% of the Big Island. Parker and his descendants would go on to become very powerful on the island.

Later, when Kamehameha III realized that Hawai'i was lacking in people knowledgeable in the ways of cattle ranching, he arranged for three Mexican cowboys to come to the Big Island and teach the locals about ranching. Nearly all Big Island paniolo traditions descend from these three cowboys.

Parker Ranch was severely neglected by subsequent Parkers. John Parker's grandson, Samuel Parker, was a flamboyant playboy who spent money like water and had a genius for making profoundly stupid investments. Unlike King Midas, everything *he* touched turned to manure. As the aging Parker II saw money pouring down Samuel's many ratholes, he began to squirrel away funds as fast as he could. But when the time came to retrieve the money, the old man could not remember where he had hidden most of it. To this day, much of the fortune Parker II hid away has never been found. In 1900 the family hired a Honolulu attorney to manage and rejuvenate the ranch. This he did with a vengeance, turning a dying relic into a powerful and very lucrative operation.

The serenity of Waimea was broken in the 1990s when Richard Smart, the descendent of John Palmer Parker, died, leaving some of his $450 *million* estate to his family, but the bulk of the land (139,000 acres) to a non-profit trust. Lawsuits started flying from disgruntled family members angry about their share, and it was beginning to look as if the ranch might be broken up and fed to the lawyers and tax collectors. Fortunately, the dispute was finally settled, and peace once again returned to sleepy little Waimea.

Parker Ranch Shown in Dark Areas

19
200
190
Mana Rd—

Most of Parker Ranch is mile after mile of rolling, grassy hills and wide open plains interrupted by rows of trees for windbreaks. Owls, pheasant and wild turkeys crisscross the ranch, while ever-chewing cows wander about. The ranch consists of several non-contiguous segments of land, and its 35,000 cattle are controlled by a mere 12 paniolo (Hawaiian cowboys). The road across from the 55 mile mark (see Waimea map, on previous page, or graphic below) slices through Parker Ranch. Called **Mana Road**, it goes 44

DIVERSION ALERT!

miles around Mauna Kea mountain to Mauna Kea Road (off Saddle Road). 2WD vehicles can drive it for the first part to see what the ranch looks like. After 18 miles there's a 5-mile segment that requires 4WD (it'll seem like more than 5), plus there's an area with confusing but *presumably* parallel roads. Otherwise, you can go as far as your desire takes you. Close any gates that you open (all 4 of them). According to the county, it is a *public* right of way, despite any signs you may see that *imply* the contrary. Avoid it if it's been too rainy; some of the puddles can be big enough to waterski in.

A successful cattle ranch is first and foremost a grass farm. After being raised on sweet Hawaiian range grass for 5–6 months, most of the cattle are shipped by 747 to the mainland or by boat to Canada, then fattened in various areas before slaughter. (Ironically, cattle class on a 747 has more leg room than what you had in coach.) In the old days, just getting the cows to the ship was a traumatic process. They were driven to Kawaihae, forced into the ocean, then lashed to the outside of small boats, which ferried them to the main ship where they were belly-

hoisted aboard. Now they simply walk onto an old cruise ship, into stalls, and off they go to Canada, where they are then trucked to Texas. Why Canada, which ain't exactly *on the way* to Texas? Because no shipbuilder in the U.S. makes cattle haulers. Yet a government law from 1920 makes it illegal for a foreign-built ship to sail from one U.S. harbor to another. Hence, they gotta go to Canada.

If you want to get an idea of what Big Island beef tastes like, the best (and most consistent) source is **Waikoloa Village Market** (883–1088) located in Waikoloa Village at the Waikoloa Highlands Center. The range-fed beef is darker and stronger than grain-fed beef and is particularly good marinated. Deliveries are usually Tuesdays and Fridays. Expect to pay *double* what you would pay for beef that is flown in by jet from the mainland.

Past Waimea heading into Kohala, sights are described in the Kohala section.

HAMAKUA & WAIMEA SHOPPING

The **Parker Ranch Center** in Waimea has lots of shops, including **Journey**, a boutique, and **Reyn's**, which offers men's, women's and keiki aloha wear. **Parker Ranch Store** has all kinds of paniolo and Parker Ranch logo items. **Wishard Gallery** has works by local artists. **Giggles!** is a must if you have kids and want toys or clothes. **Waimea Surf Classics** has a small but good selection of surfwear. There is also **Foodland** grocery store (across the road is a **KTA Super Store**) and **Starbucks** here.

On Kawaihae Road is **Parker Square** with many outstanding shops. **Bentley's** has nice clothing and stuff for your home as does **Gallery of Great Things**, which also has jewelry and artwork from around the world. And browse the **Waimea General Store**; it has a little bit of everything. **Sweet Wind Books 'n Beads** has self-help and cookbooks...and beads, of course.

After leaving Waipi'o Valley lookout, drive by Kukuihaele for **Waipi'o Valley Artworks**, which features an outstanding selection of Hawaiian woodwork and other gifts. Before your stroll up the road in Honoka'a on Mamane Street, pick up some fudge or Tropical Dreams ice cream at **Hamakua Fudge Shop** (see ISLAND DINING). Try browsing **Honoka'a Trading & Antiques** or **Hula Moon**. Honoka'a **Marketplace—Mary Guava Designs** has a beautiful selection of Hawaiian quilts and just about every other item you can think of (from T-shirts to dinnerware), many designed for their store. Look at **Big Island Glass Gallery** for lava- or ocean-inspired glass pieces. Next door is **Douglas Fine Jewelry**, which has some interesting pieces. Check out **Sew Creative** for quilting supplies and join their "quilting bee" on Wednesdays from 8 a.m. to noon (no experience required). Across the street is **Symbiosis**, which carries eco-friendly products. Pick up a water bottle for you and your keiki. Hawaiian scrapbooking supplies can be found at **Island Paperie**.

HAMAKUA & WAIMEA'S BEST BETS

Best Garden—Hawai'i Tropical Botanical Garden

Best Waterfall—Umauma Falls

Best Place to Ride a Horse—Waipi'o

Best View (Easy)—Waipi'o Overlook

Best View (Hard)—From the zigzag trail on *other* side of Waipi'o Valley

Best Treats—Hamakua Fudge Shop in Honoka'a

Best Hole to Avoid—Douglas Pit

Best Picnic Table—Kolekole Beach Park

Here's one place where you don't want a foggy mountain breakdown.

Saddle Road runs between our largest volcanoes, Mauna Loa and Mauna Kea. The entire area is called the Saddle because of the saddle-shaped valley between the two mountains. It travels through some unpopulated and very surreal-looking country and is worth considering if you are driving from one side to the other.

The saddle crests at an impressive 6,578 feet. That's some saddle. The 53-mile-long road has a bad and outdated reputation. It was hastily built by the military in 1942 for strategic purposes. This was wartime, and they wanted a road connecting the two sides of the island, and they wanted it fast. They didn't design it with general traffic in mind; it was meant for military vehicles. Even today, driving on Saddle Road is prohibited in some rental car agreements, meaning your Collision Damage Waiver with them won't cover you. A few years ago their fears were quite well founded. The road had been paved by *Sadists-R-Us* and was a body shop's dream. But now it's in great shape. It's still a winding, hilly road with blind turns that aren't banked on the Kona side. Think of those parts as a roller coaster for your car. Traffic is often sparse. It's two lanes wide, but most drive the road's center (on the Kona side of the saddle) when nobody's coming their way. There are no lights. (We came out here in the middle of the night to watch a comet some years back and *got chicken skin fo days*—i.e., it was spooky. The only sound was a lone birthing cow screaming in the blackness.) The road is often licked by fog toward the center crest. But all in all, it's not as bad as when the rental car companies first made the decision to keep you off it.

The government has improved and re-aligned several portions of Saddle Road.

These newer portions are wider and better engineered. The Hilo side of the crest is excellent.

So why drive Saddle Road? Three reasons. First, it's the only way to drive to Mauna Kea. Second, it cuts between Mauna Kea and Mauna Loa and has some nice sights. The landscape is otherworldly in places and decidedly different. Third, it's kind of fun (if you like winding roads). Even back when it was in horrible shape, we'd take our own personal car on it. (As we all know, *drive it like a rental* is like saying, *drive it like it's stolen*.) And it's a shorter distance than Hwy 19, known locally as *the upper road*. We like to take Saddle Road from the Kona side and return from Hilo on the upper road. In 50 miles the terrain goes from dry lava scrub land to rolling green hills and plains to young lava fields to dripping fern-covered forests. With this in mind, we'll describe it from west to east. There's no **gas** on this road; get it in Waikoloa Village or Waimea in the west, Hilo in the east.

Look at the foldout back cover map to familiarize yourself with the route and to put it in context. From the intersection of Saddle Road (200) and Hwy 190, you leave lava land behind and enter rolling plains of grasses. Keep an eye out for wild turkey (the bird, not the booze) and pheasant, which are plentiful here.

As you ascend to the crest of this saddle, you'll get an idea of the scale of Mauna Kea on your left and Mauna Loa on your right. The military often drive this road in their HUMVEES and other camouflaged vehicles. If you stop and listen, you'll often hear the booms of artillery from the Pohakuloa Military Training Area. Sometimes you'll see their choppers swooping low like a scene out of *Apocalypse Now*. Tanks and Armored Personnel Carriers also use this road on occasion. (We respectfully suggest that you *always* give armored tanks the right of way.) They have even used B2 Stealth Bombers to drop unguided inert bombs from 18,000 feet.

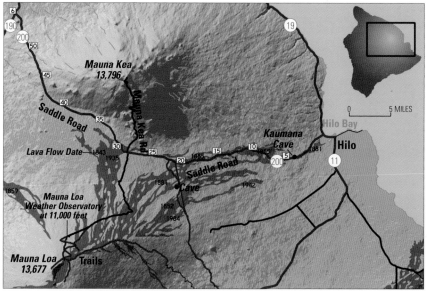

Mauna Kea State Park is near the 34 mile marker. After you turn into the park, there are restrooms and a phone to your right. Cabins are available (See CAMPING on page 179.) Restrooms here are rustic at best, and they've literally torn the sinks out due to a lack of water.

You'll find the road up Mauna Kea (on your left) is marked by a large mound, called **Pu'u Huluhulu** (hairy hill). This pu'u is a good place to stretch if you want to walk the ⅔ mile round trip to the top. (If you have kids, this is a good place to let 'em burn off some of that extra energy.) It's an old cinder cone created long ago by Mauna Kea and has been surrounded by more recent lava flows from Mauna Loa. (You can tell by scars on the side that it was once mined for its cinders.) The main trail is on the far (east) side of Pu'u Huluhulu, just off the road to Mauna Loa, on your right. There are several trails on top of this forested mound, but it's kind of hard to get *too* lost. You can go around the top and connect to the trail you took coming up. The splendid view,

as well as the birds, makes it a short but worthwhile diversion.

MAUNA KEA

If someone asked you to climb from the base of Mauna Kea to the summit (which is more than 13,000 feet above sea level), you'd have to climb over 30,000 feet. (The base of Mauna Kea just happens to be 17,000 feet *below* sea level.) Those wimps who climb from the base of Mt. Everest to the summit only have to climb a mere 12,000 feet. (Its base just happens to start at 17,000 feet *above* sea level.) Everest, too, is located in a warm latitude, 28°, as far south as sweltering Orlando, Florida. But people still freeze to death in the summer on Everest because the summit's high altitude (29,035 feet) offsets the warm latitude.

The second of the five surviving volcanoes to create the island, Mauna Kea (meaning White Mountain) pokes its head 13,796 feet above the ocean. In its prime, half a million years ago, Mauna Kea was 3,500 feet higher. But

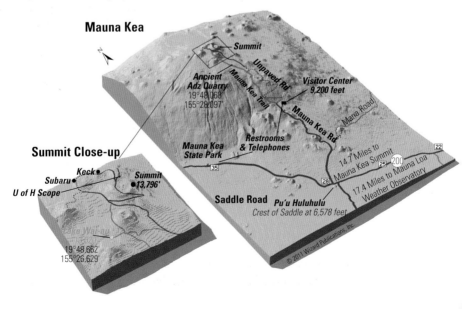

Mauna Kea

Summit

Ancient
Adz Quarry
19°48.068'
155°28.097'

Mauna Kea Trail

Unpaved Rd.

Visitor Center
9,200 feet

Mauna Kea Rd.

Mana Road

Summit Close-up

Keck●
Subaru●
U of H Scope

Summit
●13,796'

Mauna Kea
State Park

35

Restrooms
& Telephones

28

14.7 Miles to
Mauna Kea Summit

25   200

22

17.4 Miles to Mauna Loa
Weather Observatory

Lake Wai'au

19°48.662'
155°26.629'

Saddle Road   Pu'u Huluhulu
Crest of Saddle at 6,578 feet

© 2011 Wizard Publications, Inc.

With clouds below you and clouds above you, the summit of Mauna Kea feels like you're halfway to heaven.

it gets shorter with age. It shrinks every day, settling under its own weight, and bending the ocean floor beneath it. The ancient Hawaiians considered it the home of Poli'ahu, the snow goddess. She and Madame Pele, next door on Mauna Loa, didn't always get along very well, and the saddle between Mauna Loa and Mauna Kea was said to be their battleground. The ancient Hawaiians were uncomfortable in this region, not wishing to get in the middle of this domestic disturbance.

Atop the mountain, the air is thin and incredibly clear. Scientists recognized this spot as possibly the best place in the world to observe stars and have been placing the world's finest telescopes up here for years. (The *twinkle, twinkle* of the little star is caused by air turbulence, and the air above Mauna Kea is some of the least turbulent in the world—windy, but not turbulent.) With little precipitation (except for the occasional blizzard), little in the way of city lights below, and rela-

tively easy access, Mauna Kea is the pride of the astronomical community. Two dozen of the finest telescopes in the world are sprinkled about the summit or are in the works. One area up there is called Millimeter Valley since its peepers are designed to look not in the optical wavelength, but rather at the high end of the radio band, in the much longer millimeter and sub-millimeter wavelength. This allows scientists to look through cosmic clouds and watch stars being born. Some of these telescopes can look at objects over 12 billion light years away, meaning that the light they are seeing left those objects long before the earth and sun were even born. The mighty Keck telescope has a 33-foot wide viewing surface. The moveable part weighs 300 tons but is so perfectly balanced that it can be moved *with one hand.*

Here's a thought for you: Look around at all the infrastructure necessary to look at the stars—the roads, the buildings, the computers, the people, the research, the scopes themselves. All of these things and the hundreds of millions of dollars they cost are here for a single purpose: to hold *one tenth of an ounce* of metal in a specific shape. That's how much aluminum coats the giant mirrors that gather all the starlight and where all the information comes from.

Tours of the **Subaru Telescope** are available 15 days a month. You have to reserve a week in advance from their web site. Call 935–6268 for a recorded weather update of Mauna Kea. Except during summit tours, visitors won't be able to visit the inside of any of the telescopes except Keck (labeled on map), which has a visitors' gallery open weekdays 10 a.m. to 4 p.m., as well as restrooms. You'll get a glimpse through the window of the telescope itself there. (As cold as it gets outdoors, it feels even colder in the temperature-controlled rooms housing the telescopes.)

The view from atop Mauna Kea can only be described as majestic moonscape. The Apollo astronauts did considerable training up here because it was deemed uniquely moon-like. Looking down on the clouds *below* is mesmerizing. It's a cliché but true—you feel like you're on top of the world! Off in the distance, the still-active volcano of Mauna Loa seems bigger than life, especially from a place about 2 miles down the road from the summit. Ironically, Mauna Loa's massive size makes it appear smaller than Mauna Kea. *(Huh?!)* Because Mauna Loa rises so gently to its 13,677-foot height, you don't get the sense of size that you would if it were steeper, like Mauna Kea. But that very gentle slope hides a volume of rock far greater than Mauna Kea—10,000 *cubic miles* of stone. From atop Mauna Kea, the islands of Maui, Moloka'i and Kaho'olawe can be seen on clear days. From this area people ski down the mountain to link up with the road below. The actual summit is a quick (5–10 short-of-breath minutes) hike from the University of Hawaii Ob-

The only one of its kind—a tropical lake fed by permafrost.

servatory. (You'll see the trail if you look over the railing.) Sunsets from up here when clouds cooperate are an unrivaled splendor of unequaled expansiveness. The summit appears utterly lifeless except for a few unlucky bugs blown up from below and a few flightless native insects that feed on them. No trees, no plants. Just a lifeless void. The mountain last erupted 4,500 years ago and is considered dormant. (If it erupts when you are up there, please disregard this last statement.)

Also located near the top are two oddities. **Lake Wai-au**, at 13,020 feet, is one of the highest lakes in the United States and at first its existence defies explanation. What could be feeding it? There are no rivers at the top of a mountain, and natural springs need a higher source to gravitationally feed them (like water in a siphon tube). Rain and snow are insufficient, though they do help some, and the lake is here year round. The answer is *permafrost.* During the last Ice Age (and until 13,000 years ago), Mauna Kea was covered by a 20-square-mile glacier that was up to 350 feet thick and extended 3,200 feet below the summit. It carved and scoured the mountain and left permafrost several feet below the surface. Each day, as the sun heats up the mountain, it melts a fraction of the permafrost, which then works its way into Lake Wai-au. Though shallow, the ancient Hawaiians thought the lake was bottomless—probably because they couldn't find anyone crazy enough to venture into it at this frigid altitude. Lake Wai-au can be accessed by a 15–30 minute walk from the road. (See map and turn right when the trail intersects another trail. The upper trail, near the hairpin turn on Mauna Kea Road at

the 7 mile marker, is the easier trail.) Many of the gulches you see on the side of Mauna Kea were created when the glacier melted, sending the snowmelt to scour the sides of the mountain.

The other oddity up here is **Keanakako'i**, an ancient Hawaiian adz quarry. (Adz is a stone cutter used for shaping wood.) When Mauna Kea erupted during the last ice age, the glacier cap cooled the lava very quickly. The result is the densest and hardest rock in all the islands (tougher than spring steel) and was the hardest substance in the state (except for the bread at a Kona restaurant we reviewed recently). What's impressive is that the ancient Hawaiians discovered this site (at 12,400 feet) and were able to successfully mine it for generations, trading it to other islanders for assorted goodies. The only trail to the adz quarry is down from Lake Wai-au. Coming back up involves a grueling 800-foot ascent, a genuine 'okole kicker at this altitude.

DRIVING UP TO MAUNA KEA

From Saddle Road it's 14$\frac{7}{10}$ miles to the summit. About 2 miles into Mauna Kea Road is a dirt road on your right called **Mana Road**. It leads 44 miles *around* Mauna Kea Mountain all the way to Waimea and passes through tranquil forest. There's rarely anyone on Mana Road, and you need 4WD (or a mountain bike) to take it. The **Onizuka Center for International Astronomy** is 6 miles up Mauna Kea Road at 9,200 feet. Ellison Onizuka was a native of Kona and part of the crew of the Space Shuttle Challenger in 1986 that *"slipped the surly bonds of Earth to touch the face of God."*

The Visitor Information Station has a few displays and small telescopes that they break out at night for visitors. They also sell warmies (for those who came in

As the snow begins to melt, the summit of Mauna Kea becomes a land of many contrasts.

shorts) and brake fluid (for brake-riders coming down the mountain), as well as water and some snacks like freeze-dried ice cream (really weird). Their staff has improved a lot. In the past, trying to get information out of them was like interrogating a Klingon POW. These days we find them much more friendly and helpful. There are restrooms available (the best in this region). About 50 people live up here (tending the 'scopes), and they have to bring their water in several times a week by truck.

While driving up this part of Mauna Kea Road, watch out for mindless, wayward cows occasionally wandering onto the road.

After the Visitor Center the road is unpaved for 5 miles before it becomes paved again for the last 3⁷⁄₁₀ miles. You are allowed access to the top of the mountain in any vehicle. 4WD is what astronomers are *hoping* you're driving because it causes less road wear, but countless regular cars drive it anyway. 4WD is also nice because the unpaved portion of the somewhat steep road coming down

can get a bit slippery at times, especially when wet. 4WD vehicles usually have a gear low enough to obviate this situation. We've found, however, that 4WD vehicles seem to fishtail *going up* more than 2WD cars do. The road is a bit washboardy, and they'll often close it for a short time after a snow until they can plow it. (Finding a good snowplow repairman in Hawai'i must be about as easy as finding a good surfboard shaper in Anchorage, Alaska.)

If you don't want to drive it, several companies will pick you up on the west side and take you to the summit for sunset, then come down a bit for some stargazing and hot chocolate sipping. They'll provide warm coats for you, and the total time is 7½ hours. See STARGAZING on page 224 for more.

Those who *really* want a challenge can opt to hike the trail from the Visitor Center to the top. (See map.) It's 15 miles round trip and a *very* tough day hike, even for the fittest. You need a very early start and should take precautions mentioned in the hiking section. Expect blinding headaches, extreme nausea and bewildered looks from anyone who ever finds out that you did it.

If you drive up, drink *plenty* of water before, during and after, as dehydration is a severe problem at that altitude. Children, pregnant women and those with respiratory problems should avoid the summit. Try to avoid soft drinks and (how do I put this delicately?) foods that produce gas. (You figure it out.) Bring a can of unopened Pringles with you and watch how they explode when you open them up top. And consider chewing gum on the way down to help with your ears. Don't come up here within 24 hours of a SCUBA dive. As far as your nitrogen is concerned, you're flying. Altitude sickness can strike anyone, causing weakness, dizziness and nausea. Some claim that ibuprofen *before* the trip will help this, similar to the way aspirin is said to forestall hangovers, but we won't swear by it. (Well, we'll swear to the *hangover* part.) Go slow and don't exert yourself too much. Acclimating for a half hour or so at the 9,200-foot visitor center can help.

Then there's the cold. Between November and April, snow is not uncommon. Even summertime brings the occasional freak snowstorm. During the rest of the year, it's often bone-chilling up there. Dress warm. *(Like you packed your parka for your Hawaiian vacation!)* The wind can be exceptionally fierce. It's often warm and calm up there, but you shouldn't *count* on it being this way. During the winter, you can snow ski short distances. See SNOW SKIING in ACTIVITIES. When it snows, local residents often rush up the mountain to frolic. We've seen people dashing down the hill below the summit on every conceivable mode of transportation: skis, snowboards, sleds, boogie boards, surfboards, tarps—we've even seen people sliding down in *ocean kayaks,* complete with paddles!

According to King Kalakaua, the Hawaiians had their own version of the Ironman Triathlon. Here, the objective was to climb Mauna Kea during the winter, grab all the snow you could carry, bolt back down the mountain, and run all the way to the ocean. If you had enough snow for a snowball, you won. (If you didn't, you probably grabbed the winner's snowball and stuck it in his pants.) Ironically, this is still done. Only today people bring the snow back in pickup beds and throw a party when they get home. This may be the only place in the world where you can experience snow less than 30 miles from an 85° tropical resort area.

On your way down, a couple of miles below the Visitor Center, you *may* (clouds permitting) see the smoldering Pu'u 'O'o cone at Kilauea Volcano 30 miles to the southeast. Without question, the best views from Mauna Kea are while coming down, not going up.

MAUNA LOA

Across the saddle from Mauna Kea is the more active Mauna Loa (long mountain). This is the most difficult volcano summit on the island to access. You've got two choices, and both are a *buggah.* (See HIKING.) However, off Saddle Road a quarter mile east of the road up Mauna Kea, there is a narrow, paved road leading 17⁴/₁₀ miles up to the **Mauna Loa Weather Observatory**, just above the 11,000-foot level. From there the view across the saddle to Mauna Kea is stunning, especially if there is snow on top. Otherwise, Mauna Loa Observatory

Road offers little for you. Created in 1958, the observatory has the longest record of direct measurement of CO_2 in the world, and their findings are universally cited by climatologists to bolster arguments in favor of global warming. Built near the top of a semi-active volcano, it is protected by a first-of-its-kind lava barrier on the upslope side designed to redirect any lava flows long enough to get the scientists out during an eruption. Someone (with *way* too much time on his hands) has painted a squiggly center line on the entire upper portion of this road, creating the illusion that this is a two-lane road. (Actually, he wrote to us and said it was to help when driving in fog.) You might want to check out the pit crater across the street from telephone pole #200. It's about 50 feet from the road and 50 feet deep where lava drained after overflowing.

APPROACHING HILO

As you continue on Saddle Road, you'll descend toward Hilo. There's a pristine mile-long cave that you can hike to. See ADVENTURES on page 231. Look at the foldout back cover map to get an idea of where the lava has flowed during historic times. You'll be periodically passing through fields of it.

You're on the windward side now, and things will start to get greener. One mile after the 7 mile marker (the 6th was missing at press time) you'll have to turn left to stay on Kaumana Drive and Hwy 200; look for the sign. (Otherwise, the bypass—Hwy 2000—will take you to Hwy 11 if you remember to dog-leg to the right at the end of Hwy 2000 onto Puainako—see Hilo map on page 108.) As you approach Hilo, before Hwy 200's 4 mile marker, you'll see **Kaumana Cave** on your left. Created

by the Mauna Loa lava flow of 1881 that traveled 25 miles and threatened Hilo, this lava tube skylight is saturated with green. Full-grown trees and ferns have taken over the cave and its entrance. It stands in stark contrast to other caves throughout the island. Elsewhere, a century-old lava tube would be little changed from when it was created. But here, in lush, wet Hilo, geologic time marches at a rapid pace. The cave looks old, worn and rickety. You can take the stairs to the bottom and peer in. Once down there, most people are immediately attracted to the large opening to the right, never even noticing the cave entrance to the left. Remember, this is simply an interruption in a 2-mile long lava tube. If you have a flashlight (make that two—it's so dark you can't tell whether your eyes are open or closed) and sufficient nerve, you can go cave exploring. (Called spelunking—in case that's the only word you forgot in your last crossword puzzle.) The cave to your right has more low overhangs between long stretches of tall ceilings, but the formations are more fascinating. To your left, after an initial low overhang, the cave is more cathedral-like. Tree roots occasionally poke through the ceiling. You could spend hours exploring this lava tube if you wanted.

This flow came within 1½ miles of Hilo Bay. Princess Ruth was sent from Honolulu to save Hilo. She stood in front of the lava flow beseeching Pele to stop the lava. That night she slept next to the advancing flow, and by morning it had stopped. Today several hundred homes are built on the 1881 flow and can easily be recognized by their rock gardens.

Rainbow Falls and Boiling Pots are off Waianuenue Road in this area. See HILO SIGHTS for more on these.

In addition to the popular beaches, lesser known gems such as Kikaua Beach are scattered along the west side of the island.

The Big Island has the reputation of being the island without beaches. That's because in the past, lack of roads and lack of knowledge caused most of its more glorious beaches to go unnoticed. Granted, the island has fewer sand beaches per mile of shoreline than any of the other islands. It's newer, and plentiful beaches are the blessings of older, more mature islands. However, what beaches we *do* have, especially on the west side, are among the very best in the state. The water off the west side of the Big Island is the clearest, cleanest and often calmest water in all the islands. There is not one permanent stream on the entire west side, so cloudy river runoff is not a problem. And the shape of the island, along with the prevailing cur-

rent, often gives the west side relatively gentle water. Rough seas usually come from the northeast. Kona and Kohala's calmer waters can be dramatically seen from the air. During normal conditions, the inbound flier will notice that the transition from coarse, choppy channel waters to fine textured leeward waters is almost instantaneous, just south of the northernmost tip of the island. (By the way, flying a small airplane through that wind transition is utterly *nasty*.)

On the Big Island we have white sand, black sand, salt-and-pepper sand and even green sand beaches. As for beach quality, Hapuna Beach is consistently named the best beach *in the entire country* by travel magazines. Mauna Kea Beach is not far behind. Kahalu'u and Honaunau offer outrageous snorkeling. And secluded gems like Makalawena and Road to the Sea, along with unusual delights such as Kiholo Bay, Kapoho Tide-pools, and Green Sand Beach probably make beach-going on the Big Island the best in the state.

BEACH SAFETY

The biggest danger you will face at the beach is the surf. Though it is calmer on the west side of the Big Island, that's a relative term. Most mainlanders are unprepared for the strength of Hawai'i's surf. We're out in the middle of the biggest ocean in the world, and the surf has lots of room to build up. We have our calm days where the water is like glass. We often have days where the surf is moderate, calling for respect and diligence on the part of the swimmer. And we have the high surf days, perfect for sitting on the beach with a picnic or a mai-tai, watching the experienced and the audacious tempt the ocean's patience. Don't make the mistake of underestimating the ocean's power here. Hawai'i is the undisputed drowning capital of the United States, and we don't want you to join the statistics.

Other hazards include rip currents, which can form, cease and form again with no warning. Large "rogue waves" can come ashore with no warning. These usually occur when two or more waves fuse at sea, becoming a larger wave. Even calm seas are no guarantee of safety. Many people have been caught unaware by large waves during ostensibly "calm seas." We swam and snorkeled most of the beaches described in this book on at least two occasions (usually more than two). But beaches change. The underwater topography changes throughout the year. (White Sands Beach is a dramatic example.) Storms can take a very safe beach and rearrange the sand, turning it into a dangerous beach. Napo'opo'o

Beach vanished after a storm in 1992 and never came back. Just because we describe a beach as being in a certain condition does not mean it will be in that same condition when you visit it.

Consequently, you should take the beach descriptions as a snapshot in calm times. If seas aren't calm, you probably shouldn't go in the water. If you observe a rip current, you probably shouldn't go in the water. If you aren't a comfortable swimmer, you should probably never go in the water, except at those beaches that have lifeguards. There is no way we can tell you that a certain beach will be swimmable on a certain day, and we claim no such prescience. There is no substitution for your own observations and judgment.

A few standard safety tips: Never turn your back on the ocean. Never swim alone. Never swim in the mouth of a river. Never swim in murky water. Never swim when the seas are not calm. Don't walk too close to the shorebreak; a large wave can come and knock you over and pull you in. Observe ocean conditions carefully. Don't let small children play in the water unsupervised. Fins give you far more power and speed and are a good safety device in addition to being more fun. If you're comfortable in a mask and snorkel, they provide considerable peace of mind, as well as opening up the underwater world. Lastly, don't let Hawai'i's idyllic environment cloud your judgment. Recognize the ocean for what it is—a powerful force that needs to be respected.

If you're going to spend any time at the shoreline or beach, water shoes are the best investment you'll ever make. These water-friendly wonders accompany us whenever we go to any beach. Walmart or Kmart in Kona sell cheap ones, perfect for your short-duration usage. Even on sandy beaches, rocks or sea life seem magnetically attracted to the

bottom of feet. With water shoes, you can frolic without the worry. (Though don't expect them to protect you from everything. Some beaches are backed by kiawe trees, and their thorns could probably penetrate an armored car.)

The ocean here rarely smells fishy since the difference between high and low tide is so small. (In other words, it doesn't strand large amounts of smelly sea plants at low tide like other locations.)

Theft can be a problem when visiting beaches. Visitors like to lock their cars at all beaches, but piles of glass on the ground usually dissuade island residents from doing that at secluded beaches. We usually remove anything we can't bear to have stolen and leave the car with the windows rolled up but unlocked. That way, we're less likely to get our windows broken by a curious thief though leaving it unlocked *may* leave your insurance company off the hook. Regardless, don't leave anything of value in your car. (Well... maybe the seats can stay.) While in the water, we use a waterproof box or bag for our wallet, phone and keys, and leave everything else on the beach. We don't take a camera to the beach unless we are willing to stay there on the sand and babysit it. This way, when we swim, snorkel or just walk, we don't have to constantly watch our things.

Consider a disposable underwater camera. Even if you don't go in the water, they will withstand the elements. Their quality is better than most people think. And waterproof digital cameras are getting pretty cheap, as well.

Use sunblock early and often. Don't pay any attention to the claims from sunblock makers that their product is waterproof, rubproof, sand blast proof, powerwash proof, etc. Reapply it every couple of hours and after you get out of the ocean. The ocean water will hide sunburn symptoms until after you're toast. Then you can look forward to agony for the rest of your trip. (And yes, you *can* get burned while in the water.) Gel-based sunblocks work best in the water. Lotions work best on land.

People tend to get fatigued while walking in sand. The trick to making it easier is to walk with a very gentle, relaxed stride while lightly striking the sand almost flat footed.

Always remember that in Hawai'i, all beaches are public beaches. This means that you can park yourself on any stretch

Tell me a lawyer didn't write this beach sign!

of sand you like. The trick, sometimes, can be access. You might have to cross private land to get to a public beach. We'll try to point out a way to nearly all beaches

In general, surf is higher and stronger during the winter, calmer in the summer, but there are exceptions during all seasons. When we mention that a beach has facilities, it usually includes restrooms, showers, picnic tables and drinking water.

Lastly, remember that just because *you* may be on vacation doesn't mean that residents are. Consequently, beaches are more crowded on weekends.

To get **ocean safety information**, visit: www.oceansafety.ancl.hawaii.edu or call 327–3570 on the west side of the island and 961–8689 on the east side.

Beaches that are *supposed* to have **lifeguards** are highlighted with this ✚

symbol. Those that had year-round lifeguards at press time were:

West—Hapuna, Kahalu'u, White Sands
Puna—Ahalanui (north of Isaac Hale), Isaac Hale
Hilo—Honoli'i, Richardson's

Those with lifeguards on weekends and holidays:

West—Spencer
Hilo—Onekahakaha, Carlsmith

Those with lifeguards on weekdays only:

South—Punalu'u

We'll start our descriptions at the end of the road at the top of the island and work our way counter-clockwise. The first few beaches have marginal swimming.

❖ Pololu Beach

Located at the end of Highway 270 on the northern end of the island, this beach is very pretty. High surf and currents usually make this a poor swimming or snorkeling beach. Access is via a 15–20 minute trail from the Pololu Valley Overlook 400 feet up. No facilities.

❖ Keokea Beach Park

Although the swimming is usually poor, the exception is a small cove created by a manmade boulder breakwater. It was constructed as a community project by locals with the help from some heavy equipment donated by a long-gone sugar company. Not worth driving to unless you're in the neighborhood. Access road near the 27 mile marker on Highway 270 in North Kohala. Full facilities.

❖ Kapanai'a Bay

Tell anyone outside North Kohala that there is a beach below Kapa'au, and they'll look at you like you're crazy. Kapanai'a Bay is one of the best-kept secrets in North Kohala. This small pebble-and-sand beach is backed by trees and was carved out of the cliffs by a small brook. Even during moderate surf, you may see keiki boogie boarding in the back part of the bay. Surfers venture farther out where the waves are completely unobstructed. While there's not much sand and the water is a bit murky, the bay is very picturesque and a wonderful place for a picnic. The catch is that the access road requires a 4WD vehicle and the nerve to punish it. See map on page 46.

❖ Kapa'a Beach Park

No sand at this beach, just rocks and a little coral rubble. The attractive assets here are the exceptionally clear water for snorkeling and SCUBA, usually abundant fish (sometimes large pelagic fish), coupled with somewhat protected waters except during periods of high surf (which can bring rips and surges). Be careful of surge here. Clear water makes it a good place to take underwater fish pictures. Not much coral but plenty of life. Rarely visited during the week, but easy to access just north

of the 16 mile marker on Highway 270. Facilities include possibly dilapidated restrooms, as well as a BBQ and picnic tables. Excellent view of Maui and a nice place to watch the sunset. Bees and wasps are sometimes a problem here.

❖ Mahukona Beach Park

When the seas are calm, it's *really* calm here. Not a beach, but an old abandoned sugar company harbor, Mahukona boasts crystal clear water and ridiculously easy access for snorkeling or swimming. You can practically drive up, open your door and fall in. (But use the ladder at the entrance to the right, OK?) Though there's not much coral, the underwater relief is interesting. There's usually a large variety of fish, as well as abandoned sugar equipment (giant chains, wheels, etc.) and sparse remains of an old shipwreck. If the

Normally placid, Spencer Beach Park is a popular place for families with keiki (kids).

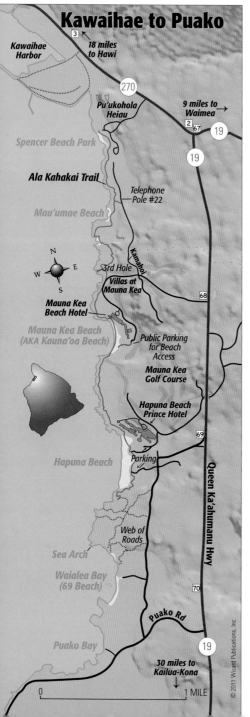

Kawaihae to Puako

Kawaihae Harbor

18 miles to Hawi

270

Pu'ukohola Heiau

9 miles to Waimea

Spencer Beach Park

Ala Kahakai Trail

Telephone Pole #22

Mau'umae Beach

3rd Hole

Villas at Mauna Kea

Mauna Kea Beach Hotel

Mauna Kea Beach (AKA Kauna'oa Beach)

Public Parking for Beach Access

Mauna Kea Golf Course

Hapuna Beach Prince Hotel

Hapuna Beach

Parking

Web of Roads

Sea Arch

Waialea Bay (69 Beach)

Puako Rd

Queen Ka'ahumanu Hwy

Puako Bay

30 miles to Kailua-Kona

19

0   1 MILE

© 2011 Wizard Publications, Inc.

surf's up, don't go. When it's calm, check for surginess. During the week you'll most likely have it all to yourself. Facilities, except drinking water. (Don't drink the shower water!) The dirt road from the other side of the harbor (to the left of the old, giant former sugar building) heading north leads to the navigational heiau shown on page 14. See map on page 46.

❖ Lapakahi

We feel kind of funny putting this in the beaches section. Located in Lapakahi State Historical Park near the 14 mile marker on Highway 270, this is a reserve and there is no real beach here. (See page 51.) But the *snorkeling* is exceptional. The water is clean and clear in Koai'e Cove between site 11 and site 7 near the coconut grove (see brochure). Not much coral but usually *lots* of fish. Stay inside the cove; the waters get unfriendly outside of its protection. Speaking of unfriendly, don't expect to be overwhelmed with aloha from park personnel. They seem to resent snorkelers here. And don't bring towels or chairs, or you'll get stink eye.

❖ Kaiholena (Sapphire) Cove

There's an unpaved road between the 11 and 12 mile markers that leads to a parking area, which is an easy 750-foot walk to a beautiful cove that has inviting waters, lots of fish and sometimes fairly easy entry. The area itself is hot, harsh and prone to a particularly annoying small fly, especially in the mid to late summer, that may not leave you alone on the land. But the waters here are incredible. Stay in the cove as it gets rougher and more exposed outside. Morning is best, but even afternoons can bring great snorkeling memories.

✪ Spencer Beach Park

A great family beach. Located just south of Kawaihae Harbor, the beach is protected by a long offshore reef and the extensive landfill of the harbor to the north. The beach slope is very gentle, and the swimming is usually quite good. Keiki (kids) enjoy the usually calm waters of Spencer. Though the water is a bit cloudy due to its proximity to the harbor, this shouldn't deter you from enjoying the ocean here. If you snorkel, you will probably see miniature underwater volcanoes from small amounts of cold freshwater seeping from the floor. The amenities include several showers, restrooms, a pavilion, lifeguard, picnic tables, barbeques, a lawn area, lots of shade and basketball/volleyball courts. Camping is permitted by county permit (see CAMPING). As you approach the park from the access road between the 2 and 3 mile marker on Hwy 270, you can go to the right or left side of the park. Whether by design or not, the right (northern) side seems to be used mostly by locals and the left side by visitors. Expect this park to be a little messier than other, more pristine beaches.

Just north of here is a small beach in front of the Pu'ukohola Heiau called **Pelekane Beach**. No swimming or sunbathing is allowed there out of deference to the sacred heiau complex.

The **Ala Kahakai Trail** between **Spencer** and **Hapuna Beach** hugs the shoreline. It crosses hole #3 on the golf course but otherwise is easy to follow and passes some pretty shoreline.

❖ Mau'umae Beach

Pretty, secluded, uncrowded during the week and decent swimming when calm. Nice place for a picnic, and you may have it to yourself during the week. Snorkeling is only fair due to slightly cloudy water. Access is through the Mauna Kea Resort entrance, right on Kamahoi, park at pole #22. 10-car maximum is rarely a problem (see map). Less than 5-minute trail walk from your car. No facilities. Usually pronounced MOW-MY. This is one of the most underrated and unknown beaches in this part of the island. Winter usually thins out the sand a bit. Sometimes frequented by nudists.

❖ Mauna Kea Beach (AKA Kauna'oa Beach)

A REAL GEM This is a great beach! Probably the most classically perfect beach on the island. This gorgeous crescent of sand over ¼-mile long offers *very fine swimming* and boogie boarding during calm seas. On the left side of the beach is a bunch of rocks, creating a linear reef that offers outstanding snorkeling. Don't venture too far out unless calm (the outer portion of this reef is more surgy and unpredictable). The northern (right) side of the beach also offers interesting snorkeling but is more exposed and should only be snorkeled by strong swimmers. There is a big light there that attracts plankton at night, which in turn sometimes attracts large manta rays. Try to resist the urge to swim over to them in the shallow water near the light; it just scares the buggas away. This beach and Hapuna are the two best frolicking beaches on the island, if not the state. Mauna Kea is usually less windy than Hapuna. Full facilities. Only 40 cars allowed in the Mauna Kea Resort parking lot at a time, which is usually a problem, so try to arrive before 10 a.m. or take the 1-mile shoreline trail from the north end of Hapuna Beach. Located 32 miles north of Kona in the Kohala resort area off the 68 mile marker. See map on page 152.

⊕ Hapuna Beach

If you close your eyes and picture a perfect beach, there's a good chance you'll see

Luscious Mauna Kea Beach offers some of the best swimming or frolicking on the Big Island.

A REAL GEM Hapuna in your mind's eye. Half a mile long and 200 feet wide during the summer, beautiful Hapuna is the ultimate frolicking beach. You know how frenzied dogs can get when they go to the beach? That's how most people act when they come to Hapuna or Mauna Kea Beach. It's a beach to savor. Fine golden sand slopes gradually into the ocean. Clean, clear water and excellent swimming conditions during calm seas, full facilities, easy access and gorgeous scenery. The **boogie boarding** here, when the surf's not too high, is exceptional. These are some of the elements that account for the fact that *Condé Nast Traveler* magazine has often voted this beach the best in the entire nation. During the week it usually isn't too crowded, but weekends and holidays bring lots of locals who know a great beach when they see one. Most people who live here bring their guests to Hapuna at least once to gloat. The north lifeguard tower is near the sign saying that there's no lifeguard on duty. Swimming is not safe during periods of high surf, which will kick the living daylights out of you. Also note that the wind sometimes kicks up in the afternoon. We've noticed that the southernmost (left) part of the beach is usually more protected during strong winds, but the north end is usually less crowded. The only shade *on* the beach is a tree at the southern end. (Though there are shaded pavilions behind the beach.)

For the more advanced snorkelers on calm days, the area directly south of the sand beach offers superb snorkeling, and it's usually empty during the week because no one knows about it. The waters are usually teeming with fish, and coral is abundant. The sea is unprotected here, so don't go in if it isn't calm, or you'll get beaten up. Check for currents. If it starts to get rough, get out. We often start at the southern end of the beach and snorkel along the rocky coastline all the way to a little black gravel cove half a mile down the coast near a sea arch. Then we walk back along the shore in our water shoes via a poor trail or use the dirt road (don't do it bare-footed). Be careful of the wicked kiawe thorns—they can penetrate nearly any shoe and probably most bulletproof vests. If you have some energy left, keep snorkeling past the little gravel cove to Waialea (69) Beach. The area just past the cove is absolutely heavenly. The north end of the beach can also be awesome.

Hapuna is located 30 miles north of Kailua-Kona in the northern part of the Kohala mega-resort area near the 69 mile marker off Highway 19. The restrooms by the parking lot usually look like they're from the third world. Use the ones behind the north lifeguard station. An unimpressive concessionaire near the parking lot has food and beach supplies. There may be a parking fee at Hapuna.

❖ Waialea (Beach 69)

A REAL GEM *Sigh!* Just another kickin' Kohala beach. This beach slopes gently into the water, giving it nice swimming conditions most of the year when the sea is calm. Not as long or as well known as Hapuna or Mauna Kea, this beach is popular with *akamai* (savvy) residents who sometimes bring their families for a day at the beach on weekends. To the north (right) of the main beach is a secluded little cove, which people sometimes claim for the day, sometimes sans clothing. The snorkeling around the northern part of the beach can be excellent. There's a sea arch at the northern tip, but refrain from walking on it; it looks like it's getting ready to go. Located 30 miles north of Kona near the Kohala resort area off Puako Road. (See map on page 152.) The short road is near telephone pole #71 (it used to be pole #69— hence the name). Facilities include toilets and showers. High surf occasionally strip mines the beach of its sand, which can take months to naturally replenish itself.

❖ Puako

Great snorkeling and SCUBA (see page 217 for directions to best spots, and photo of the reef), but the swimming is marginal. The reef at Puako is *very* extensive. The somewhat cloudy water on entry usually gives way to very clear water at the reef's edge. You stand an excellent chance of sharing the water with multiple turtles. (Oh, yeah, what's a multiple turtle?) The tops of the reefs are not the most interesting part (and can subject you to the prospect of being raked over them). The best fish and scenic action are at the outer edges of the reef. Check for currents and give the ocean respect. People occasionally bring their dogs to this beach (which end up chasing the catfish, no doubt). Wind often creates chop on the water here, but that doesn't usually affect the underwater experience much. There are nine legal public accesses along the bay from the boat launch. Some may be *conveniently* unmarked. A check of the county tax map and a site check shows us that they are by telephone poles #101, 106, 110/111, 115, 120, 123, 127/128, 131/132 & 137, plus the dirt road at 143.

❖ Mauna Lani

The Mauna Lani Bay Hotel and the Fairmont Orchid both have small, manmade (or enhanced) beaches, such as Pauoa Bay, which has lots of fish. The Mauna Lani Bay Hotel beach to the south is usually *very* protected. Access is via the public parking lot shown on the map on page 53. You'll have to walk for about 15 minutes, but the trip through the fishpond area is worth it.

❖ Honoka'ope Beach

This small salt-and-pepper beach is located between the Hilton Waikoloa and the Mauna Lani. Go south from the Mauna Lani roundabout and turn left on Honoka'ope Place. Open 8 a.m. to 5 p.m.; the lot holds 20 cars. It's a 2-minute walk from your vehicle. Like other beaches in this area, it can get windy in the afternoon. If you're seeking a hike, the ancient

Ala Kahakai shoreline lava trail takes 30–60 minutes to reach the beach. (See map on page 53.) This trail segment, which starts near the Mauna Lani fishponds and ends here, goes through some fabulous lava cliff scenery. When surf's up, waves explode onto the twisted, gnarled lava fragments in the ocean. Facilities.

At the beach the swimming and snorkeling are fair if it's calm, ugly if it's rough. (Visibility is often poor here.) If the surf's right (not too big, not too small), you can float face down with a mask and snorkel at the surf's edge. As the waves rake you back and forth, listen as the black pebbles mixed with the sand make a great sound as they, too, are raked back and forth.

❖ 'Anaeho'omalu Bay

A REAL GEM Another nice Kohala beach. (Even those born and raised here usually call this 6-syllable tongue-twister *A Bay*.) This long, curving salt-and-pepper sand beach is popular with both locals and visitors. The swimming is best in the sandy center, whereas the snorkeling (though not great) is best on the right side past the sandy area. The water is not as clear as what you'll find at other nearby beaches, but it's so tranquil here, you won't care. Protected by an offshore reef, this bay is usually safe except during very high surf. Windsurfing is popular here. Say *meow* to the wild cats that live near the restrooms.

'Anaeho'omalu is well known throughout the islands for its two large fishponds. These exceptionally picturesque and placid pools were used by ancient Hawaiians for raising mullet. Hawaiian royalty were the beneficiaries of these ponds—commoners weren't allowed to partake. The ponds are ringed by palm trees, making sunset photos from behind the trees a sure-fire winner.

There's a pleasant paved path on the mauka side of the fishpond that's worth a stroll. Numerous signs along the way give information about the fishponds and the

While not as flashy as some of the other beaches in the area, Honoka'ope Beach is a good place to listen to what's going on under the water.

area in general. Toward the center of the path are the remains of an ancient dwelling, probably a combination of sleeping and eating quarters as well as a shrine. The pond itself contains brackish water; fresh water flows from a natural spring and mixes with ocean tide water. The ancient Hawaiians covered the opening to the fishpond with a grate, which allowed small fry to enter from the ocean. Once inside, they gorged themselves on algae and small shrimp and became too fat to get back through the grate, at which time they were sitting ducks (so to speak) for the Hawaiian pond keepers.

On the right (northern) side of the beach is a hut that rents snorkel gear, kayaks, boogie boards, windsurfers, etc. (at confiscatory rates). They also have guided snorkel and SCUBA tours. If you're hungry, the restaurant at the Waikoloa Beach Marriott behind the beach has pricey but available burgers and hot dogs.

There's a marvelous shoreline trail north between the two Waikoloa hotels that leads through sand, lava and large amounts of brilliant white coral rubble. All along the trail you'll find various tide-pools tucked against the shoreline. Turtles tend to hang out at one particular tide-pool just a few feet from shore. At the north end of this trail is the Hilton Waikoloa. What a way to see this place for the first time! A sunset stroll along this path is unforgettable. Footwear is a must. There is an alternative place to park along this stretch—see map on page 53.

A few minutes walk south of A Bay on a narrow ribbon of sand leads to **Kapalaoa Beach**, a series of sand pockets. There is shade and a pleasant cove for snorkeling at the last pocket. If the surf's not high, the cove is amazingly protected. The short walk to this beach goes by numerous Hawaiian petroglyphs, some ancient and some modern. The more ambi-

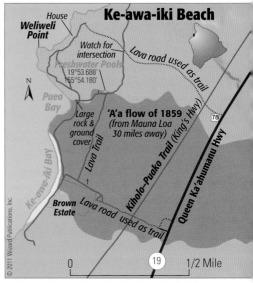

tious will want to take the lava trail farther south for about half an hour until you reach a lone palm tree in the lava, less than a hundred feet from the shore. Here, you are rewarded with an outstanding spring-fed brackish pool with lots of charm. It is very deep in spots and is great for dipping after a hike. You will rarely see anybody else here as it is only accessible by foot, and it's a favorite stopping place of ours. The lava trails in this area offer good hiking, but they can get a bit hot in the middle of the day. The trail leads mostly along the shoreline for miles, all the way to Ke-awa-iki below.

❖ Ke-awa-iki Beach

This black sand-and-gravel-lined bay is never crowded due to the access—to get there you have to walk on a lava road half the time, and a rougher 'a'a trail to the right of the fence the other half. Few on the island even know it's there. (It takes about 15 minutes to walk to it.) The water off the left (south) is clear and offers good snorkeling when calm, but be wary of currents. There's also some shade there (and sometimes a swing from one of the trees). The best snorkeling is usually in the center of the bay. If you keep walking past the southern edge of the bay, there are lots of tide-pools to explore on an older, smooth pahoehoe lava shelf at low tide. (This is a good place to be wearing water shoes.) Past that are numerous salt deposits from evaporated seawater. These deposits attract goats from the dry scrub inland who warily come and lick the salt off the rocks. Past the right (northern) side of Ke-awa-iki Bay is **Pueo Bay**, lined with black pebbles and semi-protected with nice swimming on calm days. There are off-shore fresh-water springs here, causing areas of perturbations in the water, visible as waves of underwater distortion. You will almost certainly have this bay to yourself. No shade here because it's backed by an 'a'a field. If you feel like an extended stroll, you can walk past Weliweli Point and take a lava road inland to circle back to the highway. Mauka of Pueo Bay are some beautiful golden pools, described under Hiking on page 203 and shown on page 55.

Both of these beaches were created in 1859 when 'a'a from Mauna Loa drooled down the mountain and exploded when it hit the ocean, creating black sand. The eruption only covered half the bay and some white sand is still sprinkled at the southern end because there hasn't been enough time to evenly distribute the newer black sand. The entire area has a desolate but pretty character to it and is one of the least known beaches on the west side of the island. The only pockmark is the Brown Estate lining the center part of the beach with its barbed wire fence and its unwelcome feeling. Francis I'i Brown was an influential and beloved Hawaiian businessman in the early 1900s, and in turning his estate into a historical landmark, they seem to have taken away all its charm. They have tours of it for a few hours on the third Tuesday of every month. (Gee, *that's* convenient!) Located 20 miles north of Kailua-Kona just after the 79 mile marker.

❖ Kiholo Bay

A REAL GEM More of a region than a beach, and there are a few surprises. Access to much of it requires a little hiking. See Hiking on page 200. It's certainly worth it.

❖ Ka'upulehu Beach

Most of this long sand beach is fronted by a lava bench, making the swimming poor, but there is a pocket of sand in front of the Kona Village that allows easier access to the water as well as two protected coves (man-made) in front of the Four Seasons. You can access this beach from either of these two resorts. From the Four Seasons it's only ¹⁄₁₀-mile walk, but there are only 10 Beach Access stalls lumped in with employee parking, and the stalls tend to be filled with cars that *don't* look like rentals. From Kona Village there are plenty of stalls, but it's a ½-mile walk from your car to the beach. (Not "1 mile" as we've been told from the guard shack.)

❖ Kuki'o Beach

Near the Four Seasons Resort between Kona and the Kohala Resort area, this is yet another pretty Kohala beach. This long, fringing crescent of white sand is backed in parts by palm, ironwood, and kiawe trees offering inviting shade. At the southern end of the bay is a small, but very protected sandy cove. The swimming in the bay itself is only fair during calm seas, and the snorkeling offers somewhat murky water. **Turtles** commonly beach themselves here. There is public access from the resort area (see map on next page). While Kuki'o Bay might sound like a pretty name, in

Hawaiian it means to *stand and defecate* (traditional definition) or *settled dregs* (modern definition). You probably won't be seeing *that* on the back of a postcard. The reason behind the *lovely* name has been lost to the generations, but it's probably safe to say that whoever named it was having a bad hair day.

❖ Kikaua Beach

A REAL GEM One of the things that makes the Big Island so different is its ever-changing nature. Active volcanoes sometimes create new beaches overnight. But in this case, we have modern man—developers, no less—to thank for this one. Kikaua Point was once an isolated area with a pretty, but rocky, cove defining it. A few years ago a private golf and beach club was built behind this point, and it seems obvious that a lot of sand was been transported to this cove, whether by man or by nature we can't say. But the result is a dreamy, softly padded sandy bottom and a protected cove that offers easy swimming and wading most of the time. The 27 parking spaces fill up on weekends, but weekdays are usually not bad. To get there, take the Kuki'o Nui Road just south of the 87 mile marker. Although this is private property, just tell the nice guards at the gate that you're exercising your beach access rights. It's a 5-minute walk from your car. Full facilities.

❖ Manini'owali/Kua Bay

This is one of our favorite beaches. (Most on the island know it as **Kua Bay**, but the state has been pushing Manini'owali Beach as its name.) Off the beaten path, beautiful fine white sand, clear, clean water, gentle slope and a picturesque setting. When the ocean is calm, the swimming is fabulous. The snorkeling

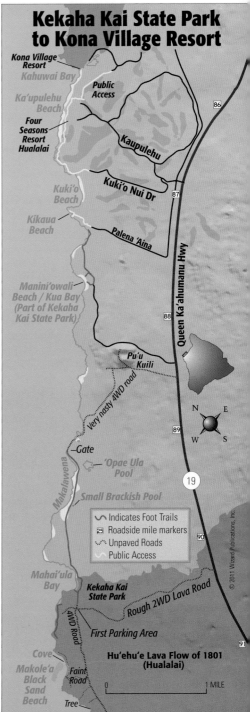

Kekaha Kai State Park to Kona Village Resort

Kona Village Resort
Kahuwai Bay
Ka'upulehu Beach
Public Access
Four Seasons Resort Hualalai
Kaupulehu
Kuki'o Nui Dr
Kuki'o Beach
Kikaua Beach
Palena 'Aina
Manini'owali Beach / Kua Bay (Part of Kekaha Kai State Park)
Pu'u Kuili
Very nasty 4WD road
Gate
'Opae Ula Pool
Makalawena
Small Brackish Pool
Queen Ka'ahumanu Hwy
86
87
88
89
19
90
91

⤳ Indicates Foot Trails
25 Roadside mile markers
⋰ Unpaved Roads
⤳ Public Access

Mahai'ula Bay
Kekaha Kai State Park
Rough 2WD Lava Road
4WD Road
First Parking Area
Cove
Makole'a Black Sand Beach
Faint Road
Tree
Hu'ehu'e Lava Flow of 1801 (Hualalai)
0   1 MILE

© 2011 Wizard Publications, Inc.

N E W S

The clean, clear waters of Manini'owali/Kua Bay.

off to the right (north) is interesting not for its coral, but for the underwater relief. **Boogie boarding** is excellent during moderate surf, but the waves can be strong and deserve respect. There is sand here most of the time, but it is most abundant during the summer months. During the winter, high surf sometimes shifts the sand offshore for a time, leaving the area rocky and undesirable. Many residents consider this one of the best swimming beaches near Kona when calm, and on weekends they sometimes make their presence known. Crowds are less common during the week. From Hwy 19 take the paved access road between the 88 and 89 mile markers. Open 9 a.m. to 7 p.m., *closed Wednesdays*. Note that the waves here have a lot of power, so if the surf's up, don't go in. No shade *at the beach*, but restrooms and shaded picnic tables are available behind it.

❖ Makalawena

A REAL GEM To many, this is the choicest beach on the island…if you don't mind walking to it. In fact, Makalawena is as idyllic a beach as you will find anywhere in the islands. Gobs of superfine, clean white sand, plentiful shade and no crowds. The setting is utterly beautiful. Consisting of a number of coves and rocky points united by a long, curving stretch of beach, the best swimming is in the largest inlet backed by high sand dunes. **Boogie boarding** can be great here. There's a freshwater pond (see map on previous page) where we like to rinse off the saltwater before walking back. A herd of wild goats visits this area often, so keep an eye out for them.

Backed by private (Bishop Estate) land, you get there over the trail from the red houses behind Mahai'ula Beach (about a 20-minute walk). It's a lava trail through an 'a'a field, and the footing is fairly annoying. As you walk this trail, try to imagine how ridiculously difficult it would be to walk through the field itself without the trail. Then imagine doing it *barefoot,* as the ancient Hawaiians did. As you approach Makalawena from the Kekaha Kai side, the 'a'a trail suddenly gives way to sand dunes. But if you climb the dunes to the left, rather than finding ocean, you find more 'a'a, indicating that this had been shoreline until a lava flow of 'a'a came along and added more real estate, cutting off the dunes from the sea.

If you have a 4WD (and your fillings are tight), you can take the nasty and intimidating road from the highway between the 88 and 89 mile marker. Locals do in their stock pick-ups and JEEPs all the time without even blinking, but readers constantly write to us saying it's impassable in their rental JEEPs. It'll take you just north of the beach before a gate forces you to walk like the rest of us dogs. By the way, because it's so isolated, people sometimes travel light to this beach, omitting such extraneous things as their bathing suits. (Yeah, *that* must be the reason.)

❖ Kekaha Kai State Park; Also Mahaiʻula/Kaʻelehuluhulu

This beach is outside of Kona town and pretty. It's usually not too crowded. **Mahaiʻula**

A REAL GEM **Beach** (which you access after a 5-minute walk to the north from the first parking area) offers good swimming and interesting strolling. Just around the southern corner is a pocket of sand called **Kaʻelehuluhulu Beach** (park at the second parking area at end of the lava road), not as good as the northern beach. The entire area was once owned by a promi-

nent part-Hawaiian family called the Magoons. They sold the land to a Japanese investor who had visions of a resort. When the state refused permission, the investor sold it to the state, which turned it into a park. The abandoned Magoon house is still located at the northern end of Mahaiʻula Beach. This area abounds with freshwater springs that bubble to the surface, occasionally forming ponds. At the farthest northern part of the beach near some palm trees and a rock wall, you may see strange indentations in the sand at low tide. Here, freshwater gurgles right out of the sand and into the ocean. The snorkeling is only fair because the water can be a bit cloudy, especially during spring, and wild goats are common here. This is a good beach to get away from it all, yet still have fairly easy access. There's plenty of shade at the backshore. Access is via a bumpy, but *usually* driveable, semi–paved 1½-mile road halfway between the 90 and 91 mile markers on Queen Kaʻahumanu Highway north of

Isolated and unknown, Makalawena is one of the finest beaches on the island. Access requires a 15–20 minute walk or a 4WD.

Kailua-Kona. The only negative is the occasional plane overhead as it lands at Kona Airport. Facilities include picnic tables and toilets. Bring your own water. The gate to the beach is open 9 a.m. Look at the signs to see what time they close it. Note that the closing of the gate is one thing state workers are *guaranteed* to do promptly. *Closed Wednesdays.*

Legend states that before 1801 there was a 3-mile-long fishpond here. That year an old lady came to the village and asked for fish. The village overseer refused, saying that it *all* belonged to the chief. On her way out she was stopped by one villager who gave her food. After eating, she told the kind stranger to place kapu (forbidden) sticks outside his house. That night lava from Hualalai roared down the mountain to the village, destroying the great fishpond but sparing the man who fed her. The villagers realized that the old woman was the volcano goddess Pele, avenging the selfishness of the chief.

Check out some of the lava on the road leading to this beach (you'll certain-ly be driving slowly enough). There are lots of interesting formations where different flows meet. It has patches of gold/rust colored lava, streaks of blue, red and other colors indicating the presence of numerous elements and gases present during cooling.

❖ Makole'a Beach

A REAL GEM Ask a hundred residents of Kona about a black sand beach just north of town named Makole'a Beach, and you'll get a hundred blank stares. Aside from a handful of shoreline fishermen, few seemed to have known about this beach—until we stumbled upon it for a previous edition. Created during the 1801 lava flow of Hualalai, this small pocket of jet black sand is the only black sand beach on this part of the island.

To get there you have two options. After driving to Kekaha Kai State Park (see page 161), those with 4WD can take a left at the first parking lot and drive the lava road heading south. Look at the sign

Did you spring for 4WD? If so, Makole'a Black Sand Beach near Kona is all yours today.

The quiet tide-pools of Wawaloli Beach at the Natural Energy Lab are an excellent place to go when the surf's pounding.

to see what time they close and lock the gate and *believe* in their promptness. Just under ⁷/₁₀ mile is a faint car path marked by some coral that leads 1,100 feet over lava to the sea. (Though driveable, you can walk this last part if the lava there dissuades you.) The other way is to park at the beach at Kekaha Kai State Park and walk along the shoreline for 15–20 minutes. At one point the sandy trail is interrupted. Best to walk on the smooth pahoehoe lava behind the beach boulders for this part. Just before the black sand beach is a small cove protected at low- to midtide during calm seas. It's a perfect place to take a quick dip. The snorkeling and SCUBA diving are great at the black sand beach. Though the visibility is only fair (it's better when you get away from the beach), there is a beautiful field of coral to the north (right) of the beach and to the south farther out. Enter at the sandy part in the center, and beware of unchecked waves. If you walked here, consider cutting across the lava field on your return for different scenery.

This beach, while certainly not on par with Mauna Kea or Kua Bay, deserves the GEM rating because it's the *only real black sand beach* anywhere near Kona, it's not overly difficult to access, and you are likely to have it all to yourself on weekdays. (Some fishermen use it on weekends and sometimes leave their beer bottles.) It's that rare treat—an undiscovered black sand beach.

❖ Wawaloli Beach

A REAL GEM This is our favorite tide-pool area on the west side of the island (shown above). The instantly accessible sand beach is cut off from the ocean by a large tidepool that offers warm swimming when the surf is too high elsewhere. There are restrooms and showers here, making it popular with local families who bring their keiki (kids) to play in the mostly protected area. The largest pool (mostly sand-lined) is best near high tide most of the year, only best at low tide if the surf's cranking. The other, less protected tidepool is better at low tide. A water channel in the lava closer to the restrooms can be fun to wander in. In late afternoon you might want to pick up a pizza on your way out, bring the kids, if you have 'em, and watch the sunset. Take the road to the Natural Energy Lab (near the 94 mile marker on the main highway north of Kailua-Kona), and park just as it veers to the right along the shoreline. Some equipment to the south is an eyesore, but try to ignore it, and airplanes sometimes shatter the quiet.

Near here is a 4WD road that leads a mile south to **Pine Trees** (Hawaiian name Kohanaiki), one of the island's premier surf spots. It's so named because of the mangrove in a brackish pool. Surfer dudes thought they were pine trees. The road is fairly poor.

❖ Kaloko-Honokohau

Honokohau is an area rich in archaeological treasures. This part of the coast was inhabited for centuries and is filled with relics. Consequently, it was made a national park in 1978 in an effort to preserve what remains (entrance is free). At first it might seem surprising that people thrived here. Barren and rocky with particularly harsh 'a'a fields in many areas, the draw here was the freshwater springs. The Hawaiians took advantage of the water to create

large fishponds to raise mullet and other fish.

Located just south of the airport (see map on this page), you can access the park between 8:30 a.m. and 4 p.m. from a parking lot near the 97 mile marker on Hwy 19 just north of Kailua-Kona or a gravel road between the 96 and 97 mile markers that leads to **Kaloko Fishpond**. You can also access the park from **Honokohau Harbor**, off the paved road between the 97 and 98 mile markers. From the harbor, a brief walk north will take you to **'Ai'opio Beach**. There are scads of turtles munching on grasses in the cloudy cove water. This was an ocean fish trap in ancient days, where fish entered at high tide and were easily captured. A protected area here is perfect for keiki (kids). An impressive heiau called Hale o Mono rests at the south end. Park at the north end of the harbor (past the restaurant) and take the trail for a minute or two. Turn toward the ocean before you reach the restrooms. This is a nice beach for relaxing. Farther north is **Honokohau Beach**. You may read elsewhere that this is a nude beach, but it is no longer permitted and they cite violators. This long stretch of salt-and-pepper sand offers reasonable swimming at the center. One nearby highlight is known as **Queen's Bath**. (Even locals get confused by Queen's Bath. There are several of these scattered throughout the islands. Essentially, any place that was considered an outstanding place to bathe was called Queen's Bath.) This 15-by-20 foot natural lava pool of brackish water was lovingly enhanced by the Hawaiians to make it a fine place to congregate and splash in relatively fresh (and very cool) water. They lined the pool, located in the middle of a harsh 'a'a field, with smoother stones, built areas to sit, and generally made it a pleasant place to visit. These days, it is only sporadically visited by hikers and

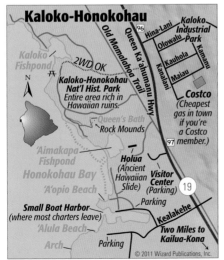

beach-goers from the nearby beach. To get there from Honokohau Beach, walk north along the beach. At 200 yards past the *end* of the beach you'll come to a rock wall. Look mauka (toward the mountain), and you will see numerous large piles of rocks. These are also ancient in origin— the largest is 10 feet high and 15 feet thick—and are part of 12 rock piles placed in a rectangle around the Queen's Bath, possibly used for lookouts. The trail to them from the south end of the wall is along the dividing line between the lava and yellow clumps of grass. Go toward, then between, the two largest mounds. The pool is about 100 feet north of the largest mound near the only large green shrub in the area. Enjoy!

At the south end of the Honokohau Harbor is **'Alula Beach**, a small, pleasant crescent of sand, which is fairly protected during calm seas—a good sunning beach. A short walk south of here leads to a large, impressive sea arch.

❖ Old Kona Airport Beach Park

This beach park is located at (do we *really* need to say it?) the Old Kona Airport, closed **A REAL GEM** in 1970 because it was unable to accommodate larger aircraft. You park anywhere on the runway (you may taxi as long as you like) and enjoy the patchy beach and full facilities. On the south end are ball fields where Little League parents battle for supremacy. The long beach is an easy one to access, and the sunsets from here are nice. Though you won't be overwhelmed by an abundance of thick sand, it's rarely crowded *during the week*. Located ½ mile (15–20 minute walk along the lava coastline) north is the finer **Pawai Bay**. The **snorkeling** in Pawai Bay is very exciting, especially for the experienced snorkeler. There's a little of everything with crystal clear water, lots of life, cav-

Old Kona Airport Beach Park
(is one mile north of Kailua-Kona)

99 Kmart
Queen Ka'ahumanu Hwy — Luhia St — 19
Makala Blvd — Kaiwi St
Small Cove
Old Airport Runway — Kuakini
Pawai Bay — Cove — Ball Field
0   ½ MILE
© 2011 Wizard Publications, Inc.

erns, sea arches, drop-offs, small caves and some pinnacles along the shoreline. Here you may see the elusive and extraordinary frog fish (an angler fish) on the coral and Spanish dancers (a contorting nudibranch). During tricky surge, novices should stay away from the more interesting shore. Some snorkel boats bring groups. If you walk here, you will find the cove in the center of the bay is the best way to enter. Be careful of the channel that leads out to the bay; it can be surgy. The shady backshore of Pawai Bay has plush camping facilities that are private and belong to the Queen Lili'uokalani Trust, used for Hawaiian children. We occasionally get e-mails from readers saying they've been told by (presumed) Trust personnel that *the beach* is private. We'd like to take the occasion to remind those folks that in Hawai'i, *all* beaches are public up to the vegetation line.

The walk to Pawai Bay from the Old Airport is best experienced at low tide. Lots of puka (holes) in the lava are exposed, creating fissures where water often surges and air escapes in loud gasps. This lava fractures easily, which is why the underwater relief along here is so good.

❖ Kailua Bay

Located in the heart of downtown Kailua-Kona. (See map on page 61.) Usually areas around piers have nasty water. This one is surprisingly clean due to the daily flushing action of the sea. There's a sur-

Good reef protected by a boulder breakwater have made Kahalu'u the most popular snorkel site in Kona.

prising number of fish in Kailua Bay. We've seen super-schools numbering in the many thousands off Hulihe'e Palace. On calm days we like to snorkel from the pier to the sand pocket across from Kona Islander Inn or the boulder beach across from Lulu's. If you are looking for *exceptionally* calm water and a sandy beach, the very small **Kamakahonu Beach** to the right of the Kailua Pier (in front of the King Kamehameha Hotel) is perhaps the gentlest and safest water on the island (with the *possible* exception of your hotel bathtub). Children love frolicking in the water here, though freshwater springs sometimes make it cold. This is where King Kamehameha chose to spend the last years of his extraordinary life, so you gotta figure it has something going for it. His personal 'Ahu'ena Heiau is right in front of you. The sand at the beach doesn't extend very far into the water, but it is shallow the whole way. If you swim out from the beach, you'll notice a private

ocean entrance to the right. It leads to a house owned by billionaire Paul Allen, the less famous co-founder of Microsoft. He bought this gloriously located house in the 1990s for $11 million. (Don't worry, it was probably a mere rounding error in his checkbook.) That was 10 years before the land boom-turned-bust. A recently discovered map hints that this might be the location of Kamehameha's tomb, but if so, it was probably destroyed when the shoreline was rearranged in the 1950s.

There is a concessionaire at Kamakahonu renting various beach accouterments at the usual confiscatory prices—but it's convenient. Large schools of fish sometimes congregate on the other side of the heiau. It's about 300 yards from the public parking lot to the beach, so you may want to drop off your stuff (and a person) at the pier first.

To the left (south) of the pier is another pocket of sand. (They sometimes do SCUBA intros there.) It's a bit less protected but still relatively calm. Boogie boarders like to ride the normally small but long lasting swells. The grueling Ironman Triathlon (see page 60) starts here. They swim 2⁴/₁₀ miles before starting their 112-mile bike ride and 26-mile marathon run—*all in the same day!* (Makes you sore just thinking about it, huh?) If it's rained recently, snorkelers should look for little calderas of what looks like boiling sand, like mini volcanoes. They're caused by small amounts of cold freshwater bubbling to the surface.

❖ **Pahoehoe Beach Park**

Though there's little sand here to speak of, this is a nice place to have a picnic and enjoy the surf and sunset from the benches. We've never seen it crowded. Backed by pretty trees and a lawn, there is a small gravel entrance to the water, but swimmers are discouraged from entering unless equipped with snorkeling gear. Even then, advanced snorkelers only need apply. That's because there are numerous holes, arches and pockets on the lava shelf offshore, making exploration very exciting. But surf can sometimes rake you over and even under the reef, making it *too* exciting. Lots of fish here, as well. Located north of the 4 mile mark on Alii Drive in Kailua (just north of White Sands Beach).

➕ **La'aloa Bay Beach Park**

Also known as **White Sands**, **Magic Sands** and **Disappearing Sands**. Located just north of the 4 mile mark on Alii Drive in Kailua, this small beach has particularly nomadic sand that retreats at the first sign of a surf assault, settling in a repository just offshore. Once the surf subsides, the sand slowly drifts back onto the shoreline until the next high surf. This occasional flushing of the sand tends to keep it clean and white. Those who live here can tell you of countless instances where the entire beach washes away in less than a day. Much of the time there is a shallow sandbar just offshore, making the swimming and boogie boarding quite good. (The best wave break is on the left [south] side of the beach.) Watch for undertow and some rocks at the end of the ride. When the sand's thick, the frolicking is good. (But water shoes are recommended in case you step on a rock.) When there's no sand or it's in the process of disappearing (i.e., when the surf's high), there is a strong rip current, making water activities hazardous. This small beach tends to be pretty crowded. Lifeguard and facilities are here along with some shade trees. On calm days, the snorkeler will want to check out the area to the right (north), in front of Kona Magic Sands condominiums. Especially large schools of fish sometimes hang out there. We've also seen more moray eels here than at any other place on the island. *(If an eel bites your hand, and you bleed in the sand... that's a'moray.)*

Just south of here right at the **4 mile mark** is a **small cove** where the SCUBA diving is excellent, offering short, easy access and good underwater relief and caves. The snorkeling is not bad either. Just offshore from this location we often see a pod of dolphins patrolling the waters. Why they hang out there, we don't know, but whatever the reason, keep an eye out for them.

➕ **Kahalu'u Beach Park**

A REAL GEM This is one of the nicer snorkeling spots on the Big Island. It is teeming with fish and offers more variety of sea life than any other easily accessible spot in Kona. Among the many fish present are wrasses, parrotfish, convict tang, porcupinefish, needlefish and puffers, as well as the occasional lobster, eel, and octopus. Outside the reef you may occasionally see deep sea life, such as tuna, marlin and dolphin jumping about. When you first enter the water you might think, "What's all the hubbub about?" Well...it's about 100 feet offshore. The perimeter of this small, sheltered bay has numerous freshwater springs, making the near-shore water cold and cloudy. But once you swim out toward the middle, it gets warmer and clearer, and life is abundant. One reason is the Menehune breakwater offshore. Built in ancient times, it has been partially disassembled by countless waves, creating an excellent fish environment. There's usually a truck at the beach where you can rent snorkel gear. Almost across the street is the Kona Surf School that will rent snorkel gear "only if the surf business is too slow." They also have boogie boards (but the boogie boarding here is not good—just surfing), and you can usually take surfing lessons at the beach. There is a full range of facilities. There's also a lunch truck with hot dogs, ice cream and bad shave ice. A family of turtles calls Kahalu'u home, and they usually won't dart away from you if you don't harass them. (We've noticed that near high tide, they often work the grasses that are otherwise exposed on the

left/southern side of the bay.) Your odds of swimming with turtles are probably greater here than anywhere else on the island, with the possible exception of remote Punalu'u Beach. The best way to keep a turtle from fleeing is to act disinterested—like you don't give a flying fish. (*Ooo*, sorry.) If you scope him out, he'll run off. If you pretend to eat the same grasses he eats, you aren't a threat. The more intrepid might venture around the breakwater on very calm days where life is also abundant. Exceptionally large mixed schools of fish sometimes congregate just outside the reef, but you expose yourself to the possibility of being strained through the reef—better stay inside unless it is real calm or you are real confident.

Crowds accumulate at Kahalu'u, but it's *usually* less crowded than White Sands Beach. During periods of high surf, large waves can wash over the reef and form a rip current flowing out the reef opening at the north end of the bay, making it unsafe.

Though this has traditionally been a popular place to feed fish, conservationists are making a concerted effort to end the practice here. See SNORKELING for more.

To the left is a **tide-pool** in front of the Outrigger Keauhou Beach Resort. The water there is sometimes as warm as bathwater as it gets heated by the sun, a natural black-bottom pool. Cruise around in the shallows and look for eels, which like to be fed by people at the railings of the hotel.

Eight hundred feet to the left (south) of Kahalu'u is **Makole'a Beach**. (Not to be confused with the beach described on page 162 with the same name.) There are several heiau along this beach that are under restoration. The salt-and-pepper sand and gravel beach is usually empty and has a lonely, forgotten feel. The swimming is poor since you are facing large

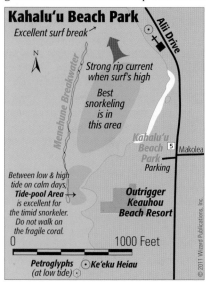

Kahalu'u Beach Park

Excellent surf break

N

Menehune Breakwater

Ali'i Drive

Strong rip current when surf's high

Best snorkeling is in this area

Kahalu'u Beach Park

5 Makolea

Parking

Between low & high tide on calm days, **Tide-pool Area** is excellent for the timid snorkeler. Do not walk on the fragile coral.

Outrigger Keauhou Beach Resort

0   1000 Feet

Petroglyphs (at low tide) ⊙   ⊙Ke'eku Heiau

© 2011 Wizard Publications, Inc.

tide-pools. Look for the gory petroglyphs mentioned on page 65.

❖ Napo'opo'o Beach

Well, it *used* to be a beach. It disappeared when Hurricane 'Iniki sideswiped the island *way* back in 1992, and the surf wiped the beach clean, depositing boulders there. You'll find little more than a small patch of sand. This beach will probably never return to its former glory—part of the ever-changing nature of the Big Island. Across the bay is the Captain Cook Monument, described on page 69. Slightly south is **Manini Beach** (shown on map on page 66). Coral rubble sprinkled with 'a'a lava, and poor swimming make this another must-miss beach.

❖ Ke'ei Beach

Between Kealakekua and Honaunau (see map on page 66), this pretty but small stretch of sand is backed by numerous coconut trees. Though picturesque, poor swimming and difficult parking mean that it is used almost solely by the small, adjacent community and by visiting SCUBA divers. This area seems to have been a magnet for historical events. Local legend (bolstered by old Spanish records) states that foreigners washed ashore here during the 1520s. Several big battles took place nearby, including the one where Kamehameha became king. (See page 71.)

❖ Pu'uhonua o Honaunau

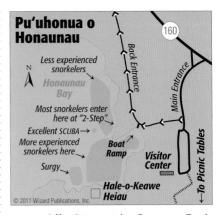

Pu'uhonua o Honaunau

160

N

Less experienced snorkelers

Honaunau Bay

Most snorkelers enter here at "2-Step"

Excellent SCUBA →

More experienced snorkelers here

Surgy

Back Entrance

Main Entrance

Boat Ramp

Visitor Center

Hale-o-Keawe Heiau

To Picnic Tables

© 2011 Wizard Publications, Inc.

A REAL GEM This is a popular place to visit for reasons other than its water. It was the Place of Refuge in ancient times. See detailed description on page 72. For ocean lovers, the snorkeling and SCUBA just north of the boat launch (at a place commonly called **Two Step** because of its easy entry) are incredible, perhaps as good as the more difficult-to-reach Captain Cook Monument at Kealakekua Bay, making it some of the best in the state when conditions are good, though it's deeper. There are also picnic tables near the shoreline at the southern half of the park that make for absolutely splendid sunset picnics. We've made good use of the BBQs there and can recommend them highly.

❖ Ho'okena Beach Park

A REAL GEM South of Kona between the 101 and 102 mile markers is a paved road leading 2³⁄₁₀ miles to Ho'okena Beach Park. We are deeply impressed with what they've done with this park. Not too long ago this beach had a reputation for being unfriendly to visitors. The local community gathered together, petitioned the county to turn park operations over to them, and they have transformed it into a family-friendly gathering place for locals and visitors alike. You can tent camp (328–7321) for $5 per night, rent kayaks, snorkel gear or boogie boards, purchase food and the facilities include showers, restrooms, picnic tables and shade. This pocket of fine salt-and-pepper sand is hot on your feet. Keiki (kids) ride the waves on calm days and splash about in a few tide-pools adjacent to the sandy beach. Decent snorkeling is to the left. If you walk 250 yards along the shoreline to the north, you'll come to a small inlet, the size of a swimming pool, that is *sometimes* protected from the stronger ocean. Keep walking north to the end of the houses, and you find one of the nicest sea arches on this whole coastline.

❖ Pebble Beach

Located down a *very* steep road. (You lose 1,050 feet of elevation in 6,000 feet of driving—that's almost as steep as the notorious road into Waipiʻo Valley.) It's at the bottom of Kona Paradise (off Highway 11 between the 96 and 97 mile markers 20 miles south of Kona) and is one of the most violent beaches we know of. Even when calm, it will kick your ʻokole. We've seen fish tossed out of the water on calm days. *(Seriously!)* The "beach" is actually countless large water-worn pebbles, which make a great sound when the surf's up. If you've got the nerve, it's fun to let the surge pull you up and down the steep beach (but stay away from the shore break).

A 5-minute walk to your right leads to a small cove with smaller pebbles and black and green sand beneath them. Not good swimming but secluded and private. Unlike the Pebble Beach rumble, this one fizzes like a glass of soda.

❖ Miloliʻi Beach Park

Located 30 miles south of Kailua-Kona, this is considered a very local beach, meaning that *on weekends* it's best to leave it to them. There is a very tight local community here, and, though Hawaiʻi is as friendly a place as you will find, you may get a little stink eye if you visit during "their time"—like crashing someone's family barbeque. This community beach sports a pavilion used by local bands playing outstanding Hawaiian music on week-

ends and holidays. There's not much sand, but the surfing is good, and the facilities are well-developed. (The sand was removed by a storm in the 1970s. The same storm also removed many houses. Some homeowners made the mistake of bulldozing their crumpled houses and were not allowed to rebuild. Shrewd owners knew that to stay that close to the water, they were required to keep and repair the *original* structure.)

Take the winding, one-lane paved road just south of the 89 mile marker. Drive slowly at the end of the road, and watch for local kids.

❖ Honomalino Bay

A REAL GEM Ask most people who live here where Honomalino is, and they'll probably tell you it's on Maui. This lovely black-and-white sand beach is not well known. It's 150 yards or so long, backed by scads of coconut trees, decent swimming when calm (which is often), usually deserted, and is a 20-minute walk from your car. Though one of the larger *south* Kona beaches, it eroded considerably during the 20th century (as black sand beaches naturally tend to do—see explanation on page 174) and will probably be mostly a memory a hundred years or so from now. To get there, start at Miloliʻi Beach Park (see previous beach). Go to the end of the road, and you'll see bathrooms and a yellow church. The public access is between them. (A left fork is private property; the right fork is yours.) When we asked nearby residents about the KEEP OUT and NO TRESPASSING signs at the trailhead, we were told this was indeed the correct public access and that it was "a *looong* story and related to four *decades* of litigation." About 3–4 minutes into the trail after some tide-pools and a palm-backed spit of sand, follow the fenceline on your left up and over the black rock at the back of the beach and continue south for 15 minutes. There may be a few fallen trees to hop over. The snorkeling on the right side of the bay is interesting when calm in the cluster of rocks. There is a small cave there where a 6-foot white-tipped reef shark often rests. Don't worry, he's not a man eater—yet. (He's been there a long time, so maybe it's his family estate.) If you plunge your hand into the sand at the water's edge at the south end of the beach, the sand's cold. That's freshwater (called a basal spring) percolating into the sand from below.

One of Honomalino's little-known joys is the pod of **dolphins** that sometimes cruise the sand-lined bay in the morning. Scientists think that, while resting, dolphins are able to turn off half their brain (including the half that runs their echolocation abilities). They do a sort of snooze and cruise, counting on the fact that the shallow water and light bottom will alert them to predators in the absence of their sonars. This means that, in the morning, dolphins are literally operating on half a brain. (Come to think of it, so am I before my coffee.)

❖ Road to the Sea

A REAL GEM This is one of Ka'u district's best-kept secrets. In BASICS we mentioned that having a 4WD can come in handy. Here's a perfect example why. First, if you don't have a 4WD, you *probably* won't make it. It depends on the level of cruelty you normally inflict on rental cars. The access road is ⅔ mile past (south of) the 80 mile marker on Hwy 11. The first of two beaches is at the end of this 6-mile long dirt road with only a 20-foot stretch in the middle, which will probably cause even the most ambitious 2WD driver to turn around. Remember, you're far from Kona. If you get stuck, the first thing the tow truck driver will ask is, "Do you own your own home?"

Honomalino Beach on a crowded day.

Sure, you can 4WD right up to the second Road to the Sea beach. But only if you're willing to beat your vehicle like a rented mule (as the driver above apparently did). Best to walk the last mile.

County maps show this as a *public* access, though we've seen hand-made KEEP OUT signs in years past.

Anyway, these two beautiful black-and-green sand beaches are nearly always deserted, especially during the week. The first beach is at the end of the road. Swimming *during calm seas* is fair, and the beach is inviting; enter it from the left (south) side. Harmless plankton-eating whale sharks are sometimes seen in the area. To the right of the end of the road is a *deep* tide-pool—7 to 9 feet in spots. It makes a *great* wading pool, and there's even some coral in it—unusual for a tide-pool.

The second beach is reached via a 1-mile long *rough* 4WD road ⅓ mile back up from the *very* end of the road. Don't take the first Fool's Road to the left (which only leads to sorrow). Take the one with the yellow gate. If you find it too rough for your driving tastes, walk the mile to the second beach. It's worth it. The road leads to a much longer and finer black-and-green sand beach. (See Green Sand Beach next page for an explanation of green sand.) At the end to the right is a freshwater pool. This one is saltier than most, but is great for dipping. There is some shade at the back part of the beach. Stay close to shore; the water can get tricky further out.

This is a great beach to get away from it all, and you *may* have it all to yourself.

The entire area out here is lifeless, arid and desolate. It was utterly assaulted by savage lava flows 250 years ago and on paper isn't worth a hill of beans. Yet despite this (or perhaps because of it), it is alluring. The lava field looks young and raw, and the beaches are desirable. If you have 4WD, it is a recommended trip. Located 40 miles south of Kona; see map.

By the way, shade is provided courtesy of the way winds wrap around Mauna Loa. Almost every day during normal tradewinds between 10 a.m. and 11 a.m. a shearline cloud forms about

5,000 feet above the beach, creating shade the rest of the day.

❖ Green **Sand (Papalokea) Beach**

A REAL GEM

(Literally!)

So you say you've seen white sand beaches. You've seen plenty of golden sand beaches. Maybe you've even seen a black sand beach. But when is the last time you frolicked on a *green* sand beach? This unusual beach owes its name and color to a large deposit of a semi-precious gem called olivine liberally mixed with black sand. After ancient volcanic eruptions created Pu'u o Mahana, a small littoral cone containing thick veins of the stuff, the ocean went to work dismantling it. It has already broken through one side, and when the surf is up, each wave rakes at the back side, revealing more and more olivine. Though most of the gemstones are in the form of sand particles, people occasionally find large nuggets. (Actually, your best chance of finding a nugget is at the rarely visited adjacent cove on the far side of Green Sand Beach. Access is from the far [northeast] side). See map of South Point on page 79.

Located near South Point, which (this will stun you) is at the southernmost point on the island, access to the beach requires a 2¼-mile (each way) walk or 4WD from Kaulana Boat Launch. (The four-wheeling is sometimes pretty rough, depending on road conditions during your visit.) There are more dirt roads than we showed on the map because people are constantly creating new ones. They all go to the beach and beyond. You'd have to try real hard to get lost since you always stay within sight of the shore. Keep an eye out for the remains of several Hawaiian structures dotting the area.

Once at the cone, most people take a "path" on the closest (southwest) side (see map), which requires a short hop off a rock at one point. Unfortunately, the path is more evident from the beach than from the top and might be tough to spot. Others walk down a path from about the middle of the cone, which can be slippery due to sand particles on the hard surface. Don't try to walk from the highest part of the cone; it's treacherous. Use your best judgment. Everyone from small keiki to the elderly goes to the beach, but you are on your own in evaluating it. Check to see that the waves are not inundating the entire beach before you go down. The ocean is unprotected, so the waves are at full strength. Many books tell you that you will drown if you even *think* about swimming there. We swam there plenty of times, and if the surf's not up, it's not bad. The sand bottom is thick and there are few exposed rocks. We have yet to encounter nasty currents *in the bay,* but we're not stupid enough to venture out of the bay where the prevailing current will give you a splendid tour of Antarctica. Again, use your best judgment. There is a shorebreak, and the undertow can be harsh. You might see plenty of local kids (or us) playing in the surf, but this is not Waikiki. And if the surf is high, definitely stay out. Those same large waves that expose the olivine could pull you in. There's no shade here, and the wind, which has beautifully sculpted the eastern side of the

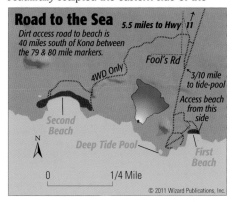

Road to the Sea *5.5 miles to Hwy 11*

Dirt access road to beach is 40 miles south of Kona between the 79 & 80 mile markers.

Fool's Rd

4WD Only

3/10 mile to tide-pool

Access beach from this side

Second Beach

N

Deep Tide Pool

First Beach

0   1/4 Mile

© 2011 Wizard Publications, Inc.

bay, is also the same wind that might get on your nerves if it is blowing hard, particularly in the late afternoon. Go earlier if you can. No facilities. Please resist the urge to take any of the sand with you. We've seen people taking large amounts, and the supply is finite.

The spooky snorkeling at **South Point** itself is described on page 81.

❖ Whittington Park

Located off the road between the 61 and 62 mile marker on the southern part of the island. Very pretty from a distance. Formerly run down, but they've spiffed it up recently. Think of it as a pit stop with restrooms and picnic tables.

⊕ Punalu'u **Black** Sand Beach

A REAL GEM

This is the most easily accessible black sand beach on the island (now that Kaimu Beach is under 75 feet of lava). Backed by palm trees and a freshwater pond, the sand is *genuine* black sand—the kind created when a chunky 'a'a lava flow meets the ocean and shatters into small pieces on contact with the water. These small chunks are quickly pulverized by the ocean, forming a delicious black sand. This differs from older black sand beaches where the sand is made up of lava chipped from a river bed by coursing water. Genuine black sand beaches are relatively fleeting since the source of the sand ends as soon as the lava flow stops. This contrasts with white and golden sand beaches, which have organic sources (coral or shells) that continue to build up sand over time. (In fact, one large, coral-munching parrotfish can produce three *tons* of white sand per year by himself!) That's why you don't see genuine black sand on old islands—the black sand erodes into the ocean over time and cannot be recovered.

The swimming is a bit different here than at many other island beaches. Cold freshwater springs bubble up from just offshore. Consequently, the top 8–12 inches of the water is guaranteed to freeze your 'okole off. You can usually see the floating freshwater while swimming and will be tempted to swim below to get a semblance of warmth. The visibility here is only fair, and you need to be conscious of rip currents. Generally, you want to stay fairly close to shore and be aware of currents during all but the calmest seas. Past the boat launch on the left (north) side of the beach, the rips can be a problem.

So why swim here at all? Well, one of this beach's lesser-known treats is its **turtles**. The waters can get almost crowded with them. We've been here when you could see small groups of turtles every couple of minutes. They munch on limu that clings to rocks on the sea floor. Please remember not to disturb or play with them. In addition to the possible harm, it might cause them to find a less accessible beach to frolic.

Near the southern tip of the island between the 56 and 55 mile markers on Hwy 11. The facilities at the south end parking lot get heavy use from the local community as well as tour buses. The less-used north lot is more convenient.

EAST SIDE BEACHES

Past Punalu'u your choices for beaches diminish along with their caliber. Put simply, the east shore, which is exposed to more hazardous surf and lots of river runoff, has fewer and mostly poorer beaches. Therefore, we are breaking them up into regions and deviating from our previous rules by describing many in the tours of the various regions.

❖ Puna Beaches

Located near the extreme eastern part of the island, **Kehena Black Sand Beach**, ➕ **Issac Hale Beach Park**, ➕ **Ahalanui Warm Springs**, and **Kapoho Tide-pools** are described in HILO & PUNA SIGHTS because you won't encounter them unless you are touring that area anyway.

❖ Hilo Beach Parks

To the east on Kalanianaole (where highways 11 and 19 meet) are Hilo's most popular beach parks starting with **Keaukaha**. During summer months it's a tent and tarp city with long-term campers. The rest of the year it's simply a great park to avoid. ➕ **Onekahakaha Beach Park** has a boulder-enclosed pool that is popular with local keiki (kids). The sand-lined pool is utterly protected except during very high seas. The pool to the left is rockier and has lots of urchins on the floor. Past Onekahakaha is **(James) Kealoha Beach Park**. Though picturesque, the swimming is poor, and you're likely to share it with young toughs drinking too much and giving you stink eye. Best to move on to ➕ **Carlsmith Beach Park** just across the bay. There are full facilities and a nice lawn area. The swimming is marginal around the lifeguard tower. Go to the far right side where the water is more protected, and keep an eye out for turtles. Instead of the parking lot, if you drive past the Mauna Loa Shores condo to an unmarked lot, you can access the park from a short but *very* cool jungle trail. (Bring bug spray for it.) Farther east is **Wai'olena and Wai'uli Beach Parks**. This last area contains ➕ **Richardson's Ocean Center** at the far end and is particularly attractive with freshwater pools sprinkled about. The county Aquatics Division is located here, and they are friendly and full of helpful information. This is an excellent place for a picnic, though sometimes the (James) Kealoha crowd spills over to here. There's a small black sand cove where you can enter the water. It'll be cold from freshwater intruding into the area. Some of Hilo's better snorkeling is here. Dolphins often frequent the area, and turtles usually congregate a little further down the coast toward Hilo. Check with lifeguards because this area is subject to strong surf.

Other beach parks north of Hilo are ➕ **Honoli'i**, **Kolekole Beach**, **Hakalau Bay**, **Waikaumalo Park**, and **Laupahoehoe Point**. Farther north is the difficult to access but beautiful black sand beach of **Waipi'o Bay**. All are described in the HAMAKUA & WAIMEA SIGHTS chapter.

Kua Bay
White Sand

Green Sand
Beach

New Black
Sand Beach

White Powder
Sand from Florida

The Big Island is a snorkeler's paradise. This is at the Captain Cook Monument in Kealakekua Bay.

Take a deep breath and do some stretching before you read this chapter, because the Big Island has so much to see and do that you're likely to pull something just reading about it all. Among the more popular activities are fishing, golfing, snorkeling, SCUBA, hiking, horseback riding, kayaking, helicopter tours, boat trips, submarine rides and whale watching. Whatever you're into—even snow skiing!—you're likely to find it here on the Big Island.

Activities can be booked directly with the individual activity providers or through activity companies. *Sometimes* you can get better deals through activity companies or online. Many resorts have activity directors and booths, sometimes run by the activity providers themselves, so be aware that their "recommendations" are sometimes biased. Many of the booths spread around the island are actually forums for selling timeshares. That's not a dig at timeshares; it's just that you need to know the real purpose of some of these booths. They can be very aggressive. (Don't get skewered by one of the long metal hooks.) Free breakfasts and "island orientations" are often similar to activity booths. So if you are steered to XYZ helicopter company and assured that they are the best, that's fine, but consider the source. We walk up to these booths frequently. Some are reputable and honest, and some are outrageous. We have no stake in *any* company we recommend; we just want to steer you in the best direction we can.

ATVs

These are those 4-wheeled things that look like Tonka Toys on steroids with knobby tires. They are often used by ranchers these days to chase cows, and they're quite a bit of fun to ride. **ATV Outfitters** (889–6000) is our favorite. They'll take you around private land near the northern tip of the island on ATVs. For $129 you cruise along for 1½ hours, taking in the coastal scenery. They'll provide beverages and long pants (if you left them at home) for a fee. The ATVs are easy to operate with automatic transmissions. (Riding wimps will do fine on these.) You need to weigh between 90–300 pounds. They also have a 22-mile, 3-hour deluxe tour for $249. All in all, these trips are lots of fun, and the coastal scenery they show you is great. They also have a 2-hour waterfall ride for $179 that's even more fun. If you have two people on one ATV, ask for the side-by-side model, unless you want to ride super slow or are interested in bouncing out your spouse.

Also available but less interesting is **Kahua Ranch** (882–7954) that has 1½-hour tours for $105.

Ride the Rim (775–1450) is a great and incredibly misleading name for an ATV company. The impression left by their brochure is that you'll be cruising along the rim of beautiful Waipi'o Valley. I guess it's easier to market than *Buy the Farm*, which is what you're *really* doing—buying a dirt road tour of a eucalyptus tree farm with only *two* views of Waipi'o Valley, if the clouds are cooperating, and one small, pretty falls and pool. Nearly all of the 15-mile

circuit is among the skinny trees as you scoot along at 16–18 MPH for about two hours. Nice folks and all, but there are *way* better things you can do with your $159 per person.

BIKING

With a moniker like the Big Island, you would expect an endless variety of biking choices. Sure enough, many of the highways, such as Queen K where they run the Ironman, have nice bike lanes so you can cruise long distances. But be prepared for strong crosswinds in Kohala. If it's **mountain biking** that you prefer, and you are willing to transport a mountain bike somewhere, these three rides can be fun:

South Point—See map on page 79 and the description of the area. You can ride from South Point past Green Sand Beach on the 4WD roads—lots of fun. The wind is usually with you coming back. This is wide-open country with good mountain bike roads.

Volcano—There's a dirt "escape" road that leads through beautiful rain forest from Thurston Lava Tube to Chain of Craters Road and the Mauna Ulu Trailhead. (See maps on pages 92 and 197.) The 4-mile road is well maintained and very scenic, with green assaulting your eyes from both directions. Return on the escape road, or take Chain of Craters road back up (right) 1½ miles, then take Hilina Pali Road as far down as you want to go before returning.

Mana Road—This road leads through Parker Ranch in Waimea and winds around Mauna Kea to near Saddle Road. It starts near the 55 mile marker on the main highway in Waimea. See maps on pages 124 and 135, and back foldout map to get an idea of the route. It's a 44-mile dirt road to Mauna Kea Road near Saddle Road. Unless you are motivated and arrange for transportation from Saddle Road, you'll probably just want to take it as far as you like, then turn around and come back. The first 18 miles are relatively easy and pass through *fairly* flat, sometimes foggy, quiet plains of grass and cows. Past 18 miles, it gets hillier and bumpier and enters a beautiful forest reserve. Be sure to close any gates you pass (all 4 of them) that are already closed. Cleverly worded or placed signs sometimes *imply* that you may not traverse the road. Actually, it's a public right of way. At 10⁴⁄₁₀ miles is a fork—take the right one.

If you are staying in Kona and want to ride on the street, cruise down Alii Drive along the coast. If you're staying in Hilo, Stainback Highway (described on page 111) is a great road to sail down on a mountain bike. You could then take North Kulani to Hwy 11 where the shoulders coming back to Hilo are usually wide.

Guided Tours

Several companies offer a variety of guided tours. **Orchid Isle Bicycling** (327–0087) has tours for $125–$145, plus some week-long trips including lodging for up to $3,000. And **Bike Volcano** (934–9199) does tours of Volcanoes National Park for $130. Their advertising photos—showing Pu'u 'O'o from the air and surface flows of fountaining lava—are a bit over the top for a *bike* tour.

A boogie boarder rides his first...and last wave of the day.

Bike Shops

In Kona, the best bike shop we know is **Bike Works** (326–2453), visible from the highway, off Kaiwi Street. Excellent selection of bikes and bike accessories. Full suspension mountain bikes (the best you'll find on the island) rent for $60 per day; front suspensions are $40. (Prices drop if you rent for longer.) **Hawaiian Pedals** (329–2294) rents cruisers for $20. In Kohala, **Bike Works Beach and Sports** (886–5000) in the Queen's MarketPlace has Specialized road bikes for $30–$60, depending on the type and duration of rental. **Mountain Road Cycles** (885–7943) is in Waimea on Hwy 19 near Kamamalu. Mountain and street bikes are $20–$50 per day. If you're a serious biker and want to bring your own from home, **Hilo Bike Hub** (961–4452) will receive and assemble it, then pack it back up for you for about $80. Adjustments are extra as are cartons.

BOAT TOURS

See OCEAN TOURS on page 211.

Boogie boarding (riders are derisively referred to as *spongers* by surfers) is where you ride a wave on what is essentially a sawed-off surfboard. It can be a real blast. You need short, stubby fins to catch bigger waves (which break in deeper water), but small waves can be snared by simply standing in shallow water and lurching forward as the wave is breaking. If you've never done it before, stay away from big waves; they can drill you. Surf is usually highest in winter months. Smooth-bottom boards work best. Men who don't do this often should—*this is important*—wear shirts, otherwise you can rub your *da kines* raw. (Women will already have their *da kines* covered, except at Kehena Beach.)

The section on BEACHES describes whether a beach is good for boogie boarding. Our favorite is **Hapuna** in Kohala. Conditions are usually excellent. We also like Mauna Kea, Manini'owali/Kua Bay and White Sands Beach. You won't have any trouble finding places to rent boards, so we won't bother mentioning them individually. Just keep an eye out for signs. Expect to pay $5–$8 per day, $15–$20 per week. You can buy them at Costco, Walmart, etc. for $40+.

There's a drive-up campground at the **Kilauea Volcano** called **Namakani Paio**, just outside the park entrance at 4,000 feet. (See map on page 92.) They have 10 simple cabins for $55 each. Each has a couple of beds, community showers (good thing it's not the other way around) and a BBQ. 967–7321 for reservations, though they were closed at press time for renovations. Tents are also permitted for free, and there's almost always plenty of space. No reservations. There's a campsite (pit toilet only) in the park called **Kulanaokuaiki** on Hilina Pali Road.

Also in the park are several campsites that require long hikes. (Halape is awesome.) Contact the park directly at 985–6017 to see which ones are open. You can pick up your permits when you get there, and there's usually not a problem getting them.

Off Saddle Road at a chilly 6,500 feet, cabins are available in **Mauna Kea State Park**. Call 974–6200 for reservations.

Campsites—County Sites in Black, State Sites in Red, National Park Sites in Yellow

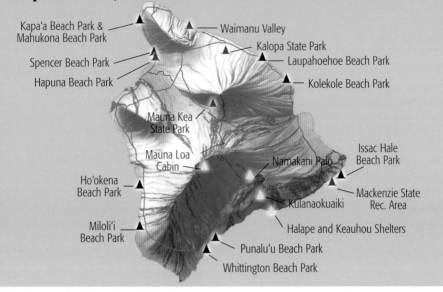

Kapa'a Beach Park & Mahukona Beach Park

Spencer Beach Park

Hapuna Beach Park

Mauna Kea State Park

Mauna Loa Cabin

Ho'okena Beach Park

Miloli'i Beach Park

Waimanu Valley

Kalopa State Park

Laupahoehoe Beach Park

Kolekole Beach Park

Issac Hale Beach Park

Namakani Paio

Mackenzie State Rec. Area

Kulanaokuaiki

Halape and Keauhou Shelters

Punalu'u Beach Park

Whittington Beach Park

They're $80 per night for up to six people, and have two bedrooms (no linens/towels), range, refrigerator, toilet but no cookware or running water. Some are heated. They close them for long periods during droughts. Available weekends only.

Kalopa Native Forest State Park has decent cabins for $90 and covered campsites for tents. The limited hiking is good, and the park is in beautiful shape.

Many of the beach parks around the island are available for camping with a county permit. Ho'okena (page 169) stands out. They are shown on the map on this page. Hapuna has A-frame cabins available from the state, but they're pretty bleak and $50 per night. There were other sites at press time that were too disgusting to recommend, so we left them off the map. Tent camping at state parks is $18 per family per night. Some beach parks, such as Punalu'u and Miloli'i, might not be as peaceful as you'd like. **MacKenzie** in Puna can be nice.

Waimanu Valley is utterly remote and stunningly beautiful. It'll take most of a day to go down into Waipi'o Valley, up the trail on the cliff, then down into Waimanu.

See ADVENTURES on page 239. For other **state campsites**, call Division of Forestry and Wildlife at 974–4221 or State Parks (974–6200). For **county campsites**, call Parks and Recreation at 961–8311.

OK, so technically we should have put this under *spelunking*, but we had a sneaking suspicion that it might get overlooked there.

The Big Island is the land of lava tubes. The other islands had them, too, but most collapsed over time. Lava tubes are a characteristic of young, growing islands. And they don't get any younger than the Big Island.

In the ADVENTURES chapter and HIKING section we've identified some lava tubes that you can hike through *on your own*. If that prospect seems too much trouble or too risky for you, there are guided lava tube hikes that you may want to consider. They are in the southern or eastern part of the island since it's the most geologically active. We list them in order of our preference. Contemplate bringing your own bright light since the one provided might not be that great.

Kazumura Cave Tours (967–7208) takes you along part of Kazumura Cave near Glenwood, the longest lava tube known in the world. The guide's knowledge of geology is the best of the bunch, and he reminds us of our favorite teacher from high school. The walking is pretty easy (with a few ladders), and you'll learn a lot. $10 per person. Their 4-hour tour—more physical with some rock scrambling—is $20 and well worth it. Closed Sundays. You have to wear long pants and closed shoes, or you'll be turned away by the guide's mother.

Kula Kai Caverns (929–9725) in Ka'u is a different experience. They have a short 30-minute tour for $15, which we *don't* recommend. That portion of the cave is lighted but lacks the punch of the longer tour. For $95, they take you to a harder-to-reach portion where you get to walk in the footsteps of the ancients. In days of old, living in Ka'u was hard, and finding freshwater was even harder. Hawaiians used to place hollowed-out gourds to catch water from the dripping ceilings, and some of their remains, including burned out torches, gourds and spent kukui nuts (for lamp oil) are still evident. There is nothing else like this in Hawai'i, and the owners are serious cavers who have a passion for conservation. They have other tours for different prices.

Volcano Cave Adventures (960–5664) has an unusual cave from a Mauna Loa flow in Glenwood. Though their geology knowledge is poor, the tube is a bit more interesting. It's unusual in that there's lots of mud and some water flowing through it. The footing is much more awkward here (and the lights are weak, too), but it's fun and they're friendly, if a bit unorganized. $25 per person—2-person minimum. Available when the owner isn't too busy. Try to call him after 5 p.m.

Our last choice would be **Kilauea Caverns of Fire** (217–2363). It's 10 miles south of Hilo. Their stretch of lava tube is less interesting than the others, and their command of the geology is highly suspect. It's $29 for the 1-hour tour.

If you had to pick the one sport Kona is most famous for, it would probably be its big game fishing. The waters off the Kona coast drop to great depths quickly and are teeming with big game fish. When there's a strike, the adrenaline level of everyone on board shoots through the roof. Most talked about are the marlin *(very hard fighters known for multiple runs),* including blue, stripers and the occasional black. These goliaths can tip the scales at over 1,000 pounds. (Virtually all marlin above 300 pounds are female.) Also in abundance are ono, also called wahoo (one of the fastest fish in the ocean and indescribably delicious—they strike very hard but tire quicker), mahimahi (vigorous fighters—excellent on light tackle), ahi (delicious yellowfin tuna) and spear-fish. With calm sunny conditions 300 days per year, quick access to the fishing areas, and strong competition among over 100 fishing companies, Kona has become a magnet for first-timers wishing to try their hand at catching the big one.

A Few Things You Should Know

Fish are plentiful year-round but more numerous in the summer, a bit less so in the winter.

The largest blue marlin ever caught in the state was a hull-popping 1,805 lbs.

Most boats leave out of Honokohau Harbor, just north of Kona. A surprising number of the thousand pounders (granders) have been caught just outside the harbor. This is probably because the harbor is flushed every day by freshwater springs, making the water clean and clear. This natural flushing expels the contents of the harbor on a daily basis. Perhaps passing fish like to hang around the harbor entrance to scoop up the results of that day's fish cleaning.

Most boats troll nonstop. Licenses aren't required. You will probably have to bring your own food and beverages.

Most boats here don't target a particular fish—they just troll for whatever they can get.

Most passengers on Kona fishing boats are novices, so don't feel self-conscious if you have no idea what you are doing. Deck hands will handle all of the arrangements; just sit back and relax.

You will either go on a shared charter (with other folks) or do a private charter. Nearly all charter boats are licensed for six people. Since boats range from 26–60 feet, how big a boat you charter will determine how roomy you feel. The fewer people on your boat, the greater the chance that *you* will be the one reeling in the fish since you share the lines with fewer people.

There are half-day (morning or afternoon) charters available, full-day, and overnighters. If this is your first time, do a half day to see if boat travel agrees with you. Mornings offer best conditions. Shared charters are getting harder to find.

Sea Wife II has them for $95. Camelot has them for $110, and they distinguish themselves by promising that you can keep part of the catch if you like. You can do a private half-day charter for $420–$650. Full-day private charters go for $600–$1,000 or more for the big boats. *Usually,* the bigger the boat, the higher the price. Individual boat rates can change often depending on the season, fishing conditions and whims of the owners. Consequently, we'll forgo listing individual boat rates since this information is so perishable and instead list a few companies that we recommend. Call them directly to get current rates.

If you're easy-queasy, take an anti-seasickness medication. There are people who never get sick regardless of conditions, and those who turn green just watching *Deadliest Catch* on the DVR. Nothing can ruin an ocean outing quicker than being hunched over the stern feeding the fish. Scopolamine patches prescribed by doctors can have side effects, including (occasionally) blurred vision that can last a week. Dramamine or Bonine taken the night before and the morning of a trip also seems to work well for many, though some drowsiness may occur. Ginger is a mild preventative. Try powdered ginger, ginger pills or even *real* ginger ale—can't hurt, right?

Tipping: 10–15% split between the captain and deck hand is customary if you are pleased with their performance. If the captain is a jerk and the deck hand throws up on you, you're not obligated to give 'em diddly.

You should know in advance that in Hawai'i, the fish belongs to the boat. What happens to the fish is entirely up to the captain, and they usually keep it. You may catch a 1,000-pound marlin and be told that you can't have as much as a steak from it. If this bothers you, you're out of luck. If the ono or another small fish are striking a lot and there is a glut of them, you might be allowed to keep it—or half of it. You *may* be able to make arrangements in advance to the contrary, but I doubt it.

If you want to catch and release, or tag and release, make sure in advance that your boat will accommodate you. Most will, but some don't. If you do, use lures—live bait usually results in the fish coughing up its stomach, which kills it.

You might want to go down to the fuel dock at Honokohau Harbor around 11 a.m. or 3:30 p.m. for fish weigh-ins to see what's being caught and by whom. The boats hoist flags on their way back, each one representing a different species of fish caught on that trip.

If you fish from Kawaihae, expect ono and mahimahi rather than bigger stuff.

Whether you catch fish or not, it's great being out on the Kona Coast.

Popular boats can get booked up in advance. Making arrangements before you arrive can maximize your chances of getting a good boat.

Captains and deckhands come and go. Below are some boats that we've had good experiences with or that have good reputations as of press time. If you have a contrary experience with any one of them or have an experience with any company that you'd like to share with us, please contact us at the address listed on page 4 so we can stay on top of these boats. The number after each name is the boat length.

For the big stuff, try:

Camelot (34').....................936–9515
Foxy Lady (46')..................960–3009
Ihu Nui (35').......................325–1513
Sea Genie II (39') 325–5355
Sea Strike (31')..................895–1972
Sea Wife II (38') 329–1806

For light tackle, try:

Reel Action (25').................325–6811

To cut through the maze of companies, a reputable charter service company can be invaluable. Unfortunately, these come and go with amazing rapidity. **Charter Services Hawai'i** at 334–1881 has helpful personnel who gave the facts without the nonsense.

As a rule, we are always leery of activity booths—some are helpful and knowledgeable, but some are scoundrels. However, at Honokohau Harbor, you might want to call 329–5735. They are right at the harbor, they have *lots* of boats to choose from and usually have the skinny on what's going on there.

Kona's famous **International Billfish Tournament** is held each year in August. Fishermen from all over the world come to compete for top prize. As a result, boats tend to fill up faster during this time.

Shoreline Fishing

The entire shoreline is available to you. If you want, you can find a secluded spot off any ugly-looking lava road on the island. Otherwise, on Hilo side, Hilo Bay, especially near the mouth of the Wailuku River, is good. South Point is excellent. In Kailua-Kona, the seawall in front of Hulihe'e Palace is a great place and easy to access. As snorkelers, we've seen schools numbering in the many thousands congregate off this area.

Yama's Specialty Shop (326–2934) is located in Kona. They are your best source for supplies.

And remember: Never say, "I'm going fishing." Say, "I am going to the woods." Hawaiian legend holds that the fish will hear and avoid you if you warn them.

Course	Par	Yards	Fees
Hamakua Country Club (X2)	66	4,920	$15
Hapuna Golf Course	72	6,029	$135*
Hilo Municipal Golf Course	71	6,006	$29–$34
Hualalai Golf Club	72	6,032	$250
Kona Country Club Mauka	72	5,976	$150*
Kona Country Club Ocean	72	6,281	$165*
Makalei Country Club	72	6,161	$85*
Mauna Kea	72	6,358	$250*
Mauna Lani North	72	6,057	$260*
Mauna Lani South	72	6,025	$260*
Naniloa Golf Club (X2)	70	5,615	$30*
SeaMountain at Punalu'u	72	6,045	$25*
Volcano Golf & Country Club	72	6,190	$53*
Waikoloa Beach	70	5,958	$165*
Waikoloa Kings'	72	6,010	$165*
Waikoloa Village	72	6,230	$80*
Waimea Country Club	72	6,195	$55*

*Indicates golf cart included in price. Yards are from the men's regular tees.

GOLFING

The Big Island is rapidly becoming known as *the* island to visit if you want to golf till you drop. This actually presented a problem for us in evaluating the individual courses. It would have been easy to froth at the mouth over most of them because compared to courses elsewhere, most are outstanding. But that would have missed the point. So with elevated expectations in mind, we have reviewed the courses *relative to each other*. This is important because if we get less than excited about a particular course, it doesn't mean it's a dump. It just means that you can do better elsewhere on the island.

Prices at the top courses are higher than many are used to. If you stay at a resort near the course, you'll probably be eligible for much cheaper rates.

A Few Tips

Wind is often a factor at Kohala courses and is usually stronger in the afternoon. Sunshine is *almost* guaranteed in Kohala. Conditions are usually best in the mornings at all courses around the island.

Greens tend to break to the ocean, even when they look uphill.

Kona has a driving range **Swing Zone** (329–6909) near Old Kona Airport.

If you're looking to master this game (yeah, good luck with *that*), there's a good golf academy called **Darrin Gee's Spirit of Golf** (887–6800).

Some courses offer big discounts after noon or 3 p.m. Check with individual courses for these or other discounts.

We also list kama'aina rates here. These are fees that Hawai'i residents pay. Though less, bear in mind that there are often restrictions on playing times.

Mauna Kea Golf Course (882–5400)

According to local lore, in the early 1960s, Laurence Rockefeller flew Robert Trent Jones, Sr., to an isolated, barren, mostly unknown place on the Big Island called Kohala. He took him out to an 'a'a lava field, pointed to the rock and asked, "Can you build me a golf course out of that?" Jones supposedly knelt down, picked up two pieces of 'a'a and ground them together. They crumbled. He then said, "Mr. Rockefeller—you've got yourself a golf course."

Opened in 1964, Mauna Kea is still the course by which all others are compared. Fairly open and forgiving rolling terrain, this course epitomizes what a Big Island course can be. The layout is brilliant, the location is dazzling, and the course is just plain fun. Number 3 is a signature hole that hugs the shoreline—a very difficult hole. The view from the black Ts alone is worth the risk of losing your ball. Number 9 shoots downhill toward the hotel. Hole 11, a par three, drops precipitously downhill—consider yourself lucky if you par. Hole 17 is 538 beautiful curving yards. If you were on island visiting us, this might be the course we'd take you to. (Of course, we'd probably make *you* pay.) The rolling scenery and the time-tested play seem ageless.

Located at the Mauna Kea Resort just south of Kawaihae—the turnoff is near the 68 mile marker on Highway 19. Fees are $250 for standard, $225 for resort guests. Carts are included; walking is allowed (but still discouraged) only in the afternoon.

Hapuna Golf Course (880–3000)

This is the other course at the Mauna Kea/Hapuna Prince resort complex. Designed by Arnold Palmer and Ed Seay and opened in 1992, it features narrower fairways, so bring more balls than you would at Mauna Kea. The course is well marked, well organized and well kept. Don't expect to be overwhelmed with hazards, however. The narrowness is your challenge. The course is ensconced in an older lava field filled with scrub, rather than the starker, yet more attractive newer lava fields, such as the Mauna Lani's South Course.

Hapuna is a very pleasant and well-run course, though not overly remarkable. (Services, however, are excellent.) Standard fees are $135, resort guests pay $95, and the kama'aina rate is $60. Carts are included and mandatory.

Mauna Lani Resort (885–6655)

Called the Francis H. I'i Brown South Course and the North Course, these two courses are the result of the 1991 splitting of the 1980 course. North and South each got nine and added nine. They have some days where they allow people to play "the old course," meaning the best 9 from both courses. Call to find out if they're doing it during your visit, because it's fantastic. Of the two current courses, the **South Course** is by far the most popular. It is closer to the ocean and is nicely incorporated into the stark lava. Fingers of 'a'a seem to reach out and grab your ball, so the accuracy-challenged will want to bring more than usual. 'A'a is a notorious ball eater and shoe wrecker. The course is well maintained, and some of the holes are highly memorable. Number 13 is quintessential Hawai'i. Driving toward and along the ocean, make sure you drive *your cart* on the left side for incomparable ocean views. Look back toward hole 7 and Honoka'ope Beach—a stunning hole by anyone's definition. At 15 you can count yourself among the elite if you can make par. It shoots over a respectable ocean cove onto greens guarded by cleverly placed traps. Par 3...we'll see.

Whereas the South Course is more open and expansive, the less used **North Course** has more trees and a more "traditional" use of lava boundaries. There are several lava tubes sprinkled about, and the kiawe trees often define the fairway. (Remember to be careful of their penetrating thorns when looking for an errant ball.) Make sure you hit solid on number 4—the scrub-filled lava gorge is laden with muffed drives. Number 17 is a short 119 yards from the tournament tees, but the narrow channel and well-placed traps call for lots of concentration.

Mauna Lani courses are the best-maintained courses on the island. If you can only play one, make it the South. Otherwise, you'll find that playing both will offer very different and enjoyable games. Our biggest gripe is that both courses are poorly marked, and the free map is not very accurate. Standard fees for South & North courses at $260. Resort guests pay $170. Kama'aina rate is $105. Discounted during certain times. Between the 73 & 74 mile markers on Highway 19 in Kohala. See map on page 53. Carts are included.

Waikoloa Resort

You have your choice of the **Waikoloa Kings'** or the **Waikoloa Beach**.

Waikoloa Kings' (886–7888) is probably our second favorite Kohala course. This links-style course is the tougher of the two. Features include deep bunkers, clever use of lava terrain and confiscatory lava boundaries. You stand little chance of retrieving your ball in this 'a'a from hell. They made good use of lava balls (you'll know them when you see them). Golf balls seem magnetically attracted to them.

Hole 5 is deceiving. There are two enormous lava balls nestled in a sand trap larger than many Kohala beaches. The cup is 327 yards away, and if there is a wind at your back and you are in a hard-driving mood, you might make it over the lava—or you might want to chicken out and use two strokes to get over them... anything to avoid being *behind* them. From most of the course on a clear day, you can see five volcanoes—Kohala, Mauna Kea, Hualalai, Mauna Loa and Haleakala on Maui. Palms and plumeria are scattered about among the trees. Though challenging, this is a course to be savored.

Waikoloa Beach (886–6060) gets far more golfers than Kings'. That's probably because it is in a location that affords more visibility and because it is closer to the ocean. Kings' is not seen from as many hotel rooms. Waikoloa Beach is a par 70, and its resort style layout is a bit more forgiving. It has less personality than the Kings' but is a fine course nonetheless. Check out the petroglyphs on your left on your way to number 9.

Both courses are well groomed and surprisingly well watered, sometimes to the point of being soggy (as evidenced by the number of golden plovers during the winter months). These two courses can get more crowded than other Kohala courses because they actively seek local players. Standard fees are $165, resort guests pay $135, kama'aina rate is $75. Near 76 mile marker in Kohala. See map on page 53.

Hualalai Golf Club (325–8480)

Opened in 1996, this course is private, meaning that only those staying at the Four Seasons Resort or at the adjacent residential community (including

*Over the water and onto the green.
Mauna Kea's hole #3 is vintage Hawaiian golf.*

Kona Village) can play. This Jack Nicklaus course is more player-friendly than most of his designs. There's a constant 5% grade toward the ocean, so there's lots of ocean views from the lushly manicured fairways. Very fast greens and a bit less wind than most Kohala resorts. Rates are $250.

Waikoloa Village (883–9621)

Up mauka of the Kohala resort area, three words come to mind here—cheaper, windy and walking. At $80 for standard rates, it's cheaper than the big boys in Kohala. (And I'll tell you right now that you are better off at Waimea Country Club if the weather is cooperating.) This course is popular with locals for the $45 Big Island kama'aina fares (cheaper with specials). As for the wind, you may see a bird on this course lay the same egg three times. Play *early* if you want to avoid the wind. Lastly, you can walk the course if you so choose, unlike most Kohala courses.

There are more trees here than many other courses. Some like to compare it to a very good municipal course, which sounds fair. It is adequately maintained (though poorly marked—you may even get lost on occasion). Overall, you get what you pay for here. Look for lots of wild goats and turkeys here.

Waimea Country Club (885–8777)

One of the most underrated courses on the island. You may think you are in Scotland rather than Hawai'i. You are a long way from and above the ocean. *Wide* open fairways, plush, well-watered grass, fog and mist often, and a delicious rolling terrain. These, along with a visitor rate of $55, make it one of the better golf bargains you'll find. The caveat is the weather—it rains a lot here, so call and ask if it looks like it will be *pumping* that day. Or better yet, just play early. A windbreak of eucalyptus trees surrounds the course. Geese, pheasant and quail all grace the course's water hazards. Number nine is as picture-perfect as you will find. A graceful curving fairway rambles down, around and up to the green.

If you're scared off by the fees the big boys charge elsewhere, this is a nice alternative—weather permitting. The course is located between the 51 and 52 mile markers on Highway 19 in Waimea.

Makalei Country Club (325–6625)

This is one of the lesser-known Big Island courses. Located 2,100–2,900 feet upslope, it's cooler and less windy up here than at the Kohala courses. There are beautiful views down the coast, and bougainvilleas dot the cart paths. The course is carved nicely into the forest. Wailing peacocks are scattered about, as well as pheasant and turkeys. Number 4 has a low rock wall to act as a speed bump for low shots. Hole 10 wanders 580 yards with impressive views of the coastline below. Makalei is a fun course. You won't get pounding Pacific surf, but you will get a moderately challenging course that's well maintained and easy to recommend. Designed by Dick Nugent. (Any relation to Ted?) $85 for standard fees, kama'aina is $45. Seven miles north of Kona on Hwy 190. Carts are included and mandatory.

Kona Country Club (322–2595)

The four sets of nine here were built over a period of 25 years, and their personalities are all different. Courses are split into the **Ocean Course** and the **Mauka Course**.

The **Ocean** has some fine ocean and upslope views. Number 12 is a signature hole that skirts the ocean, with enough palm trees to remind you of why you came to Hawai'i. At 13, look for the blowhole near the handicap tees. Note the fantastic corkscrew-shaped palm tree near the white tees at 14. The 124-yard number 17 shoots over a lava gorge— one of the few lava hazards. There is a flock of wild parrots at this course, so keep an eye (or ear) out for them.

The **Mauka** is more modern, making use of, rather than denying, the natural lava in this area. Number 14 drops 62 feet, over a water hazard and onto the green, with smashing views down the coastline. In fact, holes 14–18 all sport nice coastline views.

Someone must have gotten scared by a lawyer here once. There are more warning signs at these courses than any we've seen. Since this is the only course in Kailua-Kona, expect more people here. There are plenty of signs to prod you and keep it moving. *(If you are at this hole, you better have done it in 45 minutes.)* The fairways for both courses could use a little TLC. Greens seem fine. All in all, the course is only fair. If you pay the full standard price, you paid way too much. But check for specials—they often have one or two. Standard fees are $165 for the Ocean, $150 for the Mauka. Carts are included and mandatory.

SeaMountain—Punalu'u (928–6222)

The layout and promise were excellent here, but the course appears to be a victim of the fortunes (or lack thereof) of the developer. As a result, it's getting pretty mangy in spots, and we haven't seen much evidence that the current owners are keen to make it a grand course. The lack of water as well as lack of maintenance create a fairly sad golf experience. But the price is cheap, and you won't have to fight the crowds. Located near Punalu'u Beach on the southeast side of the island, 56 miles from Hilo and 65 miles from Kona. Fees are $25 for everyone. Carts are included.

Volcano Golf & Country Club (967–7331)

Who would ever think that you could have a lush course just 1 mile from the main crater of the most active volcano on earth? Bring your warmies—the 4,000-foot altitude brings a chill to the air. The play is straightforward with few hazards. Mother Nature and the groundskeepers keep the grass green and healthy. Unlike other courses, the afternoons here *may* be better in the summer. Mist and fog sometimes make it interesting, but wind is usually low. Remember to club down since the ball travels farther up here. This is a nice course offering a moderate challenge and a peaceful setting. Standard fees are $53, kama'ainas are $28 weekdays and $31 weekends.

Naniloa Golf Club (935–3000)

Much of the infrastructure is run down and dilapidated, but the course, aided by the fertile Hilo climate, is in fairly nice shape. This is a nine-hole course, but at least it's lightly used. Overall, forgettable. Standard fees are $15 to do the nine holes twice. Carts are $15 per 18 holes.

Hilo Municipal (959–7711)

Fairly flat layout and no sand traps (too much rain) are the hallmarks of this course. The play is not overly hard and the setting is quite pretty. It gets soggy after a heavy rain, so consider this beforehand. This course is usually pretty crowded and about half the players walk, so weekends should be avoided for the delays. Standard fees are $29–$34. Kama'aina rate is $12–$15. Carts extra.

Hamakua Country Club (775–7244)

Built as a community course in the formerly sugar-rich area of Hamakua, this *small* 9-hole course is popular with locals who come to play and talk story in the "clubhouse." Greens fees are $15. (You're on the honor system—just drop your money in the box in the clubhouse and grab a hand-drawn scorecard.) The holes are very close together and amazingly well tended. The community takes

Not all golf courses are created equal. Some, such as SeaMountain, aren't exactly worth the long drive to get there.

This ain't no sightseeing tour. You'll actually be flying this powered hang glider.

obvious pride in caring for it. You won't find a lot of challenges (and you won't find club rentals or power carts), but you will find a gentle course set in a gentle, friendly community.

From the main highway (19) east of Waimea, turn just before (west of) the gas station between the 42 and 43 mile markers on Opuhe Road, and take the frontage road 100 yards to the "clubhouse."

Unlike most activities that I can review *anonymously*, powered hang gliders (known as trikes) are aircraft that I fly myself, and I'm familiar with pilots of these aircraft since we're all members of the small flying community. So this is one of those rare cases when it's not possible for me to review the company without them knowing who I am.

Don't confuse this with hang gliding. This craft has an engine, it's bigger and more stable, and some even have a powered parachute attached to the craft... just in case (a safety feature that only a handful of traditional airplanes have). Trikes take off and land on regular runways, and the ease and grace of the craft are glorious. (Rent the movie *Fly Away Home* if you want to see what they're like.) It's as close to flying like a bird as any form of flight I know. Although I also fly traditional aircraft between the islands, I came to love trikes for the pure joy of flying, and in my opinion, they are the safest form of microlight flight available. (I'm not a daredevil and wouldn't fly them myself if I felt unsafe in them, though any time you're in the air, you're potentially at risk, even on the airlines.)

Advanced Recreation (775–9393) gives lessons in a powered hang glider. Pilot Jeff Hoff is an accomplished pilot who has been flying for many years, both microlights and fixed-wing airplanes. It's $125 for a 30-minute instruction flight in the back seat. After that it's $175 per hour. You can cruise along the lightly populated shoreline heading north, or opt for a longer flight where you'll see the dramatic Hamakua Coast.

HELICOPTERS

If you've been on a helicopter or airplane flight on another island, especially Kaua'i, you've been treated to wall-to-wall, tongue-wagging sights. The Big Island, however, has lots of fantastic areas spread about with less interesting areas connecting them. The northeast side is a lush wonderland, the southeast side is where the active volcano is, and the west side is dominated by lava. That's why limited tours are so different on each side of the island.

Here, more than most islands, your tour is affected by the passion (or lack thereof) of the pilot. A boring pilot will sound something like this: "On your left is such and such valley, and on your right is such and such hill, and in front is the such and such lava flow." *So what?!* What you really want is a knowledgeable pilot with a command of the island who also knows to speak only when it improves the silence. We're biased toward companies that let you ask the pilot

questions through a microphone, as opposed to those where the pilots tells you "everything you need to know."

Years ago helicopters were allowed to skim the ground. Now, air tour operators are restricted to flying 500 feet or higher over unpopulated areas. That doesn't mean that you won't walk off the aircraft with drool running down your shirt from the mesmerizing experience. It can still happen; you just aren't *assured* of it. When the music, helicopter, pilot and sights all come together, it'll still blow you away. We've flown with pilots who have an undisguised passion for the island and those who may as well be driving a flying bus. Unfortunately, most companies don't use the same pilots all the time, so it's sometimes hard to steer you toward the good ones.

In general, we recommend that helicopter tours be taken from Hilo. Tours that leave from Kona bound for the volcano spend too much time over less interesting areas, and you'll pay through the nose. The exception is Blue Hawaiian's trip from Waikoloa to the Hamakua coast (described below).

A-Star helicopters are the most popular. They hold six passengers, with four in back and two beside the pilot up front. The middle seats in the back are so-so; the others are good. Think of the A-Star as a pleasant tour bus. One company is also using **Eco-Stars**, a much larger, quieter and cushier cousin to the A-Star.

Company	Phone #	Departure	Helicopter Type	2-Way*
Blue Hawaiian	961-5600	Waikoloa, Hilo	A-Star, Eco-Star	Yes
Tropical Helicopters	961-6810	Hilo, Kona	Bell Jet, Hughes	Yes
Sunshine	882-1223	Hapuna, Hilo	A-Star	No
Safari Helicopters	969-1259	Hilo	A-Star	Yes
Mauna Loa Helicopters	334-0234	Kona	Robinson R22, R44	Yes

Companies toward the top are recommended higher than the ones toward the bottom.
✱ Indicates whether craft has a microphone for you to talk to the pilot.

Air tours give you a perspective on the volcano that you can't get any other way.

Hughes, Eco-Stars and A-Stars. We're luke-warm on Bell Jets.

Afternoon tours are sometimes bumpier. I can tell you that as a pilot myself, I do most of my flying on the Big Island in the morning when conditions are usually best. You may want to also.

If you want to get around the altitude restrictions, think about *chartering* the aircraft. It's worth considering if you have a group, or if you strike up a friendship with other travelers. It might not cost any more than a regular tour, and *you* get to call the shots. (Leave the doors off if you want on the Hughes.) Make sure you rent one that has two-way communication with the pilot.

The Companies

Blue Hawaiian (961–5600) uses nice A-Stars and Eco-Stars out of Waikoloa, near the Kohala resort area, and out of Hilo. They use the expensive Bose Acoustic Noise-Canceling headphones and have DVDs of your trip for an extra $25. (Pretty poor quality, though.) The two-hour volcano and Hamakua Coast tour, which lands in Hilo, is $531 and uses roomy **Eco-Stars**. (It's $107 cheaper on their A-Star.) They also have a Waikoloa to Hamakua Coast trip for $277. No volcano, just lots of beautiful valleys you won't see on a volcano flight. Overall, the most tightly-run outfit of the

Windows are larger, so you'll have better views, and it's noticeably roomier inside. The downside is the price. Since these birds are so expensive, you may pay a hefty premium of around 20% more for the comfort. **Hughes 500Ds** have two passengers in the somewhat cramped back and two *outstanding* front seats next to the pilot. This copter feels like a sports car, and the side views from the back are excellent. Windows come off if you want. They are less popular because they are less profitable for the operators. Some companies, like Tropical, have them but use them more often for non-tour business. **Bell Jet Rangers** are less comfortable with three in back and one passenger up front. The back middle seat is a poor seat indeed. We like the bunch. Their online discounts can be pretty decent.

Tropical Helicopters (961–6810) is our second choice. (They also go by the name **Paradise Helicopters**.) They use a Hughes from Hilo. They have a 35-minute quickie trip to the volcano from Hilo for $152, as well as a more comprehensive (and really fun) volcano experience from Hilo *with no doors* for $203. Less recommended trips from Kona in their Bell are also available.

Sunshine (882–1223) uses A-Stars, but it's hard to justify their prices—$200–$260 for their 35- to 45-minute volcano trip from Hilo, $455–$530 for the trip from Kohala at the Hapuna Heliport. If you can't get a deep discount, head elsewhere.

Safari (969–1259) leaves from Hilo. We've always been a bit lukewarm toward their product and still are. Their prices seem unjustifiably steep. Their 55-minute A-Star volcano tour is $249; the 40-minute is $194. Online rates, however, can be dramatically cheaper.

Mauna Loa Helicopters is a little different. *You* fly the beast. It's a 2-person chopper and they give lessons, or you can charter it *relatively* cheap.

Airplanes

Because of its size and relative flatness, the Big Island makes airplane tours an acceptable alternative. Some, like Big Island Air, use large tour planes. The volcano experience is certainly diminished from a plane (since you rush by things), but if you insist on leaving from Kona, the price is tempting.

Iolani Air Tour (329–0018) uses small (four- and six-person) airplanes out of Kona and Hilo for aerial sightseeing. Flights are cheaper and shorter from Hilo ($160 for 45–50 minutes) than Kona (2½ hours for $275). The more expensive Kona flight is round-the-island, so you'll get to see the awesome valleys of the Hamakua Coast. Overall, a good company.

Big Island Air (329–4868) flies large (nine-passenger) planes from Kona on

Hamakua Coast by air is the only way you'll be able to see its waterfalls.

round-the-island tours (well...*mostly* around) for $330. They do a pretty good job, the routes are interesting, and the pilot does his narrating well. As with Iolani, it's bumpy at times, so consider motion sickness medicine. (Morning is definitely best.)

Renting an Airplane

Iolani Air Tour rents 150s and 172s for $119–$139 per hour wet plus $55 for the hour-long instructor check ride.

The Big Island has plenty of hiking to keep you happy. You can wander through a lush rain forest, walk on a volcano crater floor, puff up a frigid, snow-covered mountain, hike along an empty tropical beach, teeter on the edge of steep canyons, or saunter along an old Hawaiian lava trail. The possibilities and diversity are incredible.

Footwear—We do much of our hiking here in hiking sandals or light trail shoes. For really muddy conditions we occasionally use boots lined with Gore-Tex. And for stream hiking, nothing beats tabis. These look like green fuzzy mittens for your feet and stick to wet, mossy rocks better than any other kind of footwear. (Though without much stiffness, tabis may leave the bottoms of your feet feeling a bit sore.) You'll find tabis for about $25 at Walmart in Kona, Walmart or Longs in Hilo, KTA in Waimea.

If you're looking for the topographic maps of the island (it takes 74 to cover the island!), **Basically Books** (961–0144) in Hilo or **Hawai'i Forest & Trail** (331–8505) in Honokohau (on the high-

way north of Kona behind Chevron) are your best bets.

We hike a lot and have become big fans of hiking sticks. We'll use two on some long hikes and find that they greatly ease the hikes and give us better balance. They have saved us several times from falling on nasty lava. Some have straps on the handles and are telescopic.

Lastly, it's nice to be able to visually see *where* you are on a trail and know you're going in the right direction. But many of the trails on the island do not show up on a typical GPS or Google maps. *Well,* it just so happens that we GPSed every trail on the island, and they are in our iPhone app available on iTunes.

KILAUEA VOLCANO HIKES

Much of the best hiking on the island is found in and around Hawai'i Volcanoes National Park. In VOLCANO SIGHTS we've described lots of strolls of 30 minutes or less. They include **Bird Park** (a nice 30-minute walk through the forest), **Devastation Trail** (see how the volcano wiped out part of a forest with flying, frothed lava and how it is coming back), **Pu'u Loa Petroglyph Trail** (less than 2 miles round trip, it heads to a massive field of ancient rock carvings—this one takes a bit more than 30 minutes), **Thurston Lava Tube** (see what lava sees as it travels underground) and a few others. We've also described a trip to a pristine **Rain Forest Lava Tube** and a trek to the edge of the smoldering **Mauna Ulu Crater** in ADVENTURES.

Kilauea Iki

This is a great hike! If you are only able to do one hike while you are on the Big Island, this is one we'd recommend. It goes from ancient rain forest to a

First through lush rain forest, then across the eerie crater floor, the Kilauea Iki hike is smashing!

newly lava-paved crater and back through rain forest. At a little over 3 miles, it can take anywhere from two hours if you hoof it without distractions, to four hours if you stop and gawk as much as we do and enjoy lunch on the crater floor. It is a *reasonably* easy hike (well...maybe moderate) with only about 15 minutes of gentle but constant incline toward the end when you ascend about 450 feet. Before hiking, read some background on this crater and its attention-grabbing past in VOLCANO SIGHTS.

We like to start this hike at the Kilauea Iki Overlook and go counterclockwise, through the forest first. The trip is gentler this way and is preferable to going into the crater first. (You could also start from the Visitor Center and get there via the Earthquake Trail and Byron Ledge Trail—see page 197.) You will go through a gorgeous and ancient fern and 'ohi'a forest as the trail skirts the edge of Kilauea Iki Crater. Take your time here, and enjoy the beauty and grace of the forest and birds. All along are short spur

trails offering magnificent views of the crater. Judging size and distance is surprisingly difficult here until you see people walking on the crater floor. The abrupt contrast between the ancient fern forest and the newly created maw of the crater floor couldn't be greater. Though the forest is lush and cool, the 4,000-foot altitude seems to prevent mosquito problems here (though it's always a good idea to bring a repellent, just in case). Before the trail veers away from the crater for a bit, take a look across at Pu'u Pua'i and you will appreciate the scale of the eruptive event. Just keep to the left whenever you encounter a trail intersection. The descent into the crater is somewhat steep, but there are steps carved into the trail in spots and a few railings to help ease the way.

In a heartbeat you go from lush forest to barren lava. The trail bears to your left for a bit, then goes right. Cairns (piles of rock) mark the path across the floor. The lava here is more jagged since it contains remnants of lava spatters rather

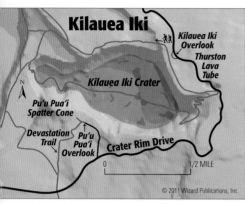

Kilauea Iki

Kilauea Iki Overlook

Thurston Lava Tube

Kilauea Iki Crater

Pu'u Pua'i Spatter Cone

Devastation Trail

Pu'u Pua'i Overlook

Crater Rim Drive

0   1/2 MILE

© 2011 Wizard Publications, Inc.

than the smooth lava farther ahead. Keep an eye out for a small sign pointing to the actual vent, where lava fragments are accumulating. Where you see steam escape from cracks, you will notice minerals leaching from the rock. The steam seems inoffensive compared to the nasty stuff that comes out of parts of Halema'uma'u. We like to have lunch near a steam vent about ⅓ of the way across the crater floor.

The crater floor is quiet and peaceful. You may be hot, cold, wet or dry here, depending on the weather. (Gee, *that's* a useful piece of insight.) Sounds bounce around the crater in an unpredictable way. You may hear the crunching of footsteps when no one is nearby. Plants and trees are already starting to make themselves at home in cracks on the lava floor. It's amazing to stand in this near-dead crater and to see and hear the profusion of life all around you just beyond this hostile field of Pele's destruction.

After you ascend the crater wall, keep to your left along the edge of the crater, and you are back at the overlook. Outstanding!

Napau Crater Trail

Another nice hike is the Napau Crater Trail to **Pu'u Huluhulu**. The trail (occasionally called the Mauna Ulu Trail) is the only place in the park where you can see Pu'u 'O'o, the heart of the current eruption. (There is an easier view of Pu'u 'O'o outside the park—see page 121.) This is a *long* day hike if you do the whole thing. Mauna Ulu (meaning growing mountain) erupted between 1969 and 1974, adding more than 200 acres of new land to Hawai'i's coastline, and its effects are dramatically seen on this trail. It was Kilauea's second longest flank eruption in recorded history. This trail starts on an old segment of Chain of Craters Road. (Twelve miles of this road were buried by the Mauna Ulu flow, and we've shown it on the map on the inside back cover as a stippled line.) This fairly easy trek wanders over the young Mauna Ulu flow, as well as through old forest. You'll notice stone sentries along the way, strangely shaped columns of rock. These are called **lava trees**. When lava from the Mauna Ulu flow coursed its way through here, it occasionally encountered exceptionally wet trees. These resisted the flow and the temperatures long enough for the lava to harden around the tree. When the lava level lowered, these piles remained. You will often see a circle in the middle of lava trees, the outline of the now-dead tree. Sometimes, there are half-circle outlines of the tree. These are on the upstream side of the lava, showing you which way the lava flowed.

At about 30 minutes, you come to Pu'u Huluhulu (shaggy hill), a heavily forested mound. There is a five-minute spur trail leading up to the top. From there you get an awesome view of Mauna Ulu, a third of a mile in front of you. You may see Pu'u 'O'o smoldering off in the distance (quite a bit to the left of Mauna Ulu, partially obscured by the

Kane Nui o Hamo Lava Shield—see map). Be sure to look down into the pristine, fern-filled rain forest below you in the crater. It's utterly untouched, looking much like it did a thousand years ago. Unfortunately, during our last visit, the park had let the vegetation grow, blocking your view of the crater floor. Looking off in the distance, you can see how the Mauna Ulu flow cut into the heart of the forest, going from green to black in a single footstep.

The view of Mauna Ulu is gorgeous. Looking over at it, you might be tempted to walk over to the top and peer into **Mauna Ulu Crater**. If so, check your insurance and see ADVENTURES.

Most people turn around from here. Past this point the trail footing gets more difficult and goes to the massive Makaopuhi Crater, then to Napau Crater, where camping is allowed. (Technically, you need a permit to go that far.) That's 6⅔ miles one way. Just before Napau, you will pass the remains of an old pulu factory. Pulu is the soft, down-like fuzz that covers the stems of some ferns. Someone thought it would make a great stuffing for pillows and mattresses, so they built a factory out here. Unfortunately, pulu turns to dust after a few years. Consequently, so did their business.

Another 2 miles past Napau is **Pu'u 'O'o**, and this is the best part of the trail.

The menacing volcano looms ahead of you the whole way, reminding you why you've started this 17-mile round trip hike. The trail goes nearly to the base of the active volcano, and if the trade winds are blowing in your face, you may have to contend with volcanic fumes for the last part of the trail. This is probably why this last 2 miles was closed at press time—to keep you and your lungs safe.

On the way back, you might choose to detour south onto the Naulu Trail. Parts of the trail are along the old road, so you go from lava to road segments spared from an eruption, eventually through a beautiful forest before the trail encounters Chain of Craters Road. (You'd have to hitch a ride 6 miles back up to your car.)

Earthquake Trail/Byron Ledge

There is a cluster of trails around and below Volcano House. One of our favorite combinations is described below. It sounds more complicated than it is—use the map on page 92. All told, it takes 90–120 minutes and is moderately difficult (if that). You descend, then ascend about 400 feet. This is a good hike to take on a clear day because the views of the crater can be spectacular.

From the Visitor Center, you can walk around the right side of Volcano House, eventually heading to your left as you pass in front of Volcano House. Parts of

Napau Crater Trail

Escape Rd

Pauahi Crater

Pu'u Huluhulu

Kane Nui o Hamo Lava Shield

Trail to Pu'u 'O'o closed past here.

Pu'u 'O'o Vent

Pu'u 'O'o Lava Flow

3

Chain of Craters Road

4

Trail

Mauna Ulu Lava Flow 1969–1974

Mauna Ulu
The trail to Makaopuhi Crater generally follows the old Chain of Craters Road, which was covered by this flow.

Campsite

Old Pulu Factory

Makaopuhi Crater

Napau Crater

N

0   1 MILE

© 2011 Wizard Publications, Inc.

Forests ruled by ferns and 'ohi'a trees make volcano hiking a time of wonder and magic.

the old trail and Crater Rim Road *fell into the crater* after an earthquake in 1983. This part of the road has become part of the Crater Rim Trail. It is eerie to see the road split in half, with guard-rails dangling into nothingness. Large, gaping chasms in the old road dispel any notions you may have that ground is inherently stable. Parts of the trail detour from the old road for safety reasons, but it is fascinating to try to safely glimpse as much of the crumbling road as you can, even if through the bushes at times. The best part shows the guard-rail and split road. Watch for this part as it's off the main trail. When the road forks, you'll usually take the right fork whenever you can. See map. The trail will eventually leave the road and descend through 'ohi'a forest. You'll turn right onto Kilauea Iki Trail, then right onto Byron Ledge Trail and continue to the Kilauea Crater floor. (The map and trail intersection signs make it much clearer.) On the crater floor, you'll get an idea of the texture of a skimmed-over lava lake. You are only on the crater floor for a few minutes before you head back up. It's not overly steep. On the way back up, you will pass the remains of a landslide. Look up from the big rock. You are at eye level and can almost feel the slide coming at you.

At the intersection with the **Sandalwood ('Iliahi) Trail**, you have the choice of continuing up to the right (which is a little steeper) or taking the Sandalwood Trail. We recommend the latter. It straddles the crater for a while, featuring great views and several steam vents. Then take the Sulphur Banks Trail back to the Visitor Center.

You might want to add the **Kilauea Iki Trail** to this hike. You can access it early on from the Byron Ledge Trail. See map and description of Kilauea Iki earlier.

Rain Forest Lava Tube

In the summer of 1993 park personnel discovered a beautiful, pristine lava tube in the rain forest. Even the ancient Hawaiians apparently never discovered it. Similar to Thurston Lava Tube but with far grander details, it is accessible via a fairly easy one-hour (each way) hike through lush forest. This cave is long and loaded with lava stalactites and other treasures, making it an unparalleled hiking experience. The park wishes to control access, and they have asked us not give directions for fear that some thoughtless jerk might read it and damage some of the delicate features. Consequently, they have *guided* tours of 12 or so people. (Hikes were every Wednesday at press time and the best time to call (808) 985–6017 is at 7:45 a.m. the Wednesday a week *prior* to when you want to hike.) Ask for the *Wild Lava Tube* (or Pua Po'o) guided hike; it'll knock your socks off. Note that people *physically* at the visitor center at that time sometimes fill the slots before they even answer the phone.

They will provide helmet lights. Be prepared to scramble on or around large boulders on the floor that have fallen from the roof over the years. The ceiling is usually 20 feet tall, but severe claustrophobics need not apply. Take your time and expect to spend about an hour to go from one end of the cave to the other.

Also in the Park

Consider the **Crater Rim Trail**. It circles the entire Kilauea Caldera and makes for a long day. But segments such as the one between Volcano House and the Jagger Museum are dramatic. The part from the Escape Road to Chain of Craters Road passes through an exquisite fern canopy.

From the end of Chain of Craters Road, there may or may not be a trail to an **active lava flow**. See ADVENTURES for more on that.

There are long overnight trails (with camping) at **Halape**, **Keauhou** and **Ka'aha**. (Halape is *incredible*.) Hikes are down the mountain or along the coast and go for many miles. Contact the Park Service at 985–6000 for more information.

Mauna Loa Summit

Getting to the top of Mauna Loa is tough, no matter which way you slice it. It's 13,677 feet high, and there are no roads to the summit. You can do it the hard way or the *very* hard way—it's your choice. The first is a 3- to 5-day hike from the Kilauea side up the Mauna Loa Trail. The trail starts at the end of the Mauna Loa Scenic Road. This hike has been known to humble even the most conditioned athlete. Though the gradient rarely exceeds 12°, it's 38 miles round trip through lava with mediocre footing, constant exposure to the sun and wind, and you gain 6,500 feet. Red Hill Cabin is 7½ miles into the hike at 10,035 feet, and Mauna Loa Summit Cabin is near the crater rim at 13,250 feet—another 11½ miles. This trail is in Hawai'i Volcanoes National Park, and you need a permit from them to camp.

There's no cooking gear at the cabin and no trash cans anywhere on the trail, so pack it out.

The other way up is a *tough* 13-mile round-trip day hike from the **Mauna Loa Weather Observatory** off Saddle Road. (See page 145 for directions.) You start at 11,000 feet, so you won't have a chance to get acclimated—count on altitude sickness from starting so high. (Savvy hikers often car-camp at the weather observatory the night before to acclimate.) This trail is steeper than the Mauna Loa Trail and over rougher terrain, but you can do it in a day if you're into punishment, and the views across the saddle will be superb. Make sure you get an early start.

It's always cold up there, and snow can come at any time of the year without warning. Altitude sickness is common, even among the fittest. For either of these hikes, thorough preparation is the key. Just because you are in the tropics doesn't mean you can take this mountain lightly. The *base* may be in the tropics, but the *summit* is in Alaska. And make note: The park can tell you if there's water at the cabins, but don't you dare *rely* on it. We've hiked to the top dreaming of (and *counting* on) water at Mauna Loa Summit Cabin, only to turn tail and hoof it back down after finding nothing but dry tanks and utter disappointment up there.

KOHALA AREA HIKES
Puako/Malama Petroglyph Trail

Located near the Mauna Lani Resort area in Kohala, this 10- to 15-minute-long trail (each way) through a kiawe forest has a few petroglyphs sprinkled along the way. (Kiawe thorns are evil, wicked and hateful; be careful not to let them penetrate your shoe.) The real payoff is at the end (just past a dirt road intersection) with hundreds and hundreds of lava carvings adjacent to each other in this field in the middle of nowhere. The reasons for the Hawaiians' selection of this site has been lost to the ages. Perhaps the most obvious reason is that the slabs in this area make nice canvases. Regardless, some Hawaiians say that if you close your eyes and listen to the breeze, you can hear the sound of rock scraping against rock.

Kiholo Bay

This is a fabulous place. You can catch a nice glimpse of the bay from the scenic turnout near the 82 mile marker on Highway 19. (See map on page 202.) Between the 82 and 83 mile markers a smooth gravel road leads almost to the shore. (The last short patch is rough, and some 2WD drivers may want to park the car and walk to the water.) From there you could walk 300 yards to the right along the shoreline to Queen's Bath. (See below.)

There's also a trail from the main highway just south of the 81 mile marker. If you take the latter trail, park at the north end of the guard-rail and take the trail toward the ocean. The trail from the highway to Kiholo Bay takes 15–20 minutes. When the trail becomes a gravel road, it will eventually curve to the left. (At that intersection there's a gate to your right, but it's private. The public access is a bit farther along the road. The map makes this clearer.)

Kiholo Bay is a beautiful and uniquely shaped ocean inlet. It has several points of interest that make it great for exploring. First, the lagoon offers waters that are usually dead calm (but cold and fairly cloudy due to freshwater springs leaking into the bay, kicking up fine silt). Turtles

Kiholo Bay is a fabulous place to wander around.

abound here, grazing on limu in the bay. The fishponds inland, called Wainanali'i Pond, are on private property. Turtles swim through the manmade channel to the fishponds at night, perhaps to sleep unmolested. Walking around this part of the bay offers magnificent scenery. You can usually look right into the lagoon water and see the fish.

This whole area was once a gigantic freshwater/brackish fishpond, built by Kamehameha the Great in 1810 after another fishpond (where the airport is now) was destroyed by lava from the 1801 Hualalai flow. Enormous stone walls up to 6 feet tall and 20 feet wide were laboriously erected, creating a deep pool 2 miles in circumference where all manner of deep sea fish were stocked. It was said that half the population worked to complete it, and it was considered one of the "artificial wonders of Hawai'i" at the time. The lagoon now composing the farthest reaches of Kiholo Bay was once part of that pond, and the water-worn stones were part of the wall. The Mauna Loa lava flow of 1859 traveled *30 miles* to fill in most of the pond and breach the southern wall, creating the lagoon. Freshwater, which initially fed the pond, still intrudes into the bay from springs. Since the water in the back part of the bay is usually as calm as a swimming pool, the snorkeling there, though the visibility is poor, can be surreal. If nobody has been there to disturb the water (except for the ubiquitous turtles), the swimmer or snorkeler might encounter what appears to be a pane of glass suspended horizontally in the water about a foot down. That's the lighter freshwater floating on top of the heavier seawater. Left undisturbed, the dividing line between the two can be straight, razor thin and very visible. If you swim slowly with your hand extended vertically in the middle of the joining of these two layers, the top of your hand will be cold (from the freshwater) and the bottom will be warm (from the seawater).

Walking along the gravel shoreline from the bay heading southwest, you pass several houses. One is called the **Bali House**. It was built by the guy you see on TV who runs Paul Mitchell hair care products. He paid 200 Balinese workers $1.50 a day for two years to create the intricate carvings and assemble the house. All was then disassembled and shipped to Kiholo Bay, where American and Balinese workers reassembled it. To the shock of many, they used large green logs from the *Borneo rain forest,* which shrank and split in less-humid Hawai'i, and much effort went into responding to the shrinking structure. While being built, the owner was amazingly gracious about letting people tour the house, so many on the island have gotten to see the inside. The Bali House is about midway between the row of houses on the beach, and you *will* know it when you see it.

Continuing south, you'll pass a big yellow house with security cameras, tennis courts and guards. (It was built by the guy who invented the pacemaker.) About 300 yards southwest of the house, only 80 feet from the ocean *and on state land* is a delight known as **Queen's Bath** (Keanalele Waterhole). It's just off the mauka (mountain) side of the gravel road and easy to miss. There you are, spitting distance from the ocean, in a fabulous crystal clear, spring-fed lava tube bath, open to the sky in two spots. (See photo on page 32.) It is attached to a dry lava tube cave, shown on the map. (By the way, the dry part of the lava tube has numerous petroglyphs carved into it and can be fascinating to visit, if you are careful and keep your eyes peeled.) Though filled with freshwater, its level rises and falls each day with the tides. (It goes back farther than it looks—a waterproof flashlight can make exploring it fun.) You can't help but think it doesn't get much better than this. Once you've refreshed yourself in the exquisitely cool water, you can make your way back to your car. (Our thermometer says it's 71°, but it sure *feels* colder.) By the way, if you have a lot of suntan lotion on, please consider rinsing in the ocean first, perhaps in the bay, to avoid leaving an oil slick in the bath.

There occasionally may be some yellowjackets flying around the area. Try not to make them mad.

Luahinewai

If you had a vast sea of blackened lava and found a beautiful, coconut tree-lined pond just 200 feet from a secluded black sand and gravel cove 1,000 feet long, what would you do? If you said build a

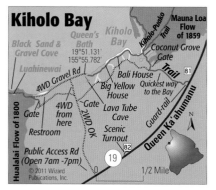

mansion, you're out of luck. Somebody beat you to it. But hey, you can still hike to it. And although the owners of this enviously located estate comically watch over what they imply is their private pond (using a high-powered camera lens, no less), you'll still get a peek at the pond and possibly have this long cove to yourself. (By the way, we seem to recall a former governor being quoted that the public has access to the pond, called Luahinewai, but we don't know if that's true.)

Anyway, the short hike of about 20–25 minutes each way is worth it. It's along the lava coastline and is pretty. Take the road toward Kiholo Bay mentioned on page 200 and toward the end take the left fork and park near the Porta-Potties. That round house you see is the old, unoccupied Loretta Lynn home. Pick up the trail to the left and follow it toward your goal, marked by lots of coconut trees.

The Golden Pools of Ke-awa-iki

How about a hike that leads to a deserted beach with white sand on one end and black sand on the other? A trail that leads over harsh 'a'a, along the beach, past a jewel-like freshwater pool and back to your car in 4 miles. We've taken friends on this hike, and they love it. It displays the raw nature of the Kohala coast, has a variety of sights you'll never forget and rewards you with a cool dip if you get warm. (See photo on page 55.)

Slightly north of the 79 mile marker on Queen K (Hwy 19) there are boulders blocking a road on the fresh (150-year-old) lava leading to the sea. (See close-up map on page 157.) Take the road-turned-trail toward the ocean and go around the right side of the fence.

The beach was created when lava from the 1859 Mauna Loa eruption flowed 30 miles, landing at the north end of the beach. The black sand created hasn't had a chance to mix with the previous white beach sand at the southern end, resulting in a nice blend from black to white along the stretch. Just past the south end there are tide-pools to explore if you have water shoes.

Continuing north (right) you'll come to Pueo Bay. Large amounts of freshwater enter this tiny bay from underground, creating some strange snorkeling conditions. From Pueo Bay you can either take the trail toward the highway (to the right of a very large lava rock) to the pools, or take the other trail to Weliweli Point and link up with another trail. Look for the latter to Weliweli marked with pieces of coral. (The map makes these trails easier to visualize.) The pools (there are two of them) can be seen from far away because they are marked by hala trees. (The ends of their branches look like palm tree-inspired pompoms.) Once at the pools, take a moment to savor the scene. Here in the middle of all this raw harshness is a magnificent oasis—freshwater (no hint of seawater at all) lined with golden-coated lava. (The gold comes from a growth on the rocks and makes the ponds too fragile to swim in.) If you want a quick, cool dip, walk just beyond the golden pools to the pool under the hala trees. It's sand- and gravel-lined and makes a good place to cool off your legs before taking the trail back to your car.

Pu'u Wa'awa'a

About 100,000 years ago, an explosion under Hualalai Volcano created the largest cinder cone on the island—Pu'u Wa'awa'a. Meaning "many-furrowed hill," it is known by locals as the "Jello Mold." Big hill—gotta climb it, right? Luckily there's a trail to the top, but the cone is bigger than it looks, and you can easily be humbled by the steep grade. The 3²/₁₀ mile trail ascends 1,800 feet from your car to the summit and will literally take your breath away. Equally breathtaking is the view from atop the pu'u. On a clear day, expect to see Hualalai, Mauna Loa, Mauna Kea, Kohala and possibly Haleakala on Maui. Your best chance for clear skies is early in the morning, and a picnic lunch up top can be spectacular if the weather cooperates.

The road to the trailhead is ⁶/₁₀ mile past the 22 mile marker on Hwy 190. (See map on page 45.) A white pipe fence funnels you to a gate that's unlocked 6 a.m.–6 p.m., Mon.–Fri. This is an active cattle ranch, so be sure to close the gate behind you and watch where you step. Go left at the fork and park at the hunter check-in station. There's a box here for hikers with a sign-in sheet and pamphlets describing the hike. You have two options. Walk the road all the way up or detour on the 'Ohi'a Trail adding a nature lesson and ⁴/₁₀ miles. While not very inspiring, it's a bit more scenic and less steep than the pavement. You'll go left when it reaches a gravel road called Miki's Road. After a long climb, you come out of the forest at the base of Pu'u Wa'awa'a.

Continue on the road until it reaches a rusty gate. Take the grassy path to the right. It will meander along the side of the hill, passing through a pedestrian gate, until it reaches the backside. Horses are often grazing around here, and you'll walk through a century-old corral. The grassy road curls into the crater and up the steepest climb yet to the rim. If you use the Porta-Potty, you should know that we've seen it knocked over from the wind, so get 'er done quick.

Follow the grassy road to the left on the rim. This takes you to the highest point and offers a commanding view of the island. The grass is really soft up here, so take a seat and revel in your accomplishment. Hiking back down is hard on the knees. Add the sweat you expended on the way up, and you have a strenuous 7 miles round trip. Give yourself four hours for this hike and start early for best viewing conditions.

KONA AREA HIKE
Arch City Coastline

We usually like to offer you certain distractions that are easy to get to with a pleasant reward, like a beautiful sea arch along a rocky coast. But this place takes the cake with over a dozen arches in a mile of shoreline. The coast is so riddled with holes that you'll also find hissing blowholes, surging cracks and picturesque coves along the way. It's located just north of Honaunau Bay near Pu'uhonua o Honaunau National Historical Park in South Kona.

Just before the entrance to the park is a one-way street that passes by Honaunau Bay. After you pass the people and driveways, you'll see a gravel trail through the brush on your left before the one-way road ends. (You may have to park at the bend at the end.) Take the trail to the shore, turn right and follow the coast.

You won't see arches at first, but there are holes where the ocean surges in and out and some sniffing and snorting cracks in the rock if the surf's up. There is no defined trail on the shore, and the terrain undulates with footing that is never level, making this hike moderately strenuous. Since you're looking down at your feet a lot, stop often to look around. The lava shoreline here has more character than most if you take your time.

For the next mile (it'll seem like more since the going is slow), 20-foot tall cliffs dominate the shoreline. In some places the vegetation gets close to the cliff's edge. Use common sense out here. If rocks are wet, that means waves have splashed or crashed on them recently, and you don't want to be there when it happens again.

After a giant lava mound there's a very picturesque arch, perfect for photographing from the land. (Our shot is of a different arch that was taken from the water.) Five to ten minutes later, look for a black lava rock wall on your right next to a lava road that ascends into the brush. You've seen the archiest part of the coastline. (Yeah, I know that's not a real word—but it fits, doesn't it?) You can walk this road ⅓ mile back to Hwy 160, turn right and head back to the one-way road and your car, or (if you miss it) just go back the way you came. The gravel road climbs up through the Moku'ohai Battlefield where Kamehameha defeated Kiwala'o to become ruler of the Big Island (more about that on page 71). The loop is less than 2¼ miles and should take around 2–3 hours, longer if you follow the shore back. Bring water and take advantage of the easy swimming at Honaunau Bay when you finish.

HILO & PUNA HIKES
Wai'ale Falls

Many people come to Hawai'i looking for an idyllic pool or waterfall to frolic in. Well, here it is, and it's only a 10-minute hike to get there.

Wai'ale Falls itself is a pretty and fairly high volume waterfall. Above the falls lie several beautiful pools and some small falls that can be a delight to play in (if the flow's not too high).

Over a dozen arches in a mile of shoreline make Arch City the most puka-strewn piece of shoreline we've ever found in Hawai'i.

You start on Waianuenue Avenue past Boiling Pots. You'll see the falls (700 feet away) from the bridge that crosses the river. (See map on page 108.) The trailhead is just past the bridge. The trail itself is plagued with mosquitoes, but once at the water we've haven't found them to be a big problem. Bring bug juice just in case. Follow the narrow trail up through the strawberry guava lining the north bank of the Wailuku River. There are several offshoots that allow you to visit the large pool below the falls (if you wish) and some false trails that can be confusing. The trail ends at the *top* of those falls. Remember that spot for your return.

At the top, pools and small falls await. The footing is much less slippery than many other stream banks around the islands, thanks to the consolidated lava here.

INSTRUCTIONS FOR WATERFALL USE: Prance, frolic and have fun. Repeat if necessary.

Stay out of pools that have a fast moving exit. Other pools are farther upstream. And, of course, always be aware that a flash flood can occur anywhere in nature. So if you see a large wall of water coming your way...well, you're already screwed, so what does it matter?

Leleiwi Tide-pool

At the end of Kalanianaole Street in Hilo, past all the beach parks, you'll find a large gravel cul-de-sac near the shore. Beyond this is a unique coastline that hides a gem of a tide-pool. The Leleiwi Tide-pool has a sandy bottom with an easy entry and is perfect for a dip. Plus it has a surreal backdrop of pine trees growing on large tilted slabs of volcanic rock with everything covered in pine needles. Although it's only ¼ mile away from the end of the road, it will take you 20 minutes or more to get there.

What makes this hike different is that if you time it right, you're walking in the

Leleiwi is a calm tide-pool protected from the restless ocean.

water most of the way. (That's good, not bad.) A couple hours before high tide the water is snaking its way inland. Wear water shoes and hike up your shorts when necessary, then embrace the tide. You could mess around trying to stay dry in the jungle, but that misses the point. The tide-pools and the tide itself are the real jewels here.

From the parking area at the end of the road, walk ahead slightly toward the ocean. Almost immediately you'll encounter a tide-caused stream. Get your feet wet and slowly slosh your way along the tide-pool. Take your time—Leleiwi ain't far. The water is usually clean, and you might see disturbances where freshwater is percolating from the ground, mixing with seawater. Try to notice if you can see the tidal changes or the slight currents in the shallow pools.

Once at Leleiwi (look at the photo to orient yourself), you can take a cool dip in the sand-lined pool. Waves crash violently on the outer rocks that protect the pool, but inside, the waters should be perfectly still. You may see local families already swimming here, but the main pool is big enough to share. Bring a lunch and enjoy an afternoon of pristine relaxation here. There's no need to venture past the pools since it's only stark lava shoreline.

Ironically, this serene area, *Leleiwi Point*, refers to an alter on which the bodies of human sacrifices were left on display.

OTHER BEACH HIKES

For other beach hikes, often to secluded spots, check out **Honomalino**, **Makalawena**, **Green Sand**, **'Anaeho-'omalu** (going south to the freshwater pool), and **Road to the Sea** (the second beach), all described under BEACHES.

Also consider the trail between **Spencer Beach Park** and **Hapuna**. It's along the shoreline and is vague only where it crosses the golf course at hole #3.

HIKES DESCRIBED ELSEWHERE

The hike to **Captain Cook Monument** is listed on page 71; the cold hike to **Lake Wai-au** on top of Mauna Kea is shown on map on page 140. The awesome hikes through a *pristine* rain forest to the erupting **Pu'u 'O'o Volcano Vent**, **current lava flows** and a **lava tube** hike are all in ADVENTURES.

HORSEBACK RIDING

If you want to let someone else do the walking, consider horseback riding. The Big Island has quite a tradition when it comes to horses, and we've noticed that, of all the Hawaiian islands, companies here tend to be of a higher caliber. There are lots of companies offering wildly different kinds of rides. It just depends on the type of riding and terrain you want to see.

Most stables provide a small saddle bag and rain gear, require reservations, suggest long pants and closed-toe shoes and need a minimum number of riders before they'll go. Dress in layers, bring a hat, sunscreen and lip balm. Most have 230-pound weight limits.

Na'alapa Stables–Waipi'o (775–0419) has excellent rides in Waipi'o Valley. You can take a 4WD van tour or take a horse-drawn carriage in the valley, but riding through it on horseback is what riding dreams and movies are made of. If you have ever imagined fording a stream on horseback, here's your chance. You take 4WD van to their corral down in the valley. It's muddy and messy, so boots or trashable sneakers are recommended.

The nose-to-tail walking ride follows mostly shaded, single-lane dirt roads that meander along ancient taro fields and streams with some stretches actually going up or downstream for nice lengths of time. Morning or afternoon 2½-hour rides are $85. These same folks have another stable, **Na'alapa Stables–Kahua Ranch**, on the uphill side of Kohala Mountain Rd. where they run a 1½-hour ride for $65 and a 2½–hour for $85. Not as compelling.

Waipi'o on Horseback (775–7291) has a similar Waipi'o tour, but they're hard to book, not very accommodating, and they *won't* take your name if you're a single rider.

Waipi'o Ridge Stables (775–1007) has a different product. Instead of going *into* Waipi'o Valley, they walk part of the upper edge above Hwy 240. (See map on page 132.) Despite the name, most of the trip is through a tree farm, but the views from some of the overlooks are great. $85 for 2½ hours. Longer rides also available that go to the top of Hi'ilawe Falls. Eight to ten people max. It's nose-to-tail, no running. Guides are good. Morning trips have less chance of clouding over (ruining your views).

Paniolo Adventures (889–5354) has nice quality, well cared-for horses and gear. Their 2½-hour trips are $96 and take you across a wide-open working ranch featuring beautiful views. This is not one of those nose-to-tail rides. You go across open country, and you can canter if you like. (That means to go faster than a trot, for all you city slickers.) The guides aren't patronizing; they genuinely seem to want you to experience the peace of the Hawaiian countryside. Rides have be-

tween 2 and 14 people and aren't at all gimmicky. This is a working ranch, and if it's calving season, you might get to see a calf being born. They also have 3-hour picnic rides for $124. Lunch is included in the price. Thick dusters and the like are available for free, but it's a good idea to bring a sweatshirt and long pants. Located ²/₁₀ mile north of the 13 mile mark on Hwy 250 in Kohala. Easy to recommend.

Dahana Ranch (885–0057) has 1½-hour tours of their 2,500-acre ranch off the Old Mamalahoa Highway (ask for directions) in southern Waimea for $70. You see lush, rolling pastures from open country, not from a trail. Bring warm clothes; it's sometimes misty or rainy in this part of Waimea. (You might want to call them for a weather check.) They also have a range station ride for $135. This is not the kind where you sit there while they do all the work. For at least 2½ hours, your group will do all the hard work from horseback while they bark out orders, and you'll probably have a great time doing it. Four people are necessary for this. (Call them to see if any others have signed up.) Dahana Ranch has a 300-pound weight limit, and kids over 3 are welcome (except on the round-up ride). Well run by good folks.

Lastly, **Cowboys of Hawai'i** (885–5006) operates out of Parker Ranch in Waimea. The good news is they'll let you run your horse a bit if you're so inclined. The bad news is you simply putz around a boring field next to the Kamuela-Kohala Airport for two hours. Hard to get happy over this one for $79.

Mule-Drawn Wagons

You can tour Waipi'o Valley for an hour with **Waipi'o Valley Wagon Tours** (775–9518) for $55. This carriage tour works pretty well for us.

Call them Jet Skis, Wave Runners (which are brand names) or personal watercraft—whatever your name for them, these motorcycles of the sea can be rented in Kona. **Aloha Jet Ski** (329–2754) has fairly powerful 1,200cc jet skis. They seem to get most of their business from the cruise ships, and customer service improves when ships *aren't* in port. Early morning is usually very smooth, late afternoon choppy. Late morning seems a good balance to give the water some texture. It's $70 for a half hour on their small track, about the size of a Home Depot. Morning usually offers smoother waters. The half hour will tucker out most people, especially if you're like me and you drive it like it's stolen. Experiment with different ways to hold your feet while you sit. Extra riders are allowed for $14, but we recommend one person per craft. *Do* spring for the goggle rentals; your eyes will be grateful. Doubling up seems to increase the risk of the passenger falling off, from what we observed. Some people seem to feel that these craft are hazardous to the ocean; others say modern jet skis are no different than regular boats. We honestly don't know which is the case; we're just saying what it's like to rent one. They leave from Kailua Pier.

On the Big Island, kayaking is mostly an ocean affair. Although other islands, such as Kaua'i, have rivers to kayak, the Big Island lacks navigable rivers. But there are several areas on the normally calm Kona coast where ocean kayaking is excellent. Our favorite is across Kealakekua Bay to the Captain Cook Monument. (See page 69 for complete description of the bay.) The 1-mile (each way) trip often features fairly calm waters, spinner dolphins and outrageous snorkeling at the monument. This is a *great* trip! Other kayak trips are from Kailua Pier to the north or south, or from Kohala beaches such as 'Anaeho-'omalu. Old Kona Airport or Honokohau Harbor to Makalawena is a long, pleasant voyage. (See BEACHES for descriptions and locations of landings.) The area south of Keauhou Bay has numerous cavities (called "sea caves" by the more optimistic companies) that can be fun to paddle by.

Remember that the ocean, even in Kona, can be treacherous and unforgiving, especially during periods of high surf. We don't want to rain on anybody's parade, but if you don't give the ocean the respect it deserves, it can humble you quickly. Only paddle when it's calm, and always be wary near the shore where a rogue wave can beach (or rock) you.

Renting a Kayak

If you're looking for a kayak near Kealakekua Bay, the most convenient is **Ehu and Kai** (328–8775). It's a super short drive from their place to the water, and they're friendly and knowledgeable. $45 for a single, $60 for a double. They also have guided trips in an outrigger canoe if you're a family looking to stay together.

Aloha Kayak Co. (322–2868) up in Honalo just past the intersection of Hwys 19 and 180 has good gear. $35 for singles, $60 for doubles.

Kona Boys Kayaks (328–1234) prices are a bit too high. It's $47 for a single, $67 for a double. Past the 113 mile marker on Hwy 11.

Kahalu'u Bay Surf and Sea (322–4338) has $40 singles and $50 doubles across from Kahalu'u Beach Park on Alii Drive.

There's also a concession to the right of the pier in Kona that rents kayaks by the (expensive) hour for use in that area. Kohala companies rent them by the minute (OK, OK...by the hour). Among them are **Ocean Sports** (886–6666), which rents them at 'Anaeho'omalu Beach. You'll have to cash in your IRA for the Kohala rentals.

Getting a kayak to Kealakekua Bay means strapping one to your car roof on foam pads and getting it into the water. (It's illegal for vendors to rent kayaks at the bay itself.) At Kealakekua Bay, put in on the left side of the cement landing before Napo'opo'o Beach Park. (See map on page 66.) The state now requires a permit to *land* near the Captain Cook Monument. And they've made it *so* easy to get one—you can either drive to their office (974–6200) in Hilo (a convenient *5-hour* round-trip) or download a form and fax or mail it back and wait a week for one of the coveted 10 permits per day. A more practical alternative is to not *land* your kayak. You can always paddle there, slip out of the kayak and snorkel around. You can even come ashore. But you can't bring your kayak ashore without that permit. People often get around this

Watch for spinner dolphins during your kayak trip across Kealakekua Bay.

by tying their kayak from the bowline to an underwater rock *(not coral)*, though this might be against the rules, too.

The reason for the state's rule is that the area around the monument was getting too popular, with people damaging coral and leaving plastic shavings behind while dragging their kayak ashore. So whatever you do, just respect the state's understandable desire not leave any traces of your visit to this remarkable area.

It's virtually impossible to rent a kayak with a **rudder** here. While rudders make it easier to stay on track in any ocean water, their absence is particularly felt in Kohala where winds will tend to annoyingly weathercock you sideways.

Guided Tours

If you want a guided trip and want to land at the Captain Cook Monument for snorkeling, **Hawai'i Pack & Paddle** (328–8911) and **Adventures in Paradise** (800–979–3370) have the proper permits. Expect between $80 and $115 for 4–5 hours of paddling, snorkeling and relaxing at the monument area. Hawai'i Pack & Paddle also offers multi-day kayak/camping trips, as well as food on their Captain Cook Monument tour. They are a tighter outfit, but they're also pricier than Adventures.

Aloha Kayak Co. (322–2868), **Kona Boys Kayaks** (328–1234) and **Ocean Safaris** (326–4699) also do guided tours of other areas around Kona.

In Kohala, **Kohala Kayak** (882–4678) leaves out of Puako Ramp, heading north or south for snorkeling. They have some pretty cool gear, including pedal kayaks, sails and outriggers (to prevent tipping) and they're relatively inexpensive at around $70. (The prices seem to vary for some reason.)

Aspen has its ski slopes, Washington has its monuments, Orlando has Disney World, and the Big Island has the Kona Coast waters. Quite simply, if you visit the Big Island and don't ply the Kona waters, you haven't *really* been to the Big Island.

The waters off the Kona Coast are the finest in all the islands. Calmer, clearer and teeming with fish, Big Island waters make residents of other islands turn *blue* with envy. A popular way to see these waters is on an ocean tour. If you take one of the many tours along the coast, you *may* see turtles. You are *likely* to see dolphins, flying fish off the bow and whales during whale season. You *will* see smiles from fellow passengers.

You're less likely to get **seasick** on Kona's calm waters than anywhere else we can think of. Nonetheless, if you take seasickness medication, do it *before* you leave. (The night before and morning of are best. It's useless to take it once you're on the boat.) Also, avoid any alcohol the night before. No greasy foods before or during the trip. And some think that citrus is a no-no. Ginger is a very good preventative/treatment. Below deck is a bad place to be if you're worried about getting seasick. Without a reference point, you're much more likely to let 'er rip down there. Scopolamine patches work but have side effects, including (occasionally) blurred vision that can last a week. (Been there, done that, on a 10-day California–Hawai'i trip.)

Boats are usually less crowded on weekends since that's when visitors usually arrive and depart the island. And remember, most single-hull power boats are smoothest in the back.

Kealakekua Bay

The Captain Cook Monument in Kealakekua Bay is a favorite destination. Snorkeling near the monument is perhaps the best you will find anywhere in the state. If you've never snorkeled before, this is the place to start. Experienced snorkelers will be dazzled. A large number of spinner dolphins reside in the bay, and you're likely to see them—perhaps even swim with them, if you're *real* lucky. (They are called spinners because they are the only untrained dolphins that routinely leap clear of the water and spin on their longitudinal axis.) Companies sometimes offer morning or afternoon tours. Take the morning; it's calmer and the water is usually clearer.

The Big Boats

Fair Wind II (345–0268) uses a 63-foot power catamaran to bring 100 or so people. They leave from Keauhou Bay, 7½ miles north and stay tied to their mooring for a couple hours of snorkeling, BBQ burgers and general frolicking. People seem to really enjoy this trip and make good use of the short water-slide into the water, the high dive platform and the cash bar. Restrooms, hose to rinse salt off, shade, ♿ accessible. Easy entry and exit from water, SCUBA also available for extra. Continental breakfast on board. It's not as crowded on board as it looks from a distance. Unfortunately, since they troll along the way, the boat travels too far from the coast to see much of the coastal features. The sail is for decoration—you will be motoring at 10 MPH the whole way—but the boat is pretty smooth. This is a good tour, especially for those who are wary about ocean travel. $125 for the 4½-hour morning

tour, $75 or $109 for the 3½-hour afternoon tour. (The extra $34 is when they BBQ during the summer season on the afternoon trip.) Note that sodas are free *only during lunch*; they charge the rest of the time. Also, no dessert after your burgers. Part of the year they also have a sunset cruise.

Hula Kai is from the same company that runs Fair Wind II, and it also leaves from Keauhou Bay. But this power cat smokes along at 25 knots, visits two snorkel spots and travels farther south than Kealakekua. Their usual second spot has a cool sea cave you can swim in, conditions permitting. They market this as a more upscale trip with a bit more personal attention, smaller crowds, no one under 18, and slightly better food. Shade only while moored via umbrellas and, though the seating is more regimented than Fair Wind II, there isn't a bad seat on the boat and they're very comfortable. Cash bar limited to beer and wine. Overall, a very nice 5-hour morning for $155.

Sea Paradise (322–2500) has a 46-foot sailing catamaran that leaves from Keauhou Bay. They attempt to sail on every trip if there's wind. With juices and muffins in the morning, sandwiches and BYOB at lunch a friendly staff and good boat, this is an easy trip to recommend. $99 for this less-crowded alternative to the Fair Winds.

The Small Kine Boats

Sea Quest (329–7238) is totally different. They take 6, 12 or 14 passengers on their rigid-hull inflatables (which is a good design because it absorbs bumps better than a regular rubber raft) to the Captain Cook Monument and beyond to **Honaunau** (Place of Refuge) for snorkeling. It's bumpier than the

Fair Wind II, and there's no shade except in the 14-passenger boat. (But bumpier means more thrilling.) You won't have all that wandering room that you have on the Fair Wind II, and it's snacks instead of a meal. But these guys go near the coastline and do the best job of narrating what you are seeing. Along the way they poke the boat into several "sea caves" along Arch City (see hike on page 204), and show you how they are formed. We like them better than Captain Zodiac below because they snorkel in two spots; and take their time on the way back. (They can afford to because they depart from Keauhou Bay, 10 miles closer to the monument than Captain Zodiac.) $92 for the more recommended 4-hour morning trip, $72 for the 3-hour afternoon trip, which omits Honaunau. And it's $109 if you want 3 snorkel spots (and shade) over 5 hours.

Dolphin Discoveries (322–8000) has a very similar product for similar prices. They do a pretty good job, as well. Their boats have a touch of shade—seems to be more for the captain, really.

Captain Zodiac (329–3199) leaves from Honokohau Harbor. Though the crew does well, they suffer from their location. Honokohau adds 20 miles (round trip) of relatively uninteresting Kona shoreline compared to rafts that leave from Keauhou Bay. Perhaps this is why they only snorkel at one spot. The good news is that one and a half of the four hours is spent at the monument area with snacks and light deli provided. $93 per person. This is an adequate tour, but we recommend Sea Quest or the Fair Wind over Captain Zodiac. They also have a contract with the cruise ships, so on cruise ship days, boats are packed to the max.

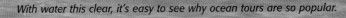

With water this clear, it's easy to see why ocean tours are so popular.

Other Boat Destinations

Body Glove (326–7122) leaves from Kailua Pier and usually cruises to Pawai Bay (which has fairly good snorkeling, but not as good as Kealakekua Bay). They take almost a hour to cruise a mere 2 miles, so it's not like you'll be covered with sea spray. The Kanoa II is a 65–foot catamaran that carries 130 passengers (it's roomy enough with less than 80). They have continental breakfast at boarding and deli lunch at the site. In addition to snorkeling, they have SCUBA (for an extra fee), both for certifieds and beginners. Good boats, crew and location make this a good deal, and we recommend it wholeheartedly when they're not at max capacity. (When they're full, expect lines getting in and out of the water.) Lots of shade, waterslide, restrooms and a full bar on board. Noodles and see–thru boogie boards for the timid. Their 4½-hour morning tour is $120. The afternoon snorkel is just 3 hours for $78. What they do best is their dinner cruise, described on page 281.

Kamanu Charters (329–2021) leaves Honokohau Harbor in their 36-foot *sailing* catamaran and heads 2¼ miles south to Pawai Bay. $90, 24 passengers at most, good snorkeling, sandwiches along with beer and wine provided. Only a little shade for this 3-hour tour (like Gilligan's Island?). Though an acceptable trip, unless you *have* to sail, you're better off on the Body Glove—better boat, longer trip.

Kailua Bay Charter (324–1749) has quickie tours (under an hour) of Kailua Bay with a glass-bottom boat for $30. No food, just a quick jaunt through the water. Leaves from Kailua Pier. Not overly compelling.

In Kohala

Ocean Sports (886–6666) has several boats but generally picks up their customers from the beach at 'Anaeho'omalu Bay in Waikoloa. Morning snorkel trips from their 58-foot catamaran **Sea Smoke** go south to the Ke-awa-iki Beach area. The 3½-hour trip includes fruit and juice in the morning, deli lunch and open bar that includes two local beers on tap. They'll usually sail for half the trip, and overall, the crew does a good job. (Avoid the pricey parking at the Marriott in favor of the free public beach parking.) Usually 30–40 people. $132. They also have a less compelling trip to Crystal Cove 5 mile to the north for the same price, no lunch.

Lava Viewing Tours

If the volcano is cooperating, two companies offer sunrise and sunset tours just offshore of the active lava flows. (Don't go midday; the visuals aren't as compelling.) **Lava Ocean Adventures** (966–4200) and **Lava Roy's** (883–1122) are the main players, though some fishing boats offer this tour at times. We've called them during periods when we *knew* there were *no* shoreline lava flows occurring and they weren't as...specific about our chances of seeing lava as we would like. Try to pin them down.

Lava Ocean Adventures has three boats, but you'll likely be in the 34-foot catamaran (which is more comfortable than Lava Roy's 8-person, rigid hull inflatable). In all, we lean a bit more toward Lava Ocean, though it's $200 vs. $150 for Lava Roy's. Either way, the ride back is usually rough, so ask for a cushion for Lava Ocean's benches. Morning trips (if you can swing the logistics of getting there) are a bit more dramatic since you arrive when the lighting (or lack thereof) is at its best. Getting close to the flowing lava in the dark or dim light is a magical experience, and if you don't want to (or can't) hike out to it, this is a great way to see it.

For **Dinner Cruises**, see ISLAND DINING on page 281. **Submarine**, see page 225.

Parasailing is where you get pulled by a boat while attached to a parachute and a long line. We've done it, and to many people (including us), it *looks* more fun and thrilling than it really is and doesn't seem worth the money. If you have your heart set on it, **UFO Parasail** (325–5836) will drag you around for $65 or $75 using a 600- or 800-foot line. You're up for 7–10 minutes. Tandem rides available.

One tip (*especially* for guys): Don't wear any slippery shorts, or you may cinch forward in your harness creating...the longest 7 minutes of your life.

Whether you're already a certified scuba diver or are interested in trying it out, you've found paradise on the west side of the Big Island. Whereas the east (windward) side of the island has poorer diving due to river runoff and rough waters, the Kona side offers some of the best in the state. There are no permanent streams on the *entire* west side (from the northern tip to the southern tip), so runoff is not a problem. Kona waters are mostly shielded from winds and the ocean's prevailing northeast swell, so calmness is the norm. Fish, coral and divers appreciate the warmer water of the Big Island, the southernmost of all Hawaiian Islands. It's 75° at its coldest in February, 82° at its warmest in October. 100+ foot visibility is common.

You have your choice of boat dives or shore dives. Boats mostly leave from Kailua Pier, Honokohau Harbor and Kawaihae Harbor. Typical dives here are two tanks at two different sites. When we list a price range in the table, it refers to those who have their own gear vs. those who need to rent it.

The island has no decompression chamber. Everyone knows not to fly after a dive, but don't forget that the heights of some of our mountains simulate flying as far as your tissues are concerned. Just the saddle *between* Mauna Loa and Mauna Kea reaches 6,600 feet. And if you decide to drive to Place of Refuge from Kona, you'll reach 1,400 feet—probably too high if you dove deep.

So you'll know our perspective when we review companies, we should tell you what we do and don't like when we go on a dive. On a bad dive, the dive master takes the group on a non-stop excursion that keeps you kicking the whole time. No time to stop and explore the nooks and crannies. Good outfits will give you a briefing, tell you about some of the endemic species here, what to look for and will point out various things on the dives, keeping it moving but not too fast. Bad outfits kick a lot. Good outfits explain the unique qualities of Hawai'i's environment. Bad dive masters may tell you what *they* saw (but *you* missed). Good

Dive Operator	Services Available	Price of 2 Tank Boat	Rent Gear Shore Dive	Camera Rental	Dive Computer	Manta Ray Night Dive	Dive Certification	Rx Masks
Big Island Divers 329-6068	Dive Shop & Boat Dives	$130–$155	$35	No	Included	$100–$130 (1 or 2 tank)	$475–$650	Yes
Hawaiian SCUBA Shack 331-8708	Dive Shop & Boat Dives	$129	$32	No	Included	$129 (2 tank dusk dive)	$325	Yes
Jack's Diving Locker 329-7585	Dive Shop, Boat & Shore Dives	$125–$159	$45	$45–$75	$9 Extra	$145–$179 (Includes 1 dusk dive)	$475–$800	Yes
Kohala Divers 882-7774	Dive Shop & Boat Dives	$129–$159	$45	$45	Included	None	$595	Yes
Kona Honu Divers 324-4668	Dive Shop & Boat Dives	$120–$150	$45	No	Included	$95–$130 (1 or 2 tank dusk dive)	$505–$625	Yes
Neptune Charlies 331-2184	Boat Dives	$119–$134	No	No	None	$99–$119 (1 tank)	$550–$780	Yes
Ocean Sports 886-6666	Boat Dives	$143–$177	No	No	None	None	$666	Yes
Pacific Rim Divers 334-1750	Boat Dives	$119–$140	No	$40	Included	None	$650	Yes
Sandwich Isle 329-9188	Dive Shop & Boat Dives	$120–$140	$45	$30	$5 Extra	$140–$165 (Includes 1 dusk dive)	$550	Yes

companies work around your needs, wishes and desires. Bad companies keep everyone on a short leash. Good dive masters know their stuff and share it with you. Bad dive masters don't know squat but imply they know it all in order to impress you. As divers, we tend to like companies that wander toward the boat for the latter part of the dive and allow you to go up when you are near the end of your tank, as opposed to everyone going up when the heaviest breather has burned up his/ her bottle. We define bad dive shop attitude as what you experience when you walk into a shop (or onto a boat), and the crew does nothing but convey the attitude, *I'm so cool, don't you wish you were as cool as me?*

During times when we feel the diving conditions are bad (poor vis or big swells), we like to call around and ask about conditions. We appreciate the companies who admit it's bad, and we hold it against those who tell us how wonderful conditions are.

The Tops in Kona

There are lots of dive outfits on the island—some good, some bad. Four of them stand apart from the rest. Any of these three would make a good choice. If we had to pick one, it would probably be Pacific Rim Divers.

Pacific Rim Divers (334–1750) is a boat-only, husband/wife team. Their enthusiasm for diving is evident and contagious. Wife Patrice is one of the best we've seen at finding critters, and her knowledge of marine life is excellent. With their warm attitude, comfortable 26-foot boat (though it needs shade) and reasonable price, we're as happy and relaxed as can be at the end of a dive. (Their killer homemade brownies don't hurt, either.)

Big Island Divers (329–6068) is a much improved dive company. We like how they pace the dives (not too fast, not too slow) and how they'll rinse your own gear if you like. We've noticed a certain fondness on their part for deep dives, and they have a pretty good black water dive. There's shade on the boat. They do a good manta dive, and we like how they post on their website how many rays showed the previous night. They use a 28- and a 34-foot boat carrying 8 or 12 divers.

Jack's Diving Locker (329–7585) is a good shop with four boats ranging from a 32-foot tin can to a 46-foot double-decker that holds 18 divers. Good ascent policy, hot shower on most, and dive masters carry slates. They do a lot of work with novices, but experienced divers will also be pleased. They are also careful with the ocean's critters. They're a *big* outfit and have had a few growing pains recently, but overall, they're still a good company.

Others in Kona

Kona Honu Divers (324–4668) has a beautiful 46-foot boat with plenty of shade for up to 18 divers. For less than 12 divers they use the somewhat less impressive 36-footer. The big boat is comfortable and

You could dive Puako every day of your trip and still not see it all.

easy to get around on. Two dive steps into the water and two showers on board. Their guides are professional. Good briefing, pineapple and cookies between dives and a relaxed pace. Our concern, echoed by reader e-mails, is that they let their equipment get a bit long in the tooth between replacement cycles. Get it new, and you'll be happy. Otherwise, maybe not.

Sandwich Isle Divers (329–9188) has an adequate shop, and their boat is a 28-foot Force. Their attitude is good. Six divers max (which is tight). They're patient with introductory dives. Cheap snacks. Sandwich makes you wait more than an hour before they put you on the boat. (Yeah, we *know* they're not supposed to take money at the harbor, but they could tighten it up a bit.)

Manta Ray Dives (325–1687) is the same company as **Neptune Charlies** (331–2184). We've had real mixed results. Sometimes fairly good. Sometimes not. We've had good manta dives with

them. We've also found them at times to be the last ones to arrive and the first ones to leave. But you should feel comforted by the fact that they know it all, have seen it all and done it all. If you don't believe us, just ask them.

Hawaiian Scuba Shack (331–8708) had the farthest to go before we'd recommend them, but they're cheap, and it's inexpensive to rent their gear if you're looking to rent and dive on your own. A certification course is only $325, all inclusive.

In Kohala

The diving in Kohala is often richer in coral than Kona. Lush finger coral gardens are plentiful. It's a bit less protected than Kona and sometimes a little bumpy, especially Dec.–April (though less bumpy than most of the other Hawaiian Islands during those months). There are only a few operators there. Your best bet is **Kohala Divers** (882–7774), which has a 42-foot Radon that leaves from Kawaihae Harbor. **Ocean Sports** (886–6666) is a big outfit that does lots of stuff, so diving isn't an integral part of their DNA. Scuba is from their 40-foot boat, up to 18 divers.

In Hilo

Yes, they *do* dive Hilo side. Though the visibility and calmness are *much* better on the Kona side, life is abundant here and often overlooked. You may see more turtles in some spots here than Kona. There's only one dive shop, **Nautilus Dive Center** (935–6939), which sells and rents gear. They cater mostly to

We took this photo at the Captain Cook Monument with a disposable underwater camera to give you an idea of the quality you should expect. Remember to get close since the lenses are at a pretty wide angle.

locals. In addition, **East Hawai'i Divers** (965–7840) gives guided 2-tank shore dives for $75. Private groups—he promises that you won't see any other divers where he takes you. He dives all over the east side. A good resource.

Manta Ray Night Dive

This dive is *so* good, we put it in the ADVENTURES chapter. If you are a diver or want to be, check out that section and make plans for the dive of a lifetime.

Blackwater Dive

If you're looking for something other than reef, consider this dive. You go out into 7,000 feet of water, and they lower you on a tether to 40 feet—*at night.* Just hang there and see what kind of exotic pelagic life wanders by. Lots of light-emitting bioluminescence, alien-like gelatinous creatures, schools of squid and perhaps even the elusive Hawaiian seahorse. **Jack's** takes small groups for $175 per person (one tank, but it's big) and had a very knowledgeable guide at press time named Matthew. **Big Island Divers** also does this after their manta dive for $220.

If You've Never Dived Before

Several companies will introduce you to SCUBA by giving instructions, then taking you down on a supervised dive. That's how we started, and we were smitten enough to get certified. **Jack's Diving Locker** does good intros. It's $55 for a one-tank shore dive, plus $25 for a pre-dive in their nifty pool with its glass wall. $175 for a two-tank boat intro. If they're full, **Sandwich Isle** is also pretty good with intros; boat dives only.

Dive Sites

Mentioning specific boat dive spots isn't particularly helpful because different companies sometimes use different names for the same spots, and you will usually go where the boat goes. As far as *shore* dive spots are concerned, here are some beauties you may want to check out on the Kona side. For Hilo side, see Nautilus Dive Center.

Crystal Cove—Also used as a boat dive area, it is in Kohala, north of Kawaihae Harbor, off the main highway. About 140 yards south of the 5 mile marker, there's a blocked road from the middle of the middle guard-rail. It's a 4-minute walk on the lava road to your entry point on the right side of the cove, if the surf's not up. (Entry is not too difficult, but it's not a breeze either.) Coral garden is thick and lush, fish are abundant. Depths are mostly less than 40 feet. If there's no boat here, you'll have it all to yourself.

Puako—Virtually every dive shop and book tells you to go to the end of the road where the pavement becomes dirt. (You actually turn right *just before* the end.) They'll say go about 25 yards on the dirt, park and swim out about 50–75 yards. Turn right (north), and you should see several large vertical holes in the reef to drop through to the bottom. Exit the tunnel on the ocean side.

That's fine, but those sources don't know about the far better area. There are several public accesses along here, but the *best* is at telephone pole #120 (kitty-corner from a church 2 miles from the highway). If the PUBLIC ACCESS sign is missing, we can confirm that it *is* a public access. Park near the road, and the water is a 175-foot walk away. Entry is easy. You can see the reef edge from the shore (polarized sunglasses really enhance it), so during the normally calm seas, kick almost straight out (slightly to the left) over the fairly shallow reef shelf so you'll end up seaward of a house with a corrugated metal roof. (Remember where you entered; other entry/exit points are harder on the diver.) Once at the reef wall (150 feet or so from shore), work your way northwest along the wall where countless chasms, arches and small caves, coupled with boundless coral, fish and the occasional turtle, create a delightful (though shallow 30–40 feet) dive. If you want to go deep (see photo where the boat is hovering), simply leave the coral behind and continue a short way farther offshore where the sand slopes relentlessly toward the abyss, broken only by vast fields of garden eels. (Approach them slowly, or they'll disappear into their holes.) If you're not too narc'd, return to the heavenly reef edge and make your way back. This is one of the few dives where you can go to 135 feet, yet still stay wet for an hour and be within your profile. Snorkelers, too, will enjoy the reef edge.

South Point—If you're a junkyard dog in search of a thrill, South Point has *lots* of fishing relics strewn about the ocean floor. Currents and surf can be unforgiving, so go only when calm. (Winter is sometimes best.) Not-so-easy entry is from rocks to the left (southeast) of the boat hoists. See page 79 for more information on this area. Stay away from the point.

Makole'a Beach—One of our personal favorites. The variety, quality and quantity of coral is exceptional. This is a *very* healthy reef, and it's unlikely you'll see it listed anywhere. We've dived it lots of times and have never seen any evidence that any other diver has been there. Unless you want to carry your gear for 15+ minutes, you'll need a 4WD vehicle to go over the lava

road. This will allow you to drive right up to this black sand beach near Kona. The best diving is about 100 to 200 feet out from the right (north) side of the beach. From there, work your way south parallel to the beach. This is a fairly shallow dive (45 feet), and visibility is not the best in Kona (50–65 feet), but the quality of the dive site is hard to beat. Follow directions on page 162. Since we're sharing a heretofore unknown dive site (one where we personally take visiting guests), please make us proud by being extra sensitive to the pristine reef.

The BEACHES chapter describes nearly all the beaches around the island. Divers should read the descriptions of Kohala beaches, such as **Kapa'a Beach Park**, **Mahukona**, and **Hapuna** (the southern end). In Kona, try the Alii Drive **Four Mile Marker** just south of **White Sands Beach** (from the cove head slightly south), **Kahalu'u Beach Park** (outside the breakwater), **Ke'ei**, and **Pu'uhonua o Honaunau** (Place of Refuge).

If you've ever gazed into an aquarium and wondered what it was like to see colorful fish in their natural environment, complete with coral, lava tubes and strange ocean creatures, you've come to the right Hawaiian Island. Hawai'i features a dazzling variety of fish. Over 600 species are found in our waters. Here's our dilemma: If we blather on and on again about how good the water can be on the west side of the island, you're probably going to get sick. But we *have* to! Because this is where Kona really pays off. Usually calm, clear and teeming with fish, the Kona side offers some of the best snorkeling in the state.

We'll admit that we're snorkeling junkies and never tire of experiencing the water here. If you snorkel often, you can go right to our list below of recommended areas. But it you're completely or relatively inexperienced, you should read on.

For identifying ocean critters, the best books we've seen are *Shore Fishes of Hawai'i* by John Randall and *Hawaiian Reef Fish* by Casey Mahaney. They're what we use. You should see plenty of butterflyfish, wrasse, convict tang, Achilles tang, parrotfish, angelfish, damselfish, Moorish idol, pufferfish, trumpetfish, moray eel, and humuhumunukunukuapua'a, or Picasso triggerfish—a beautiful but very skittish fish. (It's as if they somehow *know* how good they look in aquariums.)

We know people who have a fear of putting on a mask and snorkel. Gives 'em the willies. For them, we recommend boogie boards with clear windows on them to observe the life below.

A Few Tips

- Feeding the fish is generally not recommended since it introduces unnatural behavior to the reef, and it actually causes the variety of fish to dwindle since bolder species do well and soon crowd out meeker species. In the past it was a common practice at Kahalu'u Beach Park, but today conservationists are making a concerted effort to dissuade fish feeding.
- Use *Sea Drops* or another brand of anti–fog goop. Spread a *thin* layer on the inside of a dry mask, then do a quick rinse.

- Most damage to coral comes when people grab it or stand on it. Even touching the coral lightly can transfer your oils to the polyps, killing them. If your mask starts to leak or you get water in your snorkel, be careful not to stand on the coral to clear them. Find a spot where you won't damage coral or drift into it. Fish and future snorkelers (not to mention the coral) will thank you.
- Don't use your arms much, or you will spook the fish—just gentle fin motion. Any rapid motion can cause the little critters to scatter.
- If you have a mustache and have trouble with a leaking mask, try a little Vaseline. Don't get any on the glass— it can get *really* ugly.
- We prefer using divers' fins (the kind that slip over water shoes) so that we can walk easily into and out of the water without tearing up our feet. (If you wear socks or nylons under the shoes, they'll keep you from rubbing the tops of your toes raw.)
- Try to snorkel in calm areas. If you're in rougher water and a large wave comes and churns up the water with bubbles, put your arms in front of you to protect your head. You won't sense motion, and may get slammed into a rock before you know it.

Prices

You'll find the least expensive gear in Kailua-Kona. The business can be cutthroat, so look for coupons in the free magazines scattered around the island. If you're going to snorkel more than once, it's nice to rent gear for a week, leave it in the trunk, and go whenever you have the desire. **Miller's Snorkel & Surf** (326–1771) has decent gear for $8 per day, $16 a week. The snorkel

If you don't want to shoot fish with your disposable camera, use it to goof off, like we did with our friends here.

gear at **Jack's Diving Locker** (329–7585) is $8 per day, $42 per week. Divers' fins are available. **Snorkel Bob's** 329–0770 (near Huggo's restaurant on Alii Drive in Kona) has gear for $2.50–$9 per day, $9–$44 per week. Expect to get talked into the expensive stuff here. You can rent gear from a truck at Kahalu'u Beach Park for use there or at the concessionaire to the right of Kailua Pier.

You won't find inexpensive gear in Kohala, but you can try **Ocean Sports** at 886–6666, which has a shack at 'Anaeho'omalu Beach. Convenient, but they rent snorkel gear for (hold onto your wallet) $7 *per hour* or $14 per half day. They rent all kinds of other goodies there at rates that aren't *quite* as confiscatory.

Snorkel Boat Tours

These can be fun. They'll take you to a good spot, provide gear and show you how to use it, and sometimes provide lunch. OCEAN TOURS on page 211 reviews most of them and includes prices and where they take you. Our favorites are **Fair Wind II**, **Hula Kai**, **Body Glove** and **Sea Quest**.

Snorkel Sites

The chapter on BEACHES has complete descriptions of all beaches. Our usual bias toward west Hawai'i for water activities applies here. Clarity and calmness just can't compare on the Hilo side, but sea life can be just as abundant there.

On the west side, be sure to check out some of these beaches:

Kahalu'u—Easy access and lots of life.

Kealakekua Bay near Captain Cook Monument—Some of the best snorkeling in the state.

Pu'uhonua o Honaunau—Easy access, excellent area, lots of turtles and coral make it almost as good as the Captain Cook Monument.

Pawai Bay—Very interesting underwater relief.

Hapuna to Waialea Beach—Great stretch of reef.

Mahukona—Good underwater junk.

Puako—Very extensive reef.

Kiholo Bay—Strange conditions.

Kapa'a Beach Park—Interesting underwater sights.

Lapakahi State Park—Sometimes exceptional amounts of fish.

On the east side check out:

Punalu'u—Cold black sand conditions but *lots* of turtles.

Kapoho Tide-pools—Calm and unique.

Is this a misprint? Nope. Mauna Kea is 13,796 feet high, and in the winter it gets snow—sometimes a lot of it. **Ski Guides Hawai'i** (885–4188) rents gear for $50 on the off chance you somehow *forgot* to bring your own. Mauna Kea snow (called pineapple powder) is not reliable and neither is the company, so call them when you arrive to see if skiing is available. (It's usually tough to get them on the phone.) Granted, the conditions will be better at Aspen. But you can't go straight from the snow to the beach there, now can you? You'll need to take a 4WD to the observatory area where everyone but the driver can slide down the mountain on boogie boards or anything you think will do, while the driver takes the vehicle to the bottom to act as a ski lift.

If you're a little hesitant about trying SCUBA, consider SNUBA. That's where you swim below a raft with tanks and a 25-foot hose, regulator in mouth and an instructor by your side. **Big Island Watersports** at 324–1650 takes you on a shore dive near King Kamehameha Hotel in Kona for $89, or off their boat for $145. Groups of 2–6 per instructor; expect about 30–45 minutes of bottom time on the shore dives, a bit less on boat dives. They also have SCUBA available.

If you feel the need to lose yourself in the fog of a decadent overall body massage and treatment, you're in luck. The two best are the Fairmont Orchid and the Mauna Lani, both in the Kohala Resort area.

The **Fairmont Orchid** (885–2000) and their "Spa Without Walls" is the best *tropical* experience. We love their outdoor cabanas located at manmade waterfalls. Cabanas 4 and 5 are directly over the water with a small glass panel under your head to watch the koi fish during the day while you're on your stomach. Couples can enjoy an outdoor sunset massage right at the shoreline. Scrubs and facials take place inside. The only downside is that non-guests of the hotel won't have access to the fitness facilities or Jacuzzis. If that's important to you, **Mauna Lani Spa** (881–7922) is a great second choice. It's half outdoor thatched huts (not at the ocean) and half indoor treatment rooms. Their Lomi Lomi Hula feels like someone is doing the hula on your body with their hands. Very cool; not for the shy.

A weaker choice is the **Mandara Spa** at the **Waikoloa Beach Marriott** (886–8191). You might get good treatments, but we *consistently* have trouble with scheduling. Even when we *know* they are empty, we've been told they are "booked up."

We wish we could recommend one of the resorts in Kona. The biggest is the **Ho'ola Spa** at the **Sheraton**, and it's poorly executed. If you're looking to be pampered, go elsewhere. Facilities are limited, the only shower is in the steam room, the locker room is tiny, and they automatically charge you an extra 20% tip, even if you don't like your specific therapist.

If you want to go stargazing on Mauna Kea, home to the world's finest and most coveted telescopes, **Hawai'i Forest & Trail** (331–8505) does the best job. They'll pick you up in Kohala or near Honokohau Harbor in Kona. Then they drive you to an old sheep-shearing station at the lower altitudes of Mauna Kea for a pretty good catered dinner, take you to the summit for sunset, then bring you back down to the Visitor Center for stargazing from their own telescope. While you sip hot chocolate and eat cookies, their knowledgeable guides do a good job pointing out—with lasers—the night sky. It's 7½ hours altogether for $189.

Another company, **Mauna Kea Summit Adventures** (322–2366), has a similar product, but it's not executed nearly as well. It's $192, and you get a hot meal at the Visitor Center. **Star Gaze Hawai'i** (880–3155) will let you peek through their scopes at the Hapuna Beach Prince Hotel, Hilton Waikoloa or Fairmont Orchid for $30. Kind of hard to get excited about that one.

You won't *Run Silent, Run Deep.* There won't be the sound of sonar pinging away in the background. And it's unlikely that anyone will shoot torpedoes at you. But if you want to see the undersea world and *refuse* to get wet, *dis is da buggah.* **Atlantis Submarine** (329–6626) has a 48-passenger sub that ambles about over a very healthy reef in Kailua Bay. This is the opposite of an aquarium—this is *their* world, and *you* are the oddity. This 35-minute, $99 ride is a kick. Kids ($45) like it. Adults like it. Even certified divers like us like it. Claustrophobics will probably be too busy staring through the windows to be nervous. Photographers will want to use fast (at least 400 speed) ISO, and turn off the flash. Mornings are usually best. Wear a bright red shirt, and watch what happens to its color on the way down.

Dudes, the most gnarly surfing on the west side is at **Pine Trees** just north of Kailua-Kona. (See Wawaloli on page 163 for directions.) It takes a 4WD vehicle to get there, but the breaks are outstanding. In Kona, the break off the "little blue church" near **Kahalu'u** is one of the most dependable. **Banyans** on Alii Drive just south of Kona Bali Kai has excellent waves. Other great surf spots are **Ke'ei** and **Old Kona Airport**, described in BEACHES. You should know that Banyans and Lyman's (just around the bend) are notorious for surfers with bad attitudes. Outsiders will be as welcome as reef rash.

(By the way, a collection of surfboards is known in surfing lingo here as a *quiver.* A little kid surfer who doesn't have a job or a car yet is called a *grommet.* Double *overhead* is when the waves are huge, and if you get good enough, you might get a chance to visit the *green room.* If someone says your girlfriend is *filthy,* it's a compliment. And a *landshark* is someone who says he surfs… but doesn't.)

In Kona, **Pacific Vibrations** (329–4140) rents boards for $15–$20 per day. For lessons, **Hawai'i Lifeguard Surf Instructors** (324–0442) does an excellent job at Kahalu'u Beach Park. It's $120 for about 2½ hours, though that price seems to vary *a lot.* It's usually cheaper. Also consider **Ocean Eco Tours** (324–7873) and **Kona Surf Company** (217–5329). They charge $95–$99 per person for a group lesson.

Stand Up Paddling, or **SUP**, is the latest craze in the surfing world. The hardest part about learning to surf is standing up on the board while it's moving. This sport has made things easier by giving you a board big enough to dance on. SUP boards are wider, thicker and longer than the biggest longboards people commonly learn to surf on. SUP instruction focuses on keeping your balance while using a tall paddle to move you into the waves. (This provides an excellent central core workout, with your feet—of all things—hurting the most.) The sight of people standing and dipping long paddles in the water has earned SUP surfers the subversive title "janitors" or "moppers" from traditional surfers. The size of the board, as well as the fact that you are already standing up, gives you an advantage in catching waves early. You don't have to drop in exactly where the wave is breaking. Moppers can catch waves behind the lineup, but all surfing rules apply once you've caught the wave. Traditional surfers will be more inclined to drop in on your wave since they'll feel that you didn't work as hard to get it as they did.

Because it's a relatively new sport, rates are unpredictable. Call the surfing guys listed above.

TENNIS

If you feel like a lively game of tennis (or you simply like chasing the ball), the Big Island has plenty of courts. The WHERE TO STAY chapter mentions whether each resort has courts, lighted or not (and the phone numbers for each). The nicest courts on the island are at the **Fairmont Orchid** (887–7532). This fine tennis complex even has a stadium court. (Crowds are extra.) Rates are $15 per day per person. In Kailua-Kona, **Island Slice** (322–6112) at the Outrigger Keauhou Beach Resort costs $10 per person. Lessons are $50 per hour. In Hilo, your best bet is the county **Hoʻolulu Park** (961–8720). Three indoor and five outdoor courts. Indoor courts (preferred) are $2–$4 (day/night) per hour.

There are 42 *free* municipal courts scattered around the island. Rather than go into mind-numbing detail about all of them, just call the county at 961–8720 and ask for the courts nearest you.

Humpback whales are common in Hawaiʻi between December and March or April. Humpbacks don't eat while they're here and may lose a third of their body weight during their Hawaiian vacation. (I doubt that many *human* visitors can make that same claim.) They're here to take advantage of Hawaiʻi's romantic atmosphere and mate in our waters (so don't stare), returning the following year to give birth. Though whales are more numerous off Maui, the Big Island is still a splendid place to see them blow and breach. From shore, you may see humpback whales causing a ruckus or just generally frolicking. But out on a boat, you can sometimes get up close and personal. Additionally, there are several other species—including giant sperm whales, pilot whales, false killer whales, beaked whales, pygmy killer whales and melon-headed whales—that reside here and require boats to see.

Captain Dan McSweeney's Whale Watch (322–0028) is our resident expert. He has spent approximately 1½ zillion hours studying whales off Kona. For $90, you and up to 39 other passengers take their 40-foot boat offshore for 3–4 hours of whale watching and education. Snacks provided, restroom on board. They "guarantee" a sighting or you can come back for free and *claim* a 90% success rate in finding whales. **Living Ocean Adventures** (325–5556) offers year-round trips for up to 6 people in their 31-foot Bertram (a fishing boat). Like Captain Dan, the owner/operator is always present. Except during humpback season, they troll three lines while they whale watch—if they get a strike, you may get to reel it in. Only bottled water provided, restroom on board. $85 for 3½-hour trip. They need four people to go out. Several other boat companies listed under OCEAN TOURS provide whale watching during humpback season, but these two companies do it year round and have more experience.

Lastly, during humpback season, we like to swim out beyond the sound of the breakers (say, 100 feet past the breakwater at Kahalu'u Beach) and listen to those soulful giants sing the blues. You certainly won't get to *see* them underwater, but their concert is often the best in town. (But I sometimes wonder if the fish all around me are thinking, "I *hate* it when the humpbacks come to town. They make such a racket when we're trying to sleep!") You can hear whales from much farther distances if your ears are a few feet underwater. (Hint: Hang upsidedown.) Some years, the whale crowd is pretty raucous, constantly breaching, blowing and singing. Other years the behemoths may be strangely quiescent.

WindSurfing

Geography and winds conspire to make windsurfing and kitesurfing somewhat difficult on the Big Island. In Kona there usually isn't enough wind. And in Kohala there's usually too much of an *offshore* component to recommend kitesurfing or windsurfing unless the weather's unusual. (Offshore winds can be unsafe because they'll drag you away from the land.) At press time we couldn't find anyone consistently doing kiteboarding or windsurfing that we could recommend on the Big Island. Those

If you don't scream at some point on this one, you gotta check your pulse.

passionate about it should look to the Mecca of these sports, Maui.

Ever seen movies where military commandos don a harness, hook a pulley onto a steel cable and zip down into the action? This is similar—without the hostile fire at the end.

Ziplining has become a big business on this island, but not all zips are created equal. We zipped these four companies and found that two do a great job, and two are pretty avoidable. By the way, don't wear too-short shorts or the harness will get under your skin (so to speak). Minimum age is 10.

The most dramatic is the **Umauma Experience** (930–9477). They zip along and over the spectacularly beautiful Umauma Falls and gulch 15 miles north of Hilo. (See photo on previous page.) Zips #2 and #4 are probably the most dramatic ziplines in the state. After #4 (which had me zipping at 42 MPH over a distance of 2,000 feet) you have four anticlimactic zips before ending it on impressive #9. Because of this, you might want to save money by only doing the first four lines for $149 as opposed to all nine for $189. The first takes 1½ hours, and the second twice that, and the van ride to the ziplines is very short. Their harnesses are good, and they'll let you go *upside down* for short periods if you like. After you're done, you can use their 60-foot swing for $15 (for two people), which will *really* get your pulse pounding. You need to be between 80 and 260 pounds.

Another good one is up north in Hawi called **Big Island Eco Adventures** (889–5111). Their raw stats aren't as good as Umauma, with shorter lines that aren't as fast, and they lack the dramatic gulch. But they make up for this with a *beautiful* forest environment and a really nice and accommodating staff. After zip #6, you have snacks in an utterly idyllic shack overlooking a waterfall. Eight zips for $159. It takes 4 hours, one of which is getting to and from the zip course in their fun, bouncy 6WD vehicle. Bring a raincoat and borrow one of their packs to carry it, in case it rains. Only complaint? They need to do something about their stinky helmets. Gotta be between 80 and 270 pounds.

Right next to Umauma Experience (but a million miles away in terms of quality) is **Zip Isle** (963–5427). To be blunt, we can't think of anything we liked about this product. Their terrain is boring (it's *not* over Umauma), groups are up to 16 people (so there are longer waits between zips), their harnesses feel less reassuring than others, and the first six zips average a ridiculously short 300 feet at 13 MPH. Number 7 is 1,100 feet but by that time you're getting restless. I zipped these guys right after zipping Umauma, and the contrast was staggering. $147. At the World Botanical Gardens 15 miles north of Hilo.

Finally there's **Aloha Zipline Express** (968–7529) at Pa'ani Ranch before the 13 mile marker on Hwy 11 south of Hilo. No amount of friendly service or family atmosphere (both here in abundance) can change the fact that the land here is not very suitable for ziplining. Picture zipping along a featureless, gently sloping field barely above the ground. Hard to get excited. Though marketed to people of all ages, only kids 80 pounds and over might appreciate it for $80.

The manta ray night dive is one of those few adventures that is even better with a crowd.

The adventures described below (except for the dolphin encounter) are for the serious adventurer. They can be experiences of a lifetime. We are assuming that, if you consider any of them, you are a person of sound judgment, capable of assessing risks. All adventures carry risks of one kind or another. Our descriptions below do not attempt to convey all risks associated with an activity. These activities are not for everyone. Good preparation is essential. In the end, it comes down to your own good judgment.

MANTA RAY NIGHT DIVE

This one may stay with you for the rest of your life. Imagine the following scene: You take a boat to a dark piece of shoreline, leaving just before sunset. When you arrive, perhaps another dive boat is already there. *Damn,* you think. They'll ruin it. As you slip into the water and approach what is affectionately called *the campfire,* numerous lights already there beckon you toward them, like a porch light calling to the moths. Then you see gigantic shadows blotting out the lights. *Mantas!* As you approach, one zooms over your head, missing you by an inch. There you sit, with all the others, mesmerized by the performance before you. One, two, maybe three stinger-less manta rays, 6–10 feet across their wings, slowly swirling, looping and soaring all about you. Like a dance performed by extra-terrestrial beings, these filter-feeding leviathans are more graceful than you could possibly imagine. They seem to understand that they are on stage, and they rarely disappoint. When you think you have gotten used to their size, a goliath 14 feet across may swoop in, its enormous maw scooping up thousands of the tiny, darting shrimp that cloud the water along with the bubbles. You struggle to resist the urge to reach up and touch them—it's best to let them initiate any touching. Above the fray, a sea of needlefish gobble up what they can. Nearby, a friendly eel might slither over to give you a kiss.

It all started 30 years ago when the Kona Surf Hotel (now a Sheraton) started flooding the shoreline with light, attracting tiny brine shrimp, a form of plankton. This plankton brought large manta rays, which gobble them by the millions. Then in 2000 the resort closed (and turned off their light), and the mantas vanished. By luck they were discovered to be congregating at a spot near the Kona Airport (perplexing dive operators since there are no lights there to attract their food source). Since the resort reopened in 2005, they've returned, but there are times that they seem to take a vacation and don't show up at all. At press time, the airport location was the most manta-laden.

You will likely have plenty of air left since the dive takes place at about 35 feet, and you move very little. Diver etiquette dictates that you leave your snorkel on the boat; the protruding tube can scratch the mantas' belly. This is one of those rare dives where a crowd, as long as it's not *too* big, actually makes it better. More lights and more wide eyes. Snorkelers who try to dive down or those who use scooters can scare them off.

If you started diving because you wanted to feel like you were floating in space, night dives provide that feeling. But for this dive, weight yourself a bit heavy; it'll make it easier to stay put. (Don't assume that if the surf is up, boats won't go.

Though usually calm, we see boats out there when the surf is high enough to make us grateful *we're* not there.) Some companies use $\frac{1}{3}$–$\frac{1}{2}$ of the 50- to 60-minute dive for roaming around. Others, like Kona Honu Divers, spend nearly all of their time with the mantas. See the chart on page 216 for a list of companies doing this dive. We've had good luck with Jack's and Big Island Divers, Boats that leave from Keauhou Bay have a convenient 600-*yard* cruise out to the Sheraton site.

Lastly, if the mantas *don't* show, the night dive at the Sheraton is fairly boring. (Sorry, but it's true.)

If you've night dived before, *do this one!* If you've never night dived before, consider doing it now! Expect to spend about $100–$179 for this dive—the best money you will ever spend underwater, *if they show.*

If you only want to snorkel with the mantas and don't want a long boat ride, Sea Paradise charges snorkelers a steep $89 for their 5-minute boat ride from Keauhou Bay. The Hula Kai (322–2788) is similar but with a nicer boat for $99.

MAUNA ULU CRATER

This short hike is not for the easily frightened or the faint at heart. Mauna Ulu erupted between 1969 and 1974. When it was all over, it left a smoldering maw 400 feet deep and 500 feet across. (That's a guess—it gets bigger all the time.) This crater is accessible via a 45-minute hike from Chain of Craters Road in Hawai'i Volcanoes National Park. See map on page 197. From there, you just walk up to Mauna Ulu Crater.

We need to stress that this is new land. The part of the hill adjacent to Pu'u Huluhulu *seems* to be the most stable, but that is a relative term. There are several areas where thin, shelly lava breaks beneath your feet. You may only drop an inch or two, but your adrenaline tells you otherwise. There may be even less stable areas around the edge. The rim of the crater is nearly straight down and crumbling all the time. If you get too close, it may break off, you may fall in, and then you're *really* out of luck. If all this doesn't dissuade you, you'll get to see a view that is beyond belief. The crater seems raw, like an open wound on Kilauea. It usually steams from several spots. There are empty lava river banks around it where huge quantities of lava coursed their way down the mountain. There are blobs where lava spattered where it fell, large cracks with heat still escaping. This is as close as you may ever get to experiencing an erupting vent—while it's not erupting. But remember, this hike is what we call an 'okole squeezer. Permits are only required if you hike beyond Pu'u Huluhulu to Napau, so you *are* allowed to hike to Mauna Ulu without a permit or permission. That's official from the park, but some park personnel sometimes erroneously tell visitors otherwise. Morning is usually best for this hike.

EXPLORE A MILE-LONG CAVE

Several readers asked us where they could explore a relatively pristine cave on their own. This one, located off Saddle Road, is one of the newest ones on the island. Formed during the same lava flow of 1881 that threatened Hilo and

created the well known, but hardly pristine Kaumana Cave 14 miles east, this might well be part of the same tube, though parts are blocked off. Called Emesine Cave, there are incredible formations inside, including lava stalactites, channels and shelves that look so perfect and smooth you'd swear they were man-made (though they're not), along with numerous surprises.

As a cave, this lava tube presents dangers that you need to respect. Though seemingly stable, any cave can have areas where rocks can collapse. Most of the cave is over 10 feet tall, but there are op-

The Mauna Ulu hike is an 'okole squeezer, not an average stroll.

portunities to whack your head. (Personally, when exploring caves, we wear a hard hat with a head-band flashlight attached to the top.) Bring *at least* two strong flashlights. (We bring three). The stronger the light, the more enjoyable the experience. You'll miss *a lot* with a weak light and increase your chances of tripping or hitting your head. Getting into the cave from the entrance is a little awkward—you'll have to judge for yourself if you're comfortable scrambling into it. And please make sure you don't harm any of the formations or take any sou-

venirs other than photos from the cave. We're making some people mad just by telling you where this cave is, so make sure you leave the cave as you found it. (Sorry to sound so preachy, but we can already hear the chorus of critics, who themselves didn't even know about this cave, saying that we shouldn't have revealed this gem.)

To get there, take Saddle Road (Hwy 200) from Kona to ⁴/₁₀ mile past (east of) the 22 mile marker. Saddle Road weather may bring mist and rain. On the south side of the road is a short 4WD road that leads to a powerline road (see map). The power poles are now cut down. Walk around the gate and take this powerline road for 2⁶/₁₀ miles. It'll seem like more because the lava road is flat with obnoxious footing and isn't very interesting. Nearing the cave, the road passes through a lush fern area (the lushest yet) and descends to newer lava. A few hundred feet after the descent ends, look to your right for the tube opening (a round collapsed pit). The tunnel passes under the road, and that's the route you want. (The other way in the cave, heading uphill, is shorter, less interesting and requires ducking too much.) Because it's a single tube, you can't get lost. (Unless you lose your light—then you're screwed.) After a short distance it opens up to another skylight. Just keep going. Make sure to stop and marvel at the formations along the way; that's what you came for.

After about a mile the cave ends at a rock collapse. Don't try to go farther.

If you don't want to cover the same boring road coming back, consider taking the longer route along the old Pu'u 'O'o Trail shown on the map. The intersection is a half mile farther up the road. Pu'u 'O'o Trail is about 4³/₁₀ miles long and more interesting but more physical (because the trail undulates most of the time). Parts are hard to fol-

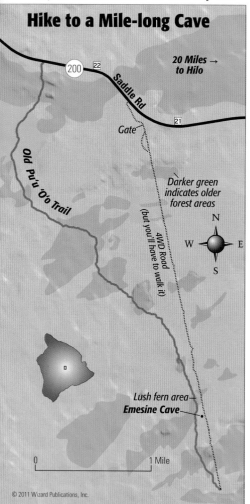

Hike to a Mile-long Cave

200 22 20 Miles → to Hilo

Saddle Rd

21

Gate

Old Pu'u 'O'o Trail

Darker green indicates older forest areas

N
W ← → E
S

4WD Road (but you'll have to walk it)

Lush fern area→
Emesine Cave

0   1 Mile

On the Pu'u 'O'o hike, the forest ends abruptly, bringing you face to face with the beating heart of the current eruption.

low; look for the tags. This is probably a good time to shamelessly plug our smartphone app that has this trail on our map and is GPS aware, so you'll *know* if you're off the trail. (Don't rely on the USGS map because their trail is wrong.) Pu'u 'O'o Trail dumps you onto Saddle Road a mile from your car.

RAIN FOREST HIKE TO PU'U 'O'O VENT

One of the few laments people voice when visiting Kilauea Volcano is that they can't readily visit Pu'u 'O'o, the origin and lava source of the current eruption. Of course, you can still see lava flowing from up close (Pele permitting) during a visit to the park, but you can't see the *actual vent* where it originates. There are places where a person can get a glimpse of the vent from a distance (see page 121), but visiting it has been a problem. Unless, of course, you happen to know the way.

Unknown to the vast majority of island residents, the Kahauale'a Trail was cut by state workers in 1990 as the quickest and most direct route to Pu'u 'O'o. It just so happens that it passes through the healthiest, most beautiful and least-hiked

rain forest on the entire island. Nowhere will you find a lovelier forest, no matter where you hike.

When we revealed this trail to readers in an earlier edition, bureaucrats at Hawai'i Volcanoes National Park fumed when they realized that we had pointed out a way to visit Pu'u 'O'o that doesn't go through their park. They even stopped selling this book in the park. Well, *that* certainly isn't going to stop us. Park bureaucrats may not *want* you on this trail because you are beyond their control, but they can't keep you off this legal *public* trail.

First things first: *Don't hike this trail unless the weather forecast is for steady trade winds* (from the northeast or north). No exceptions. Any other winds, including light and variable winds, can bring the volcanic fumes back over the trail, which could be *very* unhealthy if sulphur dioxide levels are bad enough. Note that this trail is closed for stretches when emissions levels are high. The state doesn't *like* closing the trail, but they worry about uninformed people hiking the trail when the trade winds aren't blowing.

All told, it's a 4²/₁₀-mile hike to the edge of the forest from your car. (3²/₁₀ miles as the crow flies, but you ain't no crow.) The first half of the hike may as well be through the Garden of Eden. Tree ferns and 'ohi'a trees line the way, bursting with green, many covered with a velvety moss. Even if you're not up to the whole hike, a short trek through this forest is highly memorable. There are no big climbs, just lots of tiny hills and dips. This is the rain forest of your dreams. The second half of the forest shows some signs of wild pigs and is not *quite* as perfect. (Only 98% perfect.) When you get to "the big crack" (you'll know), you're 10 minutes away.

Soon after the crack, the lush forest gives way to small clearings. The trees are looking stressed. Suddenly the forest is dying. Trees are stripped of leaves, grasses are taking over. *Something* is killing the rain forest. Then, through the trees, you see the cause—a sight as awesome as any you've ever encountered. You race to the abrupt edge of the forest and come face to face with Pu'u 'O'o a mile away. The cone, several hundred feet high and built entirely during the current eruption, angrily spews 1,500 *tons* of sulphur dioxide per day, like a snorting exhaust pipe from the center of the Earth. You are on the upslope side, and the lava should be flowing on the opposite side, so you probably won't see that. But if the wind is blowing in the right direction (which it usually is), you will have a view of the beating heart of a volcano.

If the wind is blowing toward you (which it usually doesn't), *you shouldn't be here.* You would notice a sulphur smell. These occasional winds from the south are what's killing the forest edge. Savor this view, revel in it. But don't try to get closer. Don't try to walk up and peer into the crater floor or sometimes lava lake; the risks are unacceptable. If the wind changes, it exposes you to potentially fatal concentrated fumes. If a cloud forms, the fog would disorient you to the point that you wouldn't find your way back to the forest. Plus, you might fall from the fragile land into a lava lake—a real bummer. Best to observe it from the forest edge, soaking up the sight for your memories of tomorrow.

This hike is not for everyone. It is a fairly long day hike, and conditions are often pretty muddy. This *is* after all, a *rain* forest. (The trail received rainfall of biblical proportions during one rainstorm in 2000. A frog-strangling *32 inches* fell in one day alone.) When the trail's fairly dry, it's not too difficult; when it's real muddy, it's a tiring round trip. The center section is the muddiest.

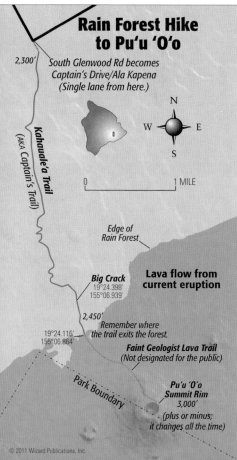

Rain Forest Hike to Pu'u 'O'o

2,300'

South Glenwood Rd becomes Captain's Drive/Ala Kapena (Single lane from here.)

N W E S

Kahauale'a Trail (AKA Captain's Trail)

0   1 MILE

Edge of Rain Forest

Big Crack
19°24.398'
155°06.939'

Lava flow from current eruption

2,450'
19°24.116'
155°06.864'

Remember where the trail exits the forest.

Faint Geologist Lava Trail
(Not designated for the public)

Park Boundary

Pu'u 'O'o
Summit Rim
3,000'
(plus or minus;
it changes all the time)

The trail has been groomed sporadically by state workers, but hunters and other users keep it in pretty good shape. A few hunter and pig trails veer off; your path is the most worn path. You may be only a few miles from your car, but if you are off the trail, it would be the longest few miles of your life. A compass or GPS is comforting, just in case. And if you pick up our smartphone app (shameless plug here), we have the track so you'll *know* if you're on the right trail. Of course, we don't guarantee the trail's condition. In fact, we don't guarantee diddly when it comes to hiking. Nature changes quickly. A strong windstorm can return a nice trail back to jungle until workers come back to repair it. We are assuming that you will use your judgment on this. Also, guerrilla gardeners (you know...alternative farmers) sometimes tend their "crops" deep in the forest. They obviously like to stay as far from people as possible. The point is that you shouldn't stray a long distance off the trail for fear of stumbling onto their "farm" (not to mention getting lost in the rain forest).

Start *early* for this hike. You will want to be hiking by 7:30 a.m. to make *sure* you aren't on the trail when it gets dark. (Some who haven't heeded this warning, starting too late, have been caught on the trail at night and needed to be rescued.) We've run into our own readers on the trail who started at 10 or 11 a.m. and have chastised them for starting too late. Personally, we leave our home in Kona at the *indecent* hour of 4:30 a.m. in order to start hiking by 7 a.m. Time the hike to be back to your car two hours before sunset, just to be safe. It'll *probably* take 2½–4 hours each way, depending on conditions and your hiking skills. Bring plenty of water. Hiking boots (especially waterproof ones) are highly recommended, and a hiking stick (for probing mud puddles and balance) is *strongly* recommended. Most people will get their feet wet due to occasionally unavoidable puddles.

Once at Pu'u 'O'o, note where the trail ends at the edge of the forest for your return. Lastly, when Pu'u 'O'o finally stops erupting, it won't be *quite* as dramatic. But you can bet it'll still be worth it. The inherent lure of this area will be here for years to come.

To get to the trailhead, take South Glenwood Road between the 19 and 20 mile markers (close to the 20) on Hwy 11 (20 miles from Hilo, 95 miles from Kona). It's just south of the Hirano Store. The road curves to the right, then left and changes its name to Captain's Drive/Ala Kapena. From the highway it's 3½ miles *to the very end* (including the one-lane part) where you'll find the trail continuing south. Some readers have had their unattended cars broken into here, so don't leave anything valuable in it.

JUMP OFF THE END OF THE WORLD

Cliff jumpers, rejoice. There's a place just past the south end of Alii Drive. (See map on page 63.) Drive to the end of the road and take the lava road by foot toward the ocean, veer toward the left, and just before the road begins to ascend (next to a short paved section), take the trail to the right to the ocean. It's only a 5–10 minute walk altogether. There at the cliff you are confronted by a 35-foot drop to the water. You have your choice—there are several elevations above the water. And beneath you is clean, clear water up to 15 feet deep. If you *want* to hit bottom, you probably can if you do your best impression of a pencil; better to spread 'em as soon as you strike water. This is your cliff-jumping opportunity, where countless locals (who named this spot) have dared the ocean. Use your best judgment in deciding whether to jump. Judgment is what

Don't like heights or falling? Not to worry; it won't last long.

Another popular cliff-jumping place is from the boat hoist area at South Point. See page 81 for directions to that. People jump from the metal ladder area and climb up the rocks to the right (looking from the water).

CLOSE ENCOUNTER WITH A DOLPHIN

You may have heard of this one. At the Hilton Waikoloa Village there's a program called **Dolphin Quest**. They have several Atlantic bottle-nosed dolphins in their lagoon where children and adults can get in the water and interact with them. (Our own local spinner dolphins need deeper water and wouldn't successfully adapt to the program.) You stand on a shallow sandy shore with three or four other folks while the dolphins come up to you. *They* decide if they like *you*. If so, you'll be treated to an experience that you will remember for life. It's hard to express the enthusiasm people have when they get up close and personal with these ocean-going mammals. But it's undeniable that the encounter is incredibly enriching. You also can't help but notice that the dolphins seem to love their contact with humans as well.

adventures are all about. The surf can rearrange the bottom, bringing in shallower boulders, so you'll have to evaluate all conditions for yourself. And there could be a critter near the surface that you could collide with. After you've jumped, do you have a nice, easy path to climb back up? No, sorry. After you hit the water in a shockingly abrupt fashion, you'll look to the left of the cave you just plummeted in front of and begin the daunting task of climbing the cliff face so you can do it all over again. Don't like those options? Then don't jump off the end of the world.

You may be thinking, "Is this program good for the dolphins?" That's a fair question and was a concern of ours. We found out that the company used to have a similar program in French Polynesia. There, the dolphins were allowed out into the open ocean (where they could easily swim off at any time). They claimed that the dolphins always returned "home" to the program. That's a pretty good testimonial. We're not experts, but the dolphins seem pretty happy to us. (We've seen other places where we couldn't make that claim.) The water in their lagoon is replaced with fresh seawater every few hours by massive pumps, keeping it very clean for them and you. The dolphins are very active and playful, reproduce when they get to the right age (wink, wink), and the trainers seem to show them extraordinary love and affection.

If you're interested, call them at 886–2875. It's not always easy to get in on this. Kids are the most desired customer here. Personnel love to introduce kids, not only to the dolphins, but also to various issues regarding the dolphins' environment (without becoming too heavy-handed). Make reservations 60 days in advance to ensure access. Cost is $210 for kids 9 and under (around ½ hour with the dolphins, 1 hour of education camp). Adults can also schmooze with the dolphins for $205–$250. Other programs are available as well.

If you want to see dolphins *in the wild,* your best chance on the island is in Kealakekua Bay. There are quite a few spinners that live in the bay. While kayaking across to the Captain Cook Monument, you stand a good chance of seeing them. We were once able to slip into the water here when 19 dolphins, including babies, were swimming and splashing all around us. You might also see them on a snorkel trip to the bay.

BOULDER-HOP TO A WATERFALL

If you spend any time in Hilo or along the Hamakua Coast, you'll see lots of waterfalls. But let's be honest—you didn't really *earn* them, did you? (Well, except for paying to come to Hawai'i, I guess.) But let's face it. You usually drive up to a parking area, walk over to a view point and take a picture. Maybe you'll take a short trail, like Wai'ale Falls. But to see *these* falls, you're gonna have to get wet

and risk falling and breaking your 'okole. Because although they're only 900 feet from your car, you can't see 'em and there is no trail. You'll have to get *in* the river and scramble upstream on big old boulders. And if you slip and fall, you probably can't even use your cell phone to call for help, so be careful.

This is not an all-day adventure (unless you drove here from Kona). It'll take most people up to an hour to struggle through the river. (Though well-balanced trail gods could probably sprint their way in 10 minutes.) Once at the falls, the beautiful, multi-tiered falls tumble into a deep pool. Take your time here, you *earned* it.

The falls are north of Hilo. Just north of the 18 mile marker, turn mauka off the highway and hang a right. The next bridge is stamped NANUE. A so-called trail on the nearside leads down to the stream. From here, head upstream as carefully as you can until there's a waterfall on your head. Flip-flops are *not* a good way to go on these rocks. Serious gear junkies

would want canyoning shoes and a pair of carbide-tipped hiking sticks. Most people, however, will do fine with some local fishing tabis (available from Kmart or Walmart) or some hiking shoes with fairly soft rubber.

An alternative is Waikaumalo Falls farther down the same road. It's a bit farther upstream (1,250 feet). Starting at Waikaumalo Park, ignore the teaser trail behind the facilities (it only leads to frustration and despair) and instead head upstream on the nearshore bank. The boulders aren't as difficult (most of the time) as Nanue, but there's a place ⅔ of the way in where you'll have to swim across a pool to continue, and the end just before the falls is pretty clumsy. This stream doesn't seem quite as clean as Nanue, but the waterfall at the end is still rewarding.

Avoid when the streams are raging, and read up on leptospirosis, listed under HAZARDS in BASICS.

Though rare, flash floods can occur in any freshwater stream anywhere in the world, and it can happen when it's sunny where you are but raining up the mountain. Be alert for them.

COMMAND YOUR OWN BOAT

There are lots of charter boats plying the waters off Kona. But what if you want to do things your *own* way? At press time, only one company rented power boats. Kona Boat Rentals (326–9155) at Honokohau Harbor rents 21-foot, single-hull boats. They're made using an amazingly tough material/process called Roplene. With their 115-horsepower outboards, they'll cut through the water at 25+ MPH. Best of all, you *don't* need prior experience. (Though they will screen you to make sure you're not a moron.) Take it as far north as Kawaihae, as far south as Miloli'i. (Check out the otherwise-inaccessible black sand beach at N19°20.512' by W155°53.168'.) They'll outfit you with fishing or snorkel gear (SCUBA is extra). Their GPS is preprogrammed with numerous moorings, and

You didn't drive to Nanue Falls. You didn't really even hike here. You just sort of...groped your way to this lovely waterfall.

You'll find crowds of wild pigs rather than crowds of hikers during your stay in Waimanu Valley.

they'll show you how to tie up to them. They'll give you some instructions, bring the boat to the harbor, and off you go.

The catch? *Price*. The half-day rental is $325; it's $450 for the day, *plus* gas. That's a big chunk of money. If you have 4 to 6 people, it's not quite as painful when you split it. Seeing the area this way is a real hoot. But nobody ever said hoots were cheap. Nevertheless, it's a great way to SCUBA, snorkel or fish *where* and *how* you want.

LOSE YOURSELF IN WAIMANU VALLEY

Hawai'i is the most isolated chain of islands in the world. If that isn't enough for you, and you *really* want to get away from it all, this is the adventure for you. Waimanu Valley has all the ingredients you would expect from a pristine Hawaiian valley, such as waterfalls, feral pigs and a black sand beach. At one time it supported a large number of Hawaiians until the 1946 tsunami ruined their taro fields. These days you'll see more helicopters here than people. Hiking in takes 5–6 hours, and you may even have the valley all to yourself, if you can make the grueling 7¾ mile trek. Don't try to do this as a day hike. Stay at least two nights to really soak in the majesty of the valley.

You need to plan this adventure a few weeks in advance by calling the Division of Forestry and Wildlife (974–4221) in Hilo for a permit. We also recommend you bring sturdy shoes, a tent and water filter or purification tablets. A 4WD vehicle is required to get down into Waipi'o Valley to start the hike. If you take your rental, be sure to leave nothing in it and the doors *unlocked* to deter any would-be criminals from smashing their way into your car. (Though leaving it unlocked *may* void your rental insurance.) If you take the Waipi'o Valley Shuttle (775–7121) down into Waipi'o, you'll have to worry about looking for a ride back up after your long hike.

Park your car behind the beach near the river, but don't put your shoes on just yet. First, cross the river where it's shallow, so you can see where you're stepping. Follow the beach or the trail through the trees to the far valley wall. Here you'll find the Muliwai Trailhead.

To say it's strenuous would be an understatement. In the first mile you climb 1,200 feet of switchbacks (also known as the Z trail, see map page 132). It's by far the hardest part of the whole trip and will take an hour or longer. The trail is rough, rocky and unrelenting, and you'll be hiking in the sun unless you start before dawn. Take breaks in what little shade there is and get some pictures of Waipi'o Valley from the lookout at the end of the 4th switchback. Once on top, the trail heartbreakingly undulates up and down as it crosses 13 gulches. As you climb up most sections of the trail, take note when you see pines needles on the ground. It means you're nearing the top. If there hasn't been much rain, the first fresh water you'll find is more than 6 miles in, so pack at least two liters per person.

As you enter Waimanu Valley, have your camera ready. From the trail you'll have stunning views of the black sand beach, the blanket of green on the valley floor and three gigantic waterfalls on the other side. From right to left, the falls are Wai'ilikahi Falls (1,080 feet), Lahomene Falls (1,800 feet) and Waihilau Falls (2,600 feet!). The last waterfall name refers to the three side-by-side falls in the back of the valley. They're only seen during heavy rains, but they're the tallest on the Big Island and third tallest in the state.

After a long descent to the valley floor, cross the river and pick a campsite. The first five sites are too close to each other; we prefer sites 6–9. Each has a fire pit, and there are two pit toilets in the area. Getting water from the river is convenient, but it tastes funky after traveling through the swamp. A spring on the opposite side of the valley has water that's infinitely better. Hike through the woods from the last campsite until you find water soaking the ground and follow it uphill to a cascading falls. At press time there was a sign saying the area was closed, possibly a long-forgotten warning from the 2006 earthquake. The trail would be very hard to follow if it wasn't marked with orange tape. Another 45 minutes along this path leads you to the base of Wai'ilikahi Falls. Its last plunge is into a verdant horseshoe valley and into a pool perfect for a refreshing swim. This will make all your hard work seem worthwhile.

We doubt you'll hike to the falls and not see any of the valley's only permanent residents. The narrow strip of land between the valley wall and the swamp is home to feral pigs. They like to drink from the spring, and you may hear them squealing at night. Remember, the pigs rule this valley, and we are merely their subjects. They're not usually aggressive, but it can be startling to see one face-to-face. Also, the mosquitoes are thick here, so make sure you bring your jungle juice.

Returning to Waipi'o Valley always seems to take less time. The climb out of Waimanu is also 1,200 feet in less than a mile, but the trail is smooth and in the shade most of the day. Expect to save an hour on the way back. Once in Waipi'o, we love to get our shoes off quickly and walk along the beach back to our vehicle. It's a beautiful stroll and a perfect end to one of the Big Island's most rewarding adventures.

HIKE TO FLOWING LAVA

This one is difficult to describe for the simple reason that we won't know where lava is flowing at the time you read this. It may be flowing right at the end of Chain of Craters Road in Hawai'i Volcanoes National Park, making this description unnecessary. But probably not. The lava flows change location all the time, so we'll tell you how to find out where they are and how to get there.

You can call the park at 985–6000 for an eruption update. We've had mixed results with the quality of their updates. You can also look at the map posted at the park visitor center. Another source is the USGS recording at 967–8862. It's usually accurate, though they often mumble on the message.

Our website at www.wizardpub.com has an updated lava flow map on it and a link to the official USGS lava flow status, usually updated daily. Check it before you leave on your trip to Hawai'i. The flows should be somewhere between the end of Chain of Craters Road in the park and the end of the lava road in Kalapana. If you hike from the park, you are nearly always permitted to hike to the unsupervised flows. They may *imply* that you can't, but it is almost always permitted.

What if it's flowing *outside* the park? If you look at the map on page 100, you'll see where Hwy 130 ends and a paved narrow road through the lava leads toward a lava-destroyed subdivision. This lava road gets you about 1¾ miles closer to the flows and was cut on top of the old state road. Until 2001, it was a junky 4WD road and access was disput-

ed. Then the county saw a way to make money: Fix it up for regular cars and charge $5 per car to drive it. (Two weeks after it opened, lava covered it again, so the $5 seems very fair given how many times they'll have to repair it.) If lava is flowing on *this* side of the volcano, this is the road to take. If it's not flowing here, the county may not have the road open during your visit. Call the county at (808) 961–8093 for an update on the road and viewing conditions.

The general rule of thumb is that eastern flows on the county side (from Kalapana) are rigorously supervised, and you won't be able to get as close. We've seen them make people walk 2 miles on the

Seeing the lava flow at night is an adventure that will stay with you for a lifetime. Walking back to your car on the undulating black lava in the dark is the price you pay.

Two hikers come upon the landslide portion of the Honokane Nui Trail—and a decision.

road and then keep them half a mile from the flows—really disappointing. In fairness, it's because county personnel are not as well-trained or confident in their lava handling, and the county is more paranoid about liability. Western flows near Chain of Craters Road are supervised by more knowledgeable park rangers, and they are pretty good about letting you get close when it's safe. Flows in the park more than a mile from Chain of Craters Road are usually *unsupervised,* and only your own common sense is there to supervise you. (And maybe your smarter spouse.)

At the flows you are presented with several dangers. Lava benches form seaward of the old seacliffs. They can collapse at any time, taking viewers with them, so *don't* go on the benches below. Collapses also can hurl rocks inland. Lava tubes travel under you. Hot water can splash on you. There may be signs where the flows enter the ocean telling you to go no farther. Heed them. There may be surface flows; watch for them.

Lava flows are *least* impressive between 10 a.m. and 2 p.m. (because the red lava is competing with the sun.) Don't hike here in the dark without flashlights. Our preference is to hike out in the late afternoon, so we get to see lava during the daylight and at night.

There are other dangers, as well, such as bad gases that trade winds *normally* blow to the southwest, and we are counting on your own good judgment to keep you out of trouble. We are not attempting to convey all the dangers present on this hike. You'll have to evaluate some on your own. The park has a brochure about viewing lava safely that you may want to pick up. This is a thrilling hike of a lifetime, but not for the faint-hearted, and bad decisions can result in tragedy. Contrary to what you might think, *smaller* lava flows, with less steam at the ocean, are much more dramatic than large ones since they're less likely to be completely engulfed by steam.

HONOKANE NUI HIKE

At the north end of the island where Hwy 270 ends you'll find Pololu Valley. (See page 49.) Though the trek into Pololu takes only 15–20 minutes, the more adventurous might want to venture beyond this beautiful valley to the more secluded Honokane Nui Valley and its accompanying stream. From the car lookout, it takes most people 90–120 minutes each way to hike into Honokane Nui. On the far side of Pololu, the trail goes up the 600-foot-high mountain, over the ridge, then drops down into Honokane. The view of Honokane Nui from the ridge top is breathtaking. Be prepared for a wet, sloppy trail going up the ridge from Pololu if it's been raining recently. (It's drier going down into Honokane.) Horseback riders occasionally take this trail and leave a few…gifts along the way. (Technically speaking, the *riders* probably aren't leaving those gifts; their *horses* are.) Usually winter is wetter.

Descending into Honokane Nui, there is a section of trail that was wiped out during the earthquake of 2006. People have put ropes in place (trust them at your own risk) to help this part that features loose dirt and rocks. This is the most difficult part of the trail and one that may turn you back. Once in Honokane Nui the trail gets vague as it goes toward the beach. Don't disturb any of the rock walls here. There is a large deposit of black sand offshore, but it doesn't do *you* a lot of good. Stay out of the ocean here; it'll hurt you. On the far side of the valley is a nice stream and pool—a perfect place to have lunch.

Although the trail continues into the next valley (Honokane Iki) it's got a number of residents (despite its remoteness), and you are less welcome there.

All in all, this is a nice hike when conditions are good. There are some ruins in the valley from days gone by when it was populated. If you are tired, you might be tempted to skirt the water's edge back to Pololu, thereby avoiding the trip up and down the ridge. If it's calm and low tide, you *might* get away with it, or you might get slammed by a rogue wave and washed out to sea, so we don't recommend it unless you're feeling lucky.

Some of the valley trail intersections can get confusing, so be observant. Bring bug juice just in case. Hiking boots are recommended. When you cross Pololu's stream in the first valley, don't do it near the ocean, but rather at a place 100 feet or so back where you can often hop on dry rocks. (Don't cross when it's raging.) Leave for this hike early. Theoretically, you could walk all the way to Waipi'o Valley from here, but the trail disappears in spots, and only those with mountain goat in their lineage will want to try it.

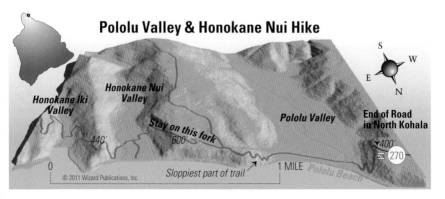

Pololu Valley & Honokane Nui Hike

Honokane Iki Valley

Honokane Nui Valley

Stay on this fork

440'

600'

Pololu Valley

End of Road in North Kohala

400'

28 270

0

© 2011 Wizard Publications, Inc.

Sloppiest part of trail

1 MILE

Pololu Beach

Aloha Deli & Ice Cream 266
Anthony's Italian & Irish 264
Anuenue 266
Ba-Le 256
Back to the '50s Highway 275
Baker Tom's 275
Bamboo Restaurant 273
Bay Terrace, The 260
Beach Tree 248
Bianelli's 254
Big Island Brewhaus &
    Tako Taco Taquiera 266
Big Island Candies 271
Big Island Grill 256
Big Jake's Island BBQ 248
Bistro Yokohama 255
Black Rock Café 272
Blue Dragon Coastal Cuisine ..260
Bongo Ben's Island Café 248
Boogie Woogie Pizza 272
Boston Basil's Italian 255
Brown's Beach House 261
Bubba Gump Shrimp Co. 248
Buns in the Sun 249
Café Concerto 270
Café Il Mondo 275
Cafe 'Ohi'a 276
Café 100 270
Café Pesto 264, 270
Canoe House, The 261
Charley's Thai Cuisine 266
Coast Grille 261
Coffee Shack 249
Costco 249
Cuz'ns 259
Don the Beachcomber 249
Fish Hopper Seafood, The 250
Giovanni's Aloha Shrimp 272
Green Flash Coffee 250
Hamakua Fudge Shop 275
Hana Hou Restaurant 277
Harbor House 250
Hawaii Calls 261
Hawaiian Ice Cones 259
Hawaiian Style Café 266
Hayashi's You Make The Roll ..255
Hilo Bay Café 268
Hilo Burger Joint 268
Hilo Homemade Ice Cream 271
Holuakoa Gardens & Café 250
Huggo's 251

Huggo's on the Rocks 251
Huli Sue's BBQ & Grill 267
Imari 265
Island Fish & Chips 261
Island Gourmet Markets 262
Island Lava Java 251
Island Naturals Market Deli ...269
Jackie Rey's Ohana Grill 251
Java on the Rock 252
Jolene's Kau Kau Korner 275
Jungle's Edge Coffee 262
Kailua Candy Company 259
Kamuela Provision Co. 262
Kanaka Kava 259
Ke'ei Café 252
Kenichi Pacific 256
Ken's House of Pancakes 269
Kiawe Kitchen 276
Kilauea Lodge & Restaurant ...276
Kiliki'i Italian Ice 259
Killer Tacos 257
Kirin Chinese Restaurant 264
Kohala Coffee/Kava Kafe 273
Kohala Snack Shack 274
Kona Brewing Co. 255
Kona Canoe Club 252
Kona Coffee Café 259
Kona Inn Restaurant 252
Kona Taeng-On Thai Food 258
La Bourgogne 254
Lava Rock Internet Café 276
Le Magic Pan 269
Leilani Bakery 267
Los Habañeros 257
Lotus Café 258
Luke's Place 274
Lulu's 253
Luquin's Mexican 273
Manago 256
Manta & Pavilion Wine Bar 262
Merriman's 267
Merriman's Market Café 263
Monstera 265
Mr. Ed's Bakery 274
New Chiang Mai Thai 271
Nihon Restaurant 270
Ning's Thai Cuisine 273
Norio's Japanese Restaurant ...263
Ocean Bar & Grill 263
Ocean Seafood 254
Ocean Sushi 270

Ocean Terrace 263
Ocean View Pizzeria 277
Orchid Court 263
Orchid Thai Cuisine 258
Original Thai 259
Pahu I'a 253
Pakini Grill 267
Pancho & Lefty's 257
Paolo's Bistro 273
Patz Pies 255
Pau 268
Pescatore 270
Puka Puka Kitchen 271
Punalu'u Bake Shop 277
Queen's Court 269
Quinn's Almost-by-the-Sea 253
Rapanui 256
Romano's Macaroni Grill 265
Rosa's Cantina & Sunset Grill ..258
Roy's Waikoloa Bar & Grill 265
Seafood Bar 263
Seaside Restaurant 269
Short N Sweet Bakery 271
Simply Natural 275
Sombat's Fresh Thai Cuisine ..271
Starbucks 264
Sushi Rock 274
Sweet Paradise Chocolatier ...266
Tacos El Unico 258
Tante's 257
Teshima's Restaurant 256
Tex Drive-In & Restaurant 276
Thai Rin 259
Thai Thai 277
Tropical Dreams Ice Cream 260
Two Ladies Kitchen 272
U • Top • It 254
Ultimate Burger 253
Village Burger 268
Volcano Golf
    & Country Club 277
Waikoloa Village Market 264
Waimea Coffee Co. 268
Whats Shakin' 274
Wilson's by the Bay 272
Woodshop Gallery Café 274
Yong's Kalbi 268

Dinner Cruises 281
Island Nightlife 278
Lu'au 278

Your table is ready...

By their very nature, restaurant reviews are the most subjective part of any guidebook. Nothing strains the credibility of a guidebook more. No matter what we say, if you eat at enough restaurants here, you will eventually have a dining experience directly in conflict with what this book leads you to believe. All it takes is one person to wreck what is usually a good meal. Many of us have had the experience when a friend referred us to a restaurant using reverent terms, indicating that they were about to experience dining ecstasy. And, of course, when you go there, the food is awful and the waiter is a jerk. There are many variables involved in getting a good or bad meal. Is the chef new? Was the place sold last month? Was the waitress just released from prison

for mauling a customer? We truly hope that our reviews match your experience. If they don't, please drop us a line. We read every restaurant comment readers send, and they help us in deciding which restaurant to re-evaluate on a given day.

Unlike some travel writers who announce themselves to restaurants (to cop a free meal, if the truth be told), we always review *anonymously* and only expose ourselves after a meal (not literally, of course) by phone if we need additional information. By their reviews, many guidebooks lead you to believe that *every* meal you eat in Hawai'i will be a feast, the best food in the free world. Frankly, that's not our style. Like anywhere else, there's ample opportunity to have lousy food served with a rotten ambiance by uncaring waiters. In the interest of space, we've left out *some* of the dives. We did, however, leave in a few of these turkeys just to demonstrate that we know we live the real world. Restaurants that stand out from the others in some way are high-lighted with this symbol.

For each restaurant, we list the price *per person* you can expect to pay. It ranges from the least expensive entrées alone, to the most expensive plus a beverage and usually appetizers. You can spend more if you try, but this is a good guideline. *The price excludes alcoholic beverages since this component of a meal can be so variable.* Obviously, everyone's ordering pattern is different, but we thought that it would be easier to compare various restaurants using dollar amounts than if we used different numbers of dollar signs or drawings of forks or whatever to differentiate prices between various restaurants. All take credit cards unless otherwise noted. When we mention that prices are reasonable, please take it in context. We mean reasonable *for Hawai'i.* (We *know* you pay less back home.) Food in Hawai'i is expensive, even if it's grown here. (You probably pay less for our fruit on the mainland than *we* do here.)

When we give directions to a restaurant, *mauka side* of highway means "toward the mountain" (or away from the ocean). The shopping centers we mention are on the maps to that area.

The difference between local and Hawaiian food can be difficult to classify. Basically, local food combines Hawaiian, American, Japanese, Chinese, Filipino and several other types and is (not surprisingly) eaten mainly by locals.

Most restaurants close around 9 p.m.

Lu'au, those giant outdoor Hawaiian parties, are described at the end.

When a restaurant requires **resort wear**, that means collared shirts for men (though nice shorts are *usually* okay) and dressy sportswear or dresses for women.

Below are descriptions of various island foods. Not all are Hawaiian, but this might be helpful if you encounter dishes unfamiliar to you.

ISLAND FISH & SEAFOOD

Ahi–Tuna; raw in sashimi or poke, also seared, blackened, baked or grilled; good in fish sandwiches. Try painting ahi steaks with mayonnaise, which *completely* burns off when BBQ'd but seals in the moisture. You end up tasting only the moist ocean steak. Generally most plentiful Apr.–Sept.

Kampachi–Raised just off the airport. In the wild these fish are called kahala; tasty but notoriously wormy. Farm-raised fish don't suffer from this problem.

Lobster–Hawaiian spiny lobster is quite good; also called "bugs" by lobster hunters. Maine lobster is revived on the Big Island, called Keahole Lobster.

Mahimahi–Deep ocean fish also known as a dolphinfish; served at lu'au; very common in restaurants. Sometimes tastes fishy, which can be offset in the preparation.

Marlin–Tasty when smoked, otherwise can be tough; the Pacific Blue Marlin is available almost year round.

Monchong–Excellent tasting deepwater fish, available year round. Usually served marinated and grilled.

Onaga–Also known as a ruby snapper; excellent eating in many preparations.

Ono–(Wahoo); *awesome* eating fish and can be prepared many ways; most plentiful May through October. Ono is also the Hawaiian word for delicious.

Opah–(Moonfish); excellent eating in many different preparations; generally available April through August.

'Opakapaka–(Crimson snapper); great tasting fish generally cooked several ways. Common Oct.–Feb.

'Opihi–Limpets found on ocean rocks. Eaten raw mixed with salt. Texture is similar to clams or mussels.

Poke–Fresh raw fish or octopus (tako) mixed with seaweed (limu), sesame seed and other seasonings and oil.

Shutome–Swordfish; dense meat that can be cooked several ways. Most plentiful March through July.

Walu–Also goes by other names such as butterfish and escolar. Be careful not to eat more than 6 ounces. The Hawaiian nickname for this oily fish is maku'u, which means—*ahem*, this is awkward—"uncontrollable bowel discharge." Eat too much, and you may pay more dearly than you intend.

LU'AU FOODS

Chicken lu'au–Chicken cooked in coconut milk and taro leaves.

Haupia–Coconut custard.

Kalua pig–Pig cooked in an underground oven called an imu, shredded and mixed with Hawaiian sea salt (outstanding!).

Laulau–Pork, beef or fish wrapped in taro and ti leaves and steamed. (You don't eat the ti leaf wrapping.)

Lomi salmon–Chilled salad consisting of raw, salted salmon, tomatoes and two kinds of onions.

Pipi kaula–Hawaiian beef jerky.

Poi–Steamed taro root pounded into a paste. It's a starch that will take on the taste of other foods mixed with it. Best eaten with kalua pig or fish. Visitors are encouraged to try it so they can badmouth it with authority.

OTHER ISLAND FOODS

Apple bananas–A smaller, denser, smoother texture than regular (Williams) bananas.

Barbecue sticks–Teriyaki-marinated pork, chicken or beef pieces barbecued and served on bamboo sticks.

Bento–Japanese box lunch.

Breadfruit–Melon-sized starchy fruit; served baked, deep fried, steamed, or boiled. Definitely an acquired taste.

Crackseed–Chinese-style, spicy preserved fruits and seeds. Li Hing Mui is one of the most popular flavors.

Guava–The inside is full of seeds, so it is rarely eaten raw. Used primarily for juice, jelly or jam.

Hawaiian supersweet corn–The finest corn you ever had, even raw. We'll lie, cheat, steal or maim to get it fresh.

Huli huli chicken–Hawaiian BBQ style.

Ka'u oranges–Locally grown. Usually, the uglier the orange, the better it tastes.

Kim chee–A Korean relish consisting of pickled cabbage, onions, radishes, garlic and chilies.

Kulolo–Steamed taro pudding.

Liliko'i–Passion fruit.

Loco moco–Rice, meat patty, egg and gravy. Specialty of Café 100 in Hilo.

Lychee–A reddish, woody peel that is discarded for the sweet, white fruit inside. Be careful of the pit. Small seed (or chicken-tongue) lychees are so good, they should be illegal.

Macadamia nut–A large, round nut grown primarily on the Big Island.

Malasada–Portuguese doughnut that is dipped in sugar. (Tex Drive-in is famous for them.)

Manapua–Steamed or baked bun filled with meat.

Mango–Bright orange fruit with yellow pink skin. Distinct, tasty flavor.

Manju–Cookie filled with a sweet center.

Musubi–Cold steamed rice, sometimes sliced Spam, rolled in black seaweed.

Papaya–Melon-like, pear-shaped fruit with yellow skin best eaten chilled. Good at breakfast.

Pipi Kaula–Hawaiian-style beef jerky. Excellent when dipped in poi. (Even if you don't like poi, this combo works.)

Plate lunch–An island favorite as an inexpensive, filling lunch. Consists of "two-scoop rice," a scoop of macaroni salad and some type of meat, either beef, chicken or fish. Also called a Box Lunch. Great for take-out.

Portuguese sausage–Pork sausage, highly seasoned with red pepper.

Pupu–Appetizer, finger foods or snack.

Saimin–Thin Chinese noodles cooked in a Japanese-style chicken, pork or fish broth. Word is peculiar to Hawai'i. Local Japanese say the dish comes from China. Local Chinese say it comes from Japan.

Shave ice–A block of ice is "shaved" into a ball with flavored syrup poured over the top. Best served with ice cream on the bottom. Very delicious.

Smoothie–Usually papaya, mango, frozen passion fruit and frozen banana, but almost any fruit can be used to make this milkshake-like drink. Add milk for creaminess.

Taro chips–Sliced and deep-fried taro; resembles potato chips.

KAILUA-KONA AMERICAN

Beach Tree
100 Kaupulehu Dr. • 325–8000

(ono) North of Kona—Fantastic beachside setting at the Four Seasons at Hualalai 14 miles north of Kona. Mixed menu of pizza, sandwiches, burgers, a couple of grilled items and salads at lunch. They have a lobster burger, but at $24 we were too horrified by the price to try it. Dinner is steak, seafood and pasta. It's pricey enough to consider their upscale restaurant **Pahu I'a** instead. $20–$30 for lunch, $20–$60 for dinner. They get an ono because it's great food. But *expensive*...

Big Jake's Island BBQ
83-5308 Mamalahoa Hwy • 328–1227

South of Kona—It's not that we don't like the food here, it's just that you pay restaurant prices but end up eating from plastic baskets on picnic tables outside. Food is pulled pork, ribs, brisket and other BBQ staples. $13–$28 for lunch and early dinner. On Hwy 11 next to a fish market at the 106 mile marker.

Bongo Ben's Island Café
75-5819 Alii Dr. • 329–9203

Kona—Fairly broad menus with expanded offerings on the usual breakfast items, burgers, sandwiches, fresh fish, wraps and salads at lunch; add steak, pork and pasta at dinner. The atmosphere is busy and noisy from the Alii Drive traffic, but your view of the water across the street isn't obstructed by much. Breakfast is what they do best. After that, the food is pretty average, and the service can be a bit unfocused. They tend to overcharge on extras. ($3 to add avocado to your burger? Hey, avo trees are *everywhere* here.) Lots of choices from the bar, though. $9–$15 for breakfast and lunch, the top end moves to $25 at dinner. Across from the seawall.

Bubba Gump Shrimp Co.
75-5776 Alii Dr. • 331–8442

(ono) Kona—This whole restaurant is based on the 1994 movie *Forrest Gump*. You'll find most of the characters' names in the menu along with lots of shrimp dishes. The Dumb Luck Coconut Shrimp is excellent but pricey at $20. We absolutely love their hush pups (different from hush puppies). Their Medal Margarita is smokin' good, and the portion is hefty. For dessert, try their Chocolate Chip Cookie Sundae, a sundae served in a cast iron skillet topped with caramel, chocolate, peanuts and whipped cream. Great views and a fun atmosphere make it a good experience, if you can tolerate the long wait at the door and the unusual service. If you want a server's attention, you have to flip the license plate to read "Stop Forrest Stop." On Ali'i Drive next to Waterfront Row in downtown Kona. **$13–$25** for lunch and dinner. No reservations.

Buns in the Sun
75-5595 Palani Rd. • 326–2774

Kona—A bakery/sandwich joint with great food for the money. Take something as simple as a French dip, put it on their sourdough hoagies, and it becomes delicious. Tasty hot and cold sandwiches, soups and great baked goods. (Love the macaroons and good coffee cake.) For breakfast they have pastries, as well as egg dishes, including kalua pig and eggs with rice (a worthy choice). Avoid the biscuits and gravy; they taste like plastic. Good, flaky croissants. Take them to their wrought iron chairs (which make an *incredible* screech when you move 'em), or grab it to go. In the Lanihau Shopping Center off Palani Road. Breakfast is a cheap **$5–$10**; lunch is **$10–$13**.

Coffee Shack
83-5799 Mamalahoa Hwy • 328–9555

South of Kona—A good place to stop on your way to the volcano—they open at 7:30 a.m. Except when we want a *big* breakfast, this is where we often stop. *Fantastic* view down the slopes of Mt. Hualalai overlooking Kealakekua and Honaunau—try to get a railing table and check out the gigantic avocado tree and the coffee trees below you. (It's nice to sit there drinking coffee grown from those very trees.) Tables are outdoors but covered, and the place is clean. Nice selection of coffee drinks, good homemade baked goods and breads (when fresh, which is not a certainty), a small selec-

tion of breakfast items and a decent selection of sandwiches and pizzas for lunch. Their home-grown coffee is usually tasty (occasionally off). **$10–$15** for breakfast and lunch. Service is often slow. On ocean side of highway in Captain Cook between the 109 and 108 mile markers.

Costco
73-5600 Maiau St. • 331–4834

Kona—You'd be surprised at how many people eat at the food stand at Costco. Their pizza is surprisingly good (they use pretty good ingredients and the crust isn't bad), and it's *very* cheap. **$10** for a gigantic pizza. They also serve hot dogs, salads and a few other items. In the back of the store they have tasty whole rotisserie chickens for **$5**. You need to be a Costco member to get in. We gave them an ONO because of the value—can't beat it. North Kona, see map on page 164.

Don the Beachcomber
75-5852 Alii Dr. • 329–3111

Kona—If you remember the original Don the Beachcomber restaurant, you probably also remember the end of Prohibition. This is the guy who claimed to have invented the mai tai in 1933. The theme has been revived here at the Royal Kona Resort. The setting offers a commanding view of Kailua Bay and Alii Drive, and the torches at night give it a nice ambiance. Food, however, is unremarkable at best, and definitely overpriced. And the $16 breakfast buffet is more of a glorified continental breakfast. Lunch is pizza, burgers and salads; dinner features pricey seafood but free, glorious sunsets. **$12–$19** for breakfast and lunch (the latter served at the bar), **$25–$40** for dinner. And yes, the original mai tais *are* good here. Personally, we prefer the killer bar location here for a sunset cocktail instead of the restaurant.

The Fish Hopper Seafood & Steaks
75-5683 Alii Dr. • 326–2002
Kona—The food has improved here. In the past we've had problems with bland flavors, but our last few visits the seasonings came out of the cabinet. Prices are pretty high, especially at dinner, but the view from across the seawall is one of the best on Alii Drive. Fish is what they do best (not surprisingly), but they also have tacos, wraps and sandwiches at lunch, and plenty of pasta and steak at dinner. Their clam chowder is excellent. And some of their drinks, such as the Bucket of Fire, are downright amazing. **$9–$20** for breakfast, **$12–$20** for lunch, **$20–$35** for dinner. Reservations recommended. We considered giving them an ONO, but $27 for seafood pasta is hard to swallow.

Green Flash Coffee
75-6000 Alii Dr. • 329–4387
ONO Kona—In front of the Sea Village Condos (see map page 63), it's a convenient spot for anyone staying along Alii Drive since you won't need to drill into town and find a place to park. They make serious coffee drinks like the Earthquake with Ghirardelli chocolate and *four* shots of espresso. It'll make your heartbeat register 7.0 on the Richter Scale. Try a breakfast sandwich served on French toast with a side of syrup. For lunch, their hot panini sandwiches are excellent. Consider the vegetable muffaletta and substitute the tapanada with pesto. Good baked goods from Mamane Bakery in Waimea. The service is friendly, but there's not much seating. A cheap **$5–$10** for breakfast and lunch. Open early every day from 6:30 a.m. So what's a green flash? Look at our description of that on page 57.

Harbor House
74-425 Kealakehe Pkwy. • 326–4166
ONO Kona—Ask anyone who frequents Harbor House why they go, and they'll give you a one-word answer—*schooners!* Located at Honokohau Harbor 2 miles north of Kona overlooking the water and boats, they serve the coldest beer on the island in ultra-thick, 18-ounce frosted schooners for around $3. (Oh, I almost forgot, they serve food, too.) This is a popular place to stop after a fishing or SCUBA excursion. The food consists of average fish and chips, fried calamari, burgers and assorted other fast food. (Good fish sandwich, though.) We didn't give 'em an ONO *because of the food;* it's just a great place to tip a cold one and watch the tranquil harbor waters while you go over your adventures of the day. If you sit near the bar, you may hear lots of watering hole talk. **$9–$15**. Head toward the harbor off Hwy 19 between the 97 and 98 mile markers and turn right at the buildings. Closes around 7 p.m.; the schooners aren't as cold near closing time.

Holuakoa Gardens & Café
76-5901 Mamalahoa Hwy • 322–2233
ONO Mauka of Kona (in Holualoa)—This is the best reason to drive up to Holualoa. Thanks to readers for tipping us off to a place we've driven by many times without noticing. They mainly use ingredients grown nearby and clearly gush with pride over the results. The menu changes nightly based on what local farmers and fishermen supply. Beef, seafood and pasta are what they do, using incredibly creative preparations. They brag that they are a "slow food establishment," so don't be in a hurry. There's no real view and you'll hear some traffic noise over the jazz music background, but you won't care. Start things out with the very unusual pizzetas. (Fantastic use of pears and sometimes figs.) The salads are from fresh-picked local greens. (Forget the heavy dressings; just enjoy the greens.) You'll want to bring a light jacket since the elevation is 1,400

feet. This is one of those restaurants that orbits around a single dominating chef—and we hope he is happy and content to keep doing this for a long time. The desserts are stupid-good with the flourless midnight torte being absolute chocolate heaven. You may have to park down the road if you can't find the parking lot above the restaurant. Closed Sun. and Mon. Reservations recommended. Brunch ($14–$20) isn't as good; stick with dinner, which is $25–$40. They also have an adjacent café for morning coffee and pastries. Almost across the street from the Kona Hotel on Hwy 180. From Hwy 11 you can cut up the mountain from Lako St. near the 119 mile marker, right when it dead ends, then left on Hwy 180 for less than a mile; mauka side.

Huggo's
75-5828 Kahakai Rd. • 329–1493

Kona—This is a very difficult restaurant to review. They have *gorgeous* open-air views adjacent to the ocean at Kailua Bay. They are so close to the water because they are grandfathered into the regulations restricting oceanside construction. The sound of the surf can get loud enough to sometimes create an arms race of sound among patrons, where the volume keeps escalating. The ocean proximity alone almost gets them an ONO. But execution is spotty. Food is often over- or under-cooked. Service can get forgetful. No doubt with their setting, they have no trouble filling their tables. And the recipes are quite good, like the tender teri beef. Add pasta, steak, seafood and some veggie items, and you have the potential for a great meal, if all cylinders are firing. Try to get a railing table where you look down onto sand, rock and water. (Preferable over the patio tables.) The adjacent lounge is a good place to enjoy a drink at sunset. Since it's so pricey and the view so important to the experience, consider them for an early dinner, because you're paying premium prices and getting a premium location with merely adequate food. $30–$45 for dinner. Off Alii Drive, downtown Kona near Royal Kona Resort. Their lunch is served next door at **Huggo's on the Rocks** and is mostly sandwiches, burgers and some off-category items such as kalbi ribs and furikake-crusted fish for $12–$20. Huggo's review didn't change much for this edition because the same problems still exist. They wouldn't have to pick it up much to get an ONO out of us.

Island Lava Java
75-5799 Alii Dr. • 327–2161

ONO Kona—An awesome—and highly popular—place for breakfast. The coffee is pretty good (though sometimes not very hot), and the food is tasty and not *too* ridiculously priced for the location. (They're right across the street from the ocean with excellent views, so you ain't gonna get a bargain.) Above average baked goods and a few breakfast items like the tasty breakfast wraps. Their cinnamon rolls are obscene and utterly massive (big enough to use as a flotation device if you fall in the water), and they taste great. An easy recommendation, although the rolls don't usually come out of the oven until around 7:30 a.m. Good (though *very* pricey) fresh-squeezed pineapple juice. Get an outdoor table. Lunch is fairly well-prepared sandwiches, soups, salads and pizzas. There used to be a Cook Island pine tree out front. It fell, smiting (I always wanted to use that word) the business for six months. Alii Drive in Kona in Alii Sunset Plaza. $5–$15 for breakfast, $10–$15 for lunch, $15–$25 for dinner.

Jackie Rey's Ohana Grill
75-5995 Kuakini Hwy • 327–0209

ONO Kona—Locals are the majority of the customers, and not just because it's not near Alii Drive. Jackie Rey's excels in every detail from well-made drinks to decadent desserts. Choose from their respectable wine list or go for the mai tai. The dinner entrées—fish, steak, pasta and short ribs—are attractively presented, and the chef knows how to combine flavors. Finish your meal with a Triple Fudge Brownie Roll. Lunch is equally good with an array of smart salads and sandwiches, burgers and some odds and ends. **$11–$17** for lunch, **$13–$35** for dinner. No lunch on weekends. On Kuakini Hwy across from Walua Road.

Java on the Rock
75-5828 Kahakai Rd. • 329-9262

ONO Kona—An espresso bar that serves a little bit of food. Only five items at breakfast. They cook their eggs using the cappuccino machine and put them in a tortilla. Is a breakfast burrito worth *$9?* Not anywhere else. But their location is *wonderful*. It's right next to the water in an ultra-relaxing atmosphere, so you're paying for that. They're not exactly lightning fast, but with this location you're not exactly in a hurry. Around **$13** for coffee and a breakfast entree. Next door to Huggo's off Alii Drive near the Royal Kona Resort. You can't linger past 11 a.m. That's when Huggo's takes over the spot, and it becomes Huggo's on the Rocks.

Ke'ei Café
79-7511 Mamalohoa Hwy • 322-9992

ONO South of Kona—Not really American, sort of a hodge-podge of items from many countries. (I guess that *is* American.) You know how you sometimes purposely get into a rut at a restaurant by ordering the same dish because you love it so much? That's how I am for the fresh fish (especially ono) on Thai curry and jasmine rice, or the (spicy) fajitas stuffed with chicken or tofu, salsa, black bean chili sauce and avocado. The decor is nicely appointed,

but passing cars from the highway are too loud. Don't worry about it, though. The flavors are unlimited. (Try the eggplant rolls with couscous inside for an appetizer or the excellent coconut shrimp rice cakes.) Also available are rib-eye steak, great pork chops and a few other items. Desserts are bread pudding, a mango cobbler and more. And they make good mango martinis. Our review doesn't change much because the place is consistent. On Hwy 11 just south of Kona in Kainaliu between the 112 and 113 mile markers. **$17–$33** for dinner. Closed Sun. and Mon. No credit cards.

Kona Canoe Club
75-5744 Alii Dr. • 331-1155

ONO Kona—Their sign reads, FISH, BURGERS AND GROG. And although we haven't found grog on the menu, they do make a powerful mai tai, if you're in the mood. It may not be world famous like they claim, but it may make you *feel* famous after just one. Great oceanside location, especially if you get a railing seat. The food is sandwiches, lots of burgers, salads and a little steak and seafood. The quality is pretty solid, and they seem to use a good grade of ingredients. Consider the fish sandwich polished off with a slice of mud pie. They're fussy about substitutions, and fries are not included with entrées. But the ocean is kind of mesmerizing from most of the tables, and overall it's a good experience. **$11–$22** for lunch and dinner; more if you get the ribs. In the Kona Inn Shopping Center.

Kona Inn Restaurant
75-5744 Alii Dr. • 329-4455

ONO Kona—Mostly seafood with a little pasta and stir-fry. Nice ambiance—a good place for a sunset dinner. Just a strip of grass separates you from the ocean. Dinner includes many varieties of fish. Consider the *super*-rich but tasty stuffed local fresh fish. At dinner, avoid the uncomfortable antique chairs in favor of the high-back wicker chairs. **$12–$20** for lunch, **$20–$45** for dinner. The food and service are usually very good. Check out the ceiling fans—all interconnected by an old belt system. Some parents like to bring their keiki here where the munchkins can play on the grass while the grown-ups can dine and keep an eye on them. Reader e-mail has gotten lukewarm on Kona Inn lately, but we've had pretty good luck so will keep the ONO—for now. Located on the ocean side of Alii Drive in downtown Kona at the Kona Inn Shopping Village. Can't miss it.

Lava Java—See *Island Lava Java*.

Lulu's
75-5819 Alii Dr. • 331–2633

Kona—Their motto is *cirrhosis at sea* or *red carpet service at shag rug prices*. With their Caribbean/South Seas-type decor, ample portions, comfort bar food and giant margaritas, Lulu's has the potential to work. But they've slipped lately, and we've had to pull their ONO. The food has gotten blah and greasy. Numerous sandwiches and burgers, they also have a large pupu selection and some good veggie items. Nice view overlooking the water. (Just pretend you don't see the enormous power lines in the way.) On Alii Drive at Coconut Grove Market Place. **$12–$22** for lunch and dinner.

Pahu I'a
100 Kaupulehu Dr. • 325–8000

North of Kona—This is one of our favorite restaurants on the island. The lanai tables (which are a bit too close together) are as close to eating on the beach as you'll get; ask for them. The menu is mostly seafood, lobster and beef. Items change often but are usually utterly delicious. Flavors aren't hit-you-over-the-head knockouts but rather super-

skillful blends of subtlety. And their warm dark chocolate cake is a fitting end to your meal. We like to arrive about 45 minutes before sunset to get a good table and to gawk at the superb beachside setting. This is a romantic place. Service is top-notch professional. They rarely do anything wrong, but, of course, you pay for that perfection, and portions are scaled back as is the norm at fancy restaurants. Breakfast is memorable but *very* pricey. If you pass on the killer $34 buffet, you can have French toast for $19, eggs with meat and 'taters for $24, etc. **$20–$45** for breakfast, dinner is **$40–$80**. Expensive? You got *that* right. But, oh, what a meal. Reservations recommended. Resort wear required. At the Four Seasons Hualalai 14 miles north of Kona on Hwy 19.

Quinn's Almost-by-the-Sea
75-5655 Palani Rd. • 329–3822

Kona—Truth in advertising. You're close to the ocean but can't really see it. Lunch offers seafood, burgers and sandwiches. The fish sandwich, especially Cajun style, is excellent, as are most seafood items. (Switch the mahi mahi sandwich for ono or ahi—it's *mo bettah*.) The clam chowder could use a little improvement. For dinner, it's the same menu plus more steak and seafood. Service is quick at lunch time. Consider the quasi-outdoor section for a nice lunch-time nautical, green ambiance. This place hasn't changed a bit over several editions. Most of the food is tastily prepared. We recommend lunch over the pricey dinner. **$10–$14** for lunch, **$10–$30** for dinner. On Palani Road across from the King Kamehameha Kona Beach Hotel in downtown Kona. Limited parking.

Ultimate Burger
74-5450 Makala Blvd. • 329–2326

Kona—They raise lots of cattle on this island, but most

burgers are made from frozen beef flown in from the mainland. Not this place. The hamburger is fresh and locally raised (which seems to have a...*beefier* flavor than standard beef). They also mix herbs into the meat, and results are wonderful. Patties are 1/3-pound, and you can get 1 to 4 of them on a bun. (For the record, we can't visualize how someone could manage to eat the 1 1/3-pound TKO burger.) The quality is excellent as are the tasty (but pricey) fries. Vegetarians can get the taro burger, and beer is also available. A good place for tasty, guilty pleasure. In the Kona Commons on Makala north of downtown Kona. **$7–$15** for lunch and dinner.

U · Top · It
75-5799 Alii Dr. • 329–0092

Kona—There's nothing else like this on the island. Everything orbits their tasty taro pancrêpes. Top 'em any way you like. Add sausage, spam, fried rice and eggs, and you have their Kanak Attack. Top the pancrêpes with tomatoes, basil, pepperoni, salami and cheese, and you have the Pizzaro. Or add chocolate hazelnut, raspberries and passionfruit sauce, and you get Pele's Passion dessert. The topping selection is vast, so it's only your imagination that stands between you and a good meal. Be creative and enjoy the novelty. They also have burgers, pork chops, teri beef and other non-crêpe items. Good Tropical Dreams ice cream. This is a great concept—what's not to love? Hidden away behind Island Lava Java on Alii Drive. **$9–$14** for breakfast and lunch. Closed Mondays.

KAILUA-KONA CHINESE

Ocean Seafood
75-5626 Kuakini Hwy • 329–3055

Kona—The food is more authentic than most Chinese restaurants, and the price is compelling. Usually well-prepared dishes, fresh ingredients and lots of attention to quality, but sometimes they drop the ball. Buffets offered most of the time—these are an *excellent* bargain. Lunch buffet for **$10**, dinner buffet **$14–$16**. Otherwise, off the menu is **$10–$20** per person. Located in the King Kamehameha Mall in Kona. See map on page 61.

KAILUA-KONA FRENCH

La Bourgogne French Restaurant
77-6400 Nalani St. • 329–6711

Kona—This *tiny* restaurant on Hwy 11 between Keauhou and Kona serves tasty and well-conceived dishes, including lamb, duck, venison, rabbit, lobster and even veal sweetbreads. Good and reasonably priced wine list. Entrée prices are in a pretty narrow range. Only dings: a bit cramped and enclosed with no view. Closed Sunday and Monday. Dinner is **$37–$47**. Reservations recommended. We haven't changed our review in a while because this place hasn't change much over time.

KAILUA-KONA ITALIAN

Bianelli's
78-6831 Alii Dr. • 322–0377

Kona—Long-time visitors might remember Bianelli's. It was one of those great places that mysteriously closed. After a six-year absence, they reopened and then moved to the Keauhou Shopping Center at the south end of Alii Drive. Although it's the same owner and recipes, the food isn't quite as good as I remember. (But memory can be a funny thing, especially with food.) They're still good, though. For the pizza, opt for the deep dish crust (the reason for the ONO) instead of the New York. And try the killer pesto and pine nut bread. By-the-slice is cheap at $3. Take-out or snag an outdoor table. **$5–$10** for lunch an dinner.

Boston Basil's Italian Restaurant
75-5707 Alii Dr. • 326–7836

Kona—A gigantic menu that'll take you awhile to navigate. You got your pizza, your pasta, various parmigianas, lots of chicken, ½-pound burgers, seafood, sandwiches and…more, but you get the picture. It's hard to do everything well, and unfortunately, the food reflects this. Items taste hastily assembled with cheap ingredients. They peak at the beginning with the tasty French bread, then it's all downhill. Some downstairs tables have a sliver of a view of Kailua Bay. Upstairs tables feel a bit pinned in, but there's live music most nights. **$12–$25** for lunch and dinner, but you can do a slice and soda for $6. Across from Hulihe'e Palace where Alii meets Likana.

Kona Brewing Co. & Brewpub
75-5629 Kuakini Hwy • 334–2739

ONO Kona—A cool place to go for some tasty brew and a pizza or salad. Twelve taps feature 9 or so different beers made there, as well as seasonal and guest beers. They range from the mild (Lilikoi Wheat Ale) to the not-so-mild (Fire Rock Pale Ale). Their best is the Hefeweissen. Most of the pizzas (except their Hawaiian style) are delicious. *Love* the Ka'u Pesto. If you normally sprinkle red peppers on your pizza, consider replacing the regular sauce with their Cajun sauce instead. In fact, they have 8 different sauces and *lots* of toppings, so the possibilities are many. As a result, we're forced to review them often so we can evaluate all the permutations. (We do it for you, only for you. Aren't we selfless?) Their Kilauea lava flow dessert is pretty criminal, and a half portion is probably enough for two. The service could use a little improvement, and we wish they could do something about the flies and gnats at the outside tables, but

overall, this is a *great* place with the best pizza on the island. **$14–$24** for lunch and dinner. At the end of Pawai Place off Kaiwi Street. See map on page 61. No reservations, and long waits are not uncommon.

Patz Pies
81-6596 Mamalahoa Hwy • 323–8100

ONO South of Kona—Yeah, now we're talking. An easy-to-miss little hole in the wall on Hwy 11 in Kealakekua that dispenses outstanding New York-style pizza for cheap prices. Grab it and go. The owner is a genuine New York pizza-maker, and the product shows pride in workmanship. A slice is $3 and a large pizza (for two or three people) is $17–$25. That means you can expect to eat well for **$5–$12**. Across from Discovery Antiques between mile markers 111 and 112.

KAILUA-KONA JAPANESE

Bistro Yokohama
75-5799 Alii Dr. • 329–9661

ONO Kona—The ambiance and clientele are very Japanese. This isn't an upscale place, however. Lunch is a variety of Japanese items (but no sushi) plus local items (such as hamburger katsu), and they have a very reasonable $8 plate lunch. Dinner brings sushi and more choices. The language barrier can be a problem here, so you may need to point a lot. **$9–$20** for lunch, **$20–$35** for dinner. Hidden away behind Island Lava Java on Alii Drive.

Hayashi's You Make The Roll
75-5725 Alii Dr. • 326–1322

ONO Kona—Tasty and cheap. The sushi is made right before your eyes and tastes great. Just a few outdoor tables, but this is the place to get your sushi fix. **$5–$10**. Kona

Marketplace Shopping Center off Alii Drive, *way* in the back.

Kenichi Pacific
78-6831 Alii Dr. • 322–6400

ono Kona—Very well-prepared sushi in a slightly ritzy atmosphere. In addition to the sushi, they also have other entrées under the fusion genre, such as steak, seafood and lamb. In fact, their mac nut-encrusted lamb is absolutely wonderful and unexpectedly unJapanese. The attention to detail is obvious. The molten cake dessert is *ultra* rich chocolate. (Oh, yeah!) It ain't cheap here, but with good service, consistently good food and a good environment, it's easy to recommend. **$15–$45** for dinner. In the Keauhou Shopping Center at the south end of Alii Drive. Open nightly from 5 to 9:30 p.m. Closed Mondays.

Teshima's Restaurant
79-7251 Mamalahoa Hwy • 322–9140

ono South of Kona—Clean, friendly place with simple but tasty Japanese, American and local items, such as bento, teriyaki beef and fried fish. There's something for everyone at this family-run restaurant, and service is usually friendly. Our only gripe is that they have a habit of bringing all the food at once, typical of izakaya restaurants in Japan. Off Hwy 11 in Honalo, just south of Kona. Lunch is **$7–$16**, dinner is **$10–$20**. Cash only.

KAILUA-KONA LOCAL

Ba-Le
74-5588 Palani Rd. • 327–1212

ono Kona—OK, so it's not really local. It's part of a chain of Vietnamese noodle shops with French bread sandwiches. But the food is good for the price. Those who aren't fond of Vietnamese flavors will probably like the sandwiches, beef stew or the roast beef croissant. Lots of veggie items. **$5–$13** for lunch and dinner. In Kona Coast Shopping Center, Palani Road, Kona.

Big Island Grill
75-5702 Kuakini Hwy • 326–1153

ono Kona—Popular with local residents and a bit loud with closely spaced tables and no-nonsense service, the food is hearty local-style with items such as chicken katsu, loco moco, tempura fish (which is great) and saimin. Portions are dependably generous, but it can take awhile to get your food. Desserts are big and deadly. (Good banana splits and excellent mud pie.) Breakfast is **$8–$18**, lunch is **$11–$20**, dinner is mostly similar with a few pricier steaks. At the corner of Henry and Kuakini. Closed Sunday.

Manago
82-6155 Mamalahoa Hwy • 323–2642

ono South of Kona—It's like eating in Grandma's kitchen. Ambiance is *so* homey, and this place never seems to change. They are famous across the island for their pork chops, which, I'm happy to say, are *not* just like Mama used to make. (Hers were always so dry.) These are moist, fatty and flavorful. (They use an ancient, cast-iron pan.) They bring your sides at the very beginning, and you share them. They also have teri steak, butterfish, liver, etc. For dessert they feature…absolutely nothing. Pick up a Snickers bar in the lobby. Closed Monday. South of Kona in Captain Cook off Hwy 11 at the Manago Hotel. Can't miss it. **$4–$7** for breakfast. **$10–$16** for lunch and dinner.

Rapanui
75-5695 Alii Dr. • 329–0511

ono Kona—We didn't know how to classify them. They call it *island food for island people*. The name comes from a beach in New

Zealand where the chef hails from. The menu from around Polynesia and Asia offers sate (skewered meat), curry and stir-fry. The beef sate is the best. Ingredients are very fresh, and we like their use of red chilies and lime in the Paw Paw Chicken. If you're allergic to nuts, be careful what you order. Most items come with peanuts, peanut sauce or cashews. Half the desserts are made with peanut butter as well. Try one of their custom–made iced teas, like the lemongrass ginger mint. Tucked in the back of the Banyan Court Mall on Ali'i Drive. **$10–$20** for dinner from 5 p.m. to 9 p.m. Closed Sundays. The atmosphere ain't much, but the food wins us over.

Tante's
75-5693 Alii Dr. • 334–1555

Kona—Local food right across the street from the seawall in Kona. With a view like that, they wouldn't need to go the extra mile...and they *sure don't*. You got local items, such as chicken katsu and kalbi ribs, Filipino items, such as pork adobo and pinakbet or burgers. Add some steak and seafood at dinner. The food tastes cheap and greasy. We can't think of any items to recommend. Both the surroundings and service are kind of blah. Not trying to be mean, just trying to warn you. **$9–$15** for breakfast and lunch, **$10–$25** for dinner.

KAILUA-KONA MEXICAN

Killer Tacos
74-5483 Kaiwi St. • 329–3335

Kona—The kind of place you'd never find if someone didn't tell you about it. Tucked away in an industrial area, the name is spot on. (Well, we've never actually seen anyone drop dead here.) Killer tacos, killer burritos, killer portions and killer prices. Pretty deadly, huh? The most expensive thing is the $7 taco salad, which is...well, you

know. Put kalua pig or the spicy ground beef in your burrito, or bag one of the fish tacos. The only thing that needs improving is the salsa—consider substituting it for hot sauce. See Kona map, page 61. Near the highway, on Kaiwi, near Luhia Street. **$5–$9** for lunch and dinner. Closed Sunday. Cash only.

Los Habañeros
78-6831 Alii Dr. • 324–4688

Kona—We're baffled by this one. We got plenty of e-mails from readers recommending this place, but we have to walk away scratching our heads. Cheap Mexican eats for sure, but it's one step below Taco Bell. With a name like Los Habañeros you'd expect the food to be bursting with flavor. Instead, it's incredibly bland unless you shower the food with salsa. Ask for extra cilantro so you have some sort of flavor to start with. We're certainly not dissing our readers. We just don't get it. In the Keauhou Shopping Center. **$7–$15** for lunch and early dinner.

Pancho & Lefty's
75-5719 Alii Dr. • 326–2171

Kona—With their ultra-prominent location on Alii Drive (the view of the ocean isn't as good as you might think from the street), this place could serve really bad food and still put people in seats. (And our previous review reflected our general lack of enthusiasm.) The menu is large and varied. (Non-Mexican items are on the "Gringo Grill" section.) The nachos are hearty, the food filling and items are more than acceptable. You won't dream about it, but it's not bad. You'd probably eat here again in a pinch...but you wouldn't tell your friends about it. Sunset sounds are filled with the squawks of flocks of mynah birds in the trees outside. Mixed drinks here are tasty and fairly potent. Overall, Pancho & Lefty's is one of those places that you can't help but notice in

Kona, and is an adequate choice for a meal. **$13–$30** for lunch and dinner.

Rosa's Cantina & Sunset Grill
75-5801 Alii Dr. • 326–1198
Kona—This place has the same owners as Pancho and Lefty's (but with better views from some tables if you ignore the ugly power lines). The menu is more creative with items like molcajete (too complicated to explain), punta nesta pasta, steak diablo plus other steak, seafood and burgers. Prices ain't cheap, and if you get a table farther from the rails you'll feel overcharged. Like Pancho, they make a pretty good nacho, and like Lefty, other items can be lacking. In Coconut Grove Marketplace. **$13–$30**.

Tacos El Unico
75-5729 Alii Dr. • 326–4033
ono Kona—You won't find fajitas at this shotgun shack. This is as authentic as it gets, right down to the little old lady making your flour tortillas from scratch. Most dishes consist of beans, rice and tortillas next to a pile of seasoned meat or seafood. Flavors are mild, and don't be surprised if you find a bone in your food. If you're not used to authentic Mexican, you may not like it. They have unusual items like goat, beef tongue and beef cheek meat. Their ceviche is good. **$10–$15** for lunch and dinner. They also have a $10 breakfast. Behind the Kona Marketplace on Alii Drive.

KAILUA-KONA THAI

Lotus Café
73-5617 Maiau St. • 327–3270
ono Kona—You won't drive by this place; ya gotta know it's there. It's literally part of an Asian wooden furniture store. (So no cheesy plastic tables here.) This is another example of readers tipping us off to a great place. The menu stresses Thai, but it also includes some Indian. Burmese, Indonesian, Vietnamese and Singaporean dishes. They use mostly organic ingredients from local suppliers. The variety of flavors is amazing. This is *not* a one trick pony. If you're having troubling picking, the taster's special has three small entrées—a nice way to go. Their Thai tea is pretty different than other Thai teas—real gingery. You'll either love it or hate it. You don't have go spicy to still get flavors here. But if you *do*, they also make their own dairy-free gelato to cool things off and offer various smoothies and blended drinks from it. Reasonably priced and great quality. At the back corner of Kaloko Industrial Park, top of the road past Costco at Kamanu and Maiau. See map on page 164. **$10–$20** for lunch and dinner.

Kona Taeng-On Thai Food
75-5744 Alii Dr. • 329–1994
Kona—Sorry, but the food's not good enough to warrant these kind of prices. Good menu but uninspiringly prepared. Service is a little cranky. You got way better Thai choices in Kona. **$13–$30**. Upstairs on Alii Drive across from Kona Marketplace.

Orchid Thai Cuisine
74-5555 Kaiwi St. • 327–9437
ono Kona—We liked them when they had a simple, spartan atmosphere buried in the back of in an industrial area because the food was so good. Now that they've moved and have a more refined ambiance, we're as happy as can be. The food is great and very reasonably priced. *Super* good chicken satay. Good curries. The portions are on the small side, but overall this is a winner. BYOB. **$10–$20** for lunch and dinner. In Kuakini Center.

Take Kuakini Hwy north, right on Kaiwi Street. Closed Sunday.

Original Thai
75-5629 Kuakini Hwy • 329–3459

 Kona—We find it ironic that a place called Original Thai would plaster the definition of *original* all over their menu, claim that their food is what original Thai tastes like, then serve burgers, wraps and coleslaw as well as Thai items. What's even more strange is that they do it so well. The larb wrap is bursting with goodness, and the burgers are made with curried meat. Even the fries and coleslaw have a hint of Thai. The curries are fantastic and come in big portions. A wonderful start is a cup of coconut milk soup. It's a shame that service can be snippy. In the Illima Court Shopping Center. **$8–$17** for lunch and dinner. Closed Monday.

Thai Rin
75-5799 Alii Dr. • 329–2929

Kona—Nice location right across Alii Drive from the ocean. The curries are their weakest item—surprisingly bland and watery. They make a pretty good garlic eggplant and the pad Thai is tasty, but overall it's an underwhelming Thai experience. Next to Island Lava Java. **$10–$25** (more for the lobster combo) for lunch and dinner. Lunch specials can knock the price down a couple of bucks.

KAILUA-KONA TREATS

Cuz'ns
75-5744 Alii Dr. • 326–4920

Kona—Smoothies here are real variable. Sometimes fairly good, sometimes way too thin and sweet. Pricey at **$5** each. You're better off next door at **Kona Coffee Café** (329–7131) where you can grab a cold frappe. (Don't let them twist your arm into buying their overpriced bags of Kona coffee.) At the back of the Kona Inn Shopping Village.

Hawaiian Ice Cones
75-5595 Palani Rd. • 895–8390

Kona—Probably the best shave ice in Kona. Good, fine ice and chilled syrups. (Necessary to avoid the dreaded *chunking* that happens if you don't chill 'em.) Add ice cream on the bottom, and for **$3** you have a *broke da mouf* experience. Next to Longs Drugs in Lanihau Center off Palani Road.

Kailua Candy Company
73-5612 Kauhola St. • 329–2522

Kona—Handmade chocolates are the specialty here. Expensive but delicious. Try the a'a lava (dark chocolate with coconut and mac nuts) or the turtles. They also make utterly indecent cheesecake with some world-class flavor combinations sold by the slice. Near Costco off Hwy 19 at the 96 mile marker. See map on page 164.

Kanaka Kava
75-5803 Alii Dr. • 327–1660

Kona—Gee, we didn't know *where* to put this one. It's a kava bar. Kava (called awa in Hawai'i) is made from a root and tastes a little like woody water. It's a mild relaxant/pain killer. Polynesians have been using it for generations, and it has cultural importance here. When you get a bowl, you're supposed to gulp it down fast; don't sip. It may make your mouth tingle. Consider it once at least for the novelty. **$6** for the kava. They also have some pupu to wash it down. (And the owner sometimes plays a mean harmonica.) On the backside of Coconut Grove Marketplace on Alii Drive.

Kiliki'i Italian Ice
75-5805 Alii Dr. • 640–4700

Kona—Don't confuse this with shave ice. Instead of

syrups poured over ice, fruit or juice is mixed in before freezing. The concoction is then ground up. The result is a coarser but more evenly distributed flavor than shave ice. Try the liliko'i or mango. **$4–$7**. In the Coconut Grove Marketplace.

Tropical Dreams Ice Cream
Various Locations

(ONO) This is the best ice cream that we've ever found in Hawai'i, and it's made on the island in Waimea. It's fairly easy to find island wide at places that serve ice cream. If you see it, snag some. It's downright wicked.

KOHALA DINING

There are a lot of ONO symbols in the Kohala dining section. That's no accident. If you're staying in Kohala, you'll find that the food choices are outstanding. That makes it difficult for us as reviewers. Normally, if we think a place is a dump, we say it's a dump. If the food or service is lousy, we say it's lousy. Unfortunately for us, most Kohala restaurants have great food and service and excellent atmosphere. This makes it hard to review without sounding like a bootlicking commercial for Kohala restaurants. The resorts go to great lengths (and expense) to feed you and keep you eating at the resort. The downside for you is that you can pay *dearly* for those ONOs. Most of the restaurants here are pricey, and you'll find that eating in Kohala will cost you more than on any other part of the island. It wasn't our intention to gush over so many restaurants in Kohala, but we can't deny the fundamental quality of their offerings at these establishments.

The restaurants at the **Four Seasons** and **Kona Village** are in the Kona dining section since they are often frequented by people staying in Kona.

If you want to cook your own meals, you'll soon learn that there are no large grocery stores in this area, just a small upscale market in Queens' MarketPlace. You *will* find a big store, however, a few miles up the road in Waikoloa Village.

When we mention that a restaurant has lunch only, or breakfast and dinner only, you should take this with a grain of salt. Resorts are constantly rearranging these options. Also, you'll find the resorts mentioned are shown on the maps on pages 53 and 152.

For simplicity, we are *excluding* restaurants in the northernmost part of Kohala (**Hawi** and **Kapa'au**). They are described under DINING ELSEWHERE.

KOHALA AMERICAN

The Bay Terrace
68-1400 Mauna Lani Dr. • 885–6622

(ONO) Mauna Lani—At the Mauna Lani Bay Hotel, the beautiful indoor/outdoor setting and outstanding food make this a winner. The breakfast buffets (**$27**) have an excellent cross section of breakfast items and fresh fruit. Or go à la carte for **$15–$25**.

Blue Dragon Coastal Cuisine & Musiquarium
61-3616 Kawaihae Rd. • 882–7771

(ONO) Kawaihae—A great restaurant if you can live without a view. The food is stupid good. They could make a radiator fluid martini and dirt casserole compelling. (But fortunately, they aren't on the menu.) Consider starting with the Hamakua mushroom polenta along with one of their uncommonly creative drinks, many made with fresh local tropical fruits and premium spirits. (They seem to craft their own drinks better than standard cocktails.) Then move onto any of their steak and seafood entrées. It's the kind of place where you have a hard time deciding, because everything sounds so good. And their chocolate flourless whatever-itscalled dessert (with ice cream) is deadly. They tend to attract some of the better live musicians on the island, and the uncovered atmosphere, surrounded by their building, is akin to being on the open deck of a large ship. Our only complaint is that service, while being super friendly, is not quite attentive enough for these prices. **$25–$40** or more at dinner with several cheaper items, but overall, that's the range. On the side of the Hwy in Kawaihae (Hwy 270). Call for days of operations.

Brown's Beach House
1 North Kaniku Dr. • 885–2000

ᴼᴺᴼ Mauna Lani—Very good outdoor setting near the beach at the Fairmont Orchid. (Sometimes it gets too breezy.) Seafood is their best bet, which they do very well. They also have steak and chicken. An easy recommend. **$35–$60** for dinner.

The Canoe House
68-1400 Mauna Lani Dr. • 885–6622

ᴼᴺᴼ Mauna Lani—The indoor/outdoor setting near the ocean at this Mauna Lani Bay Hotel restaurant, coupled with expertly prepared and presented food, make this a memorable choice for seafood plus a bit of steak and pasta. This is a great restaurant by anyone's definition and one we are happy to re-review any time we can. The sunsets from an outdoor railing table are smashing most of the year. Items change often, so we'll refrain from singling any out. It's hard to go wrong here, unless you forget your credit card. Expect **$40–$55** plus super pricey pupus. Dinner only. Reservations recommended (make them for an early dinner if you want a sunset). We've had some reader feedback complaining of bad service, but personally, we've never caught them on a bad night.

Coast Grille
62-100 Kaunaoa Dr. • 882–5810

Mauna Kea—Located at the Hapuna Beach Prince Hotel, the setting overlooking Hapuna Beach is wonderful. They have indoor and outdoor tables, but it's the outdoor ones that give it the dreamy atmosphere. It's steak and seafood here, but frankly, it's not quite up to the quality it should be for these prices. The wine list is very extensive, though. Their oyster bar has several varieties of oysters and the mac nut-crusted mahi mahi is pretty good. **$30–$45**. Open Saturdays through Mondays only.

Hawaii Calls
69-275 Waikoloa Beach Dr.
886–7470

Waikoloa—The menu tries to do a little of everything—a little steak, seafood, pasta, ribs and chicken. Service isn't as tight as other Kohala restaurants, but we've noticed that they tend to run more specials, such as two for one or 50% off all entrées when you order a bottle of wine. The food's fairly bad for these prices with overcooked fish and embarrassingly small portions on some items. The open ambiance is a combination of tropical and modern and could use a bit more vision. There are sunset views, but it's fairly filtered through the pool area and lots of scenic palm trees. **$30–$50** for dinner. At the Waikoloa Beach Marriott.

Island Fish & Chips
69-250 Waikoloa Beach Dr.
886–0005

Waikoloa—They brag about using fresh fish at this stand, but we've seen frozen mahi mahi used as the entrée. Chips along with fried fish, fried coconut shrimp, fried calamari or chicken. It's a small operation and can take a while if anyone's in front of you. The breading is tasty, but pretty thick and therefore, holds *a lot* of oil. Doesn't work for us. In the King's Shops, Waikoloa. **$11–$15** for lunch and dinner.

Island Gourmet Markets
69-201 Waikoloa Beach Dr.
886–3577

ono Waikoloa—Not actually a restaurant, it's the area's grocery store with an inventory chosen specifically with resort visitors in mind. They also have a deli that has some pretty good sandwiches, a soup bar, pizza, sushi and other items for reasonable prices. (Ahh...reasonable for *Kohala*, that is.) You can also pick up fresh fruits and cookables, and some of their specials, especially on wines, can be downright reasonable. **$7–$10**. In the Queen's Market-Place, Waikoloa.

Jungle's Edge Coffee
69-250 Waikoloa Beach Dr.
886–4070

Waikoloa—A good place for your morning fix. We like the siphon coffee. Not for the coffee, but for the cool preparation process. (Warning: It is strong and *ultra* hot.) In the Kings Shops. **$4–$6**.

Kamuela Provision Company
69-425 Waikoloa Beach Dr.
886–1234

ono Waikoloa—Steak, seafood and a token veggie item at this Hilton Waikoloa Village restaurant. The views, especially from the outdoor tables, are fantastic. Inside you'll find an upscale yet casual decor. Start everything off with the tasty but *super*-pricy ($38) appetizer platter for two, which has poached shrimp, ahi poke, two oysters and a half lobster. Dinner selections seem to change often enough that we won't recommend a particular dish. The desserts are very tasty. They have one called *Message in a Bottle*. Order it 24 hours in advance, and it'll include a note with

any message you want. (You romantic softie, you.) You may like the elevated outdoor oceanside tables for sunsets, lively indoor tables or a cocktail at the other outdoor tables near the top of the pool waterfall. Food and service quality are high, but they do disappoint on occasion. Wine list is acceptable. **$35–$60** for dinner. Reservations recommended. Resort wear with collared shirts required, but shorts are OK. Take the train *or boat* to the left from the lobby. Located in the Lagoon Tower of the resort.

Manta & Pavilion Wine Bar
62-100 Mauna Kea Beach Dr.
882-5810

ono Mauna Kea—Views from here are soothing, looking obliquely down the beach of Mauna Kea. Breakfast is a hurt-me **$32** buffet, which is awesome. (As it darned well *better* be.) And if you decide to go off the menu, you're looking at items such as $16 pancakes and a $26 continental breakfast, so you might as well go for broke (literally). Dinner continues the expensive route, but you can still feel comfortable in walking shorts and a nice aloha shirt. Steak and seafood sound so tame. But we're talking about *very* skilled preparations and presentation. The goat cheese ravioli is a great way to start it out. They pride themselves on their incredibly vast wine selection and expertise. They also have what they call the "enomatic wine experience" that allows them to sell 48 wines by the single ounce. Service is polished. They're not perfect; we've seen them drop the ball. But overall, execution is superb. They're present when you want them, not annoying you when you don't. **$40–$60** or more, especially when you start into the wine, for dinner. At the Mauna Kea Beach Hotel.

Merriman's Market Café
69-250 Waikoloa Beach Dr.
886–1700

Waikoloa—With outside seating (occasionally marred by annoying small flies), a true delicatessen and a Mediterranean-style menu, Peter Merriman has created a café that Italy would be proud of. Much like his Waimea restaurant, ingredients are fresh and local. For lunch they cover tapas, great salads, Italian such as pasta and a meatball sandwich (tasty but hard to eat), pizzas, burgers, fish sandwiches, etc. Add steak and seafood at dinner. Their professional staff will help you pick the right wine from their list with over 40 wines by the glass. Other options include lamb, steak and pasta. **$13–$20** for lunch, it goes up to **$30+** for dinner. Inside the Kings' Shops at Waikoloa.

Ocean Bar & Grill
68-1400 Mauna Lani Dr. • 885–6622
Mauna Lani—If you're at the beach at the Mauna Lani Bay Hotel and are looking for a quick bite, this is your best bet unless you want to venture far from the beach. $12 hot dogs, $14 burgers and $18 salads—that's the theme here. But the food's fairly tasty and—most important—it's convenient for lunch and a tropical drink. **$12–$22** for lunch, dinner adds a few items like pasta, fish and chicken for **$18–$28**. Behind the blue cabanas at the Mauna Lani beach.

Ocean Terrace
62-100 Kaunaoa Dr. • 882–5810
Mauna Kea—Breakfast at this Hapuna Beach Prince Hotel restaurant offers nice ocean views. Buffets (**$25** with the omelette station) bring a nice variety of items. À la carte menu includes three-egg omelettes for **$21**, waffles for **$16**, and steak and eggs for **$22**. Kind of pricey, huh? But the quality is good. (Which you'd expect at these prices.) But at dinner,

things break down. Sunsets are nice, but the problem is that dinner is off the menu, yet they still have buffets in their DNA. So, if you ask to have them hold your entrée until you've had a chance to enjoy the salad bar (a relatively uncommon thing in Hawai'i), they'll probably cook your food and simply reheat it when you're ready. And ask them to hold the onions on your panko-encrusted fish, and they'll simply withhold the entire coating...and tell you this as they're dropping it onto your table. Service is slow and unresponsive, and bartending skills are lame. So stick with the pricey breakfast or head elsewhere. **$25–$35** for dinner.

Orchid Court
1 North Kaniku Dr. • 885–2000
Mauna Lani—Breakfast buffets are **$29**. They also have various "complete breakfasts" for $16–$27, but these seem overpriced. À la carte also available. For dinner they change their name to **Norio's Japanese Restaurant & Sushi Bar**, a Japanese restaurant. Overall, a nice setting and good food. In the Fairmont Orchid.

Seafood Bar
61-3642 Kawaihae Rd • 880–9393
Kawaihae—A cool tiki atmosphere featuring souped-up bar food with a local twist. For instance, they have a poke burger (pretty good), coconut shrimp burger, (also fairly good), tempura California sushi roll, ahi sashimi, etc. The beef burgers are generous, but the meat seems a bit...overprocessed. At dinner add some short ribs, fresh fish, some steak and escargot. This place was the sister of the now-closed Kawaihae Harbor Grill, and they seem to be catering to the watering hole crowd. So expect inexpensive well drinks, margaritas and mai tais as well as beer. With the whimsical atmosphere (necessary since the view out the windows is of industrial

storage tanks) and prices in line with the product for this part of the island, it's an agreeable place for lunch or dinner and we *kinda, sorta* figgered we'd give 'em an ONO. **$15–$20** for lunch, **$15–$30** for dinner. On Hwy 270 before Kawaihae.

Starbucks
69-201 Waikoloa Beach Dr.
886–1888

Waikoloa—At the Queens' MarketPlace (but not in the food court). You know what to expect. We just wanted to let you know it's here. The baked goods there are from Mamane Bakery, so they're good.

Waikoloa Village Market
68-3916 Paniolo Ave. • 883–1088

Waikoloa *Village*—In the high-priced land of Kohala, there is some relief. This local supermarket in the Waikoloa Highlands Center has deli sandwiches, sushi, plate lunches, pastries and hot paninis, all for a good price. Plate lunches from the hot bar are popular around lunch, and most items are at their freshest during this time. Good place to stop on the go. **$4–$8**.

KOHALA CHINESE

Kirin Chinese Restaurant
69-425 Waikoloa Beach Dr.
886–1234

Waikoloa—You arrive by boat to Kirin (named after the Chinese mythical creature, not the Japanese beer) and head upstairs to the dining area, which has no view unless you get a table out on the deck (which you can reserve). Lunch includes dim sum—this can take the edge off the prices since dim sum items average around $5 each. (It's made to order, not served by cart.) Otherwise, you're looking at **$20–$50** or more for lunch and dinner. Entrées go way beyond chop suey. They have lobster served several ways, lots of seafood, duck, sizzling platters and much more. Quality is pret-

ty good (though you're *paying* for awesome, which is why we didn't give them an ONO). At the Hilton Waikoloa Village between Palace and Ocean Towers. Allow an extra 20 minutes to get there from your car—it's a *big* place.

KOHALA ITALIAN

Anthony's Italian & Irish Restaurant & Pizzeria
68-1845 Waikoloa Rd. • 883–9609

Waikoloa *Village*—Off the beaten path in the Highlands Shopping Center. The Irish portion consists of shepherd's pie or corned beef and cabbage along with the Guinness on top. Otherwise, it's Italian with pasta and pizza along with burgers and sandwiches. And although the pizza is filling, so are styrofoam peanuts. I know that sounds harsh, but they seem to take some very interesting combinations of ingredients that somehow result in a surprising lack of flavor. It's a popular local watering hole and there are no views, but it ain't priced cheap. **$15–$30**.

Café Pesto
61-3665 Kawaihae Rd. • 882–1071

(ono) Kawaihae—Excellent selection of fine Italian food. Pizzas, pastas and some calzones. Pizza is light—feather-like crust, light sauce, light toppings. It's also delicious, and they feature several unique combinations. 9-inch pizza OK for 1 person, 12-inch for hearty, half-starved appetites. Try the kalua pig-and-pineapple combination or the Oriental al Pesto with garlic, sun-dried tomatoes and Japanese eggplant. Pastas *can* be excellent but are sometimes disappointing. They can be fussy on substitutions. With those caveats, it's a great restaurant, and we recommend it wholeheartedly. In Kawaihae Center (Hwy 270 before 3-mile marker). **$13–$20** for lunch, **$15–$40** for dinner. The higher price is usually for their fresh fish special.

Romano's Macaroni Grill
69-201 Waikoloa Beach Dr.
443–5515

Waikoloa—This is part of a chain of reliable Italian comfort food, and this location is no different. The food is tasty, portions generous and the service is good. But the prices here are a bit different than what you'll find elsewhere. While eating and looking at the menu, we went to Romano's web site on our phone and found that prices here are *50% higher* than locations we looked at on the mainland. We know rent at the Queen's MarketPlace must be high, but *sheesh!* Except for the confiscatory prices, they'd probably get an ONO. And when compared to others on the Kohala coast, maybe they're not that out of line. **$16–$30** for lunch and dinner.

KOHALA JAPANESE

Imari
69-425 Waikoloa Beach Dr.
886–1234

 Waikoloa—Elegant black-and-copper decor with wood floors and shoji doors all around, you have your choice of three types of Japanese food. Teppan-yaki style (where food is prepared in front of you by a talented, knife-wielding chef), a sushi bar (tables near there will be quieter) or shabu-shabu (where items off the menu are served tableside). The ambiance is thick with Japanese culture and music, and the quality of the food is very good. If Japanese food is not your thing, they have steak, fish and chicken. Located at the Hilton Waikoloa Village, reservations required. Dinner is **$35–$60**. Resort wear with long pants and collared shirts required.

Monstera
68-1330 Mauna Lani Dr. • 887–2711

 Mauna Lani—The atmosphere is nice with general

seating and a sushi bar, which is open at dinner. We asked when we could sit at the sushi bar at lunch and were told, *Never like tell you. Sometimes can, sometimes can't.* OK. The sushi is fresh and tasty and you get a break on the pricing if you order three pieces, making family-style eating more attractive. They also have lots of non-sushi items, including whole moi (a fish) and sizzling platters. **$20–$50** for lunch and dinner. In the Shops at Mauna Lani.

KOHALA PACIFIC RIM

Roy's Waikoloa Bar & Grill
69-250 Waikoloa Beach Dr.
886–4321

 Waikoloa—Some people are born to do certain things. Roy Yamaguchi was born to run restaurants. This growing chain rarely fails to please. The food is delicious, well-conceived and nicely presented. Dishes range from dim sum appetizers, fish and beef. Specials abound and change nightly. The atmosphere is casual and somewhat noisy. The service is efficient, sometimes bordering on pestering. Prices are reasonable *for what you get*. Entrées aren't huge, so consider the delectable appetizers. Reservations strongly recommended. (Ask for a table near the glass wall overlooking the golf course pond.) Their dark chocolate soufflé is legendary. Dinner is **$30–$47**. In the Kings' Shops in the Waikoloa Resort area near Hwy 19's 76 mile marker.

KOHALA TREATS

While treats are fairly easy to come by in many of the mega resorts, if you're not staying there, you usually have to drill pretty far into them to partake. Here are some that are easier to come by.

Aloha Deli & Ice Cream
61-3642 Kawaihae Rd. • 880–1188
Kawaihae—A good place for a scoop of really good ice cream. The shakes and their other food items aren't as good. On Hwy 270 before Kawaihae.

Anuenue
61-3665 Kawaihae Rd. • 882–1109
Kawaihae—Conveniently located in Kawaihae if you're heading along the shoreline up to Hawi. The shave ice is pretty good as is the ice cream. They also have some snack food that isn't overly compelling. **$3–$5**.

Sweet Paradise Chocolatier
69-250 Waikoloa Beach Dr.
557-5358
ONO Waikoloa—The most visually attractive chocolates we've ever seen. Literally. They're almost too pretty to eat. (We said *almost*...) Their beauty is equally matched by their breathtaking prices. A box of four tiny chocolates will set you back almost *$12*. But if you're looking for something rich and beautiful, this is the place. In the Kings Shops, Waikoloa. We gave them an ONO because we're assuming you lost your ever-loving mind and don't mind paying these insane prices for some exceptional chocolates. Or maybe that describes us...

DINING IN WAIMEA

Waimea is a cool place to eat—literally. Located up at the nippier 2,500-foot level, it's a nice place to eat when you're staying in the Kohala area and want to eat away from the resorts and enjoy the views along the way.

Big Island Brewhaus & Tako Taco Taqueria
64-1066 Mamalahoa Hwy • 887–1717
Well, these guys have the record of having the longest name. It started out as a taco place and they have expanded to brewing their own beer and even sodas. (The latter is pretty novel and kind of tasty.) The atmosphere is casual and colorful. Their Mexican selection is fairly good with mixed results. Flavors are reasonably good. The spicy beef has a nice zing to it, for instance. But food is often served lukewarm, and the chips are thick and a bit too greasy. They have potential, but they need to pick it up a notch. The beer selection is not bad but for wine ya got red and ya got white...that's it. **$8–$15** for lunch and dinner. On the corner of Mamalahoa Highway and Kamamalu in Waimea.

Charley's Thai Cuisine
65-1158 Mamalahoa Hwy • 885–5591
With a name like Charley's, you're probably not *expecting* great Thai food. But that's what you *used* to get here. Yet something seems to have happened to this restaurant. The recipes taste different. We love Thai food because of all the flavors, yet the food now seems to be hollow. Hot if you like, but otherwise flat. The Queen's MarketPlace location in Waikoloa has the same problem. Lunch and dinner are **$12–$25**. The Waikoloa location has the same menu for 25%–30% more money. In Waimea Center on Hwy 19. BYOB. Avoid the lemongrass tea. It's weird and tastes kinda like...feet.

Hawaiian Style Café
65-1290 Kawaihae Rd. • 885–4295
ONO Looks like a dive on the outside. (Then again, it looks a little like a dive on the inside.) But this is probably the best deal on the island when it comes to *quantity* and heartiness. Let me give you an example. Two eggs, your choice of meat, plus hash browns or rice. Then add either toast or two fluffy pancakes (the size of hub caps). All for $7.50. Now that may be obtainable back on the mainland, but

it's utterly *unheard* of in Hawai'i. They're open from 7 a.m. to 1:30 p.m. daily (but close at noon on Sunday). The early lunch features thick burgers obscured by a towering mound of fries, as well as some other items. The food's not the best, but you ain't *paying* for the best. The atmosphere is laid-back with a few front tables (which probably aren't cleared or cleaned as often as they should be) and a large sit-down counter plus a few in back. This is how Mom used to cook before she found out it was bad for you. Sometimes we miss it. **$7–$11**. On Waimea's Restaurant Row; see map on page 135. Cash only.

Huli Sue's BBQ & Grill
64-957 Mamalahoa Hwy, Waimea
885–6268
68-1050 Makaiwa Pl., Kohala
885–7777

(ono) A straightforward BBQ joint with no pretense to be anything else. Simple, rustic surroundings, mason jars for your beverages and a classic BBQ menu of pulled pork, ribs, corn-crusted catfish, burgers and a steak. Flavors aren't subtle. Even the Tin Pan salad has their southwestern sauce in the meat. You'll either like the BBQ flavor or you won't. (They could use more sauce alternatives.) Ribs are the falling-off-the-bone type, not the chewy variety. There's no sauce at the table, so consider asking for more on the side. The banana cream pie is possibly the best we've ever had, and they make killer milkshakes. Pass on the BBQ leg of lamb though, it's too dry. Prices ain't cheap, but you *must* be getting used to that by now. **$14–$30** for lunch and dinner. Just across from the 56 mile marker on Hwy 19 in Waimea. They also have a location at the Mauna Lani Golf Clubhouse, but it's much bigger, serves pretty good pizzas and fish, and is more upscale. (And more expensive.)

Leilani Bakery
65-1158 Mamalahoa Hwy • 885–2772
Average baked goods served without a smile. For a place that serves food, they have a weird habit of closing for lunch. In Waimea Center in Waimea.

Merriman's
65-1227 Opelo Rd. • 885–6822

(ono) This is the best and most consistent food in Waimea. Peter Merriman is an excellent chef, and the recipes here are usually wonderful. Lunch includes wok-charred ahi, salads, fish, Chinese short ribs and sandwiches. The menu seems to change, so we're nervous about recommending specific items. Dinner features steak and seafood. The veggie sampler is a good appetizer to share. They have an impressive wine list, but the mark-up seems pretty extreme. And although they are fairly knowledgeable with wines, their skills are more obvious with mixed drinks. If you're in Waimea and want a great meal, this is the place to go. On Waimea's Restaurant Row; see map on page 135. Reservations recommended **$12–$20** for lunch (Mon.–Fri. only), **$35–$60** for dinner.

Pakini Grill
65-1144 Mamalahoa Hwy • 885-3333
Though the menu stresses burgers, consider some of their local style offerings, such as the char sui chicken sandwich, kale BBQ ribs, miso mahi mahi and even the roast pork with gravy. This place has real potential. They know how to cook, and the overall flavors are good. But the quality of the main ingredients feels rock bottom. (Where *do* they find turkey with that much fat in it?) Service is friendly but sometimes somewhat inattentive. However, Grandma Kathy's blueberry cream cheese pie is *wonderful*. **$12–$20** (more for ribs) for lunch and dinner. In Waimea Center in Waimea.

Pau
65-1227 Opelo Rd. • 885–6325

A casual atmosphere with a straightforward menu of super-thin 18-inch(ish) pizzas, a few pastas (love the pesto island fish), some sandwiches and very creative salads. The pizza is outstanding. Meat lovers should consider the "whole hog." Other items are similarly pleasing. Service is friendly and accommodating. Desserts are their weak point. Prices are in line with quality. Closed Sunday. **$12–$18** for lunch and dinner. In Waimea's Opelo Plaza by Merriman's.

Village Burger
67-1185 Mamalahoa Hwy • 885–7319

Gourmet ⅓-pound burgers made from locally raised beef, plus veal burgers, veggie mushroom burgers, Kobe (which is a little disappointing), ahi and sometimes taro. Quality is top notch, and you can take your food to one of the food court tables or one of the few outdoor tables. Fries are extra, and the Parmesan fries are *outrageously* good. They also make expensive but wicked shakes. **$9–$15** for lunch and dinner. In Parker Ranch Center in Waimea.

Waimea Coffee Co.
65-1279 Kawaihae Rd. • 885–8915
Waimea's best coffee shop with a limited breakfast selection. (The breakfast sandwich is good—consider it on the Parmesan bagel—but it can take awhile.) For lunch they have some paninis and several salads. The coffee is good and service...it can be one of those places where you feel invisible. You walk up to the counter, stand there for perhaps five minutes while you are never acknowledged by several employees. You finally ask about ordering, and they tell you to go to the other end of the counter where you are again ignored. Finally you place the order, and they are as friendly as can be. It's nice to be visible again. This has happened on multiple occasions. Indoor and outdoor seating, free WiFi and a drive-thru window. They also have reasonably tasty baked goods, including their almond sticky bun. In Parker Square in Waimea. **$5–$12** for breakfast and lunch.

Yong's Kalbi
65-1158 Mamalahoa Hwy • 885–8440

Korean food with a local twist. Good fried mandoo (Korean dumplings). Be brave when picking some of the odder items (but avoid the chicken katsu). **$8–$14** for lunch and dinner. Closed Sunday. In Waimea Center.

HILO AMERICAN

Fast Food
Hilo's fast food joints are mostly clustered around Puainako Town Center up Hwy 11 from town.

Hilo Bay Café
315 Makaala St. • 935–4939

First of all, it ain't near Hilo Bay—it's in a big box store center between Walmart and Office Max far from the ocean off Hwy 11. But the food is some of the best in Hilo with a diverse and very appealing menu at acceptable prices. It's hard to pick a bad item. The quality of the ingredients are high, much of it organic. Lunch is great salads, some fresh fish, sandwiches such as eggplant, kalua pork, sweet potato burgers and regular burgers, ribs and a home made pot pie. Add some osso bucco, scallops or chicken at dinner. The atmosphere is casual yet classy with a well-stocked bar serving some pretty imaginative concoctions. (Try the pear mojito.) **$12–$20** for lunch, **$15–$25** for dinner.

Hilo Burger Joint
776 Kilauea Ave. • 935–8880

 A likable place with a great selection of burgers using

lots of unusual combinations, such as the nacho burger (nacho cheese, black beans, jalapenos, tortillas and sour cream on top), curry burgers, Greek burgers, etc. All served on ⅓-pound patties from a local ranch. Don't go for just the typical burger, get creative here. They also a have a full bar and 21 beers on tap. The atmosphere is a cross between a bar and a restaurant. Service is friendly. Just south of Pauahi St. in Hilo. Parking can be a problem, but there's metered parking in the lot across the street, if it's open. **$10–$16** for lunch and dinner. Live music most nights.

Island Naturals Market Deli
1221 Kilauea Ave. • 935–5533

A health food store with a hot food bar for **$8** a pound, sandwiches and smoothies. Good organic salad bar. Prices are a bit high for what you get. At Kekuanaoa and Kilauea at the Hilo Center Shopping. (No, we didn't get those last two words mixed up. Someone *else* did.)

Ken's House of Pancakes
1730 Kamehameha Ave. • 935–8711

ono A Hilo staple, they offer a vast menu that's hard to absorb. The whole menu is available 24 hours a day—unusual for a Big Island restaurant. Service is sometimes unresponsive because the place can get crowded, but if you eat breakfast at the counter, it's fast and efficient. (Just when I need it, because I'm grumpy before my coffee.) You ain't paying for gourmet here, and you won't get it. You're paying for dependably large portions of acceptable food at reasonable prices. That's why they eked out an ONO from us in a moment of weakness, and it's for breakfast and lunch *only*. Breakfast is **$8–$15**, lunch is **$10–$15**, dinner is **$13–$25**. On Hwy 11 near Hwy 19. Open 24 hours.

Le Magic Pan
64 Keawe St. • 935-7777

ono An artsy, Frenchy kind of atmosphere with a menu that focuses primarily on crêpes at pretty reasonable prices. (We didn't put them under FRENCH, because, well, they're not *really* French.) Each crêpe is based on a different place. The Parisian is ham, mushroom and cheese on a crêpe. The Polish is sausage, tomatoes, mushrooms, olives, basil and cheese. Then ya got Greek, Alaskan, Russian, etc. They also have salads and great dessert crêpes. Lunch and dinner are **$11–$15**. Service is friendly but can be slow. An easy concept to like. At the corner of Waianuenue in Hilo.

Queen's Court
71 Banyan Dr. • 935–9361

This is the main restaurant in the Hilo Hawaiian Hotel. With giant windows overlooking Coconut Island, this should be a great restaurant...but it ain't. Try not to laugh when they put a tiny, stale roll in front of you at the beginning. (It's not much bigger than the pat of butter.) Although the menu has an appealing selection of seafood, some pasta and kalbi ribs, the preparation is consistently lacking. Lastly, their bartending skills are non-existent. We're not trying to beat them up, but they could do *way* better with their great location. **$15–$28** for dinner, it's **$36** for their thrice weekly seafood buffets. Breakfast buffets are **$16**.

Seaside Restaurant
1790 Kalanianaole Ave. • 935–8825

They built their reputation on freshwater fish raised right there in a large, serene pond, but they have mostly gravitated more toward ocean fish because, we're told, "it's less work." If you want the mullet, you have to order in advance because they need to go catch it, and odds are they'll simply say it's "not the right season." If they didn't have the view of the pond, the atmosphere would be merely adequate and a bit loud. Service is friendly. The freshwater fish that they buy from others like aholehole (we're not making that up) is served head and all. Avoid the lobster. Overall, the food's reasonable (love the butterfish, but you gotta be careful not to eat too much) but overpriced. Some tables include a show called *count how many skeeters the geckos can eat*. **$18–$35**. On Kalanianaole Avenue, east Hilo past Banyan Drive 2½ miles east of Hwy 11. Reservations recommended. Closed Monday.

HILO ITALIAN

Café Concerto
808 Kilauea Ave. • 934–0312

It's so hot inside you'll feel like a baked ziti if you don't grab an outdoor table. This is assuming they're even open. The menu is authentic, as is the owner. He'll probably come around to talk; ask him about his "homemade digestive." The flavors are there and the prices are right, but don't expect anything fancy. Good raviolis. Dinner is **$8–$15**. BYOB, no corkage fee. Open from 5:30 to 9 p.m. Closed Sunday and Monday. At Apuni St. and Kilauea Ave. in Hilo. Additional parking around back.

Café Pesto
308 Kamehameha Ave. • 969–6640

(ONO) Similar to the Café Pesto mentioned in Kawaihae on page 264. On Kamehameha between Mamo and Furneaux in Hilo.

Pescatore
235 Keawe St. • 969–9090

(ONO) This has been one of our favorites for several years. They're slipping a bit and reader e-mail has been mixed, but our most recent experiences have been good, so the ONO stays for now. Smartly conceived entrées that deviate from simple pasta and sauce.

The specials are usually delicious and often come with a dessert (such as the rich chocolate truffle cake). Try to resist filling up on the really tasty rolls. The atmosphere is subdued Italian and the service attentive. Lunch includes a good choice of pastas and sauces, as well as panini and pizza. On the corner of Haili and Keawe in Hilo. **$8–$14** for lunch, **$20–$35** for dinner.

HILO JAPANESE

Nihon Restaurant
123 Lihiwai St. • 969–1133

The building overlooks Hilo Bay, but they don't make good use of the view. This is a good place to go to be ignored. Prices are too high given the setting and lackluster service. You can do better. Sushi bar plus steak and seafood. **$9–$15** for lunch, **$15–$25** for dinner. Off Banyan Drive. Closed Sunday.

Ocean Sushi
250 Keawe St. • 961–6625

(ONO) *Ah*, Sushi lovers, rejoice. You've found a sushi place that serves killer sushi for cheap, cheap. Not much of an ambiance; just close your eyes and revel in the variety and quality. Rolls are anywhere from $2–$5, and they have platters and boxes with all kinds of selections. Service is fast and efficient. If the wasabi is still stinging, try one of their ice cream pies to put out the fire. Figure around **$10–$15** for lunch or dinner. Closed Sunday.

HILO LOCAL

Café 100
969 Kilauea Ave. • 935–8683

(ONO) Possibly Hilo's most popular eating establishment. This is the most successful local restaurant on the island. For over 60 years they've served cheap, tasty, artery-clogging food and are legendary for their loco mocos. (These consist of fried eggs over rice and Spam or a similar meat—if there *is* a similar meat—all smothered with brown gravy.) They have nearly a dozen varieties of loco moco, along with burgers, chili, stew, sandwiches and specials for as little as $2. We gave them an ONO because this is quintessential local food. But if you're watching your cholesterol or fat intake, it'll rock your Richter Scale like no other place. Grab your food at the window and eat at one of the outdoor tables. Less than $5 for breakfast, **$3–$8** for lunch and dinner. On Kilauea near Mohouli in Hilo. Closed Sunday.

Puka Puka Kitchen
270 Kamehameha Ave. • 933–2121
Tasty entrees and stuffed pitas set in a tiny hole in the wall. (Puka is Hawaiian for hole.) Food's good and the prices cheap. Even though the menu is short, it's hard to choose between the sautéed ahi, the locally raised lamb or the seafood platter. We're partial to the lamb, but they often run out. Their ahi Don is also pretty good. Get there early to increase your chances. Open 11 a.m. to 2:30 p.m. for lunch. Dinner served Thur.–Fri. Closed Sundays. **$8–$14**. On the corner of Kamehameha and Furneaux in Hilo.

HILO THAI

New Chiang Mai Thai Cuisine
110 Kalakaua St. • 969–3777
The curries and pad thai are flavorful, but the heat index of the dishes can be erratic, and the service, though *sometimes* nice, can also be comically indifferent. (A fun game can be to *bet* on how many visits to the table it takes before your server utters a single word to you.) The non-Thai entrées aren't bad, but overall, the food is mediocre. That said, it's not too often we single out a Thai restaurant for dessert, but their honey banana (with ice cream) is ex-

cellent. Lunch and dinner, both cost **$10–$20**. Dinner only on Sunday. Between Keawe and Kinoole streets in Hilo.

Sombat's Fresh Thai Cuisine
88 Kanoelehua Ave. • 969–9336
ONO *Very* good flavors and a real treat considering the prices. Don't neglect the wonderful green curry chicken—exceptionally good and complex flavors. Or the vegetables with oyster sauce. The heat level isn't overly high, so prod them if you want them to wound you. It's BYOB, and they'll even give you a nice beer glass if you bring your own. Good quality and an obvious attempt to keep things healthy, growing most of their own herbs and buying produce from local farmers. It's **$10–$23** for lunch and dinner. Next to Ken's House of Pancakes near the corner of Kamehameha and Hwy 11 in Hilo. Park around back. No lunch on Saturday. Closed Sunday.

HILO TREATS

Big Island Candies
585 Hinano St. • 935–8890
Tasty but amazingly overpriced chocolates, cakes, nuts and candies. You can also look through the glass and watch the whole process. It's a tour bus magnet, so it's either packed inside or dead, depending on your timing. On Hinano Street off Kekuanaoa, east Hilo.

Hilo Homemade Ice Cream
1477 Kalanianaole Ave. • 935–3895
Not as sweet or rich as other gourmet ice creams. Lots of exotic flavors, such as ginger, from this quaint ice cream shop. Service is slow. On Kalanianaole Avenue on the way to the beach parks in east Hilo.

Short N Sweet Bakery & Café
374 Kinoole St. • 935–4446
ONO This bakery, formerly in Hawi, is known for their

elaborate cake designs, but they caught our eye with their decadent dessert skills. The German chocolate brownie moist and tasty, as are most of the items. (Except for their disappointing banana bread.) The only thing slim here is their breakfast selection. Lunch has salads and appetizing paninis made on homemade focaccia bread. **$8–$15**, cash only. On Kinoole near Ponahawai in Hilo.

Two Ladies Kitchen
247 Kilauea Ave. • 961–4766

(ONO) These two ladies quit their days jobs to invest all their time into making mochi. It's a smooth, doughy dessert made from rice flour and traditionally stuffed with red bean paste. Here you'll find mochi stuffed with peanut butter, brownies, sweet potato or some confectionary morsel. Their best is the strawberry mochi, which cost **$2.75** each. *(Well worth it.)* You can get assortment packs of eight for **$7**. On Kilauea near Ponahawai in Hilo. Closed from Sun.–Tues.

Wilson's by the Bay
224 Kamehameha Ave. • 969–9191

(ONO) They make good and very reasonably priced shave ice. Also consider the surprisingly addictive chocolate-covered sunflower seeds (when they have them available, which seems less and less often). On Kamehameha near Haili in Hilo.

DINING IN PAHOA

Pahoa is the main place to eat when you're in lower Puna (meaning Kapoho to Kalapana). All the restaurants are on the main (and only) road going *through* town (not on the bypass). Most maps call it Government Main Road, some call it Pahoa Village Road. Once in town you can't miss 'em.

Black Rock Café
15-2872 Government Main Rd.
965–1177

American—A giant menu with burgers and subs at the low end, steak, seafood and frozen lobster tails at the high end with pizza in the middle, all in a diner-like atmosphere. Overall, the food is mostly fine, sometimes even good. Their biscuits and gravy is the best in Pahoa. (Of course, that's akin to having the greatest Mongolian food in all Ecuador.) The draft beer is embarrassingly cheap, and it's possible that fact colored our judgment; we almost gave 'em an ONO. (But when the beer wore off, we got ahold of our senses.) The Bananas Foster is their best dessert. Service can be *slooow*. **$6–$10** for breakfast, **$7–$20** (more for lobster) for lunch and dinner.

Boogie Woogie Pizza
15-2937 Government Main Rd.
965–5575

(ONO) **Italian**—New York style pizza with a bit of New York style attitude. Just a few cheap tables in a cheap environment—grab it to go. The pizza's pretty good and tastes even better if you call it in and arrive 10–15 minutes late. They'll keep it in the oven on a pan and the crust gets a tad crispy. By the slice and a side is around $3. They also have spaghetti and some sandwiches. BYOB. **$3–$10** for lunch and dinner. In short, an inexpensive pizza fix that is reliable. On main road in Pahoa.

Giovanni's Aloha Shrimp
15-2937 Government Main Rd.
965–5633

(ONO) **Local**—Anyone who's been to O'ahu's north shore is familiar with Giovanni's shrimp truck. Same food, same limited selection and profoundly indifferent service about half the time. Shrimp is peel and eat (so expect messy hands) with the delicious *super* garlicky scampi and the hurt-me spicy being the most popular. Prices are under **$15** for shrimp and garlic rice, and there are only a few canned drinks to choose from. They also have half plates available. Think of it as a truck-side experience with indoor tables and paper plates. We're giving them an ONO grudgingly—but the food's good and dependable, and it's the best place we know to get a garlic fix. On the main road in Pahoa across from Luquin's. Cash only.

Luquin's Mexican Restaurant
15-2942 Government Main Rd.
965-9990
Mexican—This place has traditionally been the busiest, most bustling restaurant in Pahoa with (consistently bad) live music on one side and lots of loud chatter on the other. Standard Mexican food, plus a few specials like tofu enchiladas and tacos, potato tacos, fish tacos (very popular) and taquitos, fish and shrimp. The food is on the bland side, but the bottle of Tapatío on the table can rectify that. They also have some American items. Prices have crept up—they aren't that cheap anymore. The service is friendly (but can be *oh-so-slow*), and the portions are large. You're likely, especially at dinner, to spend your evening dining with Pahoa's upper crust—complete with stinky dreadlocks and clothing that hasn't been washed since tie-dye was king. A pitcher of margaritas is $15, and beer is cheap. Desserts are reasonable but unpredictable—stick with the flan. Breakfast is **$8–$13**, lunch and dinner are **$11–$22**.

Ning's Thai Cuisine
15-2955 Government Main Rd.
965-7611
Thai—Good Thai food here. The food is flavorful, and they're willing to give it heat if you

ask. If you want to hurt, ask for "Thai hot." **$10–$20** for lunch. Sundays is dinner only. In downtown Pahoa; can't miss it.

Paolo's Bistro
15-2951 Government Main Rd.
965-7033
Italian—In terms of ambiance and food, it's the nicest restaurant in Pahoa. The menu is pretty limited and it's BYOB, but the food quality is very good. Pastas, a fish dish and a few specials. On main road in Pahoa. **$15–$28** for dinner. Closed Mondays.

DINING IN HAWI

Bamboo Restaurant
55-3415 Akoni Pule Hwy • 889-5555
American—Located in an old, quaint dry goods building in Hawi with a quirky, tropical ambiance, they have an eclectic menu with uniquely prepared foods. We've given them ONOs in the past, but the quality has declined in the last couple years. You can still get a great meal here, but you can get disappointed more often than we'd like. Lunch is fresh fish, BBQ pork sandwich (which is good), stir fry, burgers and sandwiches. At night add more steak, seafood and money. Prices, especially at dinner, are pretty high. I mean, $38 for a rack of ribs? Phew—pretty steep, we'd say. Our reader e-mails seem to have tracked our own observations and have turned more negative than positive. They have a gallery inside the building offering all kinds of nice, locally carved wood and other products. Lunch is **$12–$22**, dinner is **$17–$45** per person. Closed Sunday nights and Mondays.

Kohala Coffee Mill / Kava Kafe
55-3412 Akoni Pule Hwy • 889-5577
Treats—This place and the Kava Kafe to the right have the same owner. Though they have regular (and somewhat reasonably-priced) en-

trées such as burgers, some good wraps and sandwiches, what sets these two places apart are their vices. Killer Tropical Dreams ice cream, lots of varieties of fudge next door, and after 5 p.m. they break out the kava for $3 per shell. (They also have some flavored kava, though purists would turn up their nose. See Kanaka Kava review for more on kava.) Live music some nights. **$5–$10** for the food, **$3–$8** for the vices. Across the street from Bamboo Restaurant in Hawi.

Kohala Snack Shack
54-3897 Akoni Pule Hwy • 889–0099

ONO **American**—On the makai side of the highway in Kapaʻau, they have 6-, 12- and 16-inch pizzas, hot and cold sandwiches and some pretty big salads made from local greens along with cheap-tasting Roselani ice cream. The personal pizzas come with a *small* salad for around $10. The food's pretty good, the pizza flavorful, and they use nice, fresh greens for the sandwiches and salads. Service can be slow, even if no one is ahead of you. **$10–$15** for lunch and dinner.

Luke's Place
55-514 Hawi Rd. • 889–1155

ONO **American**—The atmosphere here is very relaxing, almost elegant, and it's a good Hawi dining alternative to Bamboo (with better prices). Portions are generous, but if you're looking for something small, the pork quesadilla or fish and chips pupu works well. Lunch is mainly sandwiches and burgers (the latter pretty good). Dinner is pasta, steak, ribs ($26) and seafood. Out back on the lawn (actually, it's a very convincing artificial turf) there's live music most nights. The tiki bar is inviting and has good beers on tap. Service is usually adequate with the exception of a few servers. Overall, the place works reasonably well. The ONO may be a bit generous since the food is

variable, but it's a good place to stop for a tropical drink and some live music after a day exploring the area. Adjacent to the Kohala Village Inn in Hawi. **$7–$15** for lunch and **$10–$35** for dinner.

Sushi Rock
55-3435 Akoni Pule Hwy • 889–5900
Japanese—In the last building in Hawi inside a store called **Without Boundaries** before heading toward Kapaʻau, this small operation (we're talking six *tiny* tables and some bar stools) has very fresh and nicely conceived non-traditional sushi for reasonable prices. Their Valrhona Dark Chocolate Cake comes with an unfortunate green tea glaze that ruins it. What we liked better was their homemade vodka fusions, which they use to make a mean lilikoi martini. **$12–$30** for lunch or dinner. Avoid the drink specials in favor of another piece of sushi. Closed Wed. Service can be agonizingly slow.

DINING NEAR ʻAKAKA FALLS

Woodshop Gallery Café
28-1692 Old Government Rd.
963–6363

ONO **American**—There's not much to eat between Hilo and Honokaʻa. In Honomu on the way to ʻAkaka Falls on Hwy 220, this small café has a good ahi sandwich, a taro and a garden burger, and other sandwiches. Best food in Honomu. **$5–$10**. Otherwise, **Mr. Ed's Bakery** (963–5000) has a big selection of surprisingly *tasteless* baked goods. (Of course, of course.)

Whats Shakin'
27-999 Old Mamalahoa Hwy
964–3080

ONO **American**—On the 4-mile Scenic Drive (between the 7 and 11 mile marker on Hwy 19). This is a fantastic place to get outrageous smoothies as well as a small lunch menu of dependably tasty items, such as chicken wraps, roast beef sandwich, chicken nachos and *super* fresh salads. The smoothies, their signature items, often start with frozen bananas (instead of ice) and most, such as the peanut bradduh, are wonderful. They also sell Tropical Dreams ice cream and some fruit such as papaya and pineapple. **$7–$12**.

If you don't want to get off the highway, before Hwy 19's 7 mile marker keep an eye out on the mauka side for **Baker Tom's** (964–8444). They have lots of different types of malasadas (try the blackberry), pull-aparts and sometimes the most wonderfully sweet and impossibly small tomatoes. Very reasonable prices, though lately they seem to be skimping on the fillings. At 27-2111 Hawaii Belt Road.

DINING IN LAUPAHOEHOE

Laupahoehoe is the tiny town north of Hilo and 'Akaka Falls before you get to Honoka'a. **Back to the '50s Highway Fountain** (962–0808) **American**—a '50s-style diner with burgers, loco moco, Tater Tots, roast beef and chicken. The food is pretty basic—nothing stands out. And though some items, such as the chili cheese fries are generous, others, such as the pathetic ono burger, will leave you wanting. If the food was as good as the thick, retro atmosphere, they'd get an ONO. But it ain't. Enter the town of Laupahoehoe from the road that parallels the highway mauka of Hwy 19 on either side of the 25 mile marker. **$6–$12**. Closed Monday and Tuesday. At 35-2074 Old Mamalahoa Hwy.

DINING IN HONOKA'A

Café Il Mondo
45-3626 Mamane St. • 775–7711
Italian—Pizza, calzone, lasagna, salads and hot sandwiches. Lots of different cof-

fee drinks. The pizza is pretty good (not great) with crunchy crust. Calzones are large and tasty. Fairly good meatball sandwich. Service is slow at times. One thing that rubs us the wrong way: They don't serve alcohol and encourage you to BYOB. Then they quietly charge you $2–$5.75, depending on how many are in your party, for corkage. Tacky. And oddly, medium and large pizzas are *only* available to go. Can't eat 'em at the café. On Mamane Street (240) in Honoka'a, ocean side. **$10–$15** for lunch and dinner. Closed Sunday. No credit cards.

Hamakua Fudge Company
45-3611 Mamane St. • 775–1430
ONO Treats—Let's keep this short and sweet. They make the fudge right there, and it's rich enough to make you sweat. Work for you? (Awesome liliko'i fudge.) Great ice cream, too. **$3–$5**. On Hwy 240 in Honoka'a.

Jolene's Kau Kau Korner
45-3625 Mamane St. • 775–9498
Local—A simple, homey, cheap atmosphere. This is a mom and pop (well, mom, at least) diner-type restaurant with cheap food and…well, that's it. Cheap food. And it ain't bad. Items like shrimp and tempura vegetables for $12 are a reasonable deal around here. Burgers (which you should avoid) for $4, plate lunches, teriyaki chicken, saimin, etc. **$6–$14** for lunch. They squeaked out an ONO for the last edition, but quality has inched down while prices have inched up, so no ONO. On Hwy 240 in Honoka'a.

Simply Natural
45-3625 Mamane St. • 775–0119
American—A health food restaurant that serves eggs and pancakes for breakfast (try the taro banana pancakes), sandwiches, soups and salads for lunch. The taste isn't compelling, but it's not bad. **$5–$10** for breakfast (coffee is pretty weak), **$8–$12**

for lunch. On Hwy 240 in Honoka'a. Cash only. Closed on Sunday.

Tex Drive-In & Restaurant
45-690 Pakalana St. • 775–0598

ⓄⓃⓄ Local—Every good restaurant does at least one thing well, and Tex is a perfect example. Most of the food is merely adequate fast food, such as burgers, teriyaki chicken, 12-inch pizzas, etc., for lunch; cheap (and it tastes that way) breakfasts. But Tex *excels* at making the best malasadas (a Portuguese doughnut dipped in sugar) on the island, served fresh and warm throughout the day. The plain ones are delicious, but they also have them filled with Bavarian chocolate, tropical fruits, etc. We *never* hesitate to stop by when we're in the neighborhood. Located on Hwy 19 near Honoka'a and the 43 mile marker. Sometimes the wait (even if nobody is ahead of you) can be long. Don't overlook the drive-in window. **$7–$12** for breakfast, lunch and dinner (cheaper for the malasadas).

DINING AT KILAUEA VOLCANO

Cafe 'Ohi'a
19-4005 Haunani Rd. • 985–8587
American—A simple, tiny place with a simple, tiny menu and the tiniest side salads we've ever seen. Basic sandwiches, chili and the occasional special while they last (such as lasagna or the roast pork.) The chili's not bad (no spice, though). They have some pretty scrumptious pies for dessert. The few outdoor tables are pretty basic. (They don't need to clean them off—the birds seem to do it for them.) But the price is cheap. **$7–$12** for lunch and early dinner. Behind Kiawe Kitchen on Haunani in Volcano Village.

Kiawe Kitchen
19-4005 Haunani Rd. • 967–7711

ⓄⓃⓄ Italian—A small but appealing menu of pizzas, salads (which, alas, are their weak point), pastas, steak, seafood and some specials at dinner. It's pizzas and sandwiches at lunch. As for those pizzas, they have *incredibly* thin crusts and are very tasty. They come with traditional red sauce, pesto sauce (yummy) or as white pies (olive oil-based). Add a pleasing, slightly jazzy atmosphere (and really good mojitos), consistently good food, and you have an easy place to like. It's a bit overpriced, but that seems to be common in this part of the island, so *what are ya gonna do?* On corner of Huanani and Old Volcano Road; can't miss it. **$10–$20** for lunch, **$20–$30** for dinner.

Kilauea Lodge & Restaurant
19-3948 Old Volcano Rd. • 967–7366

ⓄⓃⓄ American—This cozy restaurant in the sometimes chilly village of Volcano serves delicious food in a warm atmosphere. The owner/chef was a make-up artist on *Magnum P.I.* when he bought this place. He went to Europe to learn how to cook and has excelled nicely. Dinner items, such as fresh fish, steak, venison, antelope, rabbit, ostrich and chicken, are all expertly prepared and presented. Though I love fresh fish, this is the place I like to go for a good *red meat* experience. Expensive, but *very* good food and *very* good service. One of the best restaurants on the island. We like to get a table near the "International Fireplace." **$10–$15** for breakfast and lunch, dinner is **$25–$40**.

Lava Rock Internet Café
19-3972 Old Volcano Rd. • 967–8526
American—Admirable selection of hearty burgers, sandwiches, chili, salads (try the liliko'i dressing), chicken, fajitas (which you can avoid), fresh-tasting taco salad, stir fry and more. Many items are veggie and most cost about $8–$10 with generous portions. (Good milkshakes.) Breakfast items include some clever omelettes and

French toast with 'ohelo berry. Lunch and dinner are pretty hit or miss—like great club sandwiches and utterly horrible French dip. Service is so-so. They have Wi-Fi access for $10; hence the name. An amazingly variable restaurant. You may get a good experience, or you may get ticked off. Feeling lucky? **$7–$11** for breakfast, **$9–$13** for lunch, **$12–$22** for dinner. Right in Volcano Village. No dinner on Sunday and Monday.

Thai Thai
19-4084 Old Volcano Rd. • 967–7969

ONO Thai—Excellent menu of curries, soups, stir fry, noodle dishes and vegetarian items. It's probably safe to say they're overpriced, but the quality is top notch, so consider it a splurge. They have good Pad Thai. Curries are unusual, and curry lovers (like us) will either like the novelty (we do) or dislike the flavor. (Avoid the red.) Good (and generous) summer rolls. If you like heat, they'll wound you here. Thai hot *means* Thai hot, so go milder unless you've got an asbestos-lined tongue. Our only concern is the service can be uneven. Rushed at times, slow at others. If you catch 'em at the right pace, you'll like the place. Desserts are sparse—get the tapioca pudding. Decoration is beautiful and calming. **$15–$30** for lunch and dinner. In Volcano Village. Closed Wednesdays and for one full month each year when the owners go back to Thailand.

Volcano Golf & Country Club
99-1621 Pii Mauna Dr. • 967–8228

American—At the sometimes misty Volcano Golf Course just outside Volcano Village, the food has gone downhill. Burgers, chicken, beef—the teriyaki beef is *kinda-almost-maybe* good. The macadamia nut pie (similar to pecan pie) is great, though. Breakfast menu is small. You have better options in Volcano Village. **$7–$10** for breakfast, **$10–$14** for lunch.

DINING NEAR SOUTH POINT

Ocean View Pizzeria
525 Lotus Blossom Ln. • 929–9677

ONO Italian—Pizza, sandwiches, some baked goods and ice cream. The pizza is just OK, but their hot deli sandwiches are good and the reason for the ONO. (Your choices are meager around here unless you want to hit the grocery store.) In fact, the Italian sausage Parmesan with marinara on garlic bread is delicious. In the big shopping center on the mauka side before the 77 mile marker. **$5–$10**. Cash only.

DINING IN NA'ALEHU

Hana Hou Restaurant
95-1148 Spur Rd. • 929–9717

ONO American—Na'alehu is a pretty remote place on your way to the volcano, and it's surprising and gratifying to have great food in the middle of nowhere. We've seen them have off days, but not often. Breakfast includes different kinds of hash browns and corned beef hash, homefries with salsa, sour cream and eggs, etc. Lunch and dinner include plate lunches, sandwiches (including a surprisingly good grilled cheese) and specials. Consider their tasty lilikoi lemonade. And lastly, it's *mandatory* that you try their homemade pies. Better than your own grandmother's. **$7–$10** for breakfast, **$10–$20** for lunch and dinner. Look for a sign on the ocean side shoulder of the road in Na'alehu.

Punalu'u Bake Shop
95-5642 Mamalohoa Hwy • 929–7343

ONO American—Though their namesake sweetbread doesn't really work for us, most of their other baked goods sure do, such as the delicious the liliko'i-glazed Portuguese malasadas and the wonderful apple turnovers. They also have hot and cold sandwiches. On the highway, can't miss it. **$5–$10**.

ISLAND NIGHTLIFE

Not in the same league as what you'll find in Honolulu or any other big city, but on the Big Island we don't exactly spend *all* our evenings watching old reruns of *Gilligan's Island*. (Well… maybe Fridays.) There *is* life after sunset here.

Kona

Kona has the liveliest nightlife. Every Friday, the Entertainment section of the local newspaper, *West Hawai'i Today*, lists everything that's happening for the week ahead. Very handy. Much of the action takes place on Alii Drive. It's easy to walk downtown and check out what's shakin'. Directions to these places are in their reviews. For cocktails, the **Billfish Bar** at the King Kamehameha Hotel is famed for their cheap drinks. **Don's Mai Tai Bar** at the Royal Kona Resort has a great happy hour. Most of their mai tais are excellent, especially the Original, Pele's Volcanic and the Don Jito. (That's just our hard work ethic shining through.) Service can be thin, but the location works. **Huggo's** can be very romantic, and they often have live music. Jazz on the left side and a local guitarist on the right at **Huggo's on the Rocks**. But the best place in Kona for a sunset cocktail has to be the **Verandah Lounge** at the Outrigger Keauhou Beach Resort (322–3441) at the south end of Alii Drive. Some good tropical drinks (consider the Tropical Itch or the Hula Girl), and the location is absolutely incredible. It's surrounded on three sides by a shallow, protected lagoon that actually meanders *under* the building. Fish, eels and sometimes turtles amble about. Add a sunset and the one that you love, and you'll find this place irresistible. Note that the potency of the beverages seems to vary considerably here. They

also make a heck of a French dip sandwich. **Kona Brewing Co. & Brewpub** (334–2739) on Kuakini and Palani behind Kona Business Center is a good place for a cold, locally made beer. A dozen or so different brews and some wines. (No mixed drinks.)

The **Aloha Theatre** south of Kona up in Kainaliu often has fun local plays. Call 322–9924 for more information.

Big Island Comedy Club (329–4368) is a roving comedy act (find them mostly at restaurants and hotels around Kailua-Kona). Call for locations and dates.

Moviegoers will want to call **Keauhou Cinemas** (324–7200) or **Makalapua Cinemas** (327–0444) in Kona to see what's playing.

Kohala

Nightlife is a resort affair (so to speak). Many of the mega-resorts have lounges. Good places to have a drink include **Kamuela Provision Company** at the Hilton Waikoloa Village, **Brown's Beach House, Kahakai Bar** and **Luana Lounge** at the Fairmont Orchid, and the **Beach Tree** at the Four Seasons (325–8000).

Outside the resorts in Kawaihae, check out **Blue Dragon** (882–7771) for their consistently excellent live music along with their awesome food. (Pricey, though.) Call for days of operation.

Hilo

Hilo Burger Joint (935–8880) at 776 Kilauea Ave. has some very good live music most nights, and their bartending skills tend to be pretty high. (Great burgers, too.) **Cronies Bar & Grill** (935–5158) at 11 Waianuenue is a pretty good sports bar with good beers, bar games and a young, lively atmosphere. Food is adequate.

LU'AU

We've all seen them in movies. People sit at a table with a mai tai in one hand and a plate of kalua pig in another. There's always a show where a fire dancer twirls a torch lit at both ends and hula dancers bend and sway to the beat of the music. To be honest, that's not far from the truth. Lu'au can be a blast, and, if your time allows for one, they are highly recommended. The pig is *usually* baked all day in an underground pit called an imu, creating absolutely delicious results. Shows are usually exciting and fast-paced. Although lu'au on O'ahu can make you feel like cattle being led to slaughter, the lu'au on the Big Island are smaller, more intimate affairs of usually 100–200 people. Most lu'au include all you can eat and drink (including alcohol) for a set fee (except where noted below). If the punch they are serving doesn't satisfy you, they usually have an open bar to fill your needs.

Different resorts hold their lu'au on different nights. These change with the whims of the managers, so verify the days we list before making plans. Many lu'au advertise that they are rated number one. By whom? At any rate, this is what we thought of them. We noticed that for this edition, several lu'au have taken a *dramatic* turn for the worse, especially in Kona. We've never seen such a downturn in quality and can only chalk it up to cutbacks and changing attitudes.

In Kona, the only good lu'au is actually 10 miles outside Kona to the north. The **Kona Village Lu'au** (325–5555 ext. 266) on Fridays is also the most expensive. It's **$98** (one mai tai included), and the cash bar is expensive (but heavily poured). The grounds are absolutely beautiful. *This* is how lu'au grounds should look. Add to this really good food and a great and enthusiastic show, and you have the ingredients for a wonderful evening. They start letting cars in at 4:45 p.m., and it's first-come-first-served seating at 5:30 p.m. They also have a different Wednesday lu'au. More Hawaiian and less flashy, but to be honest, we prefer Friday's show.

In Kona town itself, there are no *good* lu'au at the current time, but they are cheaper than Kohala. **Royal Kona Resort's** (329–3111) is probably your marginal best bet. The food isn't very exciting, but it's not bad. The show is presided over by a Hawaiian lounge lizard. (But they do it pretty well.) The free bar closes around 7 p.m., and it's so poor that many people end up walking over to the poolside bar to *pay* for better drinks. The imu ceremony, when they unearth the pig, is good but it's hard to see through the crowd. When you see the torch lighters, follow them to the pit right away and stand there so you can get a better view. The location is the real star here—*right* next to the water. Like the King Kam (below), they erect a safety net for the fire knife dancer. Tables on the north (right) side are usually served last. Mondays, Wednesdays and Fridays—**$78**.

King Kamehameha's Kona Beach Hotel (329–2911). This *was* a lousy lu'au. Then they came in and improved it. Now they've cut back on the things that made it good and seem intent on charging for extras that used to be free. (Holy cow! They're acting like the *airlines*…) At press time, one of the better parts of the show—where a royal procession is brought ashore in canoes and walks through the grounds—had been nixed for quite a while because the canoe sprung a leak, and they confided that they didn't want to spend the money to fix it. The food is average, and free bar closes at 7:30. The "imu ceremony" is just two hotel cooks picking up the pig. Their show is average and they must not have much faith in the fire knife dancer, because they put a mood-killing net between him and the audience. Tuesdays through Thursdays and Sundays—**$79**. Preferred seating is an extra $15, bringing you closer to the stage.

Last (and certainly least) is **Firenesia** (it's *mandatory* to say it with a dramatic flair) at the Sheraton Keauhou Bay Resort (326–4969). The good news is they are well-organized. The bad news is...everything else. The food is mediocre. 'Nuff said. Drinks are one beer, two wines and a watered down mai tai. Dat's it. And the show? It's utterly embarrassing. They lip sync almost everything poorly, making it look like a bad Godzilla movie. The ridiculous story line is about the people of *Fireneeeesia* (did you say it dramatically?) and their battle for fire. To make matters worse, the bar closes during the show (when you really *need* it). Let's keep this simple. Just move along, folks. (**$80**)

In Kohala, the best is also the one that only does it on Tuesdays, the **Mauna Kea Beach Hotel** (882–5810). They have a good imu ceremony outside the grounds, where they pull the pig from the ground. They handle serving the food well, and the quality is very good. As soon as you're seated, you're free to head to the buffet, and getting seconds is easy. The bar is better than most, and you can get table service, but drinks are extra. (It's still open during the show, but they discourage you from ordering during that time.) The first half of the show is very strong and very Hawaiian, though the second half stalls a bit. Unfortunately, the stage is a bit low so those in back won't see as much. (And it can be pretty *loud* for those up front.) Overall, a pretty classy lu'au. **$96**.

The next would be **Fairmont Orchid's Gathering of the Kings** (326–4969). If you're looking for a traditional, old fashioned lu'au...this *ain't* it. It's a Vegas-style lu'au with modern interpretive dance and lip-syncing. Production value is very high, and they work hard, but it feels out of place. They play a recording complete with commentary that the performers follow. They try to get *everyone* in the audience on stage at the beginning, which can be awkward. The food is *excellent*. Drinks are included, and they have one of the best stocked lu'au bars we've seen, complete with blended drinks. It's **$99**. Gathering of the Kings works if you discard your notions of what a lu'au show should be, and you can accept a decidedly non-Polynesian experience.

Waikoloa Beach Marriott (886–6789) has mediocre food and a good show. They ask you to show up at 5 p.m., then make you wait an hour for no discernable reason before eating, with no entertainment provided during that time. If you don't have a food ticket in your hand, you *have* to go to the towel desk first. Although drinks are free, you may have 3 bartenders for 300 people, so expect long lines. And they don't have an imu ceremony. Located adjacent to the fishponds at 'Anaeho'omalu. Sundays and Wednesdays—**$88**.

The **Legends of the Pacific** (886–1234, ext. 54) Polynesian show at the Hilton Waikoloa Village on Tuesdays, Fridays and Saturdays is similar to the Marriott's show. But there's no view, you only get one drink, and they charge you **$99**. They charge an additional $26 for unlimited drinks, valet parking and front row seats.

And finally, this isn't really a lu'au, but we didn't know where else to put it. Called **An Evening at Kahua Ranch** (987–2108), this takes place on an 8,500-acre cattle ranch located at the 3,200-foot level of Kohala Mountain Road (250) with sweeping ocean sunset views. Instead of Polynesians dancing the hula, you'll hear a performer playing Charlie Daniels or Vince Gill, perhaps off-key, but he plays a mean fiddle. You'll also get a bit of line dancing, some star gazing, roping, branding of wood and fireside s'mores. The food is good and hearty—they do meat and 'taters well here. Drinks are beer, wine and soft drinks—no mixed drinks. But they're generous. You won't leave hungry or thirsty. It cools off more here after sunset than it does at the shoreline, so a light jacket may help. And you are a long bus ride from Kona. Some may find the entertainment hokey, but this 3-hour event is family-run and done in earnest. They say it's **$95–$145**, depending on transportation (though they charged us $130 when we drove ourselves).

DINNER CRUISES

A couple of companies in Kona offer two wildly different experiences.

Body Glove (326–7122) does it right. Their "Historical Sunset Cruise" is a 3-hour boat ride from Kailua Pier that heads to Kealakekua Bay. Along the way their impressively researched narration keeps things interesting. The food is very good, and their mai tais are better than we expected. (Only one free drink; then it's a cash bar.) You'll want to snag a table on the lower deck as soon as you board. (Preferable to the upper deck.) This is a well-oiled machine and one of the best dinner cruises we've seen. **$94**. They also have a 2-hour cocktail cruise, same price. It includes only pupu (appetizers), no history (just a DJ playing music) and no Kealakekua, but the bar is open. So decide if you want an all-you-can-eat experience, or an all-you-can-drink one.

The other company is **Spirit of Kona**, aka **Blue Sea Cruises** (331–8875). They use a glass bottom boat, which can afford cool views when they turn the lights on at night. (Though we've noticed that staring at the glass panes below seems to trigger nausea in some people.) The food's reasonably good and the staff is laid back, but they don't aren't as smooth as Body Glove (literally and figuratively). Customers seem more anxious for their 2-hour cruise to be over than Body Glove's 3-hour trip. It's **$98** and unlimited drinks are included. No kids under 8.

In Kohala, **Ocean Sports** (886–6666) has a 65-foot catamaran called **Alala** (they use the smaller **Sea Smoke** if they don't have enough customers) for dinner cruises out of Kawaihae Harbor. The

cruise is relaxing, and the friendly crew is always asking if you want anything. They motorsail much of the time, and you can chill out on the trampolines if you like. (Outdoors is preferable because their old, hazy cabin windows make the interior less desireable.) The food is acceptable—nothing more—and they start serving the simple buffet as soon as they leave port. Since serving-tray food doesn't improve with time, you feel a bit pressed to start eating, even if you want to relax with the unlimited drinks or champagne first. This nitpicking aside, this is a good 2-hour cruise for **$116**.

ISLAND DINING BEST BETS

Best Pizza—Kona Brewing Co.

Best Malasadas—Tex Drive-In

Best Use of a Pound of Sugar—One Cinnamon Roll at Island Lava Java

Best Meal Away from it All—Holuakoa Gardens in Kona or Blue Dragon in Kawaihae

Best Meal by a Fireplace—Kilauea Lodge

Best Bargain for Food *Volume*— Hawaiian Style Café

Best Use of a Crêpe—U • Top • It

Best Mexican Food—Killer Taco

Best Dinner Cruise—Body Glove

Best Use of Glassware—Schooners at Harbor House

Best Thai Fix—Original Thai or Lotus Café

Best Seafood—Pahu I'a at the Four Seasons

Best Way to Eat Your Fruit— Strawberry Mochi at Two Ladies Kitchen

Best Place to Take Your Food to Go— Sunset at Pu'uhonua o Honaunau

Best Lu'au—Kona Village

Best Sunset Cocktail—Verandah Lounge at Outrigger Keauhou Beach Resort or Don's Mai Tai Bar at the Royal Kona Resort

Alii Villas 293
Arnott's Lodge 300
Banyan Tree 294
Casa de Emdeko 294
Chalet Kilauea Collection 302
Colony One at SeaMountain 305
Country Club Hawai'i Condo Hotel 300
Country Club Villas 294
Dolphin Bay Hotel 300
Fairmont Orchid, Hawai'i 287
Fairway Villas 288
The Fairways at Mauna Lani 288
Four Seasons Resort Hualalai 288
Golf Villas at Mauna Lani 290
Hale Kona Kai 294
Hali'i Kai 290
Hapuna Beach Prince Hotel 290
Hawaiian Island Retreat 304
Hilo Bay Hostel 300
Hilo Hawaiian Hotel 300
Hilo Seaside Hotel 300
Hilo Tropical Gardens 301
Hilton Waikoloa Village 290
Holo Holo In 302
Hotel Honoka'a Club 305
Inn at Kulaniapia Falls 301
Islands at Mauna Lani 291
Jacaranda Inn 304
Kahalu'u Bay Villas 294
Kahalu'u Beach Villas 294
Kamuela Inn 303
Kanaloa at Kona 294
Keauhou Akahi 294
Keauhou Kona Surf & Racquet Club 294
Keauhou Palena 295
Keauhou Punahele 295
Keauhou Resort 295
Kilauea Lodge 302
King Kamehameha's Kona Beach 295
Kohala Club Hotel 304
Kohala Village Inn 304
Kolea 291
Kona Alii 296
Kona Bali Kai 296
Kona By The Sea 296

Kona Coast Resort 296
Kona Hotel 296
Kona Islander Inn 296
Kona Isle 296
Kona Magic Sands 296
Kona Makai 296
Kona Nalu 296
Kona Pacific 296
Kona Reef 297
Kona Seaside Hotel 297
Kona Seaspray 297
Kona Tiki Hotel 297
Kona Village Resort 292
Makolea 297
Manago Hotel 297
Mauna Kea Beach Hotel 292
Mauna Lani Bay Hotel & Bungalows 292
Mauna Lani Point 292
Mauna Lani Terrace 292
Na Hale O'Keauhou 297
Naniloa Volcanoes Resort 301
Outrigger Keauhou Beach Resort 297
Palms Cliff House Inn 301
Pineapple Park Kona 298
Royal Kona Resort 298
Royal Sea-Cliff Resort 298
Sea Village 298
Sheraton Keauhou Bay Resort 299
Shipman House B&B Inn 301
Shores at Waikoloa 292
Uncle Billy's Hilo Bay Hotel 301
Uncle Billy's Kona Bay Hotel 299
Villages at Mauna Lani 293
Villas at Mauna Kea 293
Vista Waikoloa 293
Volcano House 303
Volcano Inn 303
Volcano Village Lodge 303
Waikoloa Beach Marriott 293
Waikoloa Beach Villas 293
Waikoloa Colony Villas 293
Waimea Country Lodge 304
Wai'ula'ula at Mauna Kea 293
White Sands Village 299
Wild Ginger Inn & Hostel 301

Hotels shown in this color. Condominiums shown in this color.

Rental Agents

Abbey Vacation Rentals ....(866) 456–4252 or (808) 331–8878
ATR Properties, Inc. ....(888) 311–6020 or (808) 329–6020
Classic Resorts ....(800) 642–6284 or (808) 885–5022
Elite Property Management, LLC ....(877) 336–6751 or (808) 327–6751
Hawaii Island Bed & Breakfast Association ....www.stayhawaii.com
Hawaii Resort Mgmt./Kona Hawaii Vacation Rentals ..(800) 244–4752 or (808) 329–3333
Keauhou Property Management, Inc. ....(800) 745–5662 or (808) 326–9075
Mauna Kea Resort Luxury Vacation Rentals........................(808) 880–3490
South Kohala Management *(no cleaning fees)* ....(800) 822–4252 or (808) 883–8500
SunQuest Vacations ....(800) 367–5168 or (808) 329–6438
West Hawaii Property Services, Inc. ....(800) 799–5662 or (808) 334–1199

Room with a view...

Your selection of where to stay is one of the more important decisions you'll make in planning your Big Island vacation. To some, it's just a place to sleep, and rather meaningless. To others, it's the difference between a good vacation and a bad one.

There are four main types of lodging on the island: hotels, condominiums, bed and breakfasts, and single family homes. The vast majority of visitors stay in one of the first two types. But B&Bs and single family homes are often overlooked and can be very good values. If your group or family is large, you should strongly consider renting a house for privacy, roominess, and plain ol' value. There is a list of rental agents in the index at left, each willing and happy to send you a list of homes they represent. We also have a B&B referral service there.

Hotels usually offer more services, but smaller spaces and no kitchens. **Condominiums** usually have full kitchens, but you won't get the kind of attention you would from a hotel, including daily maid service. There are exceptions, of course, and we will point them out when they come up. You can find their locations on the various maps throughout this book.

All prices given are RACK rates, meaning *without any discounts*. Tour wholesalers and travel agents can often get better rates. Most resorts offer discounts for stays of a week or more, and some will negotiate price with you. Some won't budge at all, while others told us *no one* pays RACK rates. Also, these prices are subject to taxes of around 13.5%.

See all Web reviews at: www.wizardpub.com

These are *subjective* reviews. If we say that rooms are small, we mean that we've been in them, and they feel small or cramped to us. If we say that maintenance is poor, we mean that the paint might be peeling or the carpets are dingy or it otherwise felt worn to us.

Throughout the book we talk about the positives associated with the various areas. In deciding where to stay, here are three negatives for each major location worth considering:

Kohala: Food will cost you more and so will places to stay. You are far from the town of Kailua-Kona and its available resources. You are far from the volcano.

Kailua-Kona: Vog will be more of a nuisance in Kona. Traffic, while not *nearly* as bad as the mainland, can be troublesome at commute time. There's more noise along Alii Drive.

Hilo: Activities are less numerous. The ocean is less pleasant. Rain will probably be a companion. There are no mega-resorts on this side of the island; choices are fewer and of lesser quality in general.

The gold bar indicates that the property is exceptionally well priced for what you get.

SOLID GOLD VALUE

The gem means that this hotel or condominium offers something *particularly* special, not *necessarily* related to the price.

A REAL GEM

HOTELS

All hotel rooms described **(shown in this color)** have air conditioning, an activity or travel desk, telephones, lanais (verandas), cable TV, and have cribs available upon request. None have room service unless otherwise noted. If you are a smoker, call about smoking policies because most hotel rooms in Hawai'i are designated non-smoking.

CONDOS

One of the confusing aspects to renting a condo **(shown in this color)**, especially in Kona, is the fragmented nature of the market. Each unit usually has a different owner, they all use different rental agencies to manage them, and it changes all the time. (Spreadsheets, blinding headaches and blurred vision are all necessary to figure it out.) Therefore, when *we* review them, we may look at 10 units and get 10 winners. *You* may rent one and get a dump because the owner is using furniture from a landfill and carpet from the finish line at the Ironman Triathlon. You never truly know what you're going to get because condominium owners usually have complete autonomy in how they furnish their individual units. (Notice how we neatly cover our 'okoles, so that if you get a less-than-charming condo in a resort we recommend, we can always say you got one of the few duds there.)

Also remember that many (not *all*) condos have cleaning fees—especially in Kona. We don't list the fees because they will vary for each unit, rental agent or owner. Expect to pay $85–$250. And beware that cleaning standards in Kona condos aren't as good as other areas around the state. You may also pay a cleaning fee in some Kohala condos rented from agents, so be sure and ask.

When we describe a particular resort, we will often give the names or phone numbers of one or two companies that dominate the rental pool. But realize that this does not always do justice to the *entire* property. When we describe rates and units, they are for the rental agents

See all Web reviews at: www.wizardpub.com

we list. Different agents have different policies for the same complex.

Once you have decided where you want to stay, you can contact the resort. You may also want to contact some of the **rental agents** on page 282 to determine if they represent any units from the property you have chosen.

Many condos have minimum stays—usually three nights. We don't always list this because it changes with different rental companies. More and more rental agents are also requiring you to pay *all* of your condo rental costs before you arrive. It may make you nervous, but you might not have a choice if you're intent on staying at a particular place.

Three bedroom/two bath units are described as 3/2; two bedroom/one bath units are described as 2/1, etc. Differentiation between half baths and full baths is not made. The price spread for rooms of a given size is due to different views, different locations within the resort and seasonal fluctuations. So when you see that a 2/2 unit rents for $140–$180, you should figure that $180 units have a better view or are closer to the water. Also note that, unlike some other Hawai'i locations, Kona condo RACK rates seem more negotiable. The terms Oceanfront, Ocean View and Garden View are used rather capriciously in Hawai'i, so you should be skeptical of them.

Unless otherwise noted, all condos come with telephones, complete kitchens, coffee makers, lanais (verandas), cable TV, ceiling fans, coin-op laundry rooms, free local calls and have cribs available upon request. Maid service is only when you check out, and units won't have air conditioning or elevators unless otherwise noted. If you are a smoker, you will want to check policies before you book. Condos don't allow smoking in the units, and some even restrict you from smoking on the lanai and property, too.

BED & BREAKFASTS

Rather than describe the countless B&Bs scattered about the island, you're better off using the **Hawaii Island Bed & Breakfast Association**. Their B&B members are permitted and inspected. You can find them through their website www.stayhawaii.com. We also have lots of links to B&Bs on our website, but it's not practical to personally review them the way we do other accommodations.

WHERE SHOULD I STAY?

Kohala

Kohala is famous for its **mega-resorts**. These destination resort hotels have tons to see and do on the premises, pricey restaurants offering superb atmosphere and cuisine, and almost unending sunny weather. The developers have created oases in the lava desert where lava once stretched uninterrupted for miles.

You will notice that accommodation prices are high in Kohala. These snazzy resorts don't come cheap. We leave it up to you to decide if it's in your budget. A lot of them have REAL GEM icons next to them. We like to think of ourselves as stingy with these, but facts are facts—these *are* gems. But like the genuine article, these gems come at a price.

Picking the best mega-resort in Kohala is not a straightforward process. All of them have radically different personalities, so *your* personality is key to which one you'll like best. Most of these resorts do a great job at creating an atmosphere. The question is, is it *your* atmosphere? In our view, the Mauna Lani Bay Hotel has the best exotic tropical feel. The Fairmont

See all Web reviews at: www.wizardpub.com

Orchid has the richest, most luxurious feel. The Hilton Waikoloa Village has the most jaw-dropping elaborate, yet family-oriented feel. And 10 miles south of the main Kohala resort area, The Four Seasons has some of both Mauna Lani's and the Fairmont Orchid's assets—rich and luxurious, yet also a great tropical feel. Most of these resorts are world class, and we don't say that lightly. Choosing one just depends on what you want.

If it's a cheap **condo** you're looking for, go elsewhere. Kohala only has upscale condos for rent.

Kailua-Kona

The resorts in Kailua-Kona and the surrounding area aren't of the same caliber as the glitzy mega-resorts of Kohala, but neither are the prices. You'll find that you can stay and eat in Kona a lot cheaper than Kohala. Condos are far more numerous here than hotels. Some condos are a downright bargain, while others can only be recommended to in-laws.

Most accommodations in Kailua-Kona are along Alii Drive. This road fronts the shoreline, offering splendid ocean locations and sunsets. The penalty for staying on Alii Drive is auto noise. Cars and motorcycles scoot by, sometimes creating unpleasant reminders in *some* condos that you are still in the real world. (Other condos keep their rooms far enough from the road to keep them blissfully quiet.)

The high season in Kona is December through March, and most condos charge more at that time. Also, most condos have a minimum stay.

If you're looking for a good deal and have a little time before your trip, the Internet is the place to find individual vacation rentals. Try VRBO.com for deals from individual owners of small vacation rentals, B&Bs and houses. We have links

to some of them from our website at **www.wizardpub.com**. From the web you can also search for individual condo owners. If you're not a web person, from the mainland, you can buy an individual newspaper or get a short-term subscription from *West Hawai'i Today* newspaper (329–9311) on the west side, or *Hawai'i Tribune-Herald* (935–6621) on the east side. It'll cost you a few dollars, but you may save hundreds or even thousands of dollars on your accommodations. Just remember that you won't have the security of working with an established rental agent or company.

Hilo

Your choices in Hilo are much more limited than on the western side of the island. The number of overnight visitors here is a fraction of what the Kona side gets. The hotels are older here, and Hilo's economic woes mean once-grand hotels often have closed wings and shuttered restaurants and spas. But you shouldn't expect Kohala prices either. Hotels can be had quite cheap in Hilo, so even if you are staying on the western side, you should strongly consider staying at least a night here when you are exploring this side or visiting the volcano. That'll keep Hilo from becoming a blur during an around-the-island driving frenzy.

Most of the hotels are located along Banyan Drive. Many have outstanding views of Hilo Bay.

Volcano Village

The town of Volcano Village has a limited number of places to stay, but many of the choices you *do* have are superb. If you are spending a week on the Big Island, at least one night should be spent here. This is the most convenient place to stay when you explore the volcano. You

See all Web reviews at: www.wizardpub.com

can take your time and do the volcano justice. Remember, it gets chilly here at 4,000 feet, so bring something warm and waterproof. There are lots of B&Bs in Volcano Village, so check out the service listed on page 282 or check our website.

Other Places to Stay

Out of the main areas, accommodations are few and literally far between. **Waimea** is cool and sometimes chilly at 2,500 feet. There are lots of restaurants to choose from. The northern tip at **Hawi** has a few simple hotels and a nice inn, but your dining choices are fewer. Down at the **southern tip** you'll find an often-forgotten resort but even less dining to choose from. Finally, in **Honoka'a** near Waipi'o Valley is a cheap hotel that also has hostel beds.

WHERE ARE THE REST?

You'll notice that some of the resorts listed here don't have full reviews. That's because we reviewed more places than we have room for.

Also, we wanted to include aerial photos of the resorts. After all, a picture speaks a thousand words (and a thousand words take too long to read, anyway).

So we had a choice. Give you less info on *all* of them or do detailed reviews on only a *portion* of them. Neither choice seemed palatable.

So we came up with a *third* way: List minimal info on all (including if they are GEMS or SOLID GOLD VALUES), print full detailed reviews on *most,* and post full reviews of *all* on our website at **www.wizardpub.com**. After all, most people use this section before they come to the islands. And with the web (which has infinite space), we could do more, like post larger aerial photos of the resorts

with specific buildings labeled when appropriate, provide constant updates when necessary, and put links to the various rental agents or hotels right in the review, allowing you to go to their sites and get more photos of the rooms. You should remember, however, that resorts post photos to lure you in, and some aren't above posting modified or overly flattering shots when they were new and sparkling. Our aerials don't lie and are designed to give you a feel for their ocean proximity (does oceanfront *really* mean oceanfront?), so you'll know what kind of view to expect from a given location within the resort. Resorts whose review is posted on our website are identified with WEB REVIEW

Please remember that all these reviews are *relative to each other*. This is important. Even staying at a dump right on the ocean is still a *golly gee!* experience. In other words, *Hey, you're on the ocean on the Big Island!* So if we sound whiny or picky when critiquing a resort, it's only because their next door neighbor might offer such a better experience. It doesn't mean you'll be miserable; it just means that *compared to another resort*, you can do better.

KOHALA

Fairmont Orchid, Hawai'i
(800) 845–9905 or (808) 885–2000
1 North Kaniku Dr.

540 rooms, pool and 2 spas (one with a sand-lined area for kids to play while adults

relax), 10 tennis courts (7 lighted and one stadium court), room service, Keurig coffee

makers in rooms with free coffee daily, 5 restaurants, 5 shops, 17 conference rooms, **A REAL GEM** 2 golf courses, free fitness room, health spa, free use of sauna and steam rooms, valet parking, business center, Wi-Fi throughout, hi-speed Internet access in rooms ($15 per day), beauty salon, free 24-hour fitness room, children's program ($85 per day), empty fridge, free room safes, lu'au, wedding coordinator.

We try not to blather on about a resort—it hurts our credibility. But when it's right, it's right. The Fairmont Orchid has an intoxicating richness that permeates everything. The lush grounds have a very sculpted and precise feel. Nothing is out of place. The inside is just as flawless. The lobby, halls and rooms are all richly furnished with lots of wood and fine carpets—even the elevators are paneled in koa with crystal chandeliers. The overall effect of the resort's rooms and common areas is European-Hawaiian elegance. The entire staff seems obsessed with pleasing you. Restaurants are what you'd expect, on the higher end with delicious results. They have their own garden on property and use items they grow for their recipes. The manmade beach is usually calm and protected. Lots of activities are available. The tennis complex is the best on the island, and the two Mauna Lani golf courses are humbling and world renowned. You can get a massage next to the ocean at the "Spa Without Walls," where the sound of the surf helps you relax (as if you'll need any help) or by their waterfall with windows in the floors to watch the fish.

They have an optional $75 per adult ($60 per child) per stay activity package that'll cover snorkel gear, surfing and snorkel lessons, a kayak, etc. Parking is $17 and valet parking is $22. Local calls are free. Laundry is valet only. Casabella chairs (2 chairs with a retractable cover) by the pool are $45 and $60 by the ocean and include fruit, water and dry snacks. Umbrellas by the pool are free.

The Fairmont Orchid is exceptional in many ways. It has become popular with business travelers, and if you're looking to be pampered, consider it. Rooms (522 sq. ft.) are $292–$494. Some of the partial ocean views will require imagination to see the ocean. RACK rates are high—this ain't for the budget traveler—but they often have specials to ease the pain a bit. They also have a gold floor (for more money), which has more personalized services and its own lounge. Suites (which are *very* nice) are $614–$2,249 and are 1,050–2,752 sq. ft.

Fairway Villas
(866) 770–9497 or (808) 886–0036
(800) 822–4252 or (808) 883–8500
69-200 Pohakulana Pl.
WEB REVIEW

The Fairways at Mauna Lani
(800) 822–4252 or (808) 883–8500
(866) 456–4252 or (808) 331–8878
68-1125 N. Kaniku Dr.
WEB REVIEW

Four Seasons Resort Hualalai
(800) 332–3442 or (808) 325–8000
72-100 Ka'upulehu Dr.

See all Web reviews at: www.wizardpub.com

243 rooms, 8 tennis courts (4 lighted), 5 conference rooms, 4 pools, keiki (kid) pool, lava snorkel pool, 4 spas, coffee makers in rooms with free coffee daily, Wi-Fi in

 A REAL GEM lobby, rooms and some other areas, valet parking, free children's program, *private* golf course, health spa, 3 restaurants, 24-hour business center, free laundry room, empty fridge, 24-hour room service. This resort *shines*, even among its superb competitors. 37 one- and two-story bungalows in several semi-circles with 6–8 rooms per building, plus a few golf course buildings. They used a lot of local materials, giving the resort a very Hawaiian feel. All units (even golf course units) have nice ocean views. (Building 25 is closest to the water.) Second-floor rooms have better ocean views, but first-floor rooms have a pleasant garden on the other side of the bathroom glass with a second private *outdoor lava shower* ensconced in the garden where water gurgles over a short lava ledge. What a great place to have your morning shower! (But six of the first floor rooms *don't* have the lava shower—so be sure and ask.) This makes the first floor a better value than the higher-priced second-floor rooms. Overall, rooms are of average size, nicely furnished with cool slate floors. Some soft goods (linens, towels, etc.) updating was planned at press time.

One feature we've never seen anywhere else is a large, lava anchialine pond with 1.8 million gallons of fresh and salt water. Connected to the ocean, its level rises and falls each day with the tide. Inside are 40 species of fish, including several spotted eagle rays. You won't find a safer place to snorkel in the state. It's great to be there when they feed the fish.

If you bring your keiki, you'll find free licensed children's program for young'uns 5–12. (They also have a free teen center.) Their sand-lined kid's pool even has kid-size lounge chairs and free beach toys. The resort is the only one with a *truly* private golf course. Only guests and residents of the development are allowed to play, so tee times are spaced farther apart. It's a very nice, player-friendly, Jack Nicklaus course for about $250. The same goes for the full spa, which offers enough luxuriating decadence to melt your toenails. The resort fronts a beach, but the swimming is poor due to a lava shelf. They do have a manmade quasi tide-pool at the shore for wading. However, just a short stroll south is Kuki'o Beach with somewhat better swimming.

Services here are extraordinary, even for a Kohala resort. (An example: chilled towels at the pool, Evian spritz service, fresh fruit kabobs, sunscreen—but you have apply it yourself.) How's that for pampering? The swimming pools are scattered around the resort. Some, such as the main lip-less infinity pool, are cleverly constructed so that, while swimming, it seems to be part of the ocean. Most resort items, like self-parking, room safes and cabana chairs are free. They even have a free sunglass cleaning service and free gaming systems like Nintendo, PlayStation, GameCube and Xbox. Oddly, local calls are $1 and valet (overnight) parking is $20 (free during the day). Their restaurants, such as Pahu I'a, are excellent. No surprise there. If you have kids, the Seashell is the semi-circle you want; honeymooners (or those who want the quietest region) should choose the Palm Grove. Rooms of 635 sq. ft. are $625–$1,195. Suites (1,050–4,900 sq. ft.) are $1,375–$12,500!

See all Web reviews at: www.wizardpub.com

Golf Villas at Mauna Lani
(866) 456–4252 or (808) 331–8878
68-1122 Na Ala Hele Rd.
WEB REVIEW

Hali'i Kai
(866) 470–4254 or (808) 886–4307
(800) 822–4252 or (808) 883–8500
69-1029 Nawahine Pl.
WEB REVIEW 💎

Hapuna Beach Prince Hotel
(888) 977–4623 or (808) 880–1111
62-100 Kauna'oa Dr.
WEB REVIEW

Hilton Waikoloa Village
(800) 221–2424 or (808) 886–1234
69-425 Waikoloa Beach Dr.

1,240 rooms, 3 pools, 3 spas, valet parking, fitness room, health spa, beauty salon, 8 tennis courts, two golf courses, 24 conference **SOLID GOLD VALUE** rooms, business center, coin-op laundry, empty fridge, free room safes, hi-speed Internet access in room, Wi-Fi in some common areas, 37-inch HD TVs, room service, coffee maker in room, 9 restaurants, tons of shops, tram and a boat service, wedding coordinator.

Where do we start? How about *wow!* This is the one you've probably heard about. This resort, built in the late '80s and spread over 62 acres, is the most elaborate of them all. (By the way, despite its name, it is not located in or next to the town of Waikoloa Village.) Three separate towers are joined by a tram and boat network right out of Disneyland. A swimming pool has a pounding waterfall and an Indiana Jones-type swinging bridge overhead. There is a dolphin pool where lucky guests can get in the water with dolphins. The whole experience is described in ADVENTURES on page 236. $7 million worth of artwork is spread all over the resort. Parrots and exotic birds are also scattered about. There are multiple concierge desks around to assist in booking activities, making reservations or pointing the way to a particular part of the resort. The one thing the Hilton doesn't have is a great beach. (They have a manmade inland lagoon beach instead.) But 'Anaeho'omalu Beach is a half-mile walk or drive south. There's a large ocean-fed lagoon where guests float around in kayaks, paddle boats and rafts. In terms of amenities, the Hilton Waikoloa is an excellent place for families. Kids will *never* get bored here. There's a shallow swimming pool with a sandy beach at one end, a water slide and enough activities to wear out any teen or crumb cruncher. Their kid's camp is $60 per day (for the first child, less for second or more), and there is also a night camp. Consider a ground floor cabana room in the Lagoon Tower in front of the dolphin pool where kids can frolic on the grass. Avoid connecting rooms, unless you need them, as your neighbor can easily be heard through the closed doors—especially in the Ocean Tower.

Large groups will find the meeting facilities superb. From their 24 conference rooms to the ballroom the size of Waikiki to their business services area, which rents everything from computers to cell phones—if you're here for business, they can accommodate you. The restaurants here are excellent. 8 lounges…We could go on and on, but we're running out of room.

See all Web reviews at: www.wizardpub.com

The resort might seem overwhelming at first. It cost over a third of a *billion* dollars back in the '80s to construct, and a staggering 1,000 employees are needed to run it all. You won't see all of them running around, however. That's because they go from here to there via an extensive underground tunnel network. Tunnels have dashed lines separating the lanes—even shoulders—and when you're down there, you're likely to run into your chef in uniform cruising along on a three-wheeled bike. You may wish *you* had one to get around the property.

The entire resort is oriented inward, resulting in a destination that is self-contained. Some people who visit the Hilton Waikoloa snort that it's not real. Frankly, they miss the point. It's not *supposed* to represent reality. It's fantasy, escape, a leap into never-never land. You wouldn't sniff that Disneyland is phony, would you? The designers of the Hilton Waikoloa Village did a great job of achieving their objective—making an out-of-this-world playground/fantasyland for adults and kids. If that's what you are looking for, you will find it here in abundance. If you want to experience a calm piece of authentic old Hawai'i, you've come to the wrong place.

Rates are *reasonable* for Kohala (but the spread is huge). You may feel your pocketbook being emptied at every turn with extra charges, like Internet access at $15/day, self-parking is $15 (but motorcycles are free, as if you care), valet parking is $21 (but complimentary for hybrid cars—which ain't real easy to rent), coffee for your coffee maker is $4, cabana chairs are $50 per day by the pool, (but casabella—2 chairs with a retractable cover, are free by the lagoon), and the fitness room/spa is $20. They do offer optional resort fee packages—ranging from $4.50 to $25—which can cover some of the above extra charges. Rooms of 530 sq. ft. are $199–$599. The 55 suites (1,060–3,000 sq. ft.) range from $499–$2,499. Room updates were planned at press time.

Islands at Mauna Lani
(800) 642–6284 or (808) 885–5022
68-1375 Pauoa Rd.

Kolea
(866) 456–4252 or (808) 331–8878
(800) 822–4252 or (808) 883–8500
69-1000 Kolea Kai

126 units, a/c, pool, keiki pool, spa, BBQ on the lanai, free Wi-Fi, spa, free fitness room, washer/dryer in unit, private elevators in many. It's hard to imagine being unhappy here. These are some of the most impressively appointed condos we've seen, and it's the only condo complex in Waikoloa that's next to a beach. Rooms are richly furnished with high-end appliances, African mahogany trim and high ceilings throughout, travertine floors, granite countertops, a wall of glass that'll fold away from the 430 sq. ft. lanai (and its separate kitchen), making it part of the living space, and so much more. Even the closets light up automatically when you walk in. Although decor varies from unit to unit, we didn't see any that weren't outstanding. They have a sand bottom children's pool with its own waterfall, but it can get crowded during busy seasons.

A REAL GEM

See all Web reviews at: www.wizardpub.com

First-floor units are the least expensive, because views might be encroached upon by a home in front of you. (Third-floor units have best views, especially buildings 4–8, 10 and 12.) An easy place to love. 2/2 units (1,270–1,554 sq. ft.) are $266–$550. 3/3 units (1,716–2,147 sq. ft.) are $397–$1,099. 3-night minimum.

Kona Village Resort
(800) 367–5290 or (808) 325–5555
Queen Ka'ahumanu Hwy
WEB REVIEW

Mauna Kea Beach Hotel
(866) 977–4589 or (808) 882–7222
62-100 Mauna Kea Beach Dr.
WEB REVIEW ◆

Mauna Lani Bay Hotel & Bungalows
(800) 327–8585 or (808) 885–6622
68-1400 Mauna Lani Dr.
WEB REVIEW ◆

Mauna Lani Point
(800) 642–6284 or (808) 885–5022
68-1050 Mauna Lani Point Dr.

116 units, a/c, pool, BBQ, spa, washer/dryer in unit, sauna, Wi-Fi, daily maid service. The interiors have nice furnishings, huge master bathrooms, pleasing layouts, good location and relaxing views across the golf course. Many of the units have been nicely updated, so ask for one. Some have very good ocean views. They have done a lot building maintenance recently, and the property was looking sharp on our visit. 1/2 units (1,300 sq. ft.) are $395–$550, 2/3 units (1,700 sq. ft.) are $515–$790. 3-night minimum. Basic grocery package available for an extra fee.

Mauna Lani Terrace
(800) 822–4252 or (808) 883–8500
68-1399 Mauna Lani Dr.

80 units, a/c, pool, spa, sauna, keiki pool, washer/dryer in unit, free hi-speed Internet access, BBQ, weekly maid. Most units overlook the ancient fishponds, creating an **A REAL GEM** amazingly tranquil setting. Some units have ocean views as well. Buildings J, K and L often have nice sunset views. Many units have higher-end furnishings and some have been updated. 2- and 3-bedroom units are better. Most units have stairs leading to them—either up or down. There are two units available without stairs if you need them—one in building F and the other in building G. Master bathrooms are large. The complex is right next to the Mauna Lani Bay Hotel. Grounds are nicely groomed and mature. Even though this is an older property, it has been very well-cared for, and we still like it. 1/2 units (1,058–1,150 sq. ft.) are $356–$425, 2/3 (1,407–1,481 sq. ft.) units are $446–$575. 3-night minimum.

Shores at Waikoloa
(877) 997–6667 or (808) 886–5001
69-1035 Keana Pl.
WEB REVIEW

See all Web reviews at: www.wizardpub.com

Villages at Mauna Lani
(800) 822–4252 or (808) 883–8500
68-1025 N. Kaniku Dr.
WEB REVIEW 💎

Villas at Mauna Kea
(808) 880–3490
Kamahoi Pl.
WEB REVIEW 💎

Vista Waikoloa
(800) 822–4252 or (808) 883–8500
(866) 456–4252 or (808) 331–8878
69-1010 Keana Pl.

122 units, a/c, pool and 2 spas, free fitness room, business center, washer/dryer in unit, elevator, free hi-speed Internet access in some units, BBQ. Considering the caliber and the fact that it's in Kohala, this is a very good deal. Units are large and nicely furnished, the layout is pleasing, grounds are well-groomed, the bathrooms have nice, deep tubs. Ocean views aren't overwhelming—most are blocked by the Kolea resort or trees. But if you want a condo in Kohala, this is as close as you'll come to inexpensive yet pleasant. Buildings E & F are the best, A & B *feel* the closest to the road. 2/2 units (1,262–1,406 sq. ft. plus huge lanais) are $175. 3-night minimum.

SOLID GOLD VALUE

Waikoloa Beach Marriott
(888) 797–1907 or (808) 886–6789
69-275 Waikoloa Beach Dr.
WEB REVIEW

Waikoloa Beach Villas
(866) 956–4262 or (808) 886–0036
69-180 Waikoloa Beach Dr.
WEB REVIEW

Waikoloa Colony Villas
(877) 997–6667 or (808) 886–8899
(800) 822–4252 or (808) 883–8500
69-555 Waikoloa Beach Dr.
WEB REVIEW

Wai'ula'ula at Mauna Kea
(808) 880–3490
62-3600 Amaui Pl.
WEB REVIEW 💎

KAILUA-KONA

Alii Villas
(800) 367–5168 or (808) 329–6438
(800) 799–5662 or (808) 334–1199
75-6016 Alii Dr.

125 units, pool, washer/dryer in unit, BBQs, free Wi-Fi in most from top set of

See all Web reviews at: www.wizardpub.com

numbers. Units are fairly small, but with prices starting at $90–$185 for 1/1 units (620 sq. ft.), the value can be fairly decent. 2/2s (1,050 sq. ft.) are $149–$185. The pool is away from the ocean in the middle of the complex. Shop around with different rental agents. This ain't the greatest place to stay; it's pretty institutional-feeling, and the views feel the same from most units. 3-night minimum.

Banyan Tree
(800) 367–5168 or (808) 329–6438
(800) 244–4752 or (808) 329–3333
76-6268 Alii Dr.
WEB REVIEW

Casa de Emdeko
(800) 367–5168 or (808) 329–6438
75-6082 Alii Dr.
WEB REVIEW

Country Club Villas
(800) 367–5168 or (808) 329–6438
(800) 745–5662 or (808) 326–9075
78-6920 Alii Dr.
WEB REVIEW

Hale Kona Kai
(800) 421–3696 or (808) 329–2155
75-5870 Kahakai Rd.

39 units, pool, a/c, elevator, free Wi-Fi by pool, BBQ. Broken into two wings (the short wing and the long wing) with no grounds. **SOLID GOLD VALUE** Rooms are pleasant and clean, and the living rooms and bedrooms

both look out on the water on ocean-facing units. In ocean-facing units in the long wing, you will not get tired of watching the turtles in the tide-pools below. Many units have been updated. The pool's so close to the ocean you'll get sprayed on big surf days. Rooms ending with 07 and 08 have bedrooms that face each other, affording less privacy. There is an herb garden by the BBQ for guests to use. The solid gold value is because of their stellar ocean proximity. Definitely get an ocean-facing room here. 1/1s (648–696 sq. ft.) are $100–$185. ($20 extra gets you a pretty nice wraparound lanai.) Lots of repeat guests here. 3-night minimum.

Kahalu'u Bay Villas
(800) 367–5168 or (808) 329–6438
78-6715 Alii Dr.
WEB REVIEW

Kahalu'u Beach Villas
(866) 456–4252 or (808) 331–8878
78-6721 Alii Dr.
WEB REVIEW

Kanaloa at Kona
(800) 688–7444 or (808) 322–9625
(800) 745–5662 or (808) 326–9075
78-261 Manukai St.
WEB REVIEW ◆

Keauhou Akahi
(800) 367–5168 or (808) 329–6438
(800) 799–5662 or (808) 334–1199
78-7030 Alii Dr.
WEB REVIEW

Keauhou Kona Surf & Racquet Club
(800) 799–5662 or (808) 334–1199
(800) 745–5662 or (808) 326–9075
78-6800 Alii Dr.
WEB REVIEW

See all Web reviews at: www.wizardpub.com

Keauhou Palena
(800) 799–5662 or (808) 334–1199
78-7054 Kamehameha III Rd.

WEB REVIEW ▰▰

Keauhou Punahele
(800) 367–5168 or (808) 329–6438
(888) 311–6020 or (808) 329–6020
78-7070 Alii Dr.

WEB REVIEW ▰▰

Keauhou Resort
(800) 367–5168 or (808) 329–6438
78-7039 Kamehameha III Rd.

WEB REVIEW

King Kamehameha's Kona Beach Hotel
(800) 367–2111 or (808) 329–2911
75-5660 Palani Rd.

452 rooms, pool and spa, 2 restaurants, 4 conference rooms, 2 tennis courts, 24-hour business center, free Wi-Fi or hi-speed Internet access in the rooms, coin-op **A REAL GEM** laundry, empty fridge, free room safes, coffee maker in room with free coffee daily, 37-inch HD flat screen TVs, free 24-hour fitness room, lu'au. Built in the mid '70s, the King Kam (as it's known locally) is a Kona fixture. Located next to the Kailua Pier, the hotel is fronted by the tiny but calm Kamakahonu

Beach. The 'Ahu'ena Heiau shown on page 59 is also on the grounds. This area was the home of King Kamehameha during his latter years, and his legacy has been adopted by the hotel in paintings and artwork.

It's amazing what $35 million and a great design team have done for this aging hotel. The new owners renovated the west tower in 2009, and the balance of the hotel was finished in 2010. The results are remarkable and why it earned a REAL GEM rating for this edition. We hardly recognized the place from the lobby up. Rooms can be described as modern and fresh. The design is rooted heavily in Hawaiian nature patterns and is reflected in everything from the coffee bean fabric on the chairs to lava pattern on the hallway carpets. This design works for us and it has modern touches we like, such as hand-held shower heads and MP3 adapters. Rooms either have two queen beds or one king. The renovation did away with connecting rooms. The staff is really proud of the new look and shows it with a lot of aloha toward the guests. The redesigned infinity pool is very inviting, but we wish they had a few more umbrellas around it. Retail space and a day spa were planned at press time. Parking is $10 and local calls are $1.

King Kam is the center of the universe every October when the Ironman Triathlon takes place. Most of the athletes stay here, as do many from the television crews, and rooms are hard to get then. Ask for a "best available rate" when booking as rooms can be had for $129 and up on that rate. At that price this would be a SOLID GOLD VALUE. Rooms (348–380 sq. ft.) are $299–$449, suites (837 sq. ft.) are $799.

See all Web reviews at: www.wizardpub.com

Kona Alii
(877) 336–6751 or (808) 327–6751
(800) 367–5168 or (808) 329–6438
75-5782 Kuakini Hwy.
WEB REVIEW

Kona Bali Kai
(800) 367–5004 or (808) 329–9381
(800) 367–5168 or (808) 329–6438
76-6246 Alii Dr.
WEB REVIEW

Kona By The Sea
(877) 997–6667 or (808) 327–2300
75-6106 Alii Dr.
WEB REVIEW

Kona Coast Resort
(800) 367–5168 or (808) 329–6438
(800) 799–5662 or (808) 334–1199
78-6842 Alii Dr.
WEB REVIEW

Kona Hotel
(808) 324–1155
76-5908 Mamalahoa Hwy
WEB REVIEW

Kona Islander Inn
(800) 244–4752 or (808) 329–3333
75-5776 Kuakini Hwy
WEB REVIEW

Kona Isle
(888) 311–6020 or (808) 329–6020
(800) 367–5168 or (808) 329–6438
75-6100 Alii Dr.
WEB REVIEW

Kona Magic Sands
(800) 244–4752 or (808) 329–3333
(800) 367–5168 or (808) 329–6438
77-6452 Alii Dr.
37 rooms, pool, a/c in *some*, BBQ. You
can see and hear the ocean right from

your bed. Units are *very* small (450 sq.
ft.)—a studio with a kitchenette. The
bed area is converted
from the lanai in some
SOLID GOLD VALUE rooms, so you may just
have a railing outside your sliding glass
door. Upper floors have better views.
Units ending 01–04 have extra large
250 sq. ft. lanais, but may get noise if
the restaurant below is open. Units
ending in 01 can see (and hear) the
people on the beach next door, and
they can see *you*. Rooms can vary a
lot, so ask for a remodeled unit. The
prices have gone up and down like the
stock market and are currently $90–
$150—a good deal. The second agent
listed has some even cheaper prices. 3-
night minimum.

Kona Makai
(800) 367–5168 or (808) 329–6438
(877) 336–6751 or (808) 327–6751
75-6026 Alii Dr.
WEB REVIEW

Kona Nalu
(800) 367–5168 or (808) 329–6438
76-6212 Alii Dr.
WEB REVIEW

Kona Pacific
(877) 336–6751 or (808) 327–6751
(888) 311–6020 or (808) 329–6020
75-5865 Walua Rd.
WEB REVIEW

See all Web reviews at: www.wizardpub.com

Kona Reef
(800) 367–5004 or (808) 329–2959
(800) 367–5168 or (808) 329–6438
75-5888 Alii Dr.

130 units, a/c, pool, spa, elevator, washer/dryer in unit, free Internet access available in some and on front office computer, free Wi-Fi in common areas, BBQs. Buildings A and D are fairly quiet (except for the sound of the ocean), but units next to Alii Drive get a lot of road noise. The rooms are not bad, not great. If you're gonna stay here, try to get a corner unit—especially building A. Although there's a/c in most, it's not in the bedroom, and it may get hot in there (and not the way you intend). If you need a room that's elevator-accessible, you want Building F. That's because in the other buildings, during a fit of design goofiness, the elevator only stops *between* floors, and there are a lot stairs here. Your other option is a ground floor unit in Building A or D for access without stairs. 1/1s (611–651 sq. ft.) are $250–$305. 2/2 units (905–1,120 sq. ft.) are $410–$510. Those RACK rates are insane, but few pay them since discounts are as easy to get as a sunburn. 2-night minimum. The second set of phone numbers has *much* cheaper prices and a 3-night minimum.

Kona Seaside Hotel
(800) 367–7000 or (808) 329–2455
75-5646 Palani Rd.
WEB REVIEW

Kona Seaspray
(808) 322–2403
78-6665 Alii Dr.
WEB REVIEW

Kona Tiki Hotel
(808) 329–1425
75-5968 Alii Dr.
WEB REVIEW

Makolea
(800) 367–5168 or (808) 329–6438
78-216 Makolea St.
WEB REVIEW

Manago Hotel
(808) 323–2642
82-6155 Mamalahoa Hwy, Capt. Cook
WEB REVIEW

Na Hale O'Keauhou
(800) 367–5168 or (808) 329–6438
78-6833 Alii Dr.
WEB REVIEW

Outrigger Keauhou Beach Resort
(800) 688–7444 or (808) 322–3441
78-6740 Alii Dr.

309 rooms, pool and keiki (children's) pool, restaurant, lounge, 6 tennis courts (2 lighted), 4 conference rooms, free fitness room, **SOLID GOLD VALUE** free hi-speed Internet access in rooms and Wi-Fi in lobby, coin-op laundry room, free room safe, empty fridge, coffee makers in room with free coffee daily, valet parking, day spa. Originally built in 1970 (but renovated in 2007), the hotel borders Kahalu'u Beach

See all Web reviews at: www.wizardpub.com

on one side and a tide-pool on another. The grounds are nice and include the three reconstructed heiau (temples). Many of the rooms have nice views. The ocean-front rooms are *worth every penny.* They're the only rooms on the Big Island *directly* over the water. Just look down, and you may see turtles and eels swimming in the shallow tide-pool. Other rooms are nice for the money. South facing rooms have silly little square bathtubs, while north facing rooms have showers only and views that may be dominated by the roof of the restaurant in Partial Ocean View rooms that face north. For the location, it's a great deal. Their Verandah Lounge is a truly kickin' place to have a sunset cocktail. They offer historic cultural tours on site that delve into the area, Hawaiian traditions and include a meal. Parking is $7 and valet is $10. Local calls are a buck. Rooms (420 sq. ft.) are $279–$439 and connecting rooms are available. Their one-bedroom suite (758 sq. ft.) is $609. All rates include a buffet breakfast for two. Lots of packages available here. Ask for their "Aloha Rate," which will get room rates starting at $139. That is a *Wow!* and a SOLID GOLD VALUE.

Pineapple Park Kona
(877) 800–3800 or (808) 323–2224
81-6363 Mamalahoa Hwy, Kealakekua
WEB REVIEW

Royal Kona Resort
(800) 222–5642 or (808) 329–3111
75-5852 Alii Dr.
WEB REVIEW

Royal Sea-Cliff Resort
(800) 688–7444 or (808) 329–8021
75-6040 Alii Dr.
154 units, tennis court, a/c, free room

Wi-Fi in lobby, business center, daily maid service, BBQs, local calls are $.75. The resort is run similarly to a hotel, though units are individually owned and half are timeshare. Condos are fairly large. Note from the aerial photo that the middle rooms, though many are called "Partial Ocean View," have poor ocean views. (Think of the resort as a tree and try to get a room on a branch, not the trunk.) Also, since the floors are stair-stepped, upper-floor units look down on the lanais of the floors beneath them. So behave yourself on the lanais, unless you're at the top. Some of the rooms could use some updating, but none were in poor condition and all were very clean. Be sure and bring along your sunglasses as the reflection off the white paint on the buildings can be blinding. They have lots of packages available, so you shouldn't end up paying RACK rates. There is an Aloha Party once a week with pupus. Studios (500 sq. ft.) are $219, 1/1 units (700–784 sq. ft.) are $249–$369, 2/2 units (950–1,430 sq. ft.) are $289–$409. 2-night minimum.

Sea Village
(800) 367–5168 or (808) 329–6438
(888) 311–6020 or (808) 329–6020
75-6002 Alii Dr.
WEB REVIEW

See all Web reviews at: www.wizardpub.com

Sheraton Keauhou Bay Resort
(888) 488–3535 or (808) 930–4900
78-128 Ehukai St.

521 rooms, pool, 2 spas, 2 lighted tennis courts, 24-hour fitness room, room

service, valet parking, 3 restaurants, lounge, empty fridge, 2 shops, 8 conference rooms,

A REAL GEM 24-hour business center, Wi-Fi throughout resort, coin-op laundry room, coffee makers in room with free coffee daily, free room safes, wedding coordinator, wedding chapel, seasonal children's program, day spa, lu'au. This resort was closed for three years before $80 million worth of renovations ushered in the current Sheraton back in 2005. It's best described as sophisticated, understated, islandy and a bit stark, but it embraces their oceanside location. (But no sand beach, and they could use more plants in the interior areas.) They cater to families here, and it's reflected in their multi-level water feature with 200-foot waterslide, waterfall and pool that meanders into the lobby atrium. The fitness room (for those who can't bear to be on vacation without working out) is state of the art with a killer view of the ocean. The keiki center might just be the best we've seen in the state, complete with foosball, PlayStation, basketball, ping-pong, wide-screen movie theater, craft room and more. It's $60 for a full day, which includes lunch, but is only available at peak times of the year. For older kids (and adults), they have a gaming area with pool tables and ping-pong. Casabella chairs for two by the pool are

free. They have a good wedding infrastructure, including an oceanfront chapel. Couples can get a private ocean view massage and Jacuzzi in the day spa.

There is now a *mandatory* resort fee of $16 that covers self-parking (valet is $6 extra), Internet, local calls, a trolley that will run guests all the way into Kona Town and some other items. Overall, a modern, comfortable, family-friendly getaway. Hence, the GEM. Room updates were planned at press time, including carpets, bedding and painting. Rooms (450 sq. ft.) are $159–$219, suites (925–3,000 sq. ft.) are $950–$2,550. Their partial ocean view category is worth the upgrade from mountain view. The hotel was for sale at press time.

Uncle Billy's Kona Bay Hotel
(800) 367–5102 or (808) 329–1393
75-5739 Alii Dr.
WEB REVIEW

White Sands Village
(800) 367–5168 or (808) 329–6438
(888) 311–6020 or (808) 329–6020
77-6469 Alii Dr.

108 units, 2 tennis courts, central a/c, pool and spa, washer/dryer in unit, eleva-

See all Web reviews at: www.wizardpub.com

tor, free Wi-Fi in some, BBQs. This fairly old building is right across the street from White Sands Beach Park, which is usually swimmable. Nice pool and grounds. The buildings are well maintained. They get a few extra points for the beach proximity (but don't expect much of an ocean view from most rooms because of the orientation). Smallish 2/2 units are mostly adequate. (The washer and dryer is directly across from the toilet—that's different.) The elevator doesn't go to every room elevation, so you may have to deal with some stairs. 2/2 units (875–1,010 sq. ft.) are $122–$180. 3-night minimum.

HILO AREA

Arnott's Lodge
(808) 969–7097
98 Apapane Rd.
WEB REVIEW

Country Club Hawai'i Condo Hotel
(866) 935–7171 or (808) 935–7171
121 Banyan Dr.

147 rooms, free Wi-Fi (rooms on lobby side or in lobby), lanais on most (except room numbers ending in 9, 17, 10 and 22), microwave and empty fridge, coffee maker (free coffee in lobby), washer/dryer in some others use coin-op laundry, daily maid only if you pay the daily rate, and local calls are an extra 52¢. So what are

SOLID GOLD VALUE

they—a hotel or a condo? They're a condotel with rooms owned by individuals, so expect wide variations among the rooms. Some rooms have been updated and are acceptable, but *not all*, so keep looking until you find one with surroundings you like. The day staff has improved here and shows more aloha than in the past. Parking lot may be noisy at night. Rooms (around 300 sq. ft.) are $74–$114, kitchenettes (add a hot plate) are also $74. Cheaper weekly rates available make oceanfront rooms $84. We're giving it a SOLID GOLD VALUE for this edition based on getting a decent room and view for your money.

Dolphin Bay Hotel
(877) 935–1466 or (808) 935–1466
333 Iliahi St.
WEB REVIEW

Hilo Bay Hostel
(808) 933–2771
101 Waianuenue Ave.
WEB REVIEW

Hilo Hawaiian Hotel
(800) 367–5004 or (808) 935–9361
71 Banyan Dr.
WEB REVIEW

Hilo Seaside Hotel
(800) 560–5557 or (808) 935–0821
126 Banyan Dr.

135 rooms, pool, coin-op laundry, no elevator, empty fridge, Wi-Fi or use kiosk in lobby, coffee maker with free coffee

See all Web reviews at: www.wizardpub.com

daily, lanais on deluxe rooms overlooking koi pond, free safety deposit boxes at front desk. Clean, simple (but old) rooms across from the Ice Pond. Very warm staff, well-maintained building and grounds. Rooms facing the pool (interior side of property—#16–29) are preferable since they're away from the street noise on this busy corner. As a second choice, get a room facing the koi pond. Rooms (around 350 sq. ft.) are $110–$130, with kitchenettes for $140. You will usually get a discount, and if you get a room for $82, it's a SOLID GOLD VALUE.

Hilo Tropical Gardens
(808) 217–9650
1477 Kalanianaole Ave.
WEB REVIEW

The Inn at Kulaniapia Falls
(866) 935–6789 or (808) 935–6789
100 Kulaniapia Dr.
WEB REVIEW ◆

Naniloa Volcanoes Resort
(808) 969–3333
93 Banyan Dr.
WEB REVIEW

The Palms Cliff House Inn
(866) 963–6076 or (808) 963–6076
28-3514 Mamalahoa Hwy, Honomu
WEB REVIEW ◆

Shipman House B&B Inn
(800) 627–8447 or (808) 934–8002
131 Kaiulani St.
WEB REVIEW ◆

Uncle Billy's Hilo Bay Hotel
(800) 367–5102 or (808) 935–0861
87 Banyan Dr.
144 rooms, pool, restaurant, free Wi-Fi in lobby and rooms, or you can use lobby kiosk for a fee, coin-op laundry, empty fridge, coffee makers with free coffee daily in superior and oceanview rooms, free safety deposit boxes at front desk. Owned by the same family as the Kona Bay Hotel and built in 1964 with wings added until the 1970s. Rooms are decent-sized but looked old, dated and worn on our last visit. The grounds and common areas were also in need of care—especially the pool deck, which has no lounge chairs because, we were told, "they get stolen." The lobby is funky—sort of a '50s Hawai'i as the mainland saw it. Free "light" continental breakfast (toast, store-bought muffins, papaya and coffee) is included. The kitchenette wing has no elevator for some reason. Avoid standard rooms. If you go oceanfront, get a wraparound lanai. Rooms (approx. 550–600 sq. ft.) are $104–$129, kitchenettes (approx. 600 sq. ft.) are $119–$134. Discounts are usually available.

Wild Ginger Inn & Hostel
(800) 882–1887 or (808) 935–5556
100 Puueo St.
WEB REVIEW

VOLCANO VILLAGE

Please visit our website where we include aerial photos of all Volcano Village accommodations.

See all Web reviews at: www.wizardpub.com

Chalet Kilauea Collection
(800) 937–7786 or (808) 967–7786
19-4178 Wright Rd.
6 rooms, shared lanais on most, free Wi-Fi and computers, hot tub, daily maid. Built in 1942, this inn is often called "Inn at Volcano" and is part of a larger collection of properties that have been through lots of changes over the years, sometimes good and sometimes not so good. For this edition we found current management really putting in the effort with *some* pleasing results, others not so much. The Continental Suite is a very romantic bridal suite with double Jacuzzi bathtub in the bathroom. The Treehouse Suite is two-story; a wooden spiral staircase leads to the bedroom with its dreamy view. The bathroom has a Jacuzzi bathtub and a fireplace in it. The bungalow is the most private. Though they have toned down some of the extra touches, they still offer an optional candle-lit *continental* breakfast for $6 and afternoon tea in the common area. The grounds are lush with a large koi pond. Low ceilings in the main house make rooms feel smaller, but helps keep them warmer on cold nights (which happens at this altitude). All rooms have TVs and DVD players, some rooms have LED fireplace "artwork," which feels a *bit* out of place—just for mood, really. Rooms (275–500 sq. ft.) are $105–$235. Check for specials.

They also have other properties offsite. Volcano Hale has 6 small simple rooms with TVs, free Wi-Fi and computers, shared baths, kitchen and living area for $60–$70 (good for those on a budget), the 5-room Lokahi Lodge is also a *very* good deal at $95–$125 and has larger rooms with baths, shared kitchen, living area, free Wi-Fi and computers,, maid service every third day and hot tub.

All renters may enjoy facilities at the Chalet, like the afternoon tea and breakfast. Call them for a complete price list of all their other properties.

Holo Holo In
(808) 967–7950
19-4036 Kalani Honua Rd.
2 private rooms (with bath), 2 semi-private rooms (shared bath), 12 dorm beds, shared baths and kitchen, TV room, pay-per-load laundry, free Wi-Fi and a computer, no phones, heated rooms. This was built back in the mid-1980s and is still owned by the same family. The property is not as lush as others in area and feels more utilitarian. They close daily from 11 a.m. to 4:30 p.m. to clean and ask guests to leave unless the weather is terrible outside. The hostel provides sheets and bedding, but BYOT. (bring your own towel). There is no place to lock up valuables. The dorms and semi-private rooms are old, but the private rooms are fairly new and clean. Unless your budget puts you in the dorms, you'll get more for your money elsewhere. Private rooms are $65 and sleep 2 to 3 people, semi-private rooms are $57 per couple/$17 for each additional person up to 5, dorm beds are $20.

Kilauea Lodge
(808) 967–7366
19-3948 Old Volcano Rd.
14 rooms, coffee makers with free coffee daily, free Wi-Fi, no TV or phones (except in 2/2 cottages—which are off-site), lanais on some, restaurant, centrally heated, **A REAL GEM** fireplaces in some, hot tub (except at Tutu's Cottage). Opened in 1938 as a YMCA youth camp, this quaint lodge was converted in 1986 by Albert and Lorna Jeyte. (He was a make-up

See all Web reviews at: www.wizardpub.com

artist on *Magnum P.I.*) The whole thing is very well done and lovingly maintained. There are different styles of rooms, such as the Honeymoon Deluxe (very romantic), Hale Maluna building (snug rooms with fireplaces and incredible skylights in the bathrooms), Hale Aloha building with larger rooms and a common sitting room, and three cottages (two are off-site and have full kitchens). The grounds are lush and well-tended. The staff is top-notch. Full breakfast is included in the price of all rooms/cottages. Rooms (225–300 sq. ft.) are $170. 1/1 cottage (400 sq. ft.) is $185. is 2/2 cottages (800–1,000 sq. ft.) are $200–$220.

Volcano House
(808) 967–7321
Hawai'i Volcanoes National Park
WEB REVIEW

Volcano Inn
(800) 628–3876 or (808) 967–7773
19-3820 Old Volcano Rd.
16 rooms (9 are off-site but nearby), 2 hot tubs, shared lanai, TVs, free Wi-Fi, common room with fridge, microwave, free coffee/tea (all day) and **SOLID GOLD VALUE** computer, no daily maid. Started in 1989, this is an excellent choice in Volcano. Don't confuse them with other properties with *similar* names. The grounds are lush, the rooms are very clean, but not overly Hawaiian in decor. Though the rooms vary greatly in size and amenities at the different sites, we didn't see any we would *not* stay in from the smallest budget room to the largest family room. All have electric blankets (except budget rooms), dehumidifiers, and family rooms have gas fireplaces. The family rooms and corner window rooms (off-site) also

have kitchenettes. You can enjoy their hot tubs 24 hours a day in cozy areas of the gardens surrounded by ferns and lights. Rooms (100–960 sq. ft.) are $59–$129. Discounts on longer stays. What a deal!

Volcano Village Lodge
(808) 985–9500
19-4183 Road E
5 rooms, hot tub, free Wi-Fi and computer in lobby, coffee makers with free coffee daily, breakfast included, empty fridge, microwave, TVs (only for DVD viewing from **A REAL GEM** their library), courtesy phone in lobby, daily maid. What a find! This property is small, just over 1 acre, and was originally built as an artist's workshop, but converted in 2006 with buildings added over time. The stand-alone rooms are set amid a very lush, dense tropical forest of native plantings. Each feels very private and intimate. All are lavishly furnished in differing themes with expensive bedding and fireplaces. Fresh flowers, bathrobes, slippers, flashlights, beach mats and even flip-flops are supplied. Breakfast is placed in your room the afternoon before, so you may enjoy it at your leisure and usually includes a hot dish that may be warmed in your microwave along with the usual fruit, coffee, bagels, etc. They have a masseuse on call. Great staff. Perfect for a romantic getaway. Rooms (300–600 sq. ft.) are $195–$275. 2-night minimum.

WAIMEA

Please visit our website where we include aerial photos of all Waimea accommodations.

Things get chilly up here at 2,500 feet. There's the 30-room **Kamuela Inn**

See all Web reviews at: www.wizardpub.com

(800) 555–8968 or (808) 885–4243 at 65-1300 Kawaihae Road. This is a quaint inn, but in need of an update. The setting is well-groomed, the staff is very helpful, but the small rooms (approx. 150 sq. ft.—*slightly* larger in newer wing) are *real* variable in terms of quality. If they are not full, keep asking to look at rooms until you find one that suits you. Rooms are $59–$79, kitchenettes are $89–$99, suites for $99–$185. No laundry facilities. Phones and lanais in some. Continental breakfast included, but it's nothing special.

The **Waimea Country Lodge** (800) 367–5004 or (808) 885–4100 at 65-1210 Lindsey Road. 21 good-sized (much larger than Kamuela Inn) rooms with high, knotty pine ceilings in most units, Wi-Fi ($10). It was looking *very* tired on our visit, except the new granite kitchens in kitchenette rooms. Rooms are $125–$135, kitchenettes are $155. If you don't get a kitchenette, consider getting a superior room, which has an empty fridge. No laundry facilities.

Then there's the **Jacaranda Inn** (808) 885–8813 at 65-1444 Kawaihae Rd. Built in 1897 as a Parker Ranch manager's house, it's been converted into a charming inn. Think of it as the kind of inn that Mark Twain would have stayed at a century ago. There are 8 different rooms and a cottage, each with its own theme in purple (the color of jacaranda trees) and quaintly furnished with free Wi-Fi. Each has a private bath and entrance. Most bathrooms have double Jacuzzi tubs. The grounds and common areas have been let go in recent years. Rooms (454–665 sq. ft.) are $119–$199, 3/3 cottage with kitchen (1,695 sq. ft.) is $225–$450 for 2 up to 6 people. For sale at press time, so things may change.

NORTHERN TIP OF THE ISLAND

Please visit our website to view the aerial photos of all accommodations on the northern tip of the island.

In Hawi, the **Kohala Village Inn** (808) 889–0404 at 55-524 Hawi Road is an excellent value. It's a quaint, simple, old 19-room inn with TVs and no a/c. Internet access in lobby and free Wi-Fi in rooms. Rooms are small and basic, and it's likely that if you have noisy neighbors, you'll hear 'em. Back building rooms are quietest. No phones, but they'll take messages. Rooms (200–400 sq. ft.) are $65–$95. Suites (420 sq. ft.) are $100–$150.

In Kapaʻau, the **Kohala Club Hotel** (808) 889–6793 at 54-3793 Akoni Pule Hwy was built in the late 1800s as an English gentleman's club. Left in disrepair, it has been restored by its present owner. Consider this a historic experience, *not* a lavish one. 6 rooms with TVs, no phones, but you can use the lobby's. Tiny rooms (100–120 sq. ft.) are $56. Cash only.

Also in Kapaʻau is **Hawaiian Island Retreat at Ahu Pohaku Hoʻomaluhia** (808) 889–6336 at 250 Maluhia Rd. This place was lovingly finished by the owners in 2010 as a luxury retreat for those wishing to get away from it all and find themselves. Built on 50 acres high **A REAL GEM** on a cliff overlooking the ocean, it houses 9 rooms, 5 yurts, pool, spa, health spa, fitness room, sauna, 4 meeting rooms, valet-only laundry, and free Wi-Fi. The inn was started by the same woman who opened the Spa Without Walls at the Fairmont Orchid. Even some of the antiques from that hotel adorn the lobby and rooms. They grow and manage practically everything

See all Web reviews at: www.wizardpub.com

they serve at their restaurant—from herbs to vegetables to chicken eggs to goat's milk. They pride themselves on being organic, green and sustainable, from the solar panels to composting. A unique and hearty breakfast is included. They will also do lunch and dinner, if arranged in advance. Basically, they are there for *your* needs—if you want to be left alone, so be it. If you want a historic tour of the grounds, facial and massage, they'll do that, too. The antique-filed rooms have all the modern amenities you want, like a deep soaking tub, separate shower and expensive bedding, but no phones or TVs. (They do have CD players with iPod docks.) The yurts (round tent structures) have 2 beds and a toilet, but showers are at the clubhouse or showerhouse. (Think of the yurts as upscale camping.) Overall, this is a tranquil, peaceful place and a great choice for a family reunion, wedding or small group retreat. You may not want to leave. Rooms (400 sq. ft.) are $425–$500, yurts (200 sq. ft.) are $195.

SOUTHEAST PART OF THE ISLAND

Located near Punalu'u Beach is **Colony One at SeaMountain** (800) 525-5894 or (808) 928-6200 at 95-788 Ninole Loop Rd. This property on the south side of the island is a *long* way from other towns. Please visit our website for an aerial photo. 76 units, pool, spa, free Wi-Fi in rooms, BBQ, washer/dryer in most or coin-op laundry. The condo complex is mostly timeshares (though you won't find any salesmen around) in the heart of SeaMountain, a very remote region in the southern part of the island. The grounds are pleasant and units, though not remarkable, are clean and consistent in decor through the

above agent. Think of this as an alternative place to stay if you want to explore Hawai'i Volcanoes National Park (28 miles away) but still want to stay near the shoreline where it's more tropical (though the units are not beachside). It's quiet and peaceful. Lots of stairs at this property, mostly in the units themselves. The prices used to be very good, but the local management office closed and now the prices feel high to us. You may find owners renting units at better prices, but the decor/quality will vary. Closest (not *cheapest*) grocery shopping is in HOVE. Studios (475 sq. ft.) are $93–$142, 1/1 units (700 sq. ft.) are $113–$171, 2/2s (1,000 sq. ft.) are $122–$213. Prices include tax. 2-night minimum avoids cleaning fee.

HONOKA'A

About 8 miles from Waipi'o Valley is **Hotel Honoka'a Club** (800) 808–0678 or (808) 775–0678 at 45-3480 Mamane St. 18 rooms (upstairs rooms are best with TVs and ocean views—no phones), free Wi-Fi. This place is more than 100 years old and some common areas look like not much has changed since then. They have new lo-flow toilets, but we wish they would put in new showers. This is *not* a party place, but you *probably* will hear your neighbor. No laundry facilities. For the hostel part, no lockers, but they provide sheets and towels. The breakfast is *very* basic, so skip it and head up the road. Rooms (approx. 150 sq. ft.) are $65–$106; suites (approx. 250 sq. ft.) are $120–$130. On the hostel side: beds are $20 per person, small private room with single bed is $30. Taxes included in rates. Please visit our website for an aerial photo.

A Bay **156**
A'a Field 158, 164
A'a Lava *94*, 169, 174
Accreted Land .121
Activities 176
Advanced Recreation **190**
Adventures 229
Adventures in Paradise **211**
Adz 143
Ahalanui Beach Park 117
'Ai'opio Beach 164
Air Force Station, Old South Point 82
Airline Tickets .21
Airplane, Renting 194
Airplane Tours 193
Airport, 'Upolu 49
Ala Kahakai Trail 153, 156
Alae 123
Alamo Rent a Car **22**
Alanui Kahakai Turnout 98
Algae 56
Ali'i 15
Alii Drive 17, 59, 63
All About Babies **34**
Aloe Vera Gel .30
Aloha Jet Ski **209**
Aloha Kayak Co **209, 211**
Aloha Zipline Express **228**
Altitude, Mauna Kea 140, 145
Altitude Sickness 145, 200
'Alula Beach .165
'Anaeho'omalu Bay (A Bay) 156
'Anaeho'omalu Beach 25, *43*, 55, 58
Ancient Hawaiians 39, 129, 156, 157
Anemones 31
Arch City Coastline 204, *205*
Archaeologists 14, 15
Area Code for State (It's 808) 41
Artifacts 80
Asthma (From Vog) 33
Atlantis Submarine **225**
ATV Outfitters **177**
ATV Tours 49
Avis Rent A Car **22**

Baby's Away **34**
Backpack 22
Bali House 202
Banyan Drive, Hilo 110
Banyan Trees .110
Basically Books **42, 194**
Battles, Hawaiian 72
Beach Hikes .207
Beach Safety .148
Beach Sand Creation 174
Beach 69 (Waialea) 55, 155
Beaches, Big Island 28, 147
Beaches, 15 Best . . . . *Back cover flap*
Bed & Breakfasts 285
Beef, Big Island 137
Bees 32
Best Bets 58, 75, 122, 137, 281
Big Island Air **193**

Big Island Divers 216, 217, 219,
  230
Big Island Eco Adventures **228**
Big Island Harley-Davidson **23**
Big Island Motorcycle **23**
Big Island of Hawai'i 29
Big Island Sugar 82
Big Island Watersports **223**
Bike Shops 179
Bike Volcano **178**
Bike Works **179**
Bike Works Beach and Sports **179**
Biking 177
Biking, Bringing Your Own 179
Bird, Isabella 94, 127
Bird Park (Kipuka Pua'ulu) 102, 194
Bishop Estate .67
Bishop Museum 65
Black Sand Beach *23*, 29, 119,
  124, 129, 130, 162, 174, 175
Black Sand Beach Community 121
Black Sand Beaches 78, 174
Black Sand, Creation of *87*
Blackwater Dive 219
Blue Hawaiian Helicopters **191, 192**
Blue Sea Cruises **281**
Boat, Command Your Own 238
Boat Hoists, South Point 80
Body Glove **214, 281**
Boiling Pots 109
Boogie Boarding 58, 123, 154,
  160, *178*, 179
Books 42
Breadfruit 14
Britain 20
British 16, 18
Broken Road *76*, 82
Brown, Francis I'i 158
Brown Tree Snake 33
Bruddah Iz 38
Bruddah Waltah 38
Budget Rent A Car **23**
Bugs 31
Buses 25
Byron Ledge .96
Byron Ledge Trail 197, 198

Cabins **105, 180**
Caffeine 112
Cairns 99
Camelot Sportfishing **182, 183**
Camp Menehune **34**
Campgrounds 24, 99, 180
Camping 105, 153, 179, 180
Camping, Waimanu 133
Cane Spiders .31
Captain Cook Monument 69
Captain Dan McSweeney's
  Whale Watch **226**
Captain Zodiac **213**
Car Break-Ins 25, 109, 149
Car Rentals 21, 22
Car Seats 34

Carlsmith Beach Park . . . .
Catch & Release . . . .
Cattle, Long-Horned . . . .
Cattle Ranch 135,
Cave 56, 133, 2
Caving .146,
Cell Phone . . . .
Census . . . .
Centipedes . . . .
Chain of Craters Road 86, 95,
  99, 240
Champagne Pond 114, 117,
Chants . . . .
Charter Services Hawai'i . . . .▮
Child Restraint . . . .
Children . . . .
Christian Ceremony . . . .
Christianity . . . .
Church, Kalahikiola . . . .
Church, Mokuaikaua . . . .
Church, St. Peter's Catholic . . . .
Church, Star of the Sea . . . .*120*, ▮
Citrosa . . . .
Clerke, Captain . . . .
Cliff-Jumping 2
Climatic Zones . . . .
Close Encounter With a Dolphin 2
Cloud Forest . . . .
Cockroaches . . . .
Coconut Trees . . . .
Coffee, Kona . . . .
Coffee Tours . . . .
Cold Seawater . . . .
Command Your Own Boat 2
Condominiums 2
Contact Lens . . . .
Convective Breezes . . . .
Cook, Captain James 16, 17, 18, 20,
Cook, James, Death of . . . .
Coqui Frogs 33,
Coral 13, 31,
Costco **24,**
Cove, Crystal . . . .
Cove, 4-Mile Mark . . . .
Cove, Koai'e . . . .
Cowboys of Hawai'i 2
Crater Rim Trail 198,
Cribs . . . .
Culture, Ancient Hawaiian . . . .
Currents . . . .
Curses . . . .

Dahana Ranch 2
Darrin Gee's Spirit of Golf . . . .▮
Daughters of Hawai'i . . . .
Daylight Savings . . . .
DEET 22,
Dehydration . . . .
Devastation Trail 96, *97*,
Devil's Throat . . . .
Dinner Cruises 2
Diphthongs . . . .
Disappearing Sands . . . .

Dining Index on page 244, Where to Stay Index on page 282.

...osable Underwater Camera 149, 218, 222
...ricts of The Big Island 41
...e Sites 219
...rsion Alerts 123
...s, Mac Nuts 78
...ar Rent A Car **23**
...phin Discoveries **213**
...phin Quest **236**
...phins 69, 167, 171, 175, 236
...keys 56
...ble-hulled Voyaging Canoe 13
...glas, David 134
...glas Fir Trees 134
...e-In Volcano 85
...ing Range 184
...ing Times Chart ... *Inside back cover*
...ing Tours 41
...wning 148
...land Forest 51

...ail Address **4**
...hquake Trail 197
...hquakes 17
...h's Mantle 11
...t Hawai'i Divers **219**
...Side Beaches 174
...and Kai **209**
...l Trail 73
...tricity 114
...esine Cave 231
...peror Seamounts 11
...of the World 235
...lish 36
...erprise Rent-A-Car **23**
...ption Update 241
...pe Road 96
...nic Breakdown 35
...alyptus Forest 67

...r Wind II **212**
...mont Orchid Spa **224**
...mont Orchid Tennis **226**
...s, 'Akaka 124, *126*
...s, Hi'ilawe 131
...s, Lahomene 240
...s, Nanue 126, *238*
...s, Pe'epe'e 109, *110*
...s, Rainbow *106*, 109, 122
...s, Umauma 125, *128*, 137
...s, Wai'ale 109, 205
...s, Waihilau 240
...s, Wai'ilikahi 240
...nine 17
...ny Pack 22
...mers' Markets 42
...t Food Restaurants 111
...eral Witness Protection Program ...79
...s 148, 221
...& Seafood 246
...g Feeding 221
...ing 28, 65, 80, 181
...ing Village 77

Fishponds, Ancient 156, 162
Flashlight 91
Flights, Interisland 22
Footprints 91, 102
4-Mile Scenic Route 124
4WD 23, 78, 115, 119, 130, 136, 143, 144, 151, 160, 162, 164, 171, 220, 223, 225
Foxy Lady **183**
Freshwater Springs 27
Frog Fish 165
Frogs 33
Fuku-Bonsai **122**
Fumes, Volcanic 90

Gasoline **24, 77, 97, 139**
Gecko 32
Geography, Hawaiian 28
Gilbert Islanders 39
Ginger 182, 211
Glacier, Mauna Kea 143
Global Warming 146
Go! Airlines **22**
Gods 17, 19, 20
Golden Plover (Kolea) 15
Golden Pools of Ke-awa-iki *55*, 203
Golf Courses at a Glance 184
Golfing 184
Goodyear Blimps 33
Graffiti 55
Gray Sand Beach 76
Great Britain 20
Great Mahele 20
Green Flash 57
Green Sand (Mahana) Beach 82, *83*, 148, 173, *175*
Greenwell Coffee **68**
Greeters of Hawai'i **41**
Grocery Store 34, 44
Guam 33
Guided Tours 178, 211
Guns 16

Hakalau Bay **125**
Halape Campsite 180, 199
Haleakala 12
Halema'uma'u Crater 94
Hale-o-Keawe 73
Hamakua & Waimea's Best Bets ...137
Hamakua Coast *193*
Hamakua Country Club **184, 189**
Hamakua Macadamia Nut Co **52**
Hammerhead Shark 30
Hang Gliders (Powered) 190
Happy Campers Hawaii **24**
Hapuna Beach 25, 28, 54, 147, 153, 179
Hapuna Golf Course **184, 185**
Harper Car and Truck Rental ...**23, 24**
Hawai'i Belt Road 78
Hawai'i Forest & Trail **194, 224**
Hawai'i Lifeguard Surf Instructors ...**225**
Hawai'i Pack & Paddle **211**

Hawai'i Tropical Botanical Garden ..111, 124
Hawai'i Volcanoes Nat'l Park 10, 240
Hawaiian Airlines **22**
Hawaiian Alphabet 36
Hawaiian Artifacts 57
Hawaiian Bat 14
Hawaiian Beaches Subdivision 121
Hawaiian Canoes 15
Hawaiian Chain 18
Hawaiian Cowboys 134
Hawaiian Culture 35
Hawaiian, Definition of 35
Hawaiian Islands 28
Hawaiian Language 20, 36
Hawaiian Legend 71
Hawaiian Marine Life 30
Hawaiian Music 38
Hawaiian Pedals **179**
Hawaiian Pidgin 38
Hawaiian Religion 17, 63, 67
Hawaiian Riviera 76, 78
Hawaiian Scuba Shack **216, 218**
Hawaiian Society 19
Hawaiian Style Band 38
Hawaiian Sweetbread 105
Hawaiian Time 35
Hawaiian Village 51
Hawaiian Volcano Observatory **94**
Hawaiian Volcanoes 12
Hawaiian Waters 30
Hawi 47, 287
Hawi Wind Farm 49
Heiau *14*
Heiau, 'Ahu'ena *59*, 60, 166
Heiau, Hale-o-Kapuni 54
Heiau, Hale o Mono 164
Heiau, Hiki-au 69
Heiau, Kalaea 81
Heiau, Ke'eku 65
Heiau, Ku'emanu *62*, 64
Heiau, Mo'okini 49, 50, 58
Heiau, Pu'ukohola 19, *52*, 54, 91
Heiau, Waha'ula 99
Height, Mauna Loa 142
Hele-On Bus **25**
Helicopters 191
Hertz Car Rental **23**
Higashihara Park 34
High Surf 30
Hike to Flowing Lava 240
Hiking 194
Hiking, HVNP 102
Hiking, Mauna Kea 144
Hiking Sticks 194
Hilina Pali Lookout 97
Hilo 26, 106, 107, 139, 146, 286
Hilo & Puna Hikes 205
Hilo & Puna's Best Bets 122
Hilo Bayfront 109
Hilo Beach Parks 175
Hilo Bike Hub **179**
Hilo Homemade Ice Cream 111

Hilo Municipal Golf Course 184, 189
Hilton Waikoloa 34, 155, 157
Holei Pali Lookout 99
Holei Sea Arch 99
Holoholoku 44
Holua 67
Holua Slide 58
Holualoa Coffee 67, 68
Home Rental 283
Honaunau 77
Honeymoon .25
Honoka'a 129, 287
Honokane Nui Valley 49
Honoka'ope Beach 155, *156*
Honokohau Beach 164
Honokohau Harbor 58, 164, 183
Honoli'i Beach Park 123
Honolulu, Flying From 22
Honomalino Bay 170, 171
Honomalino Beach 170, *171*
Ho'okena Beach Park 169
Ho'ola Spa .224
Ho'olulu Park 226
Ho'opuloa 77
Horseback Riding 130, 131, 137, 207
Horses, Wild of Waipi'o 130
Hotels 284
HOVE 76
HOVE Yacht Club 78
Hualalai .26, 28
Hualalai Golf Club 184, 186
Hualalai Volcano 44, 59, 67
Hula 'Auana .39
Hula Daddy Coffee 68
Hula Kahiko .39
Hula Kai 212, 230
Hula 'Olapa .39
Hulihe'e Palace 60
Human Sacrifice 15, 50, 62, 69
Humidity 26
Humuhumunukunukuapua'a 36
Hurricane 'Iniki 69, 169

Ice Cream 47, 54, 69, 125, 144
Ice Pond 111
Ihu Nui 183
'Imiloa Astronomy Center 34, 109
India 33
Insects, Mauna Kea 143
Insurance 24
Interisland Flights 22
Internet 42, 86
Iolani Air Tour 193, 194
Ironman Triathlon 60, 166
Isaac Hale Beach Park 118
Island Air 22
Island Dining Best Bets 281
Island Foods 247
Island Lava Java 42
Island Naturals Deli 122
Island RV 24
Island Slice Tennis 226

Jack's Diving Locker 216, 217, 219, 222, 230
Jack's Tours .25
Jagger Museum 94
Japanese 14
Jeeps 23
Jellyfish 31
Jet Skiing 209
Joggers 63

K-2 29
Ka'aha Campsite 199
Ka'ahumanu .17
Ka'elehuluhulu Beach 161
Kahalu'u Bay Surf and Sea 210
Kahalu'u Beach 64, 147, *166*, 167
Kahauale'a Trail 233
Kaho'olawe 12
Kahua Ranch ATV Tours 177
Kahuku Sugar Plantation 36
Kahuna Pule .73
Kaiholena Cove 52, 152
Kailua 29, 30, 59
Kailua Bay 19, 165
Kailua Bay Charter 214
Kailua Pier 59, 166
Kailua Town .59
Kailua-Kona 25, 26, 29, 30, 286
Kailua-Kona Sights 59
Kailua-Kona's Best Bets 75
Kaimu 119
Kalani'opu'u .80
Kalapana 119, 120, 241
Kalapana Gardens 99
Kaloko Drive .43
Kaloko Fishpond 164
Kaloko-Honokohau National
    Historical Park 57
Kalopa Native Forest St. Park 129, 180
Kamakahonu Beach 60, 166
Kamakawiwo'ole, Israel 38
Kamalalawalu 65
Kamanu Charters 214
Kamehameha 18, 29, 109, 166
Kamehameha, Birthplace of 50
Kamehameha Day 47
Kamehameha I 17, 107
Kamehameha II 17, 63
Kamehameha III 135
Kamehameha the Great 18, 20, 50, 60, 71, 91
Kamehameha's Fishpond 44
Kamuela (Waimea) 29, 134
Kanaenae 35
Kanaka Maoli 35
Kapa'a Beach Park 24, 151
Kapa'au 47
Kapalaoa Beach 157
Kapanai'a Bay 150
Kapoho 114, *116*
Kapoho Beach Community 117
Kapoho Tide-pools 116, 148
Kapu System 15, 17, 20, 72

Ka'u Desert Trail 91
Kaua'i 12, 13, 15, 16, 19, 28
Kauaians
Kauhola Point . . . .
Kaulana Boat Launch . . . .
Kaumana Cave 109,
Kauna'oa Beach . . . .
Ka'upulehu Beach . . . .
Kawaihae 19
Kayaking . . . .
Kazumura Cave . . . .
Kazumura Cave Tours . . . .
Kealakekua . . . .
Kealakekua Bay 18, 77, *176*, 2
    210, 212, 237
Kealakekua Trail . . . .
Kealoha Beach Park . . . .
Keanakako'i . . . .
Keanakako'i Crater . . . .
Keanalele Waterhole . . . .
Keauhou Campsite 180,
Keauhou Holua . . . .
Keauhou Shopping . . . .
Keaukaha Beach Park . . . .
Ke-awa-iki . . . .
Ke-awa-iki Beach . . . .
Ke-awa-iki, Golden Pools . . . .
Keck Telescope . . . .
Ke'eaumoku . . . .
Ke'ei Beach 16, 71
Kehena Beach . . . .
Keiki 151, 163, 164,
Kekaha Kai State Park 161,
Kekuaokalani . . . .
Keokea Beach Park . . . .
Keoua 54
Kiawe Trees . . . .
Kiholo Bay *32*, 56, 148, 158, 200,
Kikaua Beach *147*,
Kilauea Caverns of Fire . . . .
Kilauea Crater . . . .
Kilauea Iki 194,
Kilauea Iki Crater . . . .
Kilauea Iki Overlook . . . .
Kilauea Iki Trail 194, *195*,
Kilauea Military Camp . . . .
Kilauea Overlook . . . .
Kilauea Volcano *12*, 28,
    33, 85, 179, 194
King Kalakaua . . . .
King Kamehameha's Kona
    Beach Hotel . . . .
Kipuka . . . .
Kipuka Pua'ulu (Bird Park) 102,
Kiteboarding . . . .
Koa Trees . . . .
Koai'e Cove 51,
Kohala . . . .
Kohala Area Hikes 2
Kohala Divers 216,
Kohala Kayak . . . .
Kohala Lava Desert . . . .
Kohala Mountain . . . .

Dining Index on page 244, Where to Stay Index on page 282.

ala Resort Area 24, 34, 54
ala Sugar 47
ala Volcano 47
ala's Best Bets 58
a (Golden Plover) 15
kole Beach Park 125, *127*
a 17, 59
a Airport 22, 28, 30
a Area Hikes 204
a Bay Books **42**
a Blue **57**
a Blue Sky Coffee **68**
a Boat Rentals **238**
a Boys Kayaks 210, 211
a Business Center **42**
a Coffee 67, 68
a Cold Lobster 56
a Country Club **184, 188**
a, Flying Into 22
a Historical Society Museum ..**69**
a Honu Divers **216, 217, 230**
a Inn **34**
a Joe Coffee **68**
a Nightingales 56
a Side 30
a Surf Company **225**
a Stories **42**
a Winds 26
(War God) 17
Bay (Manini'owali) 159, 179
kini, Governor 60
mo'o Battlefield 17
i'o Beach 158
uihaele 124, 130, 131
a Kai Caverns **181**
anaokuaiki Campgrounds ...98, 179
aianaha 86
e Atoll 11, *16*

aloa Bay Beach Park **64, 167**
'Apuki 99
e Wai-au *142*, 143
a'i 12, 19, 20
d Access 39
akahi Beach 152
akahi State Historical Park ..51, 152
pahoehoe 110, 127
pahoehoe Point 127
pahoehoe Train Museum **127**
a Bench 90, 242
a Craters 86
a Fissure 95, 98
a Flow 28
a Fountaining 87, 95, 97
a, Molten *11, 21, 85*, 88, *89*, *103*
a Ocean Adventures **214**
a Roy's **214**
a Stalactites 96
a Swimming Pool 115
a Tree State Park 56
a Tube 12, 32, 56, 65, 87
a Tube Skylight 102, 146
a Viewing 242

Lava Viewing, Kalapana 121
Leeward Side 27
Lei Greeting 41
Leiomanu 72
Lele Ho'okau *62*
Leleiwi Tide-pool 206
Leptospirosis 32
Lifeguards 148, 150
Light Tackle 183
Light Tower, Puna 114
Lili'uokalani Gardens 110
Lili'uokalani, Queen 20
Little Blue Church 64
Living Ocean Adventures **226**
Local Food 246
Lo'ihi Seamount 12, 84
Lono 17
Lonoikamakahiki 65
LORAN Station 51
Luahinewai 202
Lu'au 58, 278
Lu'au Foods 247
Lyman Museum **107, 122**

Mac Nut **111**
MacKenzie State Rec. Area 180
Magic Sands 167
Magma 11
Magoon House 161
Mahai'ula Beach 161
Mahukona *14*
Mahukona Beach Park 151
Mahukona Volcano 43, 51
Makahiki 17
Makalawena Beach ...58, 148, 160, *161*
Makalei Country Club **44, 184, 188**
Makole'a Beach 162, 168, 220
Mana Road 134, 136, 143, 177
Mandara Spa **224**
Manini Beach 169
Manini'owali (Kua Bay) 159, *160*, 179
Manta Ray Dives **218**
Manta Ray Night Dive 229
Manta Rays 153
Manuka State Park 78
Map, Island Overview . . *Inside back cover*
Map Reference ......*Inside front cover*
Maps, Explanation of 9
Marquesan Carvings 15
Marquesas Islands 14
Maui 12, 16, 18, 29, 32
Mauna Kea 22, 28, 138, 139, 140, 142, 143, 144
Mauna Kea Beach 147, 153, *154*, 179
Mauna Kea Golf Course ..**184, 185, *187***
Mauna Kea State Park 140, 179
Mauna Kea Summit Adventures ...**224**
Mauna Lani Beach 155
Mauna Lani Fishponds 55, 156
Mauna Lani Resort (Golf) **184, 185**
Mauna Lani Spa **224**
Mauna Loa 12, 28, 29, 33, 44, 138, 139, 145

Mauna Loa Coffee Mill **69**
Mauna Loa Helicopters **191, 193**
Mauna Loa Scenic Road 102
Mauna Loa Summit 199
Mauna Loa Trail 102
Mauna Loa Visitor Center **111**
Mauna Loa Volcano 76
Mauna Loa Weather Observatory 145, 200
Mauna Ulu 98
Mauna Ulu Crater 194, 197
Mauna Ulu Hike 231
Mauna Ulu Trail 196
Mausoleum, Hale-o-Keawe 73
Mau'umae Beach 153
Mele 39
Menehune Breakwater 168
Menehune, Legend of 14
Merrie Monarch Festival **39**
Methane Explosions 90
Mile Markers 9, 41
Miller's Snorkel & Surf **221**
Millimeter Valley 141
Miloli'i 77, 78
Miloli'i Beach Park 170
Mineral Rights 114
Missile Tracking 82
Missionaries 17, 20, 36, 39
Mo'i 16
Moku-a-Kae Bay 71
Moku'ohai Battlefield 71, 205
Moloka'i 12, 19
Mongoose 32
Monkeypod Trees 83
Mosquito Repellent ..22, 32, 124, 126, 131
Motor Homes 24
Motorcycles 23
Mount Everest 29, 140
Mount Suribachi 44
Mountain Bike 96, 177
Mountain Road Cycles **179**
Muliwai Trailhead 240
Mullet 156, 164
Music 38

Na Kamalei Toddler Playground . . .**34**
Na'alapa Stables–Kahua Ranch **208**
Na'alapa Stables–Waipi'o **131, 207**
Na'alehu 77, 82
Naha Stone 107
Namakani Paio 24, 179
Nani Mau Gardens **111**
Naniloa Golf Club **184, 189**
Nanue Stream 126
Napau Crater 98
Napau Crater Trail 196
Napo'opo'o Beach 69, 148, 169
National Car Rental **23**
Natural Energy Lab ...34, 56, 163, 164
Nautilus Dive Center **218**
Navigational Heiau *14*, 51
Nematocysts 31
Nene 98

INDEX

Dining Index on page 244, Where to Stay Index on page 282.

Neptune Charlies 216, 218
Nightlife 278
Ni'ihau 12, 16, 36
No-See-Ums 32
North Pacific Current 83
Northwest Passage 16
Nudists 119

O'ahu 12, 19, 22, 29, 36
Ocean Eco Tours 225
Ocean Rider Seahorse Farm 57
Ocean Safaris 211
Ocean Sports 210, 214, 216,
218, 222, 281
Ocean Temperature 27
Ocean Tours 211
Off-Island 35
Offerings 95
'Ohi'a Forest 96
'Ohi'a-Lehua Tree 104
Old Kona Airport Beach Park 165
Old Mamalahoa Highway 133
Olivine 173
Onekahakaha Beach Park 34, 175
Onizuka Center Intl. Astronomy . . .143
Ono Rating .246
Onomea Bay 124
Orchid Isle Bicycling 178

Pa'ao 50
Pacific Ocean 16
Pacific Plate .11
Pacific Rim Divers 216, 217
Pacific Tsunami Museum 110
Pacific Vibrations 225
Pack, What to 22
Pahala 84
Pahoa 112
Pahoehoe Beach Park 64, 167
Pahoehoe Lava 87, *94*
Painted Church 73
Pakini Nui Wind Farm 80
Pali o Kulani 82
Palm Tree 67
Pana'ewa Rain Forest Zoo 111
Paniolo 134
Paniolo Adventures 208
Paradise Helicopters 193
Paradise Park 121
Parasailing .215
Park Rangers 90
Parker, John Palmer 134, 135
Parker Ranch 44, 123, 134, 136
Parker, Samuel 133, 136
Parking, Downtown Kona 59
Parrots 67
Pau Hana Estate Coffee 68
Pawai Bay .165
Pearl Harbor 29, 84
Pebble Beach 170
Pele 33, 94, 141
Pelekane Beach 153
Permafrost *142*, 143

Personal Responsibility 40
Pest Hotline .33
Petroglyphs 55, 65, 99,
157, 169, 200, 202
Phreatomagmatic 91
Pidgin Words 38
Pigs, Waipi'o Valley 129
Pine Trees 164, 225
Pineapple 20
Pineapple Island 20
Pineapple Powder 223
Place of Refuge 19, 72, 73, 169
Plate Lunch 248
Pleasant Holidays 21
Pohaku Likanaka 62
Pohakuloa Military Training Area 139
Pohue Bay 78
Polarized Lenses 41
Polarizing Filter 91
Poli'ahu 141
Pololu Beach 48, 49, 150
Pololu Valley Lookout *48*, 49
Polynesian Languages 36
Polynesians .14
Pool, Spring-Fed 157
Pool, Warm Water 118
Portuguese Man-of-War 31
Princess Kapiolani 96
Princess Ruth 62, 146
Puako *217*, 219
Puako Beaches 155
Puako/Malama Petroglyph Trail . . .55, 200
Pu'ala'a 117
Public Beaches 149
Pueo Bay 158, 203
Pulu Factory 197
Pumice Cinders 95
Puna 27, 28, 106
Puna Beaches 175
Punalu'u Black Sand Beach 83, 174
Pupu (Appetizer) 248
Pu'u Huluhulu 140, 196
Pu'u Loa Petroglyph Trail 55, 99, 194
Pu'u Loa Petroglyphs *99*
Pu'u Maka'ala Forest Reserve 112
Pu'u o Mahana 173
Pu'u 'O'o 29, 145, 196, 197
Pu'u 'O'o Hike 233
Pu'u 'O'o Vent 2, 10, 85, 233
Pu'u Pua'i 95
Pu'u Pua'i Overlook 95
Pu'u Wa'awa'a Hike 203
Pu'uhonua o Honaunau *19*, *70*, 72,
147, 169

Queen's Bath **164, 200, 202**
Queens' MarketPlace 34

Rack Rates, Explanation of . . .**21, 283**
Rain 26, 28, 118
Rain Forest Lava Tube 194, 199
Rain Shadow Effect 51
Rainbows 109

Real Gem Icon . . . .
Reel Action . . . .
Religion 17, 20
Rental Agents . . . .
Rental Cars . . . .
Republic of Hawai'i . . . .
Resort Wear . . . .
Reviews, How We Do Them . . . .
Richardson's Ocean Center . . . .
Ride the Rim . . . .
Rift Zone 87
Rip Currents 131, 148,
Road to the Sea 148,
Road to the Sea Beach *23*,
Roberts Hawai'i . . . .
Rogue Waves . . . .
Room/Car Packages 21
Roplene . . . .
Royal Gardens 99,
Russia . . . .
RV Rentals . . . .

Saddle Road **138,**
Saddle Road, Driving On . . . .
Safari Helicopters **191,**
Salt-and-Pepper Sand 147, 156,
Saltwater Swimming Pool . . . .
Samoa . . . .
Sand, Walking In . . . .
Sandalwood ('Iliahi) Trail . . . .
Sandalwood Trade, Hawaiian . . . .
Sandwich Isle Divers **216, 218,**
Satellite Weather Shots . . . .
Scooter Brothers . . . .
Scooters . . . .
Scopolamine Patches . . . .
Scorpions . . . .
Scuba 28, 155, 163, 166, 167, 169,
Scuba Companies at a Glance . . . .
Scuba Diving and Altitude 145,
Sea Arch 154, 155, 165,
Sea Genie II . . . .
Sea Paradise **212,**
Sea Quest . . . .
Sea Strike . . . .
Sea Wife II **182,**
SeaMountain at Punalu'u **184,**
189
SeaMountain Resort **76,**
Seasickness 182,
Seat Belt Use . . . .
Seawall, Kailua-Kona . . . .
Secret Pond . . . .
Settlers 13
Shaka . . . .
Sharks . . . .
Shave Ice . . . .
Shopping, Hamakua & Waimea . . . . . .
Shopping, Hilo 111,
Shopping, Kohala . . . .
Shopping, Kona . . . .
Shoreline Fishing . . . .
Silica . . . .

Dining Index on page 244, Where to Stay Index on page 282.

Guides Hawai'i 223
art, Richard 136
oothies 124
kes 33
rkel Bob's 222
rkel Sites 223
rkeling 28, 148, 151,
152, 153, 154, 155, 156, 159, 163, 165,
169, 175, 220, 221
w, Mauna Kea *144*, 145
w Ski Mauna Kea 145
w Skiing 223
BA 223
set 223
D GOLD VALUE Icon 284
th Kona Fruit Stand **77**
Point 79, 174, 177, 220
thernmost Point in U.S. 76
Without Walls **224**
ce Shuttle Challenger 143
nish Dancers (Nudibranch) 165
s 224
cies, New 13
ed Trap 84
lunking, *see also* Caving 146, 180
ncer Beach Park 24, *151*, 152
nner Dolphins 212
ng-fed Pools 56
d Up Paddling (SUP) 225
Gaze Hawai'i **224**
gazing 224
ue, Ki'i Akua 60
ue, King Kamehameha 47
am Vents 93, *112*
ne, Holehole 50
nes, Dressed 73
aru Telescope **142**
marine 225
ar Industry 20, 84
hur Banks 94
mer Solstice 63
mit, Mauna Kea *141*, 142
block 22, 30, 149
burn 30
glasses 41
set 55, 63, 73
shine Helicopters **191, 193**
(Stand Up Paddling) 225
 ....34, 148, 150
Spots 164
face Lava Flow *11*, *21*, *85*, 87,
88, *89*, 90, 103
ing 64, 123, 225
ng Zone **34, 184**

is **194**
ti 14, 15
14
, Waipi'o Valley 129, 131
es, Accommodations, *see also*
Major Gouge 283
conic Plate 11
scope Tours, Mauna Kea 142
scopes 141, 142

Temperatures, Water 27
Temples 17
Tennis 226
Tephra 95, 98, 105, 114
The Big Island 29
Thrifty Car Rental **23**
Throw-net Fishing 14
Thurston Lava Tube 96, 177, 194
Tide-pools 116, 119, 157, 163, 168, 203
Tides, High/Low 149
Tiger Shark 30
Timeshares 176
Topographic Maps 194
Trade Winds 26, 80
Traffic 25
Traffic Noise 64
Travel Agent 21
Tree House 49
Tree Molds 102
Tropical Dreams **47**
Tropical Helicopters **191, 193**
Tropical Suntans 30
Tsunami Clock 110
Tsunami, 1946 ......125, 127, 130
Tsunamis 17, 77, 106, 110
Turtles *74*, 83, 115, 157, 164, 168, 174
Twain, Mark 94
Two Step 169

UFO Parasail **215**
'Ukulele 38
Umauma Experience **228**
Underwater Volcanoes 153
United Kingdom 69
United States Annexes Hawai'i .20
University of Hawai'i Observatory 142
Updates to Book 10
Upper Road, Hwy 19 ....123, 139
Urchins 31

Vacationland, Kapoho **117**
Vancouver, Captain George 134
Velge, Father John 73
Vertical Skylight *105*
Virgin Air 114
Visitor Center, Chain of Craters ...99
Visitor Information 41
Visitor Information Station ...143
Vog 33
Volcano 12, 27
Volcano Art Center Gallery ..**97**
Volcano Cave Adventures **181**
Volcano Golf & Country Club ...**184, 188**
Volcano House **93**
Volcano, Undersea 84
Volcano Update 41
Volcano Village 104, 286
Volcano Winery **104**
Volume of Lava 88
Vw Camper Vans 24

Waiaka Pond **99**
Waialea (Beach 69) 154, 155

Waikaumalo Park 127
Waikoloa Resort (Golf) **184, 186**
Waikoloa Resorts 24
Waikoloa Village 34, 44
Waikoloa Village (Golf) **184, 187**
Wailuku River 183, 206
Waimanu Valley 133, 180
Waimea 16, 29, 134, 136, 287
Waimea Country Club **184, 187**
Waimea Park 34
Waiohinu 82
Wai'olena 175
Wai'opae Ponds 116
Waipi'o Beach 131
Waipi'o on Horseback **208**
Waipi'o Ridge Stables **208**
Waipi'o Valley 18, 23, 65,
127, 129, *131*, 133
Waipi'o Valley Road 130
Waipi'o Valley Shuttle **130, 131**
Waipi'o Valley Wagon Tours ...**131,**
208
Wai'uli 175
Water Hazards 30
Water Shoes 148, 167
Water Sports 28
Water Temperatures 27, 215
Waterfalls, East Side 123
Waterfalls, *see also* Falls ...28
Wavecom Solutions **42**
Wawaloli Beach 57, 163
Weather 25, 86, 106
Weather, HVNP 93
Web Access 42
Web Review 287
Website Wizard Publications ...**4, 25,**
42, 86, 241, 287
Weddings 25, 64
Weliweli Point 158, 203
Westerners 35
Whale Sharks 78
Whale Watching 226
Whaling 19
What's Shakin' **124**
White Sand 147, 159, 160
White Sands Beach 64, 167, 179
White-tailed Tropic Birds 94
White-tipped Reef Sharks 30
Whittington Park 83, 174
Wild Horses of Waipi'o 130
Wild Lava Tube Hike 199
Wild Pigs 96
Wind 44, 54, 80, 145, 154
Windsurfing 156
Windward Side 28
World Botanical Gardens **126**
www.wizardpub.com **4, 25,**
42, 86, 241, 287

Yama's Specialty Shop **183**

Zig-zag Trail **133**
Zip Isle **228**

The only app that knows how to find a crystal clear, volcanically-heated "Champagne Pond" without needing a cellular or wireless signal.

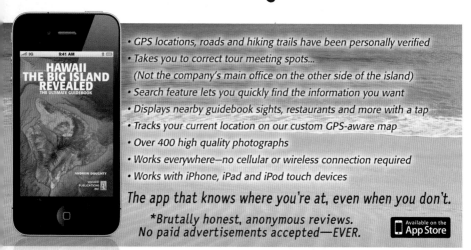

- GPS locations, roads and hiking trails have been personally verified
- Takes you to correct tour meeting spots... (Not the company's main office on the other side of the island)
- Search feature lets you quickly find the information you want
- Displays nearby guidebook sights, restaurants and more with a tap
- Tracks your current location on our custom GPS-aware map
- Over 400 high quality photographs
- Works everywhere—no cellular or wireless connection required
- Works with iPhone, iPad and iPod touch devices

The app that knows where you're at, even when you don't.

*Brutally honest, anonymous reviews. No paid advertisements accepted—EVER.

Available on the **App Store**

"A must for any serious visitor." —The New York Times

Discover Hawaii's Hidden Gems with our best-selling guides and photographic series

"The best guidebook. Every nook and cranny is explored by longtime residents."—Conde Nast Traveler

"Especially engaging collection of photographs."—Honolulu Star Bulletin

Look for our books in your favorite bookstore or online.

Visit our website for recent updates, aerial photos of resorts, helpful links to businesses, local events, weather information and so much more!

www.wizardpub.com
e-mail: aloha@wizardpub.com

WIZARD PUBLICATIONS INC *Believable Guides for Unbelievable Vacations* ®